GLOBAL JAPANIZATION?

Global Japanization? brings together a collection of articles exploring the impact of Japanese manufacturing investment and the adoption of Japanese working practices on a cross-national basis.

Key issues are explored through a range of national and sectoral studies of work reorganization and work experience within Japanese companies and their competitors. Original case studies are employed to support a wide-ranging critique of the established view of the 'Japanese model' of work organization. Alternative models, as in the Swedish and Italian cases, are discussed in depth.

Drawing on international research, this volume sheds new light on an important and often controversial debate centring on Japanese working practices. It will be of great interest to students and researchers in the sociology of work, organizational sociology and international business.

Tony Elger is Lecturer in Sociology, University of Warwick. **Chris Smith** is Lecturer in Industrial Relations, Aston Business School, University of Aston.

D0209405

CRITICAL PERSPECTIVES ON WORK AND ORGANIZATION
General editors: David Knights, Chris Smith,
Paul Thompson and Hugh Willmott

Since the appearance of Braverman's *Labour and Monopoly Capital*, the impact of labour process analysis has been experienced in the fields of industrial sociology, organization theory, industrial relations, labour economics, politics and business studies. This series examines diverse aspects of the employment relationship across the range of productive and service industries. Some volumes explore further the established terrain of management control, the intensification of work, the deskilling of labour. Others are attentive to associated topics such as gender relations at work, new technology, workplace democracy and the international dimensions of the labour process.

GLOBAL JAPANIZATION?

The transnational transformation of the labour process

Edited by Tony Elger and Chris Smith

London and New York

First published 1994
by Routledge
11 New Fetter Lane, London EC4P 4EE

Simultaneously published in the USA and Canada
by Routledge
29 West 35th Street, New York, NY 10001

© 1994 Tony Elger and Chris Smith

Typeset in Garamond by LaserScript, Mitcham, Surrey
Printed and bound in Great Britain by
Biddles Ltd, Guildford and King's Lynn

British Library Cataloguing in Publication Data
A catalogue record for this book is available from the British Library.

Library of Congress Cataloging in Publication Data
has been applied for.

ISBN 0–415–08586–1
ISBN 0–415–08587–X

CONTENTS

CONTENTS

FIGURES

TABLES

NOTES ON CONTRIBUTORS

PETER ACKERS is Lecturer in Industrial Relations at the Business School, the University of Loughborough. He has published articles on employer paternalism, employee involvement, workplace industrial relations and labour history. He is currently engaged on further research on employee involvement and the history of NACODS, the pit deputies' union.

JOHN BLACK is Principal Lecturer in Industrial Relations and Human Resource Management at Wolverhampton Business School, University of Wolverhampton. He has published a variety of articles on management control and the labour process, Japanization and managerial paternalism. He is currently researching the introduction of new working practices, and the role of the union, in the auto-components industry.

GIUSEPPE BONAZZI is Professor of the Sociology of Organization at the Faculty of Political Sciences, University of Turin, Italy. His main research interests are in the history of organization theory and the organization of work in industrial production, and he is currently coordinating a research programme on Japanese transplants in Italy. His most recent book is *Il tubo di cristallo. Modello giapponese e fabbrica integrata alla Fiat Auto* (The Crystal Tube: The Japanese Model and The Integrated Factory at Fiat Auto).

VAGELIS DEDOUSSIS is Lecturer in the division of Asian & International Studies, Griffith University and lived in Japan for eight years prior to completing his PhD in Australia.

TONY ELGER is a member of the Centre for Comparative Labour Studies and lectures in the Department of Sociology, University of Warwick. He has researched and written on labour process theory, work reorganization in British manufacturing, and the implications of restructuring for workers and trade unions. His current research focuses on the consequences of modular production and team working for employment relations.

PETER FAIRBROTHER is a member of the Centre for Comparative Labour Studies and lectures in the Department of Sociology, University of Warwick. His current research interests focus on union organization and activity in the state sector in Britain, and restructuring and union renewal in Russia. As well as articles, his publications include *Flexibility at Work: the Challenge for Unions* and (with others) *What about the Workers? Workers and the Transition to Capitalism in Russia.*

LAURIE GRAHAM is Assistant Professor of Labor Studies at Indiana University. She received her PhD in Sociology from Purdue University in 1991. Her research interests include Japanese management strategies, sociology of work, and women in the labour movement.

COLIN HASLAM teaches at the University of East London, and has collaborated with Karel Williams and other colleagues on long-term research on the manufacturing sector. They have written many articles and books on manufacturing and their next book will be *Success and Failure in the Cars Business.*

JOHN HUMPHREY is a Fellow of the Institute of Development Studies (IDS) at the University of Sussex. He has researched and written widely on work and industrial relations in Latin America, with particular reference to Brazil, and among his publications are *Capitalist Control and Workers Struggle in the Brazilian Auto Industry* and the edited collection *Quality and Productivity in Industry: New Strategies in Developing Countries.*

CHRISTOPHER HUXLEY teaches industrial sociology and comparative development at Trent University, Peterborough, Ontario. He has published in numerous journals and contributed to *Unions in Transition* (ed. S. M. Lipset). He has served as Director of Trent University's comparative development studies programme in Ibarra, Ecuador, has been a Visiting Fellow at the Industrial Relations Research Unit, University of Warwick, and is currently Visiting Humanities Fellow at the University of Windsor, Ontario.

TOSHIKO KAMADA is Professor of Sociology at Tokyo Women's Christian University and active in the Japanese Association for

Labour Sociology. She has published widely on the sociology of labour, class relations, women's work and the family, including books on *Social Class, Family Life and Labour in an Industrial City* and *Women's Work at the Turning Point.*

CRAIG R. LITTLER is Professor of Management and Head of Department in the Faculty of Business, University of Southern Queensland. He has written on Japanese management and industrial relations issues for a number of years, and is a long standing contributor to debates on the labour process. He is also the founding editor of *Labour and Industry.*

ITSUTOMO MITSUI teaches at Komazawa University in Tokyo and has published extensively on the role of small and medium enterprises in Japanese development.

ANNE CAROLINE POSTHUMA gained her PhD at the Institute of Development Studies (IDS), Sussex, and now works as a consultant in São Paulo, Brazil, and as a visiting researcher at the University of Campinas. She is currently working on issues of industrial restructuring, shop floor reorganization and their implications for training and human resource development, particularly in the automotive industry.

JAMES RINEHART is Professor of Sociology at the University of Western Ontario in London, Canada. He has written numerous articles in the field of labour studies and is the author of *The Tyranny of Work: Alienation and the Labour Process.*

DAVID ROBERTSON is a researcher with the Canadian Auto Workers union (CAW) and coordinator of the CAW Research Group on CAMI. He has written (with Jeff Wareham) *Technological Change in the Auto Industry* and *Changing Technology and Work: Northern Telecom.*

PER SEDERBLAD is Researcher and Lecturer at the Department of Sociology, Lund University. He has written research reports and articles on such topics as work groups, organizational change, staff training and industrial relations. Currently, he is studying the effects of foreign acquisitions in Swedish companies.

CHRIS SMITH is Lecturer in Industrial Relations at Aston University. He has researched and written in the areas of technical labour, management strategies and comparative labour process analysis. He is currently researching the restructuring of work in the food industry and the significance of Japanese transplants at a regional level.

BILL TAYLOR is currently a lecturer at the City Polytechnic of Hong Kong. He has lived and worked in Japan and gained his PhD in Sociology at the University of Warwick for *Work Organisation and Management Strategies in Consumer Electronics*, which focused on Japanese electricals plants in Britain.

PAUL THOMPSON is Professor in the Department of Organization Studies, University of Central Lancashire. He has a long-standing involvement in the Labour Process Conference and co-edited the volume *Labour in Transition: The Labour Process in Eastern Europe and China*. A comparative project on work organization involving colleagues in Sweden and Austria has been his main research activity in recent years. He has been working on a number of books including a second edition of *Work Organisations* (with David McHugh).

JEFF WAREHAM is in the CAW Research Department. He is co-author (with David Robertson) of *Technological Change in the Auto Industry* and *Changing Technology and Work: Northern Telecom*.

KAREL WILLIAMS currently teaches at the University of Manchester, and with Colin Haslam and other colleagues he has been engaged on a series of related research projects on developments in manufacturing industry. Their previous work includes many articles and books on manufacturing and their next book will be *Success and Failure in the Cars Business*.

ACKNOWLEDGEMENTS

Earlier versions of many of the chapters in this volume were first delivered at the International Labour Process Conference between 1990 and 1993, and the authors benefited from the discussion and debate on their papers. The editors would like to acknowledge Peter Burnham, Peter Fairbrother, Peter Meiksins, Ian Procter and Bill Taylor as colleagues with whom they have developed some of the ideas presented in their chapters. Tony Elger also wishes to acknowledge the stimulation provided by discussion of the issues with graduate students in Labour Studies, especially Nikolai Egloff, Ian Manborde and Sampson Mann.

ABBREVIATIONS

AEEU	Amalgamated Engineering and Electrical Union
AFL/CIO	American Federation of Labor/Confederation of Industrial Organizations
AIF	Annual Improvement Factor
CAMI	General Motors–Suzuki Joint Venture Auto plant, Canada
CAP	Competitiveness Achievement Plan
CAW	Canadian Automobile Workers Union
CEDACs	Cause-Efficiency Diagnosis and Control
CM	Cellular Manufacture
COLA	Cost of Living Allowance
COS	CAMI Operating Standard
CPI	Integrated Process Operator (Conduttore di Processo Integrato)
EC	European Community
EETPU	Electrical, Electronic, Telecommunication and Plumbing Union
EI	Employee Involvement
EPZ	Export Processing Zone
FDI	Foreign Direct Investment
GAT	General Aptitude Test
GDP	Gross Domestic Product
GM	General Motors
GMB	GMB Union (was General, Municipal, Boilermakers and Allied Trades Union)
GMFG	General Motors Fisher Guide Division
GNP	Gross National Product
HAF	Highly Automated Factory
HQ	Headquarters

HRM	Human Resource Management
IDS	Income Data Services; Institute of Development Studies
IF	Integrated Factory
IMTS	Injection Mold/Technical Setup (job grade)
IPEA	Institute do Pesquisas Econômicas Aplicadas, Brazil
IRS	Industrial Relations Services
JETRO	Japanese External Trade Organization
JIT	Just-in-Time production
JLC	Joint Local Committee
JOBS	Job Opportunity Bank, Security Program
JP	Joint Process
JPM	Japanese Production Management
JSSC	Joint Shop Stewards Committee
LO	Swedish Federation of Manual Unions (Landsorganisationen)
MIT	Massachusetts Institute of Technology
NIC	Newly Industrialized Country
NUMMI	New United Motors Manufacturing Incorporated (General Motors–Toyota Joint Venture)
O/D	Organizational Development
OECD	Organization for Economic Cooperation and Development
pcbs	Printed Circuit Boards
QC	Quality Circle; Quality Control
QCC	Quality Control Circle
QIS	Quality Improvement Suggestions (Fiat)
QLE	Quality, Delivery, Economy (Sweden)
QWL	Quality of Working Life
R&D	Research and Development
RSI	Repetitive Strain Injury
SAF	Swedish Employers' Confederation (Svenska Arbetsgivareföreningen)
SAP	Swedish Social-Democratic Party (Sveriges Socialdemokratiska Arbetareparti)
SEL	Secured Employment Level
SIA	Suburu–Isuzu Automotive
SOS	Standard Operation Sheet (CAMI)
SPC	Statistical Process Control
TC	Team Concept
TNC	Transnational Corporation
TQC	Total Quality Control

ABBREVIATIONS

TQM	Total Quality Management
T-S	Team Syracuse (GM)
TV	Television
UAW	United Automobile Workers Union
UK	United Kingdom
US	United States
USA	United States of America
UTE	Technological Elementary Units (Fiat)
UVA	Development Agreement on Codetermination between Swedish Employers and Unions (Utvecklingsavtalet)
VCR	Video Cassette Recorder
VIN	Vehicle Identification Number

INTRODUCTION

Tony Elger and Chris Smith

In 1980 Bill Hayden, head of Ford Europe, came back from a fact-finding visit to Japan shocked by the productivity advantage enjoyed by Japanese car producers. As a consequence he immediately started an 'After Japan' programme which sought tighter labour discipline, increased output and enhanced worker flexibility at Ford plants (Beynon 1984: 356–357). This represented a belated but sharp recognition of the changing competitive relations between American, European and Japanese transnationals, with the dramatic rise of Japanese manufacturing exports through the 1960s and 1970s.

During the 1980s, however, attention shifted increasingly from the role of Japanese firms as exporters, to their role in the establishment of transplant factories in Europe and North America. Between 1982 and 1992 Japanese car companies established eight major automobile assembly plants in the United States (Kenney and Florida 1993: 96), and by 1993 Nissan, Honda and Toyota all had major assembly plants in the UK. Nor were these developments confined to the motor industry, though most of the larger manufacturing transplants were in the auto, auto-components and electricals sectors.

The increasingly prominent role of Japanese manufacturing companies as powerful competitors, both as exporters of goods from Japan and as operators of factories across the globe, has in turn prompted considerable debate, among corporate managements and management gurus, among workers and their unions, and among policy makers and academic commentators. Sometimes the arguments have been simplistic or hysterical, even falling back on racist stereotypes of Japanese people as inherently submissive and group-minded, but at their most sophisticated and reflective they have addressed crucial questions about contemporary changes in the

1

organization of work and relations between management and employees across the globe.

This volume seeks to build on the best features of the current debate about the global role of Japanese corporations, firstly by reassessing how far such corporations are pioneering new social relations in their own workplaces at home and abroad and secondly by analysing the wider influence of their innovations in non-Japanese firms. The purpose of this introduction is to place the later chapters in a wider context, while the prologues to each part of the book introduce the specific contributions of each chapter. To provide the broader context the remainder of the introduction sets out some of the key positions in the contemporary debate about the global significance of the Japanese model of work organization; outlines major areas of controversy between these different positions; and situates these arguments in relation to the actual growth and distribution of the transnational operations of Japanese companies.

KEY CONTRIBUTIONS TO THE CONTEMPORARY DEBATE

A central issue of contention between the competing analyses of the innovations pioneered by Japanese corporations concerns the extent to which such features constitute a discrete package of organizational techniques which can be lifted from its original social and economic context and adopted and applied as a general recipe for enhanced productivity and competitiveness. While some analysts emphasize precisely the universality of this process, others have sought to highlight the importance of wider social and economic circumstances in conditioning the relevance and implications of adopting innovations pioneered by some leading Japanese firms. As we shall see, woven into these contrasting positions are also differing views about the character of competitive relations between firms and about the costs and benefits of these innovations for employers and for their workforces. Finally, almost all of the discussions of the novelty and the global ramifications of Japanese methods of work organization use the notion of Fordism as their benchmark, and we will conclude our review of analytical positions by reassessing the viability of this benchmark.

Universalistic models

The most influential exposition of the universalistic view of the applicability of Japanese production techniques is the MIT study *The Machine That Changed the World* (Womack *et al*. 1990). This argues that innovative and competitive Japanese car manufacturers have developed a distinctive form of production organization, which they title 'lean production'. This is characterized both by the minimization of stocks and work in progress through 'just-in-time production' and by an emphasis on the continuous improvement of production procedures. They claim not only that this approach produces such dramatic productivity gains in the motor industry that all surviving firms will be compelled to adopt them, but also that these innovations are equally relevant across all sectors of manu-facturing and beyond. Finally they argue that these methods are only successful with a skilled and committed workforce attuned to problem solving under pressure, providing a basis for a con-vergence of interests between management and workers.

The MIT study has had a tremendous influence. It has been instrumental in carrying the debate about Japanese production methods to countries like Germany, whose own manufacturing base has proven much more resilient than those of Britain or America, and managements in Britain have used it as a lever to redefine the terrain of their bargaining with unions over such issues as teamworking. There are, however, important problems with the MIT analysis, not least because of its reliance upon an idealized model of lean production. Thus Williams *et al*. (1992) argue that (i) the MIT team dramatically overstate the contrasts between Japanese, European and American car firms in terms of productivity and stock turnover, when in reality Toyota alone stands as the exceptional firm at one end of a spectrum of corporate performance; and (ii) they offer a one-dimensional view of the competitive advantages secured by these supposedly universally applicable production innovations, because they gloss over the significance of other bases of competitive advantage – high capacity utilization, intense work-pace, long working hours and an extensive network of low-waged components suppliers for the Japanese car producers.

Such criticisms suggest that, even within the automobile sector, the competitive relations between transnational firms hinge around a more complex repertoire of options and possibilities and sustain a more turbulent and tension-ridden rivalry than that depicted in the imagery of the evolutionary triumph of lean production. They also suggest that the production innovations celebrated by the MIT team are more likely to shift the terrain of conflicts between management and workers than to achieve a radical resolution of those conflicts.

Another, somewhat more qualified and sophisticated variant of a universalistic analysis is that provided by Kenney and Florida (1993). They too identify the leading Japanese firms as the originators of a new model for the organization of work and production. They choose to term this 'innovation-mediated production' to highlight what they portray as an unparalleled symbiosis between research and development and continuous improvement in the production process, premised upon the active mobilization of the knowledge and intelligence of all employees. Their analysis gives much greater attention to the social relations between capital, labour and the state which surrounded and conditioned the development of teamworking, JIT and continuous improvement in Japanese industry; they offer a less bland account of the implications of this system for workers, by explicitly acknowledging the pressures and constraints involved; and their investigation of the transplantation of innovation-mediated production is not confined to motors but covers several other important sectors.

Yet despite these strengths their commitment to an idealized conception of innovation-mediated production, and its allegedly general applicability, severely distorts their account. Firstly, their characterization of innovation-mediated production collapses together the social relations of the research and development process and those of the much more constrained exercise of initiative in shop floor improvements, and this conflation is reinforced by addressing 'tensions and contradictions' such as work intensity separately from the essentials of the model. Secondly, they persistently interpret variations in the application of the new production methods in terms of progress versus backwardness, thus excluding the possibility that these methods may be of varying relevance to different firms or sectors and in different social and economic conditions.

Much of the appeal but also many of the problems associated with both the MIT and the Kenney and Florida studies stem from their dependence upon one pivotal contrast, between an old and outdated production paradigm – mass production – and a new and progressive paradigm – lean or innovation-mediated production – which stands on the other side of a qualitative divide. There has

been a long history of efforts to understand the historical development of capitalist production in such terms, but this mode of thinking has gained renewed appeal in the last decade or so. This is a
period which has been characterized by the paradoxical
combination of the deepened political hegemony of capitalism, but
also persistent economic dislocations and crises. In such circumstances it becomes extremely tempting to overinterpret what are
certainly significant innovations, to read them uncritically as the
precursors of a wholesale transformation of work and employment
relations, and thus to gloss over substantial continuities, real variations and persistent sources of conflict in the contemporary restructuring of work and employment. This becomes particularly easy if
continuities, variations and conflicts are simply construed as the
remnants of a failed and backward-looking paradigm, but the
danger in this is that the ideal types become substitutes rather than
starting-points for analysis, a point we will return to in our later
comments on Fordism and post-Fordism.

Arguments about Japanization

In some respects the experience in Britain during the 1980s, marked
by economic deregulation, a precipitate decline of manufacturing
and mass unemployment, invited just this approach, and Dan Jones
of the MIT team, for example, argued that these circumstances
marked a moment of opportunity for a transition from old to new
production paradigms. The dominant terms of social science debate
in Britain have, however, diverged somewhat from this approach, to
pay rather more systematic attention to the wider patterns of social
relations which have surrounded and conditioned the organization
of work relations, both in Japan and elsewhere. This approach
probably reflects the salience of arguments about such wider institutional patterns – of union organization and workplace bargaining, of
corporate control and the social organization of management
specialisms, and of state policy – in the debates about the 'decline
of the British economy', which are long standing but gained
renewed political vigour with the rise of Thatcherism.

These concerns had increasingly been articulated from the late
1960s onwards through analyses of the distinctive social and organizational trajectories of different national economies, and debates
about the implications of different national models, especially those
offered by other European states such as France, Sweden or

Germany, for alternative political and industrial agendas in Britain. An important strength of these discussions arose from their recognition of significant and persistent differences in the institutionalized relations between employers, workers and the state in these societies, and their appreciation of the ways in which such differences influenced patterns of innovation and restructuring within companies and workplaces. At the same time it often remained unclear how far these different models were to be regarded as variations around a common theme, as much of the debate about the strengths and weaknesses of 'corporatism' implied, or how far contemporary changes in the global economy, most especially the internationalization of production and the development of a 'new international division of labour', were now placing all these national models under pressure and eroding their distinctiveness.

It was in this context that several British authors chose to talk about Japanization. In general this notion differed from lean production and the like in regarding the adoption of Japanese production innovations outside Japan as problematical, precisely because of the very different institutional and social contexts involved, though commentators differed on just how problematical such adoption might be, and sometimes the arguments fell back on the crude cultural stereotyping which can mar such national comparisons.

At one pole of the British discussion of Japanization are Ackroyd *et al.* (1988), who highlight the contrasts between the economic and social structures of Britain and Japan, not just in terms of contrasting employment systems and labour markets but also in terms of the organization of finance and investment policy. These institutional contrasts will, they suggest, place major constraints on the implementation of Japanese forms of work organization and employment relations by corporate innovators, be they Japanese or British. From this vantage point they also underline the importance of the rhetoric of Japanization, not as an adequate characterization of real changes but rather as an ideological justification for an agenda of changes which often owes little to established Japanese ways of working.

Their article provides a valuable reminder that the organizational initiatives and economic successes of Japanese corporations are embedded within a whole network of social and economic relations, and that any processes of transfer and adaptation will necessarily be conditioned by the different social and economic relations of host countries. This case is, however, developed at a quite abstract level, so that the precise character and extent of such influences remain to be explored.

This opens the way to the approach adopted at the other pole of the Japanization argument, that of Oliver and Wilkinson who are much less critical of the new production paradigm approach. The fundamental argument in their influential book, *The Japanization of British Industry* (1988, 1992) is twofold. Firstly they emphasize that the new production methods celebrated by the MIT study and Kenney and Florida do require very specific social conditions, of the sort provided by the Japanese social structure, for them to work, because of the levels of worker commitment they require and their potential vulnerability to disruption by both workers and suppliers. Secondly, however, they argue that there are various ways in which managements can cope with the resultant interdependencies; the reproduction of Japanese institutions suggested by Ackroyd is unlikely to be necessary as 'a variety of practices, many of which may not be Japanese, can act as the functional equivalents to some of the supporting conditions found in Japan itself' (Oliver and Wilkinson 1992: 69).

Unfortunately, however, there is little real elaboration of the implications of this argument in the rest of their book. Overall, they succeed in leaving the impression that Japanization in Britain is advancing on a wide front, despite significant setbacks, but the changes involved remain opaque. In particular their discussion of the potential 'functional equivalents' available to British companies merely becomes a catalogue of fashionable 'human resource management' techniques, though they emphasize that the initial adoption of such techniques was often unconnected with Japanese inspired production innovations. Thus they offer little critical inter-rogation of the extent to which human resource management genuinely reconstructs employment relations or supports inno-vations in production, or more broadly of the relationship between consent and coercion of employees in a period characterized by fears of redundancy and the marginalization of trade unions.

In this sense, then, the notion of Japanization has become a label for a fairly open-ended agenda of investigation rather than a set of strong claims about the scope and character of the spread of Japanese production techniques. This is tacitly recognized by Oliver and Wilkinson (1992: 12–19) and actively advocated by Wood (1992), and it is in this spirit that we have retained this terminology in the title of the present volume. Thus we use the term Japanization with a question mark, to underline both the disputed character of the social organization of production in Japanese manufacturing and the problematical influence of wider social, economic and political conditions on management efforts to adopt or adapt such innovations.

Toyotism: the corporate exemplar?

This leads us to a final family of concepts that have been used to characterize contemporary changes in the organization of work and employment, namely 'isms' associated with innovating managers or corporations. Of course there is a long tradition of debate surrounding the notions of Taylorism and Fordism, which remain important benchmarks in assessing the significance of Japanese production innovations, and such labels were deployed by both Womack *et al.* (Ohnoism) and Kenney and Florida (Fujitsuism) before they opted for their more universalistic sounding terminologies. However, the most cogent arguments for the use of such a label have focused on the notion of Toyotism.

Dohse *et al.*, one of the few German research groups directly to address the implications of Japanese production innovations, chose the label Toyotism for two critical reasons. First, they wish to challenge the notion of a radical transformation in work relations by reassessing the novelty of these innovations even in the exemplar company. Thus they argue that Toyota has pioneered methods which extend rather than supersede the existing logics of mass production, by providing new ways in which to rationalize and intensify the work process. Secondly, they wish to pursue the issues raised by commentators on Japanization by drawing out the connections between these innovations and the wider institutional matrix of employment relations within which they are embedded, again with particular attention to the conditions surrounding developments at Toyota.

Though developed in the mid-1980s their core argument remains a powerful one. This is that the specific institutional framework of employment relations in Japan facilitated innovations at Toyota which imposed significant new pressures on workers, and that such pressures would have met more immediate resistance in many areas of Europe or America with their different forms of trade unionism and traditions of workplace bargaining. What remains less clear in their account is the degree of novelty involved in the Toyota system, for in general they characterize it as a refinement of Fordist methods but they acknowledge that this involves a real shift towards the deployment of worker knowledge to facilitate continuous improvement. They also remain somewhat ambiguous about the extent to which Toyotism has been adopted and adapted by other companies than Toyota even within Japan.

A more recent and somewhat different argument for the analytical value of the notion of Toyotism (though he spells it Toyotaism) has been advanced by Wood (1992). His starting point is the British debate about Japanization, and in particular the evident need to distinguish between the transfer of specific innovations in the organization of production and the development or transfer of wider institutional arrangements if the issues raised by that debate are to be clarified. This leads him to define the essence of Toyotism as just-in-time production management, but to problematize both the extent of diffusion of this approach and the evolving relationship between such innovations and their wider social and economic contexts.

In pursuing the first theme he suggests that the adoption of such JIT methods has not only been quite selective and limited outside Japan but also very uneven within Japan. Thus one of the advantages of the notion of Toyotism is that it can signal the corporate specificity and variability of developments among Japanese companies, both within and beyond manufacturing, and thus avoid any assumption of a homogeneous Japanese model or generalized contrasts between Japanese and non-Japanese enterprises. Such an approach also lends itself to a more agnostic evaluation of the productivity and profitability implications of Toyotism, for on the one hand applications may be varied and selective, but on the other hand management objectives and priorities may also vary, especially once we recognize that there is no perfect production system, and that all variants will still embody real dilemmas and sources of conflict (Wood 1992: 582–585).

In pursuing the second theme Wood wishes to distinguish contemporary changes in employment practices and in inter-firm relationships from innovations in work organization, so that the connections and disjunctions between them can be investigated rather than assumed. This leads him to define a research agenda focused upon the varied and changing relationships which might exist between (i) the Toyotist organization of production, itself implemented in an uneven fashion; (ii) alternative employment systems, such as those associated with core employment in Japanese firms, or those associated with British versions of 'human resource management'; (iii) different contractual relations between firms, such as arms-length market transactions or close long-term alliances, and (iv) broader institutional relations and state policies. Thus the distinction between Japanization and Toyotism generates a valuable mapping of some of the central research issues which arise from a more critical reappraisal of the claims made by the earlier analyses, which posit the triumph of a new production paradigm or the widespread Japanization of European or American manufacturing.

There is, however, one important lacuna at the heart of Wood's research agenda, which concerns the character of the demands and opportunities faced by those who work within the Toyota system. Elsewhere Wood (1989) has emphasized that this system represents a major development in the organization of production because it recognizes the importance of the tacit knowledge possessed by ordinary workers and effectively mobilizes that knowledge within the production process, and he tacitly carries this positive assessment into his interrogation of 'Japanization and/or Toyotaism'. In so doing he shifts attention away from what should remain a key component of a critical research agenda, namely an investigation of the relationship between working smarter and working harder in Toyotist work regimes, for the evidence on Toyota itself suggests that these features were originally intimately related (Dohse *et al.* 1985; Cusumano 1985).

Furthermore, this issue of the substantive character of work relations within the labour process has important implications for the rest of Wood's agenda, for it must be central to any assessment of the tensions and conflicts which may beset JIT production systems and it must inform any discussion of the stability or fragility of the different forms of institutionalized employee integration or class compromise which may surround such manufacturing innovations.

The spectre of Fordism

As we noted earlier, all three of these broad approaches to understanding the character and influence of the new forms of work organization pioneered by leading Japanese firms treat Fordism as a benchmark. Both 'lean production' and 'innovation-mediated production' are directly defined as fundamental breaks from Fordist mass production. The debate surrounding the notion of Japan-ization widens the comparisons to include not only changes in the labour process but to relate these to distinctive forms of industrial relations and state policy, but this parallels the extension of the notion of Fordism in the French 'regulation theory' approach (Aglietta 1979), to embrace mass consumption and state welfarism as well as mass production. Finally Toyotism is an evident analogue of Fordism, though Dohse *et al.* see more of a continuity than a rupture between the two.

Thus Fordism appears as a long-established and clearly identifiable paradigm which, through contrasts and comparisons, can guide the analysis of contemporary changes which as yet remain amorphous and ambiguous. Recent reappraisals of the notion of Fordism (Tolliday and Zeitlin 1986; Williams *et al.* 1987; Clarke 1992; Williams *et al.* 1993) have, however, suggested that such appearances are deceptive, and in our view the implications of these critiques now need to be absorbed by those seeking to analyse the work relations of Japanese trans-nationals, their transplants and their imitators.

Though the commentators listed above work within different theoretical traditions, their critiques share several common themes. The first is that many usages of the notion of Fordism deploy it in an overextended fashion, to embrace not only the organization of the labour process but also mass trade unionism, centralized wage bargaining, extended working class consumption, and welfarist and Keynesian state policies. As Clarke (1988, 1992) in particular emphasizes, the central problem with such an approach is that all of these components come to be viewed as integral and mutually reinforcing features of a totality, which for a period constitute a functional whole before the onset of crisis and supercession. As a result the uneven and syncopated relations between these develop-ments are suppressed and tensions and contestation are banished to periods of transition.

Their second major argument is that even those more modest conceptions of Fordism which focus exclusively on the socio-technical organization of production operate with an over-coherent and static model of the relationships between such features as standardized production, assembly line processes, unskilled work and high wages. In practice these elements were developed in an uneven fashion over time even within the Ford plants (Williams *et al.* 1993), while the adoption and adaptation of these features by US and European competitors facing different product market, employment and political conditions spawned further temporal and spatial variation and unevenness (Tolliday and Zeitlin 1986). Such features are only compounded if we look beyond the automobile sector and seek to characterize the mass of manufacturing (or even much of the service sector) in terms of Fordism.

The third theme, which underpins the first two, concerns the problematical status of ideal types of production paradigms or production regimes, which inevitably tend to freeze specific but evolving ensembles of social relations in ways which suppress the contested and contradictory dynamics of those relations. The central implication of this critique is that our analyses of the organization and reorganization of social relations within the production process, and of the relationship of such initiatives to inter-corporate competition and the wider restructuring of social and political relations, should always be informed by a sense of the fundamental tensions and incipient conflicts which qualify any settled and generalized institutionalization of a specific production paradigm or social structure of accumulation.

This suggests that our understanding of the significance of Japanese innovations in work organization is more likely to be limited than advanced if we remain mesmerized by idealized contrasts between production paradigms or broad brush conceptions of Japanization. Even the concept of Toyotism is unlikely to be immune from such limitations if the fate of the notion of Fordism is anything to go by. This does not, however, mean that the research agenda which emerges from critiques of these typologies simply becomes an invitation to engage in piecemeal and untheorized research. What it suggests is a different analytical agenda which should inform substantive research; an agenda that should subvert the contemporary penchant for reading real but partial and contested changes, both in forms of work organization and the wider social relations of employment, as radical transformations which unproblematically transcend older competitive rivalries and class antagonisms.

The starting point for such an approach must remain what Thompson (1990) identifies as the core of critical labour process theory: the analysis of those tensions and struggles through which the open-ended potentials of labour power have been managed, through shifting patterns of coercion, accommodation and compliance, into forms of profitable production. In turn this analysis has to be linked to a dynamic disequilibrium perspective on the competitive relations between capitalist enterprises. That is one which remains sensitive to the variety of ways in which competitive advantage may be sought on the complex and uneven social terrain of globalized production, and which recognizes that even the most successful corporate strategies remain beset by substantial constraints and contradictions (what Hyman (1987) characterizes as alternative routes to partial failure). Finally, we need to develop an analysis of the terrain of global capitalist production which recognizes the distinctive features of different states and their related civil societies, for example in terms of modalities of state intervention and institutions of class accommodation, but also attends to both the internal tensions and the limited autonomy of such social forms.

So far in this introduction we have sought to contextualize the contributions of the later chapters by reviewing three major approaches to the contemporary discussion of the significance of Japanese innovations in the organization of production, and their global dissemination through the activities of transplants, emulators and competitors. Through an interrogation of these different approaches we have argued for a substantial reorientation of social analysis, away from generalized contrasts between production paradigms or the multiplication of variant types of Fordism or post-Fordism, towards an emphasis on the ways in which active but contentious processes of work reorganization and institutional restructuring continue to reconstitute the unsettled social relations of the labour process. We now turn to a brief consideration of the relationship between the debate about Japanization and the actual pattern of growth and geographical location of Japanese foreign investment.

JAPANESE FOREIGN DIRECT INVESTMENT

In this section we examine the pattern and spread of Japanese foreign direct investment (FDI), as well as its rationale, and the differing reactions to its rapid growth across nation states. We examine the depth of investment, and the extent to which genuine globalization and decentralization of core activities is taking place. We also indicate how the locational and sectoral concentration of FDI affects the interaction between Japanese practices and the local environment.

The debate around the export of the 'Japanese model' of work organization and labour–capital relations only partially reflects the material conditions of Japanese FDI. While arguments about the diffusion and adaptation of this model have followed increased volumes of

13

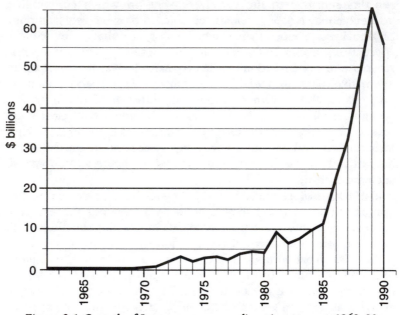

Figure 0.1 Growth of Japanese overseas direct investment, 1962–90
Source: Ministry of International Trade and Industry, *Direct Overseas Investment from Japanese Companies*, various issues.

investment, the depth and nature of the investment has not been directly mirrored in the focus of debate. Most investment has been in services, yet virtually all discussion has centred on manufacturing industries. We know little about work organization in Japanese overseas service industries, except that in Japan it is an inefficient and labour-intensive area, in contrast to the efficiency of much of manufacture. A different story of the Japanese 'miracle' would have emerged from a focus on its service industries. Debate has, however, followed investment patterns in terms of geographical location. The US has received more investment by value and number, and has also been dominant in creating interpretative schemas for studying the consequences of this investment. In Europe, Britain has gained more investment, and also theorized and analysed its meaning much more extensively than elsewhere. German exposition (e.g. Dohse *et al.* 1985; Tokunaga and Bergmann 1984; Bergmann and Tokunaga 1987) has concentrated primarily on analyses of Japanese work and employment relations, and has only recently begun to address the process of diffusion more directly (Jurgens 1989, 1992; Deutschmann 1992; and other contributions in Tokunaga *et al.* 1992; Brookman 1993). A study of French and Spanish transplants (Costa and Garanto 1993) has provided a more thoroughly disaggregated analysis by sectors than British studies, but remains relatively dependent on British theorizing. So while there is no neat correspondence between the facts of investment and terms of debate, there is a relationship which we need to examine.

The growth of Japanese FDI has been accelerating dramatically in recent years. The cumulative outward FDI between 1986 and 1989 constituted 70 per cent of total outward FDI from 1951 (Akimune 1991: 11). As Figure 0.1 shows, investment took off from the mid-1980s, having moved along in fits and starts from the mid-1960s, though the dip in 1990 underlines some continuing instability in the pace of growth.

Most investment in the 1970s was in developing countries, and much of this was oriented towards either securing primary raw materials scarce in Japan, or subcontracting labour-intensive areas of manufacturing, such as textiles and electronics. The pattern in the 1980s switched towards developed countries, and was primarily market rather than cost driven. The US was the primary investment target, followed by Europe. The combined share of US and EC cumulative outward FDI rose from 38 per cent in the 1970s to 61 per cent in the 1980s (Akimune 1991: 11).

Tables 0.1 and 0.2 indicate the flow and the accumulated share of Japanese FDI by sector/industry. Much of this investment was in the non-manufacturing and non-primary goods sectors – the cumulative share in the 1980s being 70 per cent of Japanese FDI compared with 39 per cent in the 1970s. Finance, insurance and real estate dominated this investment in the non-manufacturing sector, and this was also different from the 1970s when commerce dominated non-manufacturing investment, as Japanese TNCs established offices, branches and service outlets to manage the products which were exported. The move into finance, insurance and real estate reflects both the independent growth of the Japanese non-manufacturing sector abroad, and also the need to support Japanese firms establishing production facilities overseas.

The flow and the accumulated share of Japanese FDI by region is shown in Tables 0.3 and 0.4. They reveal that the US has been the main recipient by number of investments and value, taking 36.2 per cent of all investments and 42 per cent ($130.5bn) of the cumulative value for 1951–1990. Asia, while taking almost 30 per cent of the

Table 0.1 Flow of Japanese overseas investment by sector and industry to 1991, measured by cases

Sector/Industry	−1975	1976–1980	1981–1985	1986–1990	1991	Total
Manufacturing	1,088	533	608	2,310	296	4,917
Foodstuffs	61	31	53	147	27	333
Textiles	136	12	24	131	27	337
Chemicals	142	75	88	261	32	616
Metal Products	36	23	24	106	14	212
Gen. Machinery	93	58	61	233	26	473
Elect. Machinery	250	128	119	491	61	1,055
Autos & parts	54	43	58	283	32	471
Other	316	163	181	658	77	1,420
Non-manufacturing	1,723	960	1,503	3,712	495	8,605
Agri. forestry, fishing	39	19	13	50	7	132
Minining, construction	101	68	146	247	35	609
Commerce	1,139	620	755	1,419	208	4,230
Finance & banking	156	85	188	441	57	934
Securities & invest.	22	20	91	304	26	472
Real Estate	41	14	45	275	11	398
Transportation	113	62	113	280	35	633
Services	105	72	145	506	89	949
Stockholding & other	30	13	30	251	33	375
All industries	2,811	1,493	2,111	6,022	791	13,522

Source: Ministry of Finance

Table 0.2 Accumulated share of Japanese overseas investment by sector and industry, 1951–1990, measured by cases and value

Sector/Industry	No. of cases	%	Value ($m)	%
Manufacturing	18,531	29.38	1,613	26.3
Foodstuffs	1,771	2.8	4,085	1.3
Textiles	1,834	2.9	3,999	1.3
Chemicals	2,047	3.2	10,940	3.5
Iron, Steel, Metals	2,029	3.2	10,308	3.3
General Machinery	2,307	3.7	7,932	2.6
Electrical Machinery	3,194	5.0	20,360	6.6
Transportation equip.	1,081	1.7	10,880	3.5
Other	4,268	6.7	13,107	4.3
Non-manufacturing	44,705	70.7	229,195	73.7
Agri. forestry, fishing	2,022	3.2	2,097	0.6
Mining, construction	2,393	3.8	18,928	6.1
Commerce	14,547	23.0	31,315	10.1
Financing & insurance	2,387	3.8	65,319	21.0
Services	5,521	8.7	34,667	11.1
Transportation	4,269	6.8	17,438	5.6
Real estate	8,977	4.2	46,444	15.0
Other	4,589	7.3	12,987	4.2
All Industries	63,236	100.0	310,808	100.0

Source: Ministry of Finance

Table 0.3 Flow of Japanese overseas investment by region and selected countries to 1991, measured by cases

Region/Country	−1975	1976– 1980	1981– 1985	1986– 1990	1991	Total
North America	623	363	644	1,902	168	3,791
United States	548	339	571	1,767	163	3,467
Canada	75	25	73	139	5	324
Europe	436	283	483	1,365	247	2,877
Asia	1,185	590	735	2,201	325	5,126
Latin America	349	131	106	222	20	863
Oceania	157	82	101	270	30	651
Australia	105	63	76	197	19	468
Africa	44	25	20	43	–	136
Near & Mid East	17	19	22	14	1	78
World Total	2,811	1,493	2,111	6,022	791	13,522

Source: Ministry of Finance

cases of investment, took under 15 per cent ($47.5bn) of the value of total Japanese FDI. Asian investments were largely to take advantage of low labour costs, and not markets, as a high proportion of investments were in production facilities which produced for export, either back to Japan or to developed countries. In the EC and America, investment in manufacturing has been primarily – although not exclusively – to service local markets. Europe took 11.8 per cent of cases of investment but 19.1 per cent ($59.2bn) of the value for the same period (*Financial Times*, 20 September 1991). If we break down the European figures, then the UK has attracted most investment, 32 per cent of investment cases (2,134), and 42 per cent ($22.6bn) of value for the 1951–1990 period. This compares with Germany which gained 1,187 projects worth $4.7bn and France which attracted 1,328 projects worth $4.1bn. The Netherlands, Italy and Spain have been the other primary targets of Japanese investment in Europe.

The rationale for Japanese FDI varies by region, as does the debate which surrounds its nature. In Asia Japanese capital has taken advantage of cheap but qualified labour to create off-shore production platforms typical of strategies of other multinationals,

Table 0.4 Accumulated share of Japanese overseas investment by region and selected countries, 1951–1990, measured by cases and value

Region/Country	No. of cases	%	Value ($m)	%
North America	24,225	38.3	136,185	43.8
United States	22,944	36.2	130,529	42.0
Canada	1,281	2.0	5,655	1.8
Europe	7,425	11.8	59,265	19.1
United Kingdom	2,134	3.4	22,598	7.3
Asia	18,634	29.5	47,519	15.3
Latin America	7,194	11.4	40,483	13.0
Oceania	3,957	6.2	18.098	5.8
Australia	2,760	4.4	16,063	5.2
Africa	1,458	2.3	5,826	1.9
Near & Mid East	340	0.5	3,431	1.1
World Total	63,236	100.0	310,808	100.0

Source: Ministry of Finance

and it is therefore not surprising that we have not witnessed in these countries much theoretical debate about a distinctly 'Japanese' type of production behaviour. Kume and Totsuka (1991: 51) note that the 'search for abundant cheap labour is characteristic of investments in developing countries'. Japanese firm behaviour is no different from other multinationals in this respect (see Dedoussis and Littler, this volume). In Britain, however, Japanese capital was actively encouraged by the Conservative Government to replace and modernize ailing manufacturing sectors and discipline labour, and it is therefore, not surprising, that this country has produced an active debate around what some writers have called the 'Japanization' of British industry. As two recent Japanese commentators note: 'The British government expressed the hope that Japanese companies would introduce new industrial relations practices and transfer their manufacturing philosophy and technology to their British counterparts' (Kume and Totsuka 1991: 53). The incentives for Japanese capital entering the UK included the low demands made on it for local content and other regulations, the openness of the British market to foreign capital and ease of language – English being the world business language, the chief foreign language taught in Japan and the main language in strategic sectors such as computers. In Britain the courting of Japanese investment at a high level, and the liberal terms of entry were part of a strategy to attack organized labour.

This is in sharp contrast to the attitudes towards Japanese FDI in Germany and France, where there was no state agenda to utilize foreign investment as a national industrial strategy. The German Federal government offers no special incentives to investors, though the Länder governments do. But the more open nature of product markets and the competitive and successful high wage nature of German industry has kept open Japanese imports and not made for significant Japanese investments. The hostility of the French state towards Japanese imports, and its strong defence of strategic industries like autos, has not kept Japanese investment out, as, paradoxically, France's very hostility is an incentive to enter to placate an important state. Kume and Totsuka (1991) note that Japanese companies regard France as a central player inside the EC and therefore it is necessary not to alienate it by keeping out investment.

In general terms motivations for Japanese overseas investment relate to the need to recycle Japan's trade surpluses, the fear of growing protectionism in world markets, appreciation of the yen which reduced the cost of overseas investment, increased prices of Japanese real estate and stocks which pushed investment out, and the globalization of the trade and corporate structures of Japan's multinational companies. Between 1985 and 1988 there was a twofold increase of yen–dollar exchange value, which slashed the cost of American stocks and real estate to Japanese companies – this explains a lot of the surge in investment in the late 1980s. Trade frictions associated with Japan's accumulating trade surpluses and relatively closed home market, led to expanded overseas investment, much of which was export substitution investment in the increasingly protected sectors such as autos, VCRs and semi-conductors. Finally, many Japanese firms were seeking to globalize their operations, and establish not just sales outlets, but a financial base, production facilities and even regional headquarters in the main centres of world trade. This naturally sucked capital out of Japan. Kanda (1992: 15) notes that the proportion of foreign employees of Japanese companies rose from 10.7 per cent in 1985 to 15.5 per cent in 1990.

Critical debate on Japanese investment in America and Europe has centred on the extent of diffusion of Japanese methods, whether these are positive or negative in local terms, and how much this investment constitutes low or high value-added production. Leaving aside the evaluation of Japanese production methods both at home and abroad, evidence on the depth of Japanese investment remains controversial. While the pessimists (e.g. Williams *et al.* 1992) have emphasized the predominantly assembly nature of factories and their dependence on component sourcing from outside the country, the optimists (e.g. Kenney and Florida 1993) have argued that this is a temporary phase and is declining as local component supplies replace imported parts. Local content rules vary between European societies and between Europe and America, although EC rules are now more uniform, and attempts to get European based, especially UK based, Japanese car assemblers categorized as non-EC have largely failed. Such rules have had the effect of further internationalizing Japanese component suppliers as these follow auto assemblers. Specific research on assemblers – such as Nissan (Garrahan and Stewart 1992) – has found them highly dependent on bought-in components. Moreover, locally sourced content is frequently of low value-added items, like packaging, rather than high value-added manufactured components, which are bought in from Japan or elsewhere (*Financial Times* 20 September 1991).

The question of whether Japanese firms in Europe and America are increasing the depth and breadth of their investment profile and establishing not just sales and assembly outlets, but product support, research and development (R&D) and corporate management provision also remains controversial. While certain companies have established research institutes in Europe, for example, Nissan, Kao Corporation, Sony, Sumitomo, Toshiba and Hitachi, these are very much the exception, rather than the rule. Moreover, many of these facilities employ few staff, and do not in any way detract from the main R&D centres which remain in Japan. Statistically, the number of companies establishing R&D sites outside Japan is insignificant. Kanda (1992) uses figures from the Japan Committee for Economic Development to show that at the end of 1990 only twenty Japanese companies had basic R&D subsidiaries abroad. About 25 had product development subsidiaries, and about 50 were engaged in procurement, but this must be set against the thousands of investment sites and production bases overseas. The data indicates a rise in R&D, product development and procurement during the 1980s, but there has been a levelling off in the 1990s, due to the recession in Japan and general downturn in overseas investment from its peak in 1989. Strategic alliances between Japanese and US and European companies have been increasing, and these, more than independent research subsidiaries, are an important source of the transfer of ideas and technologies. More so than American multinationals, Japanese firms overwhelmingly retain high-value added production at home.

What of the decentralization of managerial control? Some Japanese companies, Cannon and Honda for example, have put forward the idea of four headquarters – Japan, USA, Europe and Asia – as part of a globalization strategy and an attempt to devolve power from Japan. But again, the celebrated examples exaggerate the process. Kanda (1992: 18) shows that overseas regional headquarters increased from 20 in 1981 to 68 in 1990 – 30 in the US, 20 in Europe and 18 in Asia. Hardly a dramatic change. Using research on company plans for decentralization conducted in 1990, he notes that the trend is likely to increase, although perception of the relative importance of Japanese and regional HQs indicate that for all categories of decision making Japan remains the centre. Meanwhile, the late 1980s probably represent something of a hiatus in decentralization, as the onset of recession in Japan has made retrenchment the order of the day.

One other feature of the pattern and nature of Japanese investment is worthy of note, as this affects debate over diffusion. In Britain research has indicated a distinct clustering of investment by region and product type (*Financial Times* 20 September 1991; Oliver and Wilkinson 1992; Hill and Munday 1992). This pattern is also observed in France and Spain (Costa and Garanto 1993) and across Europe (Kume and Totsuka 1991). There is tendency for production to go to depressed areas – South Wales, the North East and Scotland in Britain – as well as new towns – Milton Keynes and Telford in Britain. This is partly to take advantage of state subsidies, and partly to escape regional labour markets and work cultures in particular sectors – autos for example. The consequence of clustering is to enhance the impact of Japanese working practices on the environment – high unemployment increases choice of labour and people's willingness to accept new conditions, while clustering exaggerates the influence of Japanese firms on the local economy and indigenous working practices. Kenney and Florida (1993) observe a similar clustering in the auto sector especially in the US and also note the predilection among Japanese firms for rural areas, non-industrial labour and white workers. At the same time Milkman (1992: 162), studying Japanese transplants in Southern California, found that while the proportion of black workers was low, Mexican and Asian labour was recruited in large numbers, and suggests that the ways in which firms captitalize upon the conditions in local labour markets may vary quite markedly across sectors and regions. Such features are especially relevant in assessing the implications of the growing number of studies of transplants, but are also pertinent to the wider debate about the diffusion of Japanese management techniques, as other firms adopt, modify or convert those techniques in the light of their own priorities and circumstances.

REFERENCES

Ackroyd, S. *et al.* (1988) 'The Japanization of British Industry?', *Industrial Relations Journal* 19, 1: 11–23.
Aglietta, M. (1979) *A Theory of Capitalist Regulation*, London: Verso.
Akimune, I. (1991) 'Overview: Japan's direct investment in the EC', in M. Yoshitomi *et al.* (eds) *Japanese Direct Investment in Europe: Motives, impact and policy implications*, Aldershot: Avebury.
Bergmann, J. and Tokunaga, S. (eds) (1987) *Economic and Social Aspects of Industrial Relations: a Comparison of the German and Japanese Systems*, Frankfurt: Campus.
Beynon, H. (1984) *Working for Ford*, Harmondsworth: Penguin (2nd edn).
Brookman, J. (1993) 'Sayonara London', *Times Higher*, 26 November, p. 21.
Clarke, S. (1988) 'Overaccumulation, class struggle and the regulation approach', *Capital and Class* 36: 59–92.
—— (1992) 'What in the Ford's name is Fordism', in Nigel Gilbert *et al.* (eds) *Fordism and Flexibility: Divisions and Change*, London: Macmillan.
Costa, I. and Garanto, A. (1993) 'Entreprises japonaises et syndicalisme en Europe', *Le Mouvement Social* 162 (January–March): 95–128.
Cusumano, M. A. (1985) *The Japanese Automobile Industry: Technology and Management at Nissan and Toyota*, Cambridge Mass.: Harvard UP.
Deutschmann, M. (1992) 'Works councils and enterprise-level industrial relations in German transplants of Japanese firms', in S. Tokunaga *et al.* (eds) *New Impacts on Industrial Relations*, Munich: Luridicum-Verlag.
Dohse, K. *et al.* (1985) 'From "Fordism" to "Toyotism"? The social organisation of the labour process in the Japanese automobile industry', *Politics and Society* 14, 2: 115–146.
Financial Times, 'Japan in the UK', 20 September 1990.
Florida, R. and Kenney, M. (1991) 'Organisation versus culture: Japanese automotive transplants in the US', *Industrial Relations Journal* 22, 3: 181–196.
Garrahan, P. and Stewart, P. (1992) *The Nissan Enigma: Flexibility at Work in a Local Economy*, London: Cassell.
Hill, S. and Munday, M. (1992) 'Japanese investment: The benefits for Wales', *Anglo-Japanese Journal* 6, 1: 14–15.
Hyman, R. (1987) 'Strategy or structure? Capital, labour and control', *Work, Employment and Society* 1, 1: 25–55.
Jurgens, U. (1989) 'The transfer of Japanese management concepts in the international automobile industry', in S. Wood (ed.) *The Transformation of Work?*, London: Unwin Hyman.
—— (1992) 'Internationalization strategies of Japanese and German

automobile companies', in S. Tokunaga *et al.* (eds) *New Impacts on Industrial Relations*, Munich: Luridicum-Verlag.

Kanda, M. (1992) 'Globalisation of Japanese companies in the '90s: an overview' (March), Doctoral Working Paper no. 4, Aston Business School, Aston University.

Kenney, M. and Florida, R. (1988) 'Beyond mass production: production and the labour process in Japan', *Politics and Society* 16.1: 121–158.

—— (1993) *Beyond Mass Production: the Japanese System and its Transfer to the US*, Oxford: Oxford UP.

Kume, G. and Totsuka, K. (1991) 'Japanese manufacturing investment in the EC: motives and locations', in M. Yoshitomi *et al.* (eds) *Japanese Direct Investment in Europe: Motives, Impact and Policy Implications*, Aldershot: Avebury.

Milkman, R. (1991) *Japan's California Factories: Labor Relations and Economic Globalization*, Los Angeles: Institute of Industrial Relations, University of California.

—— (1992) 'The impact of foreign investment on US industrial relations: The Case of California's Japanese-owned Plants', *Economic and Industrial Democracy* 13: 151–182.

Oliver, N. and Wilkinson, B. (1988) *The Japanization of British Industry*, Oxford: Blackwell.

—— (1992) *The Japanization of British Industry: New Developments in the 1990s*, Oxford: Blackwell.

Thompson, P (1990) 'Crawling from the wreckage: the labour process and the politics of production', in D. Knights and H. Willmott (eds) *Labour Process Theory*, London: Macmillan.

Tokunaga, S. and Bergmann, J. (eds) (1984) *Industrial Relations in Transition*, Tokyo: Tokyo University Press.

Tokunaga, S., Altmann, N. and Demes, H. (eds) (1992) *New Impacts on Industrial Relations: Internationalisation and Changing Production Strategies*, Munich: Luridicum-Verlag.

Tolliday, S. and Zeitlin, J. (1986) 'Introduction: between Fordism and flexibility', in S. Tolliday and J. Zeitlin (eds) *The Automobile Industry and its Workers*, Cambridge: Polity.

Williams, K. *et al.* (1987) 'The end of mass production?', *Economy and Society* 16, 3: 405–439.

—— (1991) 'Factories versus warehouses: Japanese manufacturing foreign direct investment in Britain and the United States', Polytechnic of East London *Occasional Papers on Business, Economy and Society* 6.

—— (1992) 'Against lean production', *Economy and Society* 21, 3: 321–354.

—— (1993) 'Ford v "Fordism": the beginning of mass production?', *Work, Employment and Society* 6, 4: 517–555.

Womack, J. *et al.* (1990) *The Machine that Changed the World*, New York: Rawson Associates.

Wood, S. (1989) 'The Japanese management model: tacit skills in shop floor participation', *Work and Occupations* 16, 4: 446–460.

—— (1991) 'Japanization and/or Toyotaism?', *Work, Employment and Society* 5, 4: 567–600.

Part I

THE JAPANESE MODEL

PROLOGUE

The chapters in Part I address the debate about the character of the
Japanese model in Japan, and discuss the implications of our understanding of Japanese work and employment relations for analyses
of the international influence of Japanese management practices.
The first chapter provides a wide-ranging review of the major
debates about these issues, and proposes a substantial reorientation
of those debates; the second chapter develops a systematic analysis
of the distinctive features of work organization in the large Japanese
car assemblers which exemplify the most advanced forms of
Japanese management practice, but also emphasizes the importance
of the wider institutional context of these operations; and the third
chapter discusses the impact of restructuring on the employment
status and job security of the employees of large manufacturing
firms, and thereby illuminates wider shifts in the organization of the
Japanese labour market and employment.

In Chapter 1 we aim to do two things: outline our approach to
understanding the diffusion of the Japanese 'model' which has
followed in the wake of the rapid growth in Japanese FDI outlined
in the Introduction, and examine the nature of the labour process in
Japan. We suggest that concepts like 'Japanization' and the Japanese
'model' require deconstructing as they not only imply a greater
degree of homogeneity than actually exists in the labour process in
Japan, but more importantly they set up a fixed benchmark which
both obscures variations in the standard and content of Japanese
FDI and also ignores diversity in the patterns of adoption and
emulation by non-Japanese companies. We demonstrate that
Japanese innovations in work organization and employment have
themselves been the evolving and varied products of the interaction
between earlier dominant (especially American) models, specific

27

institutional ensembles embodying national class compromises and industrialization strategies, and the efforts of Japanese enterprises to cope with particular sectoral and temporal contingencies. Relatedly, the exportation and diffusion of innovations labelled 'Japanese' have to be analysed in terms of a dialogue between the broader corporate strategies of both Japanese and other transnational corporations (TNCs), the interventions of propagandists and mediators who manage the processes of codification and dissemination of specific packages of techniques, and the distinctive national, regional and sectoral conditions and social relations which structure the reception and adaptation of these techniques. We suggest a methodology for further research in the area, which goes beyond prescription and hype, acknowledges the importance of putting the sector political economy of Japanese investment in the frame, and recognizes the continuing need to be flexible in interpreting both the deepening of Japanese investment and foreign company adaptation of innovations associated with the Japanese model.

In Chapter 2 Williams *et al.* use detailed case study evidence drawn from several Japanese motor plants and a European factory operated by an American firm to develop a meticulous analysis of the distinctive character of Japanese production practices and the wider social relations which condition those practices. They underline some profound differences between Japanese and European motor firms – in operating procedures and priorities; in management organization; in the hours and intensity of labour; and in the coordination and control of the labour force – but they also register significant differences between the Japanese companies themselves. They relate the differences between Japanese and Western production practices both to specific trajectories of management organization (with divergent patterns of management expertise, careers and monitoring procedures) and to distinctive levels of worker compliance (sustained by radically different labour market and reward structures, together with company unionism). In this context they draw on material from a major Japanese study of work and labour relations, as well as their own empirical research.

This analysis allows Williams *et al.* to identify both key sources of Japanese competitive advantage and major reasons why the successful generalization of Japanese production methods and priorities among Western companies will be difficult, despite much 'ritual symbolic modernization'. Finally they place their findings within a wider context by underlining that any moves towards

Japanization represent only one aspect of what is a highly complex process of contemporary transnational competition and restructuring, a theme which they have also pursued in parallel research on the role of transplants in Britain and the US and in their critique of the notion of 'lean production' (Williams *et al.* 1991; 1992).

Finally Kamada's chapter sheds fresh light on the complex realities of Japanese employment relations by examining key features of the reorganization of work and employment resulting from the rationalization of Japanese iron and steel during the 1980s. She highlights the central importance of the 'loaning' ('shukkoh') of workers between workplaces and enterprises, as a method of partially reconciling lifetime employment practices with major workforce reductions. These moves have accompanied processes of corporate diversification, so that workers may be transferred to older subsidiaries, to newly formed companies within enterprise groupings, or to other firms outside the conglomerate. The transferred workers remain employees of the rationalizing enterprise and sometimes work on the same site, but have different jobs and often inferior working conditions. The wages paid by the receiving firms are generally lower, but the wage levels for loaned workers are made up by the loaning company, which in turn receives subsidies for 'employment adjustment' from the state. Both the remaining workers and those transferred may experience increased workloads and prolonged working hours.

Kamada sees the extensive transfer/loaning of workers by large rationalizing enterprises as a key element in a wider restructuring of Japanese employment relations. The immediate impact is a domino effect on the security and working conditions of those who already had inferior employment statuses as workers for subsidiaries or subcontractors. In the longer term large enterprises are encouraged to expand their use of subcontractors and temporary workers, while narrowing the pyramidal structure of employment and shifting away from seniority wages towards overtime and other allowances. Thus the wider web of insecure employment expands and the secure core shrinks. Workers have resented these developments, but such resentment has remained unvoiced because of the increasing fragmentation of the workforce and an atmosphere of crisis in which enterprise unions have embraced management's solutions. Nevertheless Kamada suggests that these changes are likely to stimulate some questioning of the established patterns of union organization and politics in Japan.

Thus in their different ways both her account and that of Williams *et al.* underline significant shifts, tensions and instabilities in the social relations of work and employment in Japan, and reinforce the argument that we should take care not to reify a singular and coherent Japanese model. Furthermore, both chapters point out that the very process of the internationalization of Japanese manufacturing itself threatens to exacerbate some of the difficulties and conflicts within Japan, for both rationalization and overseas investment tend to weaken the post-war social settlement and are sources of anxiety for Japanese workers and unions.

REFERENCES

Williams, K. *et al.* (1991) 'Factories versus warehouses: Japanese manufacturing foreign direct investment in Britain and the United States' *Occasional Papers on Business, Economy and Society* 6. Polytechnic of East London.

Williams, K. *et al.* (1992) 'Against lean production', *Economy and Society* 21, 3: 321–354.

1

GLOBAL JAPANIZATION?

Convergence and competition in the organization of the labour process

Tony Elger and Chris Smith

This chapter offers a framework for interpreting the diffusion of work practices associated with Japan to other capitalist societies. We begin by discussing our theoretical perspective, which argues that the organization of the labour process within capitalism is neither entirely context bound nor context free. We argue that the 'organization versus culture' (Florida and Kenney 1991) and the 'Japanization' versus 'lean production' debates (Womack *et al.* 1990; Oliver and Wilkinson 1992) are needlessly dualistic in their treatment of contextual conditions and/or universalizable work practices. Our argument is that practices identified with Japan are simultaneously the embodiment of general economic efficiencies, culturally specific institutional supports and dominant best practices of a powerful economy (Smith and Meiksins 1991).

The paper has four sections covering our theoretical framework, an outline evaluation of the Japanese model in Japan, a review of the impact of the Japanese transplants and 'adopters' in the UK and finally some concluding thoughts on the research issues raised by our analysis.

APPROACHES TO DIFFUSION

Over recent decades discussions of the Japanese model have moved from a preoccupation with national distinctiveness to an emphasis on diffusion. Dore's 1973 account of factory regimes in Britain and Japan emphasised their national-institutional distinctiveness. In Oliver and Wilkinson's 1988 book on the 'Japanization' of British industry, a dominant state was, through direct investment and emulation, extending its national practices to foreign shores. Admittedly Dore, through an appreciation of the effects of uneven development, anticipated a 'learning' from the Japanese, and rejected the idea that Japan had to 'catch up' with the 'more advanced' US or West. But it took the dramatic growth of Japanese foreign direct investment (FDI), discussed in our introduction, and the continual rise of their economic power to turn an academic debate about national distinctiveness into a political discourse on learning, borrowing and the diffusion of 'Japanese' practices. But what does it mean to 'borrow' practices from another national context? What does it mean to talk about these practices through the prefix of nationality, rather than the more universal categories of organizational and economic theory? There are a number of models of cross-national difference and diffusion which can help us unpack these issues.

Cultural uniqueness versus universalism

Some writers have criticized the idea of 'learning' between societies, suggesting instead that each society, due to the specificity of its historical and cultural development, is relatively unique and unchanging. As the products of these conditions are unique, imitation by other societies or export of the products of these conditions is not possible. Diffusion, therefore, does not arise, except where the cultural arena is extended, say through imperialism, but even then it takes a long time before the new part of the cultural arena is recognized as part of the dominant culture.

The problem with such an approach is that because capitalism has spread around the globe, and encountered and subordinated various alternative economic systems and cultural arenas, of necessity, some diffusion of technology, management methods and labour process ideas has occurred. Japan, for example, borrowed Western science and engineering, and American management practices (McCormick 1991; Warner 1992). America, in turn, borrowed and interacted with British craft practices in developing its system of management (Littler 1982; Merkle 1980). While such borrowing does not mean standardization of work organization, to deny the ability of efficiency methods to transfer from one cultural or national context to another is mistaken.

At the other end of the spectrum is the view that efficiency ideas travel from society to society because they share the same economic system, with the same 'culture-free' inputs of science and technology which act as the main influence on the shape of organizations.

In this view, system standards and measures take precedence over nation state diversity, and economics dominates politics. Countries become more or less the same as they adopt the same efficiency imperatives. Concepts like industrialization and modernization assume all societies will become similar by using shared inputs, or adopting common forms, such as large-scale organization, which are solely responsible for structuring work organizations and institutions in the society.

Based on supply side assumptions and crude technological determinism, this 'culture-free' thesis has been popular in organizational theory, especially the contingency school, but has encountered problems from cross-national studies which have revealed persistent difference between societies and sectors sharing the same political economy (Rose 1985). Despite sharing and borrowing, it seems societal specificity continues to be reproduced (Sorge 1991). We are therefore asked to explore the agencies responsible for preserving societal 'uniqueness' and those linked to forces promoting uniformity. This leads us to examine the question of mediating societal arrangements and institutions.

Institutional settlements

This approach suggests that national uniqueness or distinctiveness is created by socio-economic settlements between social agencies and institutions operating on a national terrain. In particular it focuses on institutionalized arrangements between capital and labour, state–firm relations, capital–capital relations, and distinctive factory regimes within particular societies. These conditions are less the consequence of cultural legacies than of socio-political action. Agencies within particular contexts create sets of industrial relations, education/training programmes and so on, which influence the action of the state in the economy. If the agents within these situations create distinctive competences in the economy – such as the German and Japanese stress on manufacturing, education, training – then they cannot be imitated by other capitals, only other states, and this is not simple because the product is the result of specific class settlements, responses to crisis conditions or specific time constraints, which will not exist in other socio-economic contexts. Moreover, the 'product' to be exported is a complex institutional network of state–capital–labour relations, and not something particular to factory regimes; it may be manifest in factory regimes, but does not originate there, hence cannot be borrowed at this level.

Whereas certain innovations within capitalism, such as new technologies, are capable of being detached from their original context and sold in the original state through markets on a global scale, others, such as social or organizational processes, are harder to detach, harder to put together in a different environment and inevitably open to conflicting and competing mediation and interpretation.

Where such state–capital–labour regimes have been conceived of as exportable policy packages, such as corporatism, then these political policies can be copied. However, as the British experience of fragile corporatism in the late 1960s and 1970s reveals, such new policies encounter deeper national institutional traditions which often subvert such policy formulae. This suggests that in comparison with capitalist firms, state institutions involve greater diversity and complexity which militate against the operation of standard political strategies. As we explain later, much of what is considered to be characteristic of the Japanese 'model' exists within a distinctive state–capital–labour complex, and these features of the model will be difficult to transfer.

Not all states are created equal

One mechanism of diffusion is the dominance of one state over another. Capitalism can subordinate and constrain national trajectories to international standards, but because the world is divided into capitalist blocs, this also means that economic hegemony can be exercised by one state and society over another. In particular dominant societies can extend their sphere of influence to others through processes of underdevelopment or enclave industrialism which create 'banana republics' or export processing zones (EPZs). The increasing integration of the world, and disintegration of the firm, may speed up diffusion of advanced production methods from north to south, but also reinforce patterns of subordination between developed and developing societies. As Sklair (1991: 95) shows, while investment in developing societies is slowing down, export platforms, such as EPZs, remain dynamic areas of growth, and it is these areas where the transnational corporations (TNCs) exercise great influence.

In the age of more mobile capital, the logic of industrialization in developing societies and direct investment/relocation in advanced societies is informed by a transnational company logic and not some universal economic principle as envisaged by industrial society literature. This suggests that the diffusion of best practice ideas or new production systems, which are part of a dominant state's transnational factory regime, will be differentially distributed according to this particular logic and not some set of general capitalist principles. Japanese firms will install different factory regimes in their Malaysian relative to their German subsidiaries. In other words, the international division of labour and production through transnational capital means an unequal installation of personnel practices, manufacturing techniques and training programmes typically identified with the home practices of the dominant country.

Diffusion, ownership and timing

Diffusion is influenced by the ownership character of the TNC, and the conditions of trade, transport, communication and technology across the world. In addition it is also affected by the timing of the arrival of the new entrant or practice in the host society. Dicken (1992: 405), summarizing the literature on the effects of the nationality of ownership on the labour relations in firms, notes that American and Japanese companies are more centralized in these matters relative to British and European companies. Hence there is likely to be more conformity to local conditions in British overseas transplants, relative to American and Japanese plants which bring with them national competences. This qualifies the above argument that diffusion takes place through the logic and structure of transnational capital, and suggests an intervening variable might be the *nationality* of ownership of these TNCs.

But there is also a question of the relationship between dominant states, global economic trading conditions and the social innovations brought in by the TNC. In some ways the diffusion of American best practices was made easier in the inter-war and post-war period because American firms established replica manufacturing plants where best practice could be installed and learnt. It was not possible, because of distance, available transport/ communication systems or political conditions of trade, to disaggregate and integrate design–manufacture–assembly on a global scale (at least in the advanced capitalist economies). At the same time, the impact of these American free-standing exemplars was qualified by the persistence of a semi-luxury market in Europe throughout the inter-war period, and also in Britain by a continuing management insistence on piecework payment work regimes.

However, Japanese transplants in the advanced economies are chiefly assembly operations, dependent on imports of manufactured inputs from Japan, and hence possess a continued reliance on the Japanese economy (Williams *et al.* 1991; Dedoussis and Littler, this volume). Japanese capital not only depends more heavily on disaggregated production, but has also entered global expansion under conditions of free trade, and technological circumstances which are more conducive to the spatial division of labour. This makes the spread of Japanese best practice to the West different from the 'Americanization' of Europe because their transplants are more tightly coupled to a logic which suits Japanese capital. In the British case this involves the use of cheap female and male unskilled labour to assemble products for the export market in Europe. Japanese transplants lack a 'full' compliment of engineers, technicians, skilled and semi-skilled workers typical of production at home. These specific features of the Japanese subsidiary constrain transfer or diffusion of practices associated with Japan, because in a real sense we are not comparing like with like when we discuss Nissan UK and Nissan Japan. Therefore any sense of borrowing 'best practice' or the Japanese 'model' is conditioned by a Japanese transnational capital logic and thus it is not open for all societies or firms to participate in an unqualified way.

These arguments undermine those universalistic approaches to the diffusion of Japanese manufacturing practices which focus on the potential transfer of a discrete package of expertise, judged by unproblematical efficiency standards, through TNCs operating as equivalent corporate agencies across the globe. For the diffusion of any social innovation is inevitably conditioned by its host environments, by the differing institutional complexes surrounding origins, transfer and adaptation. Furthermore, the organizational and market power relations between these different sites of innovation, between HQs and branch plants and between different national and regional locations, influence both the timing and the form of diffusion.

Diffusion as 'Japanization'

Much of the discussion of the diffusion of the Japanese model, especially in Britain, has been conducted in relation to the notion of Japanization which, as we saw in the Introduction, identifies a total package of techniques which have been developed in the Japanese context and may be more or less transferable to other settings. In some respects this approach is preferable to those which simply abstract best practice models from the Japanese experience, but it still hinges upon the construction of an ideal type against which diffusion can be assessed, and as such it tends to treat Japanese practices holistically and diffusion in a primarily quantitative and rather unilinear fashion, both of which gloss over the variety of agencies and forms of adoption and adaptation involved. Faced with such limitations, different commentators have sought to utilize the notion of Japanization in several different ways, though in our view these different usages do more to highlight the deficiencies of such an ideal type conceptualization than to repair those deficiencies. Three major approaches deserve note:

1 *'Japanization' as a 'whole package'*: Oliver and Wilkinson (1988, 1992) are advocates of this approach, as they seek to draw out the interrelated character of Japanese innovations in manufacturing methods, work organization, personnel and employment relations by constructing a catalogue of the relevant techniques. In turn this leads them to concentrate on a quantitative assessment of the extent of Japanization by counting the incidence of the different techniques through surveys of management practice and seeking to measure 'progress' in terms of approximations to the 'whole package' (Oliver and Wilkinson 1992: 18). Such an approach tends to abstract reports of the presence or absence of each technique from the real social relations surrounding their origination in Japan and their implementation elsewhere. It also implies that the partial adoption of such techniques in the Japanese transplants is a deviation, when it is more than likely part of the corporate strategy of Japanese TNCs to construct diversity across their global operations. Finally their central preoccupation with the speed and progress of adoption also directs attention away from the active processes of selective appropriation and reworking of these techniques by non-Japanese companies.

2 *Dual 'Japanization'*: An alternative interpretation splits 'Japanization' into two ideal types of corporate conduct, that characteristic of the large Japanese firm, and that of the small firm sector – generating a typology of primary (core) and secondary (peripheral) 'Japanization' (Dedoussis and Littler, this volume). This well known duality is then used to interpret Japanese overseas transplants who

are said to conform to conditions of secondary or 'peripheral Japanization'. This model sees diluted forms of Japanese practices abroad not as a deviation from the whole system, but as conformity to part of that system. Japanese TNCs retain high value-added manufacture at home, and the rest of the world is a peripheral other, where assembly and routine operations are conducted, with few of the compliment of practices operating at home. A major problem with this model is that the rest of the world, the non-Japanese space, is treated as one rather than differentiated according to market and economic opportunities. It therefore conceptualizes corporate strategy in terms of the internal Japanese socio-political environment, without allowing for both autonomous developments in foreign subsidiaries, and national locational differences in subsidiary markets. In common with other dual labour market models it also risks oversimplifying the spectrum of corporate strategies and forms of employment found even in Japan (see Kamada this volume).

3 *Disaggregated 'Japanization'*: This approach avoids such problems by treating Japanese FDI as equivalent in intent to other FDI by TNCs, in that they share similar logics of global corporate operation, and therefore Japanese firms take advantage of different regions of the globe for market and cost reasons, and selectively adjust their factory regimes to fit into these local conditions. Furthermore, different industrial sectors will reveal differences in Japanese practices, as sector logics can be more critical than national practices. In Southern California, Japanese electronics companies adopt American recruitment and union-avoidance strategies prevalent in the American firms in the sector and region, thus conforming to local and dominant practices (Milkman 1991). In the US auto sector, Japanese companies have introduced more in the way of Japanese practices, because of the competitive inferiority of American methods in the sector (Kenney and Florida 1991). However, in addition to a sector effect, there is also a TNC effect in operation, in the sense that Japanese car firms have disaggregated their manufacturing chain in such a way that assembly work goes overseas to get past protectionist laws and utilize cheap labour, but high value-added manufacturing of components stays at home (Williams *et al.* 1992).

Such different usages and contested meanings reinforce our view, outlined in the Introduction, that the label of 'Japanization' should be treated with caution, and must not become a substitute for critical comparative case studies of different national and sectoral encounters with labour process practices associated with the Japanese. It is in this light that we next seek to reassess the Japanese model in Japan, before turning to a substantive discussion of the operations of both Japanese transplants and domestic emulators, with particular reference to the British experience.

THE JAPANESE MODEL IN JAPAN

There is some diffuseness in discussions of the Japanese model even among those writers who focus specifically upon innovations in the organization of production, such as teamworking, JIT and total quality management (TQM). In part this is because the substance of such initiatives has varied across firms and evolved over time. But it also arises because *pervasive* changes in organizational relationships and cultures are deemed integral to these methods, making it difficult to abstract specific features from their wider organizational context. There is, however, considerable agreement that the pioneer and exemplar of these innovations has been Toyota. As Cusumano (1985) documents, it was in the Toyota plants that JIT, teamworking and kaizen were developed as an increasingly coherent approach, first in a more partial fashion through limited experiments in the early post-war years, but increasingly as a total approach embracing whole factories and then the components suppliers from the mid-1960s.

Toyotism

Toyota was certainly not alone in such innovations. For example it lagged behind Nissan, and indeed firms in other sectors such as steel, in developing the devolved team based quality assurance programmes which were being increasingly effectively sponsored by the Japanese Union of Scientists and Engineers from the late 1950s (Cole 1989). In the specific social and economic context of the post-war growth decades, many Japanese enterprises faced the exigencies which have been identified as pivotal in stimulating the innovations at Toyota: materials shortages, relatively constricted but differentiated markets, and the consolidation of conciliatory forms of enterprise unionism (Cusumano 1985; Sayer 1986). Furthermore, many different enterprises drew in different ways upon a complex repertoire of established approaches (fragmented tasks; time and motion study; teamworking) and more novel, often American inspired, techniques (quality assurance; advanced technology) to cope with these exigencies.

Against this background of varied and uneven innovation, however, the developments in the Toyota factories and supplier hinterland had by the mid-1960s placed it clearly at the leading edge of competitiveness among Japanese motor firms. Furthermore, the very success of Toyota represented an important model, not only for its own supplier network but for many other enterprises in Japan. As noted in the Introduction, such features lend plausibility to the label Toyotism (Wood 1992), though with two important caveats. The first is that we need to specify the sources of Toyota's lead position clearly. This cannot be done simply in terms of the benign characterization offered by the apostles of 'lean production', where a bias towards capitalizing on worker expertise – to working smarter rather than harder – arose from (i) management prowess in coping with shortages of capital and small batch sizes, and (ii) management's respect for the achievements of post-war unions in institutionalizing the position of core workers as a fixed cost. Rather we have to recognize, as Cusumano does, that the JIT and QC innovations at Toyota involved a systematic drive towards the intensification of work, premised upon the defeat of the more radical post-war unions and the capacity of Toyota to dominate its local labour market and supplier hinterland.

This suggests that Toyota's advantage resulted from a combination of more thoroughly subordinated labour, more intensive and longer working, and a more rigorous mobilization of worker initiative towards continuous improvement (Dohse *et al.* 1985; Cusumano 1985). In such circumstances team flexibility, job rotation and the deployment of worker expertise operate in the context of an intense and unrelenting workpace underpinned by persistent demanning. Thus as Dohse *et al.* (1985) argue, it is not a question of *either* work intensification *or* learning by doing, as these features are mutually implicated in procedures which increase the transparency of both any underutilization of labour and possible improvements in working arrangements.

Varieties of innovation in Japan

This brings us to our second caveat, which is that the operations of Japanese firms cannot simply be sorted into those with and without lean production, but have to be understood in terms of a more complex and evolving mix of organizational and employment relations, including continuing automation, changing forms of teamworking and the reorganization of supplier networks within and beyond Japan (Cusumano 1985; Williams *et al.* 1992). Nissan's more hesitant moves towards JIT and stronger reliance on automation throughout the post-war boom were conditioned by such features as their metropolitan location, the continuing leverage of a less compliant enterprise union, and the more dispersed character of their supplier network – and similar regional, sectoral and temporal contingencies have continued to influence patterns of work reorganization across the Japanese economy, so that (as Koike (1988) documents) teamworking, for example, may assume a very different character in a motor factory, a steel plant or an engineering workshop.

These arguments suggest that such authors as Kenney and Florida (1988) can only sustain their characterization of a ubiquitous 'Fujitsuism' by collapsing together quite diverse variants of work organization, conflating, for example, the forms of teamworking and worker initiative involved in swapping among a small family of routine assembly tasks with those involved in the operation of project teams which cross-cut research, development and production. This has evident implications for debate about the global ramifications of any of these Japanese-inspired models of production – Toyotism; Fujitsuism; lean production – because it suggests that even the globalizing Japanese enterprises will be operating with significantly varied repertoires and mixes of management practice, coloured by specific sectoral and corporate patterns of innovation.

The institutional context of Japanese corporate innovation

It is common ground in the discussions of Japanese models of production organization that the initial innovations at Toyota and elsewhere were conditioned by specific features of the social and economic structure of post-war Japanese society, and in particular what we earlier termed a distinctive institutional settlement. In going beyond culturalist accounts, some authors have pointed to the ways in which close relations between state agencies and dominant enterprise groupings have facilitated relatively concerted corporate policy initiatives on such matters as quality programmes (especially via the Japanese Union of Scientists and Engineers) and sectoral research and development priorities (especially via the Ministry for International Trade and Industry). A few commentators have highlighted the central importance of the unusually large periphery of smaller enterprises which constitute much of the extensive supplier network for key manufacturing sectors like motors (Chalmers 1989; Tokunaga 1984). Finally most writers have identified the 'three pillars' of the employment relations of core workers in the large enterprises – 'life-time' employment and enterprise based training, seniority linked wages and enterprise unionism – as pivotal social supports for flexible working and worker commitment, and thus for the evolving innovations in production arrangements since the 1950s.

As Cole (1989) emphasizes in his study of the institutional infrastructures of QC initiatives in Japan, Sweden and the USA, such an appreciation of the socially located character of innovation should serve as a constant reminder that similar processes of adaptation and transformation in the light of local circumstances, resources and constraints, will inevitably characterize the diffusion of Japanese model(s). Thus we cannot assume that packages of measures developed in specific conditions can simply be taken up and generalized across the globe, but neither can we argue that such innovations must be forever bounded by the particular social circumstances of their origination.

However, such an anodyne injunction to treat the development and diffusion of new management initiatives in a symmetrical fashion, each as creative and adaptive processes, does not take us very far. To go beyond this we need to specify more clearly the particular character of the social conditions which have been critical to the viability of these innovations in work organization, both in terms of their survival and in terms of their contribution to any competitive advantages enjoyed by Japanese corporations. At this point competing understandings of the character of what Kenney and Florida (1988) call the post-war class accord become critical, as they underpin different assessments of the costs and gains for workers and employers, not least in regard to the relationship between working harder and working smarter (Cusumano 1985; Moore 1987).

The vicissitudes of an institutional settlement

Of course, the post-war settlement itself drew upon a longer history of management strategies and worker responses, from the turn of century incorporation of subcontractors within large enterprises, through limited and precarious precursors to the 'three pillars' in heavy industry to cope with labour shortages and unrest in the 1920s, to the authoritarian regulation of labour from the 1930s (Littler 1982; Gordon 1985). However, the reconstruction of employment relations in the late 1940s took place in the context of unprecedented forms of worker mobilization, and as a result the extension and entrenchment of the 'three pillars' in this period embodied important employer concessions. Such features as reduced differentials between manual and white-collar workers, recognition of the consumption needs of married workers and inclusive forms of collective organization at plant level corresponded with the priorities of the nascent labour movement, while at the same time reinforcing an emphasis on 'factory communities' and enterprise unionism.

These developments left a lasting imprint on employment relations in post-war Japan, but it would be mistaken to characterize them as the firm foundation of a post-war settlement. By the beginning of the 1950s tight fiscal policies and increasing state hostility to a politicized labour movement had laid the basis for an employers' offensive which resulted in several prolonged strikes, marginalized many radical plant unions, and achieved a substantial reassertion of managerial prerogatives within the workplace, greater management control of pay structures and abridged guarantees of job security (Cusumano 1985; Gordon 1985). Management did not recoup their pre-war levels of discretion and the new enterprise unions retained significant (though variable) leverage over pay and employment, but the parameters of bargaining were generally set by the logic of enterprise competitiveness, so that even core workers failed to make wage gains in line with productivity increases and the unions did little to relieve widespread management pressures for intensive and extended working (Kawanishi 1992).

Clearly the relative stabilization of a version of the 'three pillars' was also strongly conditioned by developments in the wider political economy. A period of sustained economic growth, coupled for two decades with an abundant supply of labour from the countryside, sustained the conditions for a quite steep advancement of wages with service in the big firms. In addition, the limited role of state welfare reinforced the importance of corporate welfare provisions for permanent employees in the large enterprises, while the existence of an extensive periphery of temporary workers and smaller firms, characterized by low wages and continuing job insecurity, cushioned the core workforce from market fluctuations.

Furthermore, the highly concentrated character of manufacturing capital, reorganized into Keiretsu groupings, and the close links between capital and the state, helped to sustain coherent long-term investment and export strategies in key sectors.

In summary the early 1950s witnessed the consolidation of an interlocking set of somewhat distinctive institutional arrangements covering a minority of workers in Japan, which underpinned Toyotist and related innovations in work organization by placing a premium on enterprise-based skills, company loyalty and internal labour market advancement. It remains important, nevertheless, not to reify this complex of institutions. Not only have its implications been subtly different in different enterprises (such as Toyota and Nissan), but it has always been characterized by significant tensions and modifications. The tight labour market of the late 1960s, for example, led to diminished seniority differentials and an extension of permanent status, whilst the recent recessions have prompted the growth of temporary work, increased resort to the transfer of regular employees across enterprises (Kamada, this volume) and altered the operation of team based production innovations. In this sense, the moving target of Japanese innovation should not be seen simply as a hare which will always be ahead of the race, but more as an evolving repertoire of management practices which is also beset by significant tensions and constraints even on its home ground. These features have recently been underlined by noting both the potential impact of a greater cyclicality in the Japanese car market (Williams *et al.* 1992) and the role of JIT in exacerbating urban congestion (Berggren 1992).

The role of the subcontracting periphery

Finally we also have to register the extent to which the competitiveness of Japanese enterprises is rooted not only in the operation of their major plants, but also in the role played by their extensive supplier networks. Here the contrasting characterizations of working smarter or harder are transposed more starkly into working smarter or cheaper. It is generally agreed that a dominant feature of inter-enterprise relationships in Japan is an unusually heavy reliance on highly integrated networks of subcontractors, both to supply labour to work in large plants and to manufacture themselves parts and subassemblies for the final assemblers.

There is, however, considerable controversy about how far the resulting pyramidal supply chains and their associated forms of employment can be characterized in terms of subordination, insecurity and low pay (e.g. Chalmers 1989) or rather as centres of innovation, entrepreneurship and growing independence (e.g. Friedman 1988). The latter diagnosis emphasizes that some clusters of high-tech innovative firms have gained relative independence within subcontracting networks; that some male workers are themselves destined to become small firm owners; and that low-tech subcontractors have increasingly moved overseas. Despite these developments, however, firms and workforces down the supply chains remain heavily dependent upon the large firms. They face persistent pressures for cost reductions and, even with investment in new methods and equipment, they survive by using cheaper and more insecure workers with little legal protection or scope for collective organization.

Of course the relationships between large firms and their supplier networks have been no more static than the employment and work relations of the core workforce, but despite significant changes between the 1950s and the 1990s small enterprises have continued to provide real advantages to the core firms, both by delivering lower labour costs and by carrying a disproportionate share of market uncertainties. In these respects they have remained an important source of the competitiveness of Japanese manufacturing, but one which offers very different lessons to those generally celebrated by exponents of the 'Japanese model'.

TRANSPLANTS AND ADOPTERS

In looking at the ways in which Japanese models have been influential outside Japan we need to distinguish between the innovating transplant firms, which often carry a version of their own national practice, and the adopting firms operating within the domestic environment. Direct foreign investment by American and Japanese firms in particular has meant that they are carriers of new standards and repertoires which shape, but are also reshaped by, the particular conditions within their host environment. The foreign TNC can, moreover, choose relocation sites, and disaggregate the production chain so that investment flows to different societies to captitalize on different factor advantages, whether these be skilled design engineers or cheap female labour. Such transplants possess more power to impose their standards on the environment, conditioned only by the strengths of the institutions in civil society and the state, and the efficiency of domestic firms. In other words, the extent to which the different cultural and institutional contingencies within the host environment constrain them varies according to both political and economic conditions.

The logics of adoption

If in turn we examine the adopting firms within their domestic context then their acquisition of the new innovations will be mediated by their existing practices, the agencies responsible for managing innovation and what *they* interpret as the key features of the particular social innovation – itself not straightforward as we have seen – and what the power holders want from the innovation. Cole (1989) argues convincingly that social innovations, such as quality management, produce different outcomes according to the degree of sponsorship by senior management and the nature of the agencies who interpret, codify and manage the innovation. These vary between capitalist societies, where different mixes of voluntary, statutory and commercial change agencies, and of professional specialists, management generalists and consultants, interpret social innovations in ways which seriously affect their outcomes.

The rationale of management in seeking to introduce a new innovation will typically be in order to stay in the market, to withstand the competitive pressures from the new entrants and the new standards of production. But there may also be another agenda, derived from local class compromises and struggles, which under the threat from without, are pursued through the new discourse. British firms, for example, saw non-union or single union deals, flexibility, group working, attacks on rigid job territories, and so on, as old battles which were given a new legitimation through arguments about the need to keep up with Japanese standards. Similarly, American corporate interpretations of Japanese success have been filtered through an entrenched American agenda. In other words, the selection and interpretation of social innovations, such as those associated with Japan, of necessity are mediated and interact with home grown conditions and existing practices.

These existing practices may also be reinterpreted or repackaged to conform to the new language, whether this is flexibility, Japanese production methods or human resource management (HRM). For example, a personnel manager from a food TNC recently interviewed by one of us described the established practice of delaying replacing staff, in order to stretch and intensify the work of those who remain, as kanban. In the words of this manager, they 'kan-banned' the remaining staff. In a management culture where learn-ing new attitudes and vocabularies is commonplace, both genuine misunderstandings about the ramifications of such concepts and the opportunistic recodifying of existing priorities to fit the new dis-course may be typical survival strategies. This makes the job of critical research and interpretation all the more important, and reduces the validity of methods which rely upon management self-assessments through questionnaires and single interviews.

Transplants as innovators: the British experience

The British economy has long been the base for substantial overseas operations by British based TNCs, as well as being markedly open to inward investment by foreign transnationals, and both these features have long reinforced a bias towards labour-intensive manu-facturing and only modest restructuring (Nolan 1989). However, the more specific economic and political conditions of the 1980s were, as mentioned in our introduction, of crucial importance for making Britain the site of a disproportionate share of Japanese direct foreign investment in this period.

Much of the commentary on the activities of Japanese transplants has taken it for granted that they represent exemplars of the Toyota production system, and has focused on the variety of ways in which they have been able to construct a workforce amenable to the work routines imported from Japan. Particular attention has been given to the capacity of the greenfield transplants to (i) mobilize the uncritical political and financial support of local authorities in the context of fierce competition between localities to attract inward investors to replace lost jobs; (ii) captitalize on the peculiarities of local labour markets and mass unemployment by focusing recruitment on 'green workers' and using intensive selection procedures to recruit a com-pliant and committed workforce; (iii) exploit the political divisions and competition for membership among British trade unions by encour-aging 'beauty contests' and the acceptance of a tightly circumscribed role for workplace trade unionism; and (iv) deploy such management techniques as participation, teamworking, and single status to enhance the commitment of workers to enterprise goals and limit opposition.

Oliver and Wilkinson (1992) draw implicitly on 'societal effect' theory to develop the argument that such features should be seen as the functional equivalents of the 'three pillars', allowing Japanese transplant managements to pursue JIT and TQM procedures which would otherwise make these transplants vulnerable to heightened risks of disruption. There must, however, be important reservations about this argument. The first is that the specific mix of these features varies substantially between plants and sectors, not least in terms of preferred sources of labour (especially young workers or women) and union avoidance or recognition (Garrahan and Stewart 1992; Peck and Stone 1992; Morgan and Sayer 1988; Taylor *et al.*, this volume). The second is that case study evidence underlines the importance of the usual instrumental bases of worker commitment in the Japanese transplants, hinging on comparatively good wages and relative job security, rather than any more profound trans-formation of the bases of employee consent (Garrahan and Stewart 1992; Peck and Stone 1992; Oliver and Wilkinson 1992, chapter 8). The third source of reservations is that it remains unclear how far the production operations of the Japanese assemblers are peculiar in terms of their disruptability, especially as their generalized adoption of JIT procedures has been questioned by case study evidence (Oliver and Wilkinson 1992: 233; Taylor *et al.*, this volume; Williams *et al.* 1992). Finally, then, such features often appear to facilitate the pursuit of rather more mundane management priorities than is generally implied by references to Japanization, such as more intensive work regimes and greater interchangeability of labour. At the same time the hype associated with the apparent distinctiveness of the production processes in these firms undoubtedly helps to sustain their reputations for innovation and quality.

It is in this context that the wider influence of the transplants must be assessed. On the one hand the larger factories do represent sub-stantial investments in production operations within the UK, and their work and employment practices have generally differed in important respects from those of the remaining British manufacturers in their sectors. On the other hand, though, they remain a very small number of enterprises accounting for a small percentage of total employment, and the pattern of inward investment suggests that they will generally remain branch assembly plants with only limited local supplier networks.

The symbolic significance of the Japanese model in Britain

In these terms it is the symbolic significance of the transplants which has been enormous, well beyond the Thatcherite political arguments

about their role in the renewal of British manufacturing competitiveness. From 'After Japan' onwards, claims about Japanese manufacturing and lean production have become central to the rhetoric and
negotiating positions of senior managers in non-Japanese firms, as they
have sought to recast established working patterns and bargaining
arrangements (Turnbull 1986; Foster and Wolfson 1989; IDS 1988,
1990; Rover Group 1992). In turn the differing responses to the transplants among British unions have come to symbolize broader divisions
in their responses to hostile government policies and membership loss.
The notions associated with Japanization have also become major
ingredients in the ferment of management education and consultancy
which markets recipes for competitive advantage (Oliver and
Wilkinson 1992; Training Agency 1989). They have thus become significant weapons in arguments among senior executives about the recasting of management hierarchies (extolling both the strategic role of top
corporate management and the need to recast devolved supervisory
roles and responsibilities), and also among middle management
specialists (especially bearing on relationships between production
and personnel managers).

Over against this inflated rhetorical background there is considerable evidence that, as usual, British managers have generally
borrowed and adapted facets of the Japanization package in a
piecemeal fashion (Elger 1989; Elger and Fairbrother 1992; IDS
1988, 1990). These features are underlined both by the well-
documented cycles of enthusiasm and evaporation which have
characterized the experience of the quality circle movement in the
UK (Hill 1991), and by the sheer diversity of practices found to be
covered by such umbrella notions as teamworking and team leaders
(Smith 1988; Vauxhall 1990; Rover Group 1992; Peck and Stone
1992). Even the evidence for a widespread adoption of Japanese
production practices adduced by Oliver and Wilkinson actually
sustains this interpretation, for their finding of the apparently near
universal spread of 'Continuous Improvement' suggests that their
surveys have largely tapped an untypical minority of enthusiasts,
and yet the characteristic pattern remains of piecemeal adaption of
'bits of JIT' (Oliver and Wilkinson 1992: 143–149).

New variations on old themes?

In developing this argument we are not simply claiming that the
processes of adoption and adaptation of Japanese production

arrangements and personnel procedures are complex and uneven. Rather we are suggesting that the contours of this complexity and unevenness reflect key features of work and employment relations in British manufacturing. The first of these is the long-standing concern of British managements to gain greater leverage over worker effort and initiative on the shop floor by recasting both formal relations with workplace trade unionism and informal relations with workgroups – a concern which has been most strongly articulated in the development of productivity bargaining in the 1960s and flexibility bargaining in the 1980s, but which re-emerges in much of the debate surrounding quality circles, briefing groups, teamworking and modular production. The second is that, in the context of the political and economic conditions of the last fifteen years, and most particularly mass unemployment, factory closures and the collapse of manufacturing, management-defined agendas for plant survival have increasingly defined and narrowed the parameters of effective workplace bargaining even in well organized workplaces (Turnbull 1986, 1988; Terry 1989).

It is against this background that we should understand the ways in which the borrowing and adaptation of Japanese-style work organization have been coloured by the differing circumstances of specific brownfield sites and sectors and their established working practices and bargaining arrangements (Turnbull 1986; Marchington and Parker 1988; Bratton 1991, 1992). At major mass production sites dominated by male semi-skilled workers and their unions, managements appear to have clothed a quite long-standing agenda of enhanced flexibility and work intensification in the revised language of lean production, but even in the recent conditions of weakened workplace unionism they have been met with considerable scepticism and some opposition over the implementation of arrangements for teamworking and flexibility (Starkey and McKinlay 1989; IDS 1988; Vauxhall 1990). In electronics, modularization has encouraged a shift from piecework incentives to tighter performance monitoring as a way of mobilizing flexibility among a tightly circumscribed range of operations – again an agenda with an earlier history – while doing little to disturb the entrenched gendered division of labour in that sector (Morgan and Sayer 1988; Turnbull 1986; Delbridge et al. 1992). Finally, if Bratton's work can be taken as typical, in specialist batch engineering, where skilled workers predominate, cell manufacture has often encouraged forms of upskilling which build as much on existing patterns of expertise and flexibility within craft-based production as they do on Japanese models (Bratton 1991, 1992; British Timkin 1992).

Overall, then, our assessment of the significance of the Japanese transplants and the diverse emulators of Japanese methods in the UK is that they *have* been involved in significant changes in the organization of work processes, but that the catch-all category of 'Japanization' does not offer a particularly good way of understanding these changes. In part this is because there has been no simple or wholesale application of a Japanese model, even by the transplants, while the emulators have borrowed varied elements of transplant practice in a typically piecemeal fashion (Taylor *et al.*, this volume). It is also because distinctive sectoral logics have remained significant for both transplants and emulators, and have thus differentiated among the inward investors and the emulators alike. Thus enterprise and sectoral contingencies have had a profound influence on the ways in which elements of the corporate repertoire of work organization and personnel practice are selectively deployed by branch transplants and selectively adapted by locally based companies.

At the same time the overall bias of this selectivity has been conditioned by the particular features of the national political economy, both by long-term patterns of investment, employment, training and collective bargaining, and by the more immediate exigencies of the political management of economic cycles and class conflict. Our argument is that the real significance of the Japanese transplants and the wider rhetoric of 'Japanization' in Britain can only be understood in terms of the interplay between these features and the operations of both Japanese and other TNCs. This underlines that any wider view of the global significance of the Japanese transnationals and the 'Japanese model' would have to attend to the specific interactions between nationally derived repertoires of management policy, global locational and marketing strategies and the dominant features of different national political economies.

ISSUES FOR FUTURE RESEARCH

The spread of Japanese direct investment, the emulation of techniques associated with Japanese manufacture and the continued strength of the Japanese economy are reasons why the debate on 'Japanization' will continue. But we have argued in this chapter that comprehending the nature of Japanese economic growth and the 'model' of work organization associated with it, is actually hampered by the misleading paradigm of 'Japanization'. This does not invite us to consider the contradictions within Japanese practices, their historical nature and dynamics, but rather erects a functional totality impermeable to radical change. Cataloguing the contents of 'Japanization' does not consider how they change, either by internal contradictions between the social actors who reproduce these practices, or in the course of their externalization through Japanese FDI, emulation by neighbouring states (Korea, other NICs) and adaption by transnationals keen to gain the competitive advantage they appear to offer.

Not only is any process of diffusion also inevitably a process of adaptation, but the wider dissemination of innovations exposes further tensions in their operation even in those settings where they were first developed. When the sharing of the efficiency advantages of the methods is generalized, will we not see a heightening of overproduction, and other problems which continue to beset capitalist production. 'Japanization' is not the panacea to smooth these flaws. Moreover, what are the long-term effects of the export of jobs from Japan? What will be the effects of growing global trade protectionism which can only encourage this export of capital from Japan? And what of the effects of recession through the business cycle on sectors of the Japanese economy accustomed to stable and growing demand, such as the auto industry? The shift towards greater use of temporary labour and early retirements of core workers is already imposing strains on the life-time employment systems which formed the main quid pro quo for the class settlement between capital and organized labour from the 1950s. The environmental fall-out from JIT systems, with massively increased road congestion, is already forcing its pioneer, Toyota, to build warehouses, and the diffusion of such environmentally unfriendly practices can only increase tensions between industry and green movements (Berggren 1992: 253). Yet these issues are never explored as part of the contradictions of the Japanese model. It rather operates as a functional entity.

Against this meta-theorizing, we believe we need a more dispassionate middle-range investigation of the actual practices of Japanese companies and their emulators, of the sort provided by this book. Instead of building a framework for interpreting restructuring and new efficiency methods in terms of a national typology, it is more appropriate, though analytically exacting, to treat

Japanese practices in their historical national setting, and their diffusion through the agencies and sector dynamics they engage. This includes consideration of:

1 *Transnational companies.* Japanese transplants must be seen not simply as quintessentially Japanese, but more generally as capitalist enterprises facing similar exigencies to other TNCs and similar tensions issuing from the intractabilities of the relations between labour and capital. Thus, while Japanese firms manage capital–labour relations in their own particular ways, the contradictions of these social relations are not overcome – they do not become capitalist utopias. This does not require subordinating analysis to crude notions of the laws of capitalism or inherent contradictions of the system. National specificities can be recognized, but it would be foolish to ignore the linkages between the actions of Japanese capital and internationalized capital in general. Rather, we need to explore the specific manifestations of those tensions and conflicts which exist in all capitalist societies, both in relation to the 'nationality' of the transplant and its operation within another nation state.

2 *Sectors.* One implication of an analysis that considers those features which Japanese TNCs and transplants share with other transnational operations, is that Japanese transplants are not all of a piece, but clearly operate in distinctive ways in different sectors, paralleling the behaviour of other TNCs facing similar sectoral conditions. Such sectoral specificities emerge particularly clearly in the differences between Japanese electronics and auto transplants in both the US and Europe. This points towards a meso-level analysis of the sector and business cycle dynamics which lend specificity to broader TNC strategies, and which in important respects cross-cut national distinctiveness. Therefore, we would argue that before pinning national colours on action, this needs to be validated through checks on the extent of convergence with priorities and standards set by other more general levels and patterns of action.

3 *Regions.* Similarly, further attention to locational and regional specificities is evidently necessary, especially to explore the effects of clustering of investment, which has been observable in Japanese investment in the US and Britain. Such investment and sector clusters, as noted earlier, maximize environmental control for the transnational, but again, this is not necessarily special to

Japanese capital, as the American computer corporations' domination of areas like Silicon Glen in Scotland and Santa Clara Valley in California testify. TNC clustering in this way allows inter-firm cooperation on non-union strategies, non-poaching agreements and a generally more systematic and coherent management of the host environment relative to those TNCs which are geographically dispersed. Analyses which operate inside a paradigm of nationally determined forms of behaviour would have difficulty making these linkages between sectoral, geographical and transnational capital strategies and action.

4 *Temporal factors.* There is also a need to examine Japanese transplants over time. In part, this is because the 'honeymoon' effect on labour relations noted by Oliver and Wilkinson (1992: 280) may give a false impression of capital–labour practices, but also because of the possible positive effects of 'greenfield' locations and investment coming during upward curves in product life-cycles. Taking the previous debate over another nationally distinct pattern of investment – American capital in Europe – we can observe a cyclical pattern of growth and decline. Wild predictions about the 'Americanization' of Europe (Servan-Schreiber 1968), made at the highpoint of American capital formation in the late 1960s, proved rather foolish when such investment began to decline. As Dicken (1992: 60) shows, American firms have over the last decade been through an extended process of closure, withdrawal and rationalization, and there is no reason to assume Japanese capital will not follow the same pattern. Subsidiary formation does not grow indefinitely, and with the single European market, and a more thoroughly branch-plant character to Japanese capital investment, we may witness a more rapid relocation and greater volatility of capital than has occurred with American investments. Crucially, for the debate on the diffusion of Japanese practices, projections from the social character of Japanese subsidiaries during periods of upward expansion could prove short-lived when decline and rationalization begin.

5 *Comparative case studies.* Finally, there is a need for more comparative data on Japanese subsidiaries in other societies of the kind provided by this volume, including studies from both developed and developing countries. These would test the integrity of corporate practices, and measure the influence of more general and pervasive national and sector influence on what are supposedly distinct factory regimes. Such comparative analysis

could perhaps begin to develop a more accurate picture of the points of convergence and divergence between societies and regions, and the potential influence these have on the reception and mediation of the Japanese model. For example, the dual labour market in Japan is critical to Japanese firm practices, but aspects of this may be being reproduced in the West through structural unemployment, and growing wage differentials between large and small firms. The excessive hours worked in Japan, again, are signalled as unique, but convergences are also occurring as a recent book on the unexpected growth in American working hours has indicated (Schor 1991). Moreover, Britain has some of the longest working hours in Europe, and most of the Japanese investment. These elements of structural alignment should be put in the frame to avoid the limitations of some methods of comparative research, such as those of the 'societal effects' school.

CONCLUSION

The intent of this chapter has been to argue that the notion of Japanization needs to be deconstructed if we are to advance our understanding of the complex processes involved in the development, generalization and adaptation of new models of work organization and employment relations.

We have suggested that Japanese innovations in production and employment have themselves been the evolving and varied products of the interaction between earlier dominant (especially American) models, specific institutional ensembles embodying national class compromises and industrialization strategies, and the efforts of Japanese enterprises to cope with particular sectoral and temporal contingencies. Similarly, we have argued that the exportation and diffusion of Japanese innovations have to be analysed in terms of an interaction between the broader corporate strategies of both Japanese and other TNCs, the role of propagandists and mediators who manage the processes of codification and dissemination of specific packages of techniques, and the distinctive national, regional and sectoral conditions and social relations which structure the reception and adaption of these techniques.

We are therefore advocating a research strategy which dispenses with both the mythology of the decontextualized 'one best way' and the identification of distinctive national models against which to measure the progress of the rest of the world. Instead we are advocating the further development of middle-range analyses based on case studies which can explore the intersection of the global logics of TNCs, the significance of the hegemony of specific national economies on the world stage, the agencies and mechanisms of transmission of models of good practice, and the specific national and regional contexts of both innovation and reception/adaption.

Acknowledgement

An earlier draft of this chapter was first given at the Eleventh Labour Process Conference at Blackpool, March 1993.

REFERENCES

Ackroyd, S. *et al.* (1988) 'The Japanization of British industry?', *Industrial Relations Journal* 19, 1: 11–23.

Berggren, C. (1992) *The Volvo Experience. Alternatives to Lean Production in the Swedish Auto Industry*, London: Macmillan.

Bratton, J. (1991) 'Japanization at work: the case of engineering plants in Leeds', *Work, Employment and Society* 5, 3: 377–395.

—— (1992) *Japanization at Work: Managerial Studies for the 1990s*, London: Macmillan.

British Timken (1992) *Timkin Tomorrow: The Best Manufacturing Company in the World*, Associates Handbook.

Chalmers, N. J. (1989) *Industrial Relations in Japan: the Peripheral Workforce*, London: Routledge.

Cole, R. (1989) *Strategies For Learning: Small-group Activities in American, Japanese and Swedish Industry*, Los Angeles: University of California Press.

Crowther, S. and Garrahan, P. (1988) 'Corporate power and the local economy', *Industrial Relations Journal* 19, 1: 51–59.

Cusumano, M. A. (1985) *The Japanese Automobile Industry: Technology and Management at Nissan and Toyota*, Cambridge Mass.: Harvard UP.

Delbridge, R., Turnbull, P. and Wilkinson, B. (1992) 'Pushing back the frontiers: management control and work intensification under JIT/TQM factory regimes', *New Technology, Work and Employment* 7, 2: 97–106.

Dicken, P. (1992) *Global Shift*, London: Paul Chapman (second edition).

Dohse, K. *et al.* (1985) 'From "Fordism" to "Toyotism"? The social organisation of the labour process in the Japanese automobile industry', *Politics and Society* 14, 2: 115–146.

Dore, R. (1973) *British Factory, Japanese Factory: the Origins of National Diversity in Industrial Relations*, London: Allen & Unwin.

Elger, T. (1989) 'Not the polyvalent worker: the restructuring of work relations and flexible intensification in British manufacturing', Anglo-German Conference on Industrial and Urban Change in Britain and West Germany, University of Manchester, November.

Elger, T. and Fairbrother P. (1992) 'Inflexible flexibility: a case study of modularisation', in N. Gilbert *et al.* (eds) *Fordism and Flexibility*, London: Macmillan.

Elson, D. and Pearson, R. (eds) 1989 *Women's Employment and Multinationals in Europe*, London: Macmillan.

Florida, R. and Kenney, M. (1991) 'Organisation versus culture: Japanese automotive transplants in the US', *Industrial Relations Journal* 22, 3: 181–196.

Foster, J. and Wolfson, C. (1989) 'Corporate reconstruction and business unionism: the lessons of Caterpillar and Ford', *New Left Review* 174: 51–66.

Friedman, D. (1988) *The Misunderstood Miracle: Industrial Development and Political Change in Japan*, Ithaca: Cornell University Press.

Garrahan, P. and Stewart, P. (1992) *The Nissan Enigma: Flexibility at Work in a Local Economy*, London: Cassell.

Gordon, A. (1985) *The Evolution of Labour Relations in Japan: Heavy Industry 1853–1945*, Boston: Harvard UP.

Hill, S. (1991) 'Why quality circles failed but TQM might succeed', *British Journal of Industrial Relations* 29, 4: 541–568.

IDS (1988) 'Teamworking', *IDS Study* 419 (October).

IDS (1990) 'Total quality management', *IDS Study* 457 (May).

IRS Focus (1992) 'Lean production – and Rover's "New Deal"', *IRS Employment Trends* 514, June: 12–15.

Kamata, S. (1983) *Japan in the Passing Lane*, London: Allen & Unwin.

Kawanishi, H. (1992) *Enterprise Unionism in Japan*, London: Kegan Paul.

Kenney, M., and Florida, R. (1988) 'Beyond mass production: production and the labour process in Japan', *Politics and Society* 16, 1: 121–158.

—— (1993) *Beyond Mass Production: the Japanese System and its Transfer to the US*, Oxford: Oxford UP.

Koike, K. (1988) *Understanding Industrial Relations in Modern Japan*, London: Macmillan.

Kunda, G. (1992) *Engineering Culture: Control and Commitment in a High Technology Corporation*, Philadelphia: Temple.

Lipietz, A. (1982) 'Towards global Fordism', *New Left Review* 132: 33–47.

Littler, C. R. (1982) *The Development of the Capitalist Labour Process*, London: Heinemann.

McCormick, K. (1991) 'The development of engineering education and training in Britain and Japan', in H. Gospel (ed.) *Industrial Training and Technological Innovation*, London: Routledge.

Marchington, M. and Parker, P. (1988) 'Japanization: a lack of chemical reaction', *Industrial Relations Journal* 19, 4: 272–285.

Maurice, M. *et al.* (1980) 'Societal differences in organising manufacturing units', *Organisation Studies* 1: 63–91.

Merkle, J. A. (1980) *Management and Ideology: the legacy of the International Scientific Management Movement*, Berkeley: California University Press.

Milkman, R. (1991) *Japan's California Factories: Labour Relations and Economic Globalisation*, Los Angeles: Institute of Industrial Relations, University of California.

Moore, J. (1987) 'Japanese industrial relations', *Labour and Industry* 1, 1: 140–155.

Morgan, K. and Sayer, A. (1988) 'A "modern" industry in a "mature" region: the remaking of management–labour relations', in D. Massey and J. Allen (eds) *Uneven Redevelopment*, London: Hodder & Stoughton.

Munck, R. (1988) *The New International Labour Studies*, London: Zed Books.

Nolan, P. (1989) 'The productivity miracle?', in F. Green (ed.) *The Restructuring of the UK Economy*, Brighton: Wheatsheaf.

Oliver, N. and Wilkinson, B. (1988) *The Japanization of British Industry*, Oxford: Blackwell.

—— (1989) 'Japanese manufacturing techniques and personnel and industrial relations practice in Britain: evidence and implications', *British Journal of Industrial Relations* 27, 1: 73–91.

—— (1992) *The Japanization of British Industry: New Developments in the 1990s*, Oxford: Blackwell.

Parker, M. and Slaughter, J. (1990) 'Management-by-stress: the team concept in the US automobile industry', *Science as Culture* 8: 27–58.

Peck, F. and Stone, I. (1992) *New Inward Investment and the Northern Region Labour Market*, Dept Employment Research Series 6.

Reitsperger, W. D. (1986) 'Japanese management: coping with British industrial relations', *Journal of Management Studies* 23, 1: 72–87.

Rose, M. (1985) 'Universalism, culturalism and the Aix Group', *European Sociological Review* 1, 1: 65–83.

Rover Group (1992) *Rover tomorrow – the new deal at Longbridge: a Guide for Associates*.

Sayer, A. (1986) 'New developments in manufacturing: the just-in-time system', *Capital and Class* 30 (Winter).

Schor, J. B. (1991) *The Overworked American*, New York: Basic Books.

Servan-Schreiber, J-J. (1968) *The American Challenge*, London: Hamish Hamilton.

Sewell, G. and Wilkinson, B. (1992) '"Someone to watch over me": surveilance, discipline and the JIT labour process', *Sociology* 26, 2: 271–289.

Shirai, T. (ed.) (1983) *Contemporary Industrial Relations in Japan*, Madison: Wisconsin UP.

Sklair, L. (1991) *Sociology of the Global System*, London: Harvester Wheatsheaf.

Smith, C. and Meiksins, P. (1991) 'System, society and dominance effects in cross-national organisational analysis: A New Model', 10th EGOS Colloquim, 15–17 July, Vienna, Austria.

Smith, D. (1988) 'The Japanese example in southwest Birmingham', *Industrial Relations Journal* 19, 1: 41–50.

Sorge, A. (1991) 'Strategic fit and the societal effect: interpreting cross-national comparisons of technology, organisation and human resources', *Organisation Studies* 12, 2: 161–190.

Starkey, K. and McKinlay, A. (1989) 'Beyond Fordism? Strategic choice and Labour relations in Ford UK', *Industrial Relations Journal* 20, 2: 93–100.

Terry, M. (1989) 'Recontextualising shopfloor industrial relations: some case study evidence', in S. Tailby and C. Whitson (eds) *Manufacturing Change*, Oxford: Blackwell.

Tokunaga, S. (1984) 'The structure of the Japanese labour market', in S. Tokunaga and J. Bergmann (eds) *Industrial Relations in Transition: the cases of Japan and the Federal Republic of Germany*, Tokyo: Tokyo UP.

Training Agency (1989) *From Quality Circles to Total Quality Management at Prestwick Circuits Ltd*, Sheffield: Training Agency.

Turnbull, P. (1986) 'The "Japanization" of production and industrial relations at Lucas Electrical', *Industrial Relations Journal* 17, 3: 193–206.

—— (1988) 'The limits to "Japanization" – just in time, labour relations and the UK automotive industry', *New Technology, Work and Employment* 3, 1: 7–20.

Vauxhall (1990) *Vauxhall V6 Agreement*.

Warner, M. (1992) 'Japanese culture, western management: Taylorism and human resources in Japan', *Management Studies Research Paper no. 3*, Cambridge: University of Cambridge, Management Studies Group.

White, M. and Trevor, M. (1983) *Under Japanese Management: the Experience of British Workers*, Heinemann: London.

Williams, K. *et al.* (1991) 'Factories versus warehouses: Japanese manufacturing foreign direct investment in Britain and the United States', *Occasional Papers on Business, Economy and Society* 6, Polytechnic of East London.

—— (1992) 'Against lean production', *Economy and Society* 21, 3: 321–354.

Womack, J. *et al.* (1990) *The Machine that Changed the World*, New York: Rawson Associates.

Wood, S. (1992) 'Japanization and/or Toyotaism?' *Work, Employment and Society* 5, 4: 567–600.

2

HOW FAR FROM JAPAN?

A case study of Japanese press shop practice and management calculation

Karel Williams, Itsutomo Mitsui and Colin Haslam

INTRODUCTION

Japanese manufacturing now has the same international status as American manufacturing in the first half of this century; its factories are sites of international pilgrimage and its manufacturing practices are objects of emulation. The growing number of Japanese branch factories in Europe and America, plus Western attempts to transfer Japanese manufacturing practices, make Japanization an inescapable topic. Some academics claim that Western factories are increasingly like Japanese factories. Oliver and Wilkinson's (1988) book, for example, was provocatively titled *The Japanization of British Industry*. Other academics represent Japanese manufacturing as a model of technical excellence which could and should be adopted throughout the industrialized world; thus, the MIT study of the car industry (Womack, Jones and Roos 1990) has culminated in a long panegyric to 'lean production' as developed in Japan and imitated elsewhere.

This chapter raises questions about the claims and assumptions which underpin burgeoning and often uncritical literature about Japanese manufacturing and Japanization. We address the widespread misconceptions engendered by this literature by reporting the results of a case study of press shops in several Japanese car factories. Such a focused study allows us to reappraise Japanese manufacturing practice and techniques – a necessary preliminary to any discussion of transferability. The car press shop is an intelligible object of investigation because the process equipment used to produce pressed steel panels for car bodies is similar in all volume car manufacturers, and an appropriate focus because rapid die change in the press shop figures as a classic example of Japanese superiority in the Western engineering literature (Schonberger 1982, 1987; Hartley 1986).

In the summer of 1988 we visited three Japanese and one European press shop. Management cooperated on condition that individual firms were not identified and we have throughout used pseudonyms for the firms. 'Nippon Car' and 'Tokyo Motors' were two major Japanese manufacturers and we visited the press shops which produced panels for their best-selling light cars. 'Major Subcontractor' was another Japanese firm which undertook subcontract press work for medium-sized manufacturers. As a European point of reference we compared the British press shop of a large American multinational, 'Detroit Motors', which produced panels for medium and small cars. Each company completed a detailed questionnaire from which we constructed a multidimensional analysis of press shop performance and practice. This was followed up with interviews of press shop managers, focused on forms of calculation and practices of intervention. The questionnaire was translated into Japanese and most of the research interviews in Japan were also conducted in Japanese. Because information supplied by management is inevitably partial and because none of the Japanese companies had independent trade unions, we also consulted Japanese researchers who had specialist knowledge of labour and work practices in the car industry.

Our discussion is divided into two main parts. The first part analyses the difference between East and West by examining press shop practice and enterprise calculation in Japan. Our main conclusion is that the balance between physical and financial calculation in all the Japanese shops is biased very strongly towards the physical; orthodox Western cost accounting is completely absent. This bias in the forms of calculation is associated with an inter-process perspective on production and a commitment to continuous improvement. The second part of the chapter takes up the issue of Japanization by examining the conditions which would have to be replicated if Western press shops were to become like the Japanese. We conclude that effective Japanization would require changes in forms of calculation, a new management cadre and a level of workforce commitment which is probably neither possible nor desirable in the West. In fundamental respects, Western management is very far from Japan.

PRESS SHOP PRACTICE

Before we analyse press shop practice, a brief description of the pressing process and of shop layout is required. The process of panel pressing has changed little since all-steel car bodies were introduced more than fifty years ago. Mild steel sheet is delivered to the shop in coils and the coil is first fed into a blanking press which guillotines panels to the appropriate flat dimensions. Large complex panels, like wings or hoods, are then usually formed on a line of four or five 400–1,200 ton hydraulic ram presses, which stand alone and work in tandem to draw the panel into deeper and more complex shapes in successive operations; panels are automatically transferred between presses on a bed of rollers. Car press shops usually have two or more lines of tandem presses with high volume requirements met by doubling up equipment and/or opening a second shop. Scale is a less important influence than differences in age of equipment; recently re-equipped shops are likely to have a 1,500–2,500 ton automatic transfer press which can cycle much faster than the old tandem lines because the successive drawing operations are performed in the bed of one machine. Because all presses work at high speed and because car bodies are made by assembling many different panels, press lines are not dedicated. The presses are first used to run a batch of one panel type and then, after the die formers carried on the rams have been changed, the presses run a batch of another panel type.

It is widely understood that the Japanese change press dies faster, a point confirmed by our finding that the best practice Japanese firm, Nippon Car, had a ten-minute setup time against four hours on comparable presses at Detroit Motors. This observation is, however, meaningless unless it is fitted into a broader account of press shop practice; Japanese car firms are not Olympic athletes who are concerned simply with doing everything faster. Indeed, our data shows that the Japanese are not superior performers in all respects and by all criteria. If we consider throughput and operating efficiency in the single process of pressing there is remarkably little difference between Japanese and European levels of performance.

Within the press shop, the relation between the basic operating variables is very straightforward. With given capital equipment, machine throughput and efficiency equals cycle time × machine available time × length of working day. If the presses cycle faster, if down time is reduced or if the machine working day is increased, then single process efficiency is increased because more panels go down each line and through the shops. But there is little difference in these three basic operating variables between Europe and Japan. The presses cannot run faster because cycle time is technically determined by press design; if the presses are speeded up, they damage themselves. Thus in all the Japanese shops, as at Detroit Motors, the tandem presses operated on a cycle time of 6 to 8 seconds. Furthermore, the presses do not run for a much longer proportion of each day in Japan. The working day is very similar in Japanese and European shops because all car companies work their press shops more or less round the clock. The Japanese typically did this by working two long shifts of 10 to 11 hours, while Detroit Motors worked three short shifts of 8 hours. As for machine available time, that was superior in the best practice Japanese shop at Nippon Car whose presses were up and running 85 per cent of the time on each shift, but Tokyo Motors only managed 68 per cent machine available time, roughly the same as Detroit Motors in Britain.

If the residual category of down time is examined more closely, interesting differences do emerge. Machine available time is less than 100 per cent because presses never cycle continuously through the shift. Part of each day is lost as down time because (i) presses are halted for setup when dies are changed and (ii) breakdowns occur, typically when the handling gear fails to pick up and transfer panels. One Japanese shop had succeeded in reducing down time below the 30 per cent level achieved at Detroit Motors, but all the Japanese shops were using a much larger proportion of their down time for die change. This point can be established by contrasting Detroit Motors with best practice Japanese achievement at Nippon Car, where the advantage of 10-minute setup was used to make much more frequent die changes: at Nippon Car, dies were being changed 5 times a shift (or 10 times a day) while at Detroit Motors the average was once every 30 shifts (or once every 10 days). As a result, the composition of down time is very different in Japanese shops: much less is wasted on machine breakdown and panel jam and considerably more is spent on die change. Detroit Motors loses 30 per cent of each shift and that divides into 28 per cent breakdown and 2 per cent die change; by contrast, Nippon Car loses 15 per cent of each shift and that divides equally between 7.5 per cent breakdown and 7.5 per cent die change.

What does this signify? It is clear from the Nippon Car case that the aim is frequent die change without incurring the penalty of unreasonable amounts of down time. If we then ask, what is gained by more frequent die changes, the answer is much smaller batch sizes. At Nippon Car, the batches are down to 1–2,000 panels (or three shifts requirement) whereas at Detroit Motors, batch size is up to 14,000 panels, depending on order schedule. Small batches from the press shop are the foundation of a low stocks factory and the implication is that the function of the Japanese press shop is to contribute to the objective of downstream process efficiency through reduced batch size. Paradoxically, this achievement rests not on a mastery of production but on a mastery of unproductive time. More exactly, the Japanese do not seek reduced unproductive time for its own sake; instead they try to minimize the wasted breakdown down time while what we might call the 'contributing down time' of setup is used constructively to secure the downstream objective.

There are several objective reasons why smaller batches should be so important to Japanese car manufacturers. Their marketing strategies require variety in production, so stock holding becomes a major physical problem if panels are made in large batches and, more positively, low stock levels mean large financial savings. The large Japanese companies have a strategy of proliferating model variants: Nippon Car, for example, produced no less than six variants of its light saloon with substantial differences in outer body panels. The smaller manufacturers aggressively seek to maintain or extend their model line up: Major Subcontractor produced panels for the smaller Japanese manufacturers, whose model volumes were always low and whose order schedules were often erratic. At the same time, the maintenance of low stock levels saves considerable expense. In an earlier paper on stock reduction, we argue (Williams *et al.* 1989a) that the saving is around 33 cents for every dollar of stocks eliminated and show that the major cost saving arises from elimination of the overhead expense incurred when large amounts of indirect labour are employed to move, warehouse and progress chase stock. These arguments are independently corroborated by Abegglen and Stalk (1985) who show a positive correlation between faster stock turn and higher labour productivity, and that Japanese factories run with very low levels of indirect labour.

Physical versus financial calculation

The objective of Japanese press shop practice is thus to eliminate downstream indirect labour. Given this logic, we were also interested in whether and how this logic was identified and internalized in management calculation. Our research focused not only on workshop practice, but also on the operational calculations and measurements which are used by press shop managers in Japan.

This is an important subject because practice and performance are powerfully directed and influenced by shop calculation. From this point of view, Japanese press shop practice is particularly intriguing because it focuses on operational variables which appear 'invisible' in orthodox Western financial calculation. None of the management accounting textbooks elaborate the distinction between wasted and contributing down time and all the orthodox techniques compute costs for a single process. In principle, the difference in Japanese practice could be associated with either less financial calculation or more elaborate and sophisticated (non-Western) forms of calculation. When we interviewed press shop managers, we found the corollary of practice was less financial calculation; in all three companies operational calculation was biased very strongly towards physical measures.

All press shops are run, day to day, on physical measures and most strategic planning in the upper echelons of large companies necessarily relies on financial measures which allow senior management to target and compare the performance achieved by operating units. Beyond such universals there are, however, significant differences in the amount of financial calculation and how far it is used at the operational level. As we would expect from Western accounting textbooks, financial calculation was very important at Detroit Motors where financial measures paralleled physical measures of operating efficiency. Operations managers used a management accounting system which computed the cost of production of panels and determined standards of performance. Control was then effected by comparing actual financial performance against the standard. In the three Japanese press shops there was simply no sign of any such system.

This observation does not imply an absence of management accounting in these companies. Hiromoto (1988) provides graphic examples of how Japanese companies use management accounting systems instrumentally to put pressure on managers and engineers. Significantly, though, his examples are drawn from product planning and development rather than operations management, and it is important to distinguish between cost accounting for planning and cost accounting for financial control. Our point is simply that there was no sign of ex post historical control of Japanese press shops operations through management accounting (or any other financial technique).

Perhaps this is not surprising because our three Japanese car companies were not organized for financial control and it is hard to see why they should wish to exercise such control over operations. In such companies, accounting control is impossible because the specialist finance function is very small and underdeveloped. Nippon Car produces more than 2.5 million cars each year and the plant we visited produces 63,000 cars a month, but the finance department at head office employs 200 people and the finance departments in each of its major plants employ just 10 to 20 people. The Tokyo Motors plant produced 35,000 cars a month and the finance office employed just 5 people. More fundamentally, management accounting is unnecessary and irrelevant, insofar as Japanese shop practice is focused on the contribution to downstream process efficiency. Because orthodox management accounting takes a single process perspective it cannot compute the downstream costs of large batches or the downstream benefits of small batches. Why should the Japanese trouble to make measurements which are irrelevant to their practice?

Of course, the issue of costs incurred in the press shop is important and, even in Japan, shop calculation starts from financial measures of shop cost which are generated at the higher levels of the company as part of the planning process. The Japanese approach is, however, very non-Western because there is no attempt to compute a total cost of production for each batch of output and Japanese press shop managers always shift from simple cost targets to sophisticated physical measures as quickly as they can. At Nippon Car the head of the press shop explained that the finance office supplied him with two cost targets – for labour costs and materials costs. The latter target had a very low priority because styling ruled at Nippon Car, as in the other Japanese companies, and managers claimed there was little attention to panel design for economy and ease of manufacture from the coil. Labour cost was the crucial measure and the press shop manager dealt with it by immediately translating the financial target for the next time period into a physical measure of press strokes per hour: the labour cost target would be achieved if the presses worked at a rate of so many strokes per man hour. Such a translation from financial target to physical measure also took place in the two other Japanese companies, though at Tokyo Motors it occurred within the finance office and each company used different physical measures of operating efficiency. All the Japanese shop managers would have agreed with the press shop manager at Nippon Car who asserted 'I never calculate financial saving. Never ever.'

Japanese press shop managers are not accountants in disguise: they are productionist engineers preoccupied with physical performance. It has been argued that Western firms would compete more effectively if productive expertise had a more important place within the management hierarchy inside the firm and in management education outside the firm (Armstrong 1987). It is therefore important to emphasize that the Japanese do not have a simple-minded general preference for physical rather than financial measures. They have taken the trouble to develop very specific physical measures which are designed both to prevent 'cheating' and to identify the variables which management must shift. The concern with preventing 'cheating' was strongest at Major Sub-contractor, where the operational measures used were strokes per hour and die changes per month: managers sought and achieved improvement on both measures. The double measure appeared to be a safeguard against a manager who cheated by running the press shop with fewer die changes, which would raise press strokes per hour and improve process performance but sabotage the inter-process objective. At both Nippon Car and Tokyo Motors, the operating measures were more positively designed to concentrate the minds of managers on particular variables. The strokes per man hour target at Nippon Car directed attention to reducing man hours or increasing power strokes through less frequent breakdown and/or more rapid setup. At Tokyo Motors, the operational indicators of power strokes and labour hours appeared to be used separately so that the either/or choice was even clearer.

The differences in press shop calculation broaden our understanding of the contrast between Europe and Japan and the unity of Japanese calculation and practice. There is a complete antithesis between European calculation and Japanese practice. European calculation is distracted by management accounting which incidentally involves the allocation of overhead, whereas Japanese shop practice centres on the elimination of overhead generated through the employment of indirects in a high stocks factory. Equally fundamentally, there is a kind of paradoxical unity to Japanese practice and calculation. The beginning and end of the process of physical shop calculation is the removal of labour costs. If Japanese calculation in the press shop focuses effort on the removal of in process direct labour, that reinforces the effects of shop practice which aims to remove downstream indirects. The same managers who emphasize physical calculations also identify the reduction of labour costs as the sacred mission of management. At Nippon Car, the head of the press shop argued forcefully, in broken English, that 'managers should do anything to improve labour cost. If not so, what kind of job can they take? What responsibility?'

Westerners may be perplexed to find that Japanese production managers reject the form of management accounting calculations but retain the substance of accounting's traditional preoccupation with labour costs, for critics of management accounting often allege that its procedures have been rendered obsolescent by the substitution of capital for labour in manufacturing, which has reduced hourly wage costs to 10 per cent or less of total costs. This point is, however, partial and misleading as all the direct and indirect payroll costs of labour, when added up, account for 30 per cent of total costs (including bought in components) in a Western mechanical engineering firm (Williams *et al.* 1989b). Furthermore, labour's share of value added (excluding bought in components) is likely to be around 70 per cent in a Western firm, though rather lower in Japan. The 30 per cent residual share of the value-added fund must cover depreciation, net new investment, interest and profit distribution. Thus, the control of wage costs is crucial in determining the trajectory of any manufacturing enterprise, especially an expanding enterprise which seeks increased market share as many Japanese enterprises do. The preoccupation with labour costs in Japan suggests that Japanese production managers appreciate the fundamentals of the activity of manufacturing.

Kaizen and calculation

Many of our research interviews were conducted mainly or entirely in Japanese and 'kaizen', which means an improvement or step towards improvement, was the most overused concept in all the firms. In our view the aggressive search for constant kaizen improvement is as important as the emphasis on physical measurement in determining the dynamics of Japanese manufacturing. The concept of kaizen has been introduced to Western readers by Masaaki Imai (1986), but they may be puzzled because kaizen is both presented as a broad philosophy which is 'the key to Japan's competitive success' and interpreted as a narrow practical wrapping around total quality control (TQC). From our research, we would present kaizen in a different way as a workshop imperative that dynamizes the shop practice and forms of calculation which we have already described.

It would be grossly unfair to claim that Detroit Motors was not interested in improvement. The company was trying to close the gap with Japan, and since the early 1980s the press shop managers we interviewed claimed to have reduced setup time from 9 to 4 hours or less on some presses and batch size from 20 to 10 days or 5 days in one case. But two qualifications need to be registered. First, although the company was taking the easy, early gains, on its own account by 1988 it had not got to where Nippon Car was in 1968 when that company had a setup time of 2 hours and batches of 15 days. Second, although Detroit Motors was changing its shop practice, older Western ways of calculating survived completely unreformed, and this limited the pressure that was being applied for improvement.

At Detroit Motors, the emphasis was not on kaizen improvement but on policing the variances. The orthodox management accounting system rested on a computation of standard costs with subsequent measuring of variances. This was shadowed by a system of physical time accounting where the company computed a standard time for the job and then measured the variance in terms of 'off standard' hours. Under such a system, managers escape pressure for improvement if they achieve a norm of performance. Both forms of calculation encourage management by exception: only negative variances are immediately and closely examined. Furthermore, the variances are necessarily only identified ex post long after the event; they represent a system of historical control which is always backward-looking.

In the Japanese companies the emphasis was instead on forward planning which incorporated the assumption that continuous kaizen was possible; press shop managers were given aggressive targets and were expected to show constant improvement month by month. In this war, there is no discharge. Although setup time is already very low and batch size is small, these companies expect to achieve further substantial gains in the next one to three years. In the summer of 1988 Major Subcontractor was changing the dies in tandem presses in 14 minutes; by the end of 1989 this time was to be halved to 7 minutes. On batch size, Major Subcontractor's target was a 25 per cent reduction from 800 to 600 panels. The targets which are set are almost always achieved and kaizen progress is rendered visible in a variety of ways. Major Subcontractor presented us with a two-year summary of press shop performance on one side of A4: as Table 2.1 shows, performance measured in terms of power strokes and die changes did steadily improve.

Table 2.1 Press shop performance at Major Subcontractor

Performance	1986 April–Sept.	1986– Oct.–March	1987 April–Sept.	1987–1988 Oct.–March	1988 April–June
Line A (6 presses producing 4 × 4 jeep outer body panels: engine hood, back door, front fender, side body panel, etc.)					
Strokes per minute	5.4	5.2	5.5	5.8	5.9
Die change time in minutes	19.6	19.8	17.6	16.2	16.6
No. of die changes per line per month	813.0	794.0	1,071.0	1,227.0	1,026.0
No. of die changes per press per month	135.5	132.3	178.5	204.5	171.0
Line B (6 presses producing 4 × 4 jeep chassis and underbody parts)					
Strokes per minute	8.4	8.8	9.1	9.4	9.7
Die change time in minutes	23.1	21.1	20.3	19.4	17.6
No. of die changes per line per month	647.0	664.0	757.0	841.0	873.0
No. of die changes per machine per month	107.8	110.7	126.2	140.2	145.5

Although all the Japanese press shops are very much better than Detroit Motors (or any Western firm) by the relevant inter-process measures of performance, there are also significant differences in performance between Japanese firms, and they are associated with significant differences in what is targeted for kaizen improvement. At the leading edge, in the best practice firm of Nippon Car, there was a firm conviction that endless kaizen improvements were possible with the same capital stock. The press shop manager there was convinced that these improvements could help to realize his vision of a press shop where panels moved in a continuous flow, and each panel touched the next as it passed through the process. Attitudes were rather different at Tokyo Motors, where a company engineer complained that the press shop was up against the limits of what was possible with existing equipment. Our research suggested the problem was in the company not the capital equipment. Working with similar tandem presses, its two Japanese competitors were changing dies in one-quarter and one-half of the 30 minutes it took at Tokyo Motors. Interestingly, Tokyo Motors did not have any setup time reduction target for the next one to three years, but it did have an aggressive direct labour target: 20 per cent of the press shop workforce was to be taken out in the next twelve months. At Tokyo Motors, labour reduction in the press shop appeared to be a substitute for the process improvement which the press shop managers could not achieve.

These differences in press shop management and kaizen targets were associated with differences in investment philosophy. Nippon Car has long been an investment-averse, operationally obsessed organization. Much of its press shop equipment appeared to date from its opening in 1966. Press shop management was totally responsible for operating this equipment and for nothing else. The press shop manager met a question about the choice of new equipment with a terse response: 'not my department.' Nippon Car had devised a system which puts pressure on management to continuously improve the use of what they had. Tokyo Motors had a Western style philosophy of buying operational improvement through investment in new and technically superior process equipment. The plant we visited had a modern automated body shop and a showpiece automated final assembly line. In the press shop was a brand new 2,700-ton automatic transfer press which performed the necessary 3 to 5 forming operations on hood or door panels as they travelled automatically down the bed of the one machine. The new press was designed to cycle 18 times per minute which is 2 to 3 times as fast as the old tandem presses, and the advantage of rapid die change was built in: a set of dies could be changed in 7 minutes when the dies went in east to west through the long open side of the machine while the panels travelled north to south down the bed.

It is difficult to evaluate the solution of pure kaizen at Nippon Car against the solution of investment in new equipment at Tokyo

Motors. Any financial evaluation would require data on the capital cost of equipment which we do not have. Nippon Car shows that the inter-process objective of small batches can be technically achieved on tandem presses without the expense of investment in the latest generation of press shop equipment. Automatic transfer presses may be a cost-effective way of buying in extra capacity without compromising the inter-process objective; because they cycle so much faster, automatic transfer presses dramatically increase panel throughput and the advantage of rapid die change is built in to the design. But the latest equipment creates new problems for firms, which want to realise their inter-process potential by frequent die change. At Tokyo Motors we were told that the new automatic transfer press had aggravated quality problems in the press shop. Panels tracked so quickly through the press that it was difficult to detect and prevent production of a large number of defective panels when any one of the dies in the machine was out of adjustment, and batches of defectives are extraordinarily disruptive of production in a low stocks factory.

From this viewpoint investment in new equipment is not an alternative to kaizen because it needs extra kaizen to realize the potential of the new equipment. Investment in itself is not an adequate defensive response for firms which cannot realize kaizen. The implication for Western press shops is that they must adopt the Japanese style of operations management if they wish to equal Japanese performance. This brings us to the issue of Japanization which is the theme of the rest of our chapter.

CONDITIONS OF JAPANIZATION

Management calculation and intervention

Given the design of our case study and its conclusions, generalization about Japan is impossible. Case studies necessarily bring a small area into precise focus through limiting the scope of the enquiry, and thus undermine the possibility of generalization; we did not investigate Japanese manufacturing practice outside one process, pressing, in one industry, motors. Furthermore, the differences between kaizen at Nippon Car and Tokyo Motors warn against any assumption of homogeneity in manufacturing practice and forms of calculation. In this respect, our study is an antidote to the facile Western tendency to construct myths about a unitary

Japanese system through production concepts like 'Toyotism' and 'Fujitsuism' which inadmissibly read the whole through the part.

Our research did, however, reveal something more specific inside our Japanese press shops: a distinctive *a priori* of production management. The basic Japanese objective is inter-process efficiency rather than improved single process performance. This objective is secured by physical, forward-looking calculations which assume continuous improvement rather than financial, backward-looking policing of the variances. The concept of a difference in *a priori* opens up a new way of questioning the possibility and desirability of Japanization. Given the difference, what conditions would have to be satisfied before Western press shops could replicate the productive achievements of their Japanese counterparts? The answer is that several intellectual and material conditions would have to be satisfied inside the firm. Most obviously, Japanization of the press shop depends on an intellectual revolution in the forms of managerial calculation, but calculation will only become effective intervention and good practice if it is materially supported by organizational redesign and a much higher level of compliance and commitment from the workforce. Our argument about the managerial preconditions will suggest that Japanization is difficult, and our argument about the labour preconditions will suggest that Japanization is undesirable.

In discussing forms of calculation, we would begin by observing that Japanese press shop managers are generally articulate and explicit about their preferred forms of calculation; they advocate physical measures because they believe such measures are more immediately intelligible than financial measures and also help to identify what has to be improved. At Nippon Car the press shop manager insisted on physical measures which line workers could understand. In discussing his translation of labour cost into press strokes, he said 'I change the figures (because) people understand it.' Managers in the other companies added the point that financial measures only showed results and could not indicate the source of the problem or what should be done. A manager at Major Subcontractor was quite clear about why his company privileged physical rather than financial measures: 'The reason is that if the shop managers are given the financial target, they probably will have no idea what they should do, how to do it, how to improve the process.'

In the larger Japanese multinational corporations which have long-established overseas operations, Japanese managers are often well informed, and always highly critical, regarding Western forms of calculation. The press shop manager at Nippon Car had managed the press shop of an overseas subsidiary and had studied the shop practice and calculations of the big American manufacturers. He was scathing about the use of management accounting which he regarded as 'a joke' because its procedures could not generate accurate or relevant cost information. This view was not simply a personal opinion, it was company policy. We were told that a vice president of the company had warned shop managers, 'Don't calculate (in that way) because the basic theory is not correct, even if the calculation is done in the best way.' The press manager at Nippon Car also criticized the absence of kaizen in American owned factories: the Americans made improvements in efficiency every four to five years, when models were changed, but tolerated a constant standard of inefficiency.

In terms of understanding, Japanese managers are like Copernican astronomers disparaging their Ptolemaic precursors whose beliefs and practices they represent as crudely inferior. The problem is that their Western counterparts are often in the position of Ptolemaic astronomers who may have heard of, but do not understand, Copernicus. Thus, at Detroit Motors, the company had an 'After Japan' programme but the managers we interviewed had not considered privileging relevant physical indicators. They had no doubts about the capacity of the financial to represent the productive and guide production; if managers get the right set of costings, the financial numbers will tell them what to do. Thus, the size and expertise of the finance function was a matter of pride; we were told that management accounting was one of the things which the company did 'really professionally'. All of this was slightly bizarre, when management accounting at Detroit Motors was generating information whose opacity confirmed the worst suspicions of the Nippon Car press shop manager. At Detroit Motors, the press shop managers received cost information after the plant's own management accountants had worked out variances. Neither press shop managers nor plant accountants understood how the standards were determined by a third group of managers at corporate headquarters.

Detroit Motors' press shop managers believed that the Japanese managed production better, but they did not know how the Japanese conceptualized production differently. In consequence, their attempts at Japanization were spreading confusion rather than promoting kaizen; according to an internal management document, there was no improvement in the average die change over a time of 5.2 hours between January 1988 and summer 1990. In Detroit Motors there was no clarity about the hierarchy of production ends and means; rapid die change was emphasized, although frequency of die change is a more significant indicator of operating efficiency when the objective is small batches. Slow setup was accepted as an excuse for infrequent die change, although, if small batches were highly desirable, the managers should have considered incurring extra contributing down time in the interests of downstream efficiency. Above all, nobody seemed to have asked why the company wanted smaller batches or whether they would be beneficial. Smaller batches from the press shop will only produce downstream benefits if the subsequent processes can run efficiently with low stocks. If process imbalance or machine un-reliability downstream is not corrected, then smaller batches from the press shop will only lead to output loss downstream as necessary buffer stocks are removed. In the worst case, Japanization without understanding could be a form of ritual, symbolic modernization without real benefits.

If British and American managers are Japanizing without understanding, this is partly because their unconscious *a priori* is promoted and validated by a system of management education which claims to offer universal techniques for managing business. The strategy texts are built on a disparagement of the operational, and the management accounting texts impose a procrustean definition of management calculation. Many Western academics accept that orthodox management accounting is not generating relevant numbers; inside the business schools, there is a sense of crisis about the procedures and results of management accounting. But many academic critics, like Johnson and Kaplan (1987), argue the solution is better management accounting which allocates costs to product lines more accurately and more precisely. Within the Western *a priori* the obvious answer to the problems is more of the same. The answer of less (or no) management accounting comes most easily to those, like Japanese managers, who have a critical distance from the *a priori*, or those, like the trade unions at Detroit Motors, who are innocent of the *a priori*. Disillusioned with the Japanizing efforts of their own managers, the trade unions at Detroit Motors sent a group of workers to Japan who returned in 1989 with a sound general understanding of Japanese practice and a series of practical recommendations for physical improvements in the press shop.

If management education outside the firm was reformed, however, many practical obstacles to Japanization would remain inside the firm. The necessary intellectual revolution could only succeed inside large Western firms if it was supported by organizational redesign which controlled departmentalism in general and the finance function in particular. Western firms must not only reform calculation but also curb production departments which are traditionally accustomed to improving their own results at the expense of creating problems in downstream processes. More specifically, the existence of a large finance function inside the Western company creates massive problems. Finance has a vested interest in the vertical transmission of historical financial information on a single process and it is hard to see how it can be adapted to Japanese-style horizontal dissemination of timely information about inter-process physical performance. It is therefore difficult to define an alternative role for accounting and accountants. Like Doyle (1989), we would argue for the demotion of the finance function and its functionaries, but that is hardly practical politics inside large Western firms where the supply of financial control meets its own demand. The political power of accountants to force their continued presence on the rest of the organization is limited; when profits fail and cost-cutting is necessary, accountants cannot protect their own jobs. But more fundamentally, the orthodox finance function must always be protected as long as Western management demands the financial numbers, and it is hard to see that demand changing when financial expertise is an important qualification for senior management.

There are many ironies in this situation for the British. Large British firms acquired their management accounting function in imitation of the Americans, who were the best practice manufacturers of the 1940s. Productivity delegations went to America in the late 1940s and came back with the message that what Britain needed was more management accounting (Anglo American Council on Productivity 1950). As the best practice manufacturers of the 1980s, the Japanese teach a rather different lesson that management accounting is unnecessary. It is going to be much more difficult, however, to take the accounting out, than it was to put the accounting in, and, worse still, reform of enterprise calculation is not the only, or the most difficult, condition of Japanization: it is also necessary to develop a cadre of production engineers who can deliver kaizen. This requires a practical, interventionist approach to production management and substantial changes in what Western management does when it manages.

The press shop is particularly illuminating here, because there is no secret about what has to be done to achieve better performance. Whatever the framework of calculation, all press shop managers see that it is desirable to reduce unproductive time and can identify the technical means which deliver that end. Wasted down time is reduced by better housekeeping and preventive maintenance which eliminates mechanical breakdown, and also by modifying the handling gear which improves the reliability of panel transfer between tandem presses. In Japanese shops the main operating problem is panel jams caused by failure of the handling equipment to grip as newly pressed, vibrating panels are lifted out of one press for transfer to the next. Contributing down time can be used more productively if setup times are reduced. This requires attention to matters such as preloading of dies on to trolleys or roller beds, standardization of die height, unitized 'cassette' format dies, quick-release lock bolts, arrangements for quickly swinging the panel handling gear out of the way, and traffic-light systems for synchronized line die changes where red shows pre-load preparations and amber shows ready to go. These engineering practicalities are dealt with by Shingo (1985) in a classic text which was translated into English in the mid-1980s.

Why are Japanese managers better at solving the many small problems which all press shop managers can identify? In part because the Japanese have a very practical, interventionist approach to the management of production. Such a practical interventionist approach appears lost in Britain or America, but survives in the most economically successful Western manufacturing country, Germany. But, as Lawrence (1980) argues persuasively, the German approach is tied to the concept of 'technik' or the knowledge and skills relevant to manufacturing. It also presupposes a very high level of technical literacy and competence in the management cadre. It is easy to caricature the German approach to the problem of panel jams: analysis by a team of three Dr. Ing.s using the most sophisticated vibration measurement techniques, with a complex, over-engineered new handling mechanism as the preferred solution. In Japanese factories, the problem of panel jams appeared to be tackled with a lot of left hand up a bit, right hand down a bit experiment in moving panel grippers, while Tokyo Motors was also experimenting with weighting panels. The improvising approach partly reflects more rapid model change in the Japanese car industry, making expensive fixed solutions unattractive, but it is also partly a consequence of management qualifications and careers in Japan.

The Japanese educational system now produces many well qualified engineers, but many older production managers do not have much formal education. The grizzled veterans who make up the current cadre of senior production managers grew up in the 1950s and early 1960s. Their reticence about educational background encourages the surmise that many are technical high school graduates. Furthermore, the senior managers in press shops are not always functional engineering specialists. Rotation between departments and functions in the course of a managerial career is much more common in Japanese than in Western companies. At Major Subcontractor, one of the two senior managers who explained shop practice had just transferred from tool and machinery design and before that had worked in sales. Given the nature of the cadre, it is not surprising that the management style is hands on and practical without any cult of the technik. It is thus not enough to say that Japanese management integrates engineering: the way in which it does so is probably unique.

As a result the job senior departmental managers do when they manage is rather different in Japanese companies. The central part of the Japanese shop managers job is walking the press shop, identifying problems and looking for improvements. This process is led by the head of the shop, who does as much walking as anybody else. The head of the Nippon Car press shop worked an 11-hour day and said he divided his time between 5 hours walking, 3 hours sitting and 3 hours of meetings. He criticized his counterparts who managed Western press shops for spending too much time behind their desks.

> Their way is different. Western managers have a big room (office). Sitting time seven hours. They don't know the actual situation on the shop floor. The sitting time is too long. They are just controlling by the figures.

Management by walking about is, of course, not unknown in the West, but, presumably, what Western managers see when they walk about is conditioned by their calculative framework.

The Japanese approach has one further advantage from the point of view of increasing efficiency. The practical, non-technical nature of their approach makes it possible to incorporate the workers into the kaizen process. The press shop manager at Nippon Car criticized

Western workers who were allowed in a Taylorist way to 'just push the button' and complained 'Western managers don't use people's minds'. The contrast with Germany is again instructive. German line workers performing semi-skilled operations will often have craft work qualifications, but there is no way they can contribute to the efforts of the Dr. Ing.s. The Japanese approach allows greater worker participation and this is institutionalized and made compulsory by the Quality Circle (QC) system which, in one form or another, probably operates in more than half the companies in Japan. As Imai (1986: 100) observes, QCs involve ordinary workers in what the West would regard as management tasks for production or industrial engineers. Predictably, the QC system was most strongly developed at Nippon Car whose commitment to kaizen through operational improvement was total and obsessional. Nippon Car's Japanese employees were organized into 6,000 QCs and, in 1987, they came up with 32 suggestions per employee, or more than one a fortnight. Many of the suggested improvements are trivial, but some are not and all are evaluated by the practically minded managers of kaizen.

There is no doubt that production management has a higher status in Japan than in the West. At Nippon Car, the principle of 'genbashugi' is part of the Company's official ideology: genbashugi means that production sites and production skills are the most important. But Western firms who want to emulate the Japanese will have to do more than change the status of the production function; they will have to learn a new practice of management which makes every man his own engineer. This has interesting implications for ordinary line workers. Kaizen represents intensification and exploitation insofar as the QC system puts continuous pressure on the workforce for no obvious large, direct benefit. If the workers refuse to be incorporated into the post-Taylorist pursuit of kaizen, the pace of improvement must be slowed down, regardless of management calculation or practice. Thus, the existence of a compliant, committed workforce is a further condition of effective Japanization.

Workforce consent and commitment

It is difficult to research the regime of labour control which is used to secure workforce compliance and commitment inside Japanese companies. The technique of interviewing managers reaches its limits here because Japanese press shop managers, who will eagerly discuss the minutiae of rapid die change, are not so forthcoming about management's control over the labour process. As in other countries, Japanese managers regard themselves as company ambassadors who should avoid sensitive issues where the company's performance and practice could be represented as discreditable; interestingly, the managers at Detroit Motors were evasive about details of shop performance where they knew they had much to hide. We are suspicious of the engineering literature on Japanese manufacturing excellence (e.g. Hartley 1986) because it takes the company ambassadors' discourse at face value and thereby reproduces management's partial account of the Japanese achievement and its preconditions.

Thus, we do not apologize for presenting an account of labour control, in the car industry and its press shop, which is based on secondary sources. Much of the English language literature on Japanese labour control is interpretative rather than informative and concentrates on issues like the difference of Japan from an unexamined stereotype of 'Fordism' (e.g. Kenney and Florida 1988; Kato and Steven 1989). Dohse *et al.* (1985) remain the best short guide to the distinctiveness of Japanese labour control, but the absence of hard information is such that Kamata's (1983) book remains a classic in the West, even though it describes work conditions in one Japanese car company more than fifteen years ago. Our questions about whether and how work practices and labour control had changed since then were put to an independent team of University researchers, whose major study of Nippon Car was published recently (Asoa *et al.* 1988). Most of what follows is based on conversation with and papers supplied by this team, who intend to publish their work in English in due course.

The first point that needs making is that Nippon Car is something of a special case. It is based in a sprawling company town, some distance from the major urban centres. Historically, the company recruited its workforce from the underdeveloped and poor surrounding rural areas. Nippon Car has a more total control over its workforce because it operates in the community as well as the factory, and this workforce is generally supposed to be more compliant than the big city workforces of Tokyo Motors or Major Subcontractor. The extent of compliance and the fusion of community and workplace at Nippon Car are best illustrated by the way in which the company's QCs routinely punish workers who have had traffic accidents as private individuals in their own time off company premises: the bizarre punishment is an especially short haircut. Nevertheless, many of the labour control practices inside the factory at Nippon Car are not unique but operate in less extreme form in other Japanese companies.

The differences in factory labour control between Nippon Car and the rest of the industry are in themselves significant and suggestive. It is universally accepted that Nippon Car's manufacturing practice inside and outside the press shop is superior to that of any other Japanese car manufacturer. It is widely believed in radical circles that this superiority is partly or mainly the result of the more intense forms of labour control which the company operates. The causal connection between manufacturing performance and labour control is, of course, exceedingly difficult to establish. Our own cautious position would be that Nippon Car's labour control is a necessary but not sufficient condition of manufacturing superiority: without that labour control, ten-minute die changes and 1,000 panel batches on tandem presses would remain a dream. This basic point needs emphasis in the West because engineers (Schonberger 1982; Hartley 1986) who have written about Japanese manufacturing practice for Western audiences, neglect the dark, coercive side of Japanese management.

At Nippon Car, all manual workers are obliged to meet the standards of work effort and time commitment which in Western societies are only met voluntarily by some well-paid and self-motivated middle class professionals. Workshop kaizen requires that all workers be committed in two respects: first, they should intensify effort to meet the ever receding targets; second, they should be prepared to sacrifice free time, as necessary, to the company.

Intensity of effort is easiest to observe on the final assembly tracks where the workpace at Nippon Car is more intense than at Tokyo Motors or at Western plants like Volkswagen Wolfsburg. Nippon Car uses its own hard-driving foremen to set time standards for each job where Tokyo Motors uses industrial engineers, and the time allowances for assembly operations are obviously tighter at Nippon Car. In both companies yellow flashing Andon lights indicate a worker has pulled a cord because he is having difficulty in completing the assembly operation. At Nippon Car the Andon lights above the lines were constantly flashing yellow, whereas we never saw a flashing yellow light when we walked the Tokyo Motors assembly line. The difference in labour intensity and pace is reinforced by differences in stock levels. Tokyo Motors had failed to implement a kanban card system and still maintains substantial buffer stocks; there was, for example, a 350 car buffer stock at the end of the final assembly line so that it did not matter if the line stopped. At Nippon Car such buffer stocks have been removed so that, if the line stops, downstream operations and deliveries are immediately disrupted.

What goes on in the press shop is subtler and more difficult to observe, but the logic of kaizen requires intense effort in the press shops of all the companies. Most of the tasks are machine paced and machine speed in the press shop, as elsewhere in the factory, is the prerogative of management. The manager of the Nippon Car press shop claimed that if he saw the possibility of speed-up, he would tap the worker on the shoulder and get him to do it there and then. But Japanese press shop practice does not depend on speed-up in a Chaplin/Modern Times sense; as we emphasized in the section on shop practice, Japanese presses do not cycle ever faster and Japanese workers are not therefore struggling to keep up with shorter cycle times. Intensification of effort takes a different form when additional tasks are added to the direct operative's job in a shop where this year there are fewer operatives than last year. The pick and place operator of one machine survives in Western press shops but has long since been abolished in Japan where separate, skilled die change crews are equally part of industrial history. In the ideal Japanese press shop an individual operator or small crew tends automatic feed, pick and place arrangements, unloads and checks panel dimensions and finish as necessary, and undertakes routine maintenance or setup. Under the kaizen system each operator or crew is responsible for an increasing number of machines: that is the inexorable logic of demanning with unchanged capital equipment, and, if assembly line work was more relaxed at Tokyo Motors, this was not obvious in the company's press shop which had to meet tough targets for manpower reduction.

Nippon Car's management requires more than intense effort. It also requires the sacrifice of free time, even if that means working continuously for 11 hours a day, 6 days a week with the one day off in the middle of the week, at the company's convenience. In an information pack for visitors, the company claims to offer its workers an '8-hour day, 40-hour week'. This claim is somewhat economical with the truth. The standard working day is 8 hours, but the shift runs for 9 hours because it includes one hour of unpaid meal breaks. After 9 hours on shift, the workers are required to work overtime as necessary. All Nippon Car shops run on a work to finish basis; each shift has a production stint and overtime is worked to finish the stint. Workers are paid for overtime but the overtime requirement (and thus the going home time) is only put up on a board halfway through each shift. In recent years, demands for the company's product has been brisk and 2 hours of overtime are routinely required. Flexibility is built in, as management thoughtfully leaves several hours gap between the two standard 9-hour shifts. With overtime, the working day from start to finish is typically 11 hours long-from 8 a.m. to 7 p.m. on the day shift, and 8.30 p.m. to 7.30 a.m. on the night shift. Even though their day is long, workers can expect little free time for rest and relaxation in the course of the working day. The scheduled meal breaks are often taken up with company business, such as QC meetings. When the norm is 32 suggestions per worker per year, membership of an 8- or 10-person QC imposes real obligations. Workers are formally entitled to 2 days off each week, but, in recent years, they have been obliged to work 6 days so that the company can extract more output from existing capacity. Their one day off may not be completely free because loyal workers are expected to join in company sports and social events. Finally, the day off may be taken mid-week at the convenience of the company and the inconvenience of the worker's family. In the summer of 1987 Nippon Car chose to work Saturdays and Sundays because the local electricity utility charged a lower tariff at weekends.

Even in Nippon Car there are limits on management prerogatives. The experimental system of the mid-week break was abandoned in 1988 partly because of opposition by company workers and the local community; the Christian churches, in particular, complained about having to rearrange Sunday services for the middle of the week. In all other respects, though, the informal work contract for a 6-day, 66 hour week of intense effort is institutionalized and accepted by the workforce. The question which Westerners always ask is, why do Japanese workers give their consent and commitment to these arrangements?

Part of the answer is that organized collective resistance is extraordinarily difficult under a system of company unionism and guided democracy on the shop floor. At Nippon Car, for example, the balloting for union offices is open, so that it is extraordinarily difficult to vote against official candidates. Both Nippon Car and Tokyo Motors established company unions in the early 1950s after winning fierce struggles against independent unions. The resulting company union settlements have been unchallenged and stable for the past thirty years because they have operated in the context of a system of economic rewards and punishments, common to most large firms, which make individual and small group resistance very costly and damaging.

The way of consent and conformity is made easy because those who make the commitment to work are rewarded with a formal or informal guarantee of permanent employment. Much has been written about the institution of 'lifetime employment', but we would emphasize that the institution exists in a specific economic context of rapid output growth, where aggressively competitive Japanese companies have been winning extra sales on a fast expanding domestic market at the same time as their exports claim an increasing share of world markets. 'Taking labour out' is relatively painless in this context: demanned workers are not sacked but transferred to other company shops, new factories or redeployed into supplier firms. At Nippon Car most of the transfers are between company shops which employ much the same number in Japan as they did twenty years ago: between 1970 and 1988 the company's vehicle output increased from 1.6 to 4.0 million units and its total (worldwide) workforce increased from 42,000 to 68,000 workers. The guarantee of continuing employment does not apply to seasonal or casual workers at Nippon Car and Tokyo Motors, while the women who work for Nippon Car are required to give up their jobs after they marry. As is well known, many of the permanent, male workers in smaller Japanese manufacturing companies also have no guarantee of continuing employment. But as long as the growth continues, a substantial minority of the workforce can be offered a guarantee of employment, and major companies (which ruthlessly pursue the operational objective of taking labour out) are able to honour this guarantee. Indeed, growth has been so strong that this guarantee for some workers can be honoured without squeezing out other workers who are employed at the base of the pyramid of component suppliers. Between 1970 and 1987 employment in Japanese manufacturing increased from 10.6 to 15.2 million.

The rewards for consent and commitment have been well publicized in the West because major Japanese companies can present these practices in a favourable, welfarist way. For obvious reasons, the companies are less eager to publicize the punishments for dissent and nonconformity which make the consequences of individual or small group dissent intolerably high. At Nippon Car appropriate punishments were built into the payment system for individuals and for work groups. For individuals there is no such thing as a set rate for the job. Basic wages, which account for some 30 per cent of total earnings, are individualized. The basic rate is varied according to an annual merit rating of each worker's attitude and effort. All the bonuses, which account for some two-thirds of earnings, are paid out as percentage increments on the individual's basic rate. A lowly merit rating for attitude is therefore a severe individual punishment. The bonus system also involves the threat of work group punishment. At Nippon Car, roughly 40 per cent of the monthly wage is accounted for by the *seisan teate* (or shop bonus). This is not a piece-rate incentive scheme, which directly rewards work groups for getting more metal out of the door, but is a bonus paid as a reward for group cooperation with management. The group's fear is that the whole shop's bonus would be withdrawn if a handful of individuals refused to cooperate with management about speed-up or demanning; under this threat of collective punishment, it is unsurprising that uncooperative workers are widely referred to as 'destroyers of our company'. Tokyo Motors did not use this kind of bonus system as a direct sanction, but it had exactly the same philosophy of group punishment. The whole shop group of workers and managers would be punished for the sins of one or a few members of the group. At Tokyo Motors, we asked a young engineer what would happen if the press shop did not meet its kaizen targets: he replied, without hesitation, that pay and promotion prospects would suffer 'for all engineers and for all workers as well'.

These sanctions are exceedingly powerful because traditionally in Japan there has been no external labour market for workers and executives in mid-career who find it exceedingly difficult to transfer between major companies. If their career inside one major firm is blighted, they must live with the consequences inside that firm until they retire. Everybody believes that the threat of 'lifetime punishment' is not an empty one because exemplary punishment was used, at Nippon Car and Tokyo Motors, against those who supported the independent union in the early 1950s. It is alleged that many who resisted the company were not sacked but kept on and never promoted. In each shop the presence of these unfortunates served to remind younger workers that the company never forgives those who oppose the company line.

An almost infinite management prerogative over the labour process is one key precondition of Japanese press shop performance; as we have seen, in the press shop at Nippon Car, this prerogative is used ruthlessly to maintain long hours and intensify the workpace in an industrial relations system where there is virtually no possibility of individual or collective worker dissent or resistance. It is important to emphasize that this kind of labour control is criticized by many independent Japanese outside the companies: they argue, like most Westerners, that it should not be emulated in the West. In these terms Japanese management in the press shop is technically superior but in many ways socially inferior to Western practice. More immediately important, this kind of labour control could not easily be recreated in the West where there are customary limits on management prerogatives, even without resistance by independent unions.

The experience of Britain, under radical right government in a period of mass unemployment, shows that the prerogatives of labour can be eroded. In Austin Rover in the early 1980s management regained a large measure of control over the labour process (Willman and Winch 1985; Williams *et al.* 1987), and unions were forced into a position where their only role was to administer a grievance procedure and negotiate an annual pay rise. But managers in most Western firms are not in any position to secure the Japanese press shop level of consent and commitment, because they cannot apply a Japanese style system of rewards and punishments. As managers of low growth firms in slow growing economies they cannot offer the reward of a guarantee of employment: in the West, taking labour out of a process usually means redundancies. Furthermore, the Japanese philosophy of punishing all for the sins of the few would be thought unfair, not least because the all would usually include a significant number of managers. The 'successes' of macho management in the 1980s have obscured the fundamental point that there are limits on what can be captured and held as a management prerogative in Western firms. The managers of Japanese branch factories in Western economies may be in a more favourable position if they can win rapid increases in market share, but the contradiction between Western values and the press shop style of labour control must still set limits on their prerogative. When the team of Japanese researchers who had investigated Nippon Car visited the American branch factories of Japanese car firms, they were impressed by the level of concession and compromise over labour control. All these firms organized labour into a few general grades, none had instituted individualized, merit-rated pay. More systematic evidence confirms this impression: in a recent survey of Japanese manufacturing firms operating in Europe, more than 20 per cent reported problems about absenteeism and difficulties about persuading workers to accept overtime and holiday work (JETRO 1990).

CONCLUSION

We have emphasized that our research took the form of a case study of three Japanese press shops, but if this research provides no basis for generalization, it does have implications for the existing over-generalized debate on Japanization and its question 'how far from Japan'. The short answer from the press shop is 'a long way and not getting much closer'. If press shop management and labour control are representative of Japanese practice, Western firms will find it difficult to Japanize because they must learn radically new forms of calculation and management intervention. Even if the branch factories of Japanese firms have the advantage of (transferred) understanding, they will still find it difficult or impossible to Japanize because they cannot recreate Japanese levels of workforce consent and commitment.

These conditional conclusions open up an agenda for further research and debate. Inside Japan, the obvious question is whether our press shop findings are representative of Japanese manufacturing. From the point of view of transferability, the key question is how effective would the press shop style of calculation and intervention be if workforce consent and commitment is much more qualified. We have no way of knowing how much of Japanese manufacturing relies on the practices of the press shop. But we believe the question about what happens if (or when) labour control is relaxed is important to the future of Japanese manufacturing at home and abroad. Major Japanese companies are already experimenting with high-tech alternatives to their traditional forms of labour exploitation. Nippon Car, for example, has recently opened a new highly automated plant.

The outcome of such experiments is uncertain, but, meanwhile, it is important to avoid the production management centred view of Japanese manufacturing which underpins much of the existing debate about Japanization. There is room for compromise about productive efficiency insofar as Japanese firms can compete successfully in other areas. When we interviewed senior management at Tokyo Motors in 1990, they claimed their company now sought competitive advantage through quicker, cheaper model development rather than production kaizen. Furthermore, the new Japanese branch factories in Europe and America often represent investments in market access, rather than efficient low cost production: in a recent survey of Japanese branch-plant manufacturers in Europe, only two out of 270 respondents cited lower production cost as a reason for establishing a presence in Europe (JETRO 1990: 24–25). Overseas manufacture is the only way for these firms to maintain and increase market share against a background of trade friction with the United States and protectionist threats from 'fortress Europe'. Productive efficiency in these branches is not essential if Japanese parent plants supply cheap, high quality components for assembly and if new model development costs can be recovered on the Japanese home market.

It is equally important to avoid a Japan centred view of modern manufacturing. This view is partially justified in America where the Japanese firms have displaced domestic consumer electronics firms and captured a share of the car market which is rising to 30 per cent. But, in Europe, the arrival of the Japanese is a media event which has attracted academic attention that is out of all proportion. For the Japanese, Europe is a relatively unimportant and distant export market: in 1987 it took just 17 per cent of Japanese exports, whereas the United States alone took 38 per cent (Cutler *et al.* 1989). The scale of Japanese branch manufacturing is also very modest: by early 1990, for example, there were just 125 Japanese branch factories in Britain, with 25,000 employees, or roughly 0.1 per cent of the workforce (*Independent*, 30 May 1990).

The problem for British and many other European firms is not that they are technically too far from Japan; the problem is that they are geographically not far enough from West Germany. In manufacturing terms, West Germany is a regional superpower in Europe as Japan is in East Asia; with just one-sixth of the EC 12 population, the West Germans have nearly 40 per cent of EC 12 manufacturing output and their huge surplus on manufactured trade with the rest of Europe represents a substantial transfer of employment to West Germany (Cutler *et al.* 1989). Academics, who are fixated on the superiority of the Japanese, have neglected the persistent and significant differences in competence between national manufacturing sectors inside Europe and America. German success is particularly interesting because

German management combines technical efficiency with a limited social prerogative over labour. 'Germanization' would certainly represent a more congenial and appropriate future for the Western countries, and the implication is that research into the possibility of Germanization should be given much higher priority.

Acknowledgement

This a slightly revised version of a paper which was first published in *Critical Perspectives in Accounting* (1991) 2: 145–169.

REFERENCES

Abegglen, J. C. and Stalk, G. (1985) *Kaisha – The Japanese Corporation*, New York: Basic Books.

Anglo American Council on Productivity (1950) *Management Accounting*, London: Anglo American Council.

Armstrong, P. (1987) 'The abandonment of productive intervention in management teaching syllabi', *Warwick Papers in Industrial Relations*, Industrial Relations Research Unit, University of Warwick, Coventry.

Asoa, *et al.* (1988) *Jidosha Sangyo to Radoshu* (The Automobile Industry and Its Workers), Tokyo.

Cutler, T. *et al.* (1989) *1992 – The Struggle for Europe*, Oxford: Berg.

Dohse, K. *et al.* (1985) 'From Fordism to Toyotism', *Politics and Society*, 14, 2: 115–146.

Doyle, P. (1989) 'Britain's left and right-handed companies', Unpublished Paper, University of Warwick, Coventry.

Hartley, J. (1986) *Fighting the Recession in Manufacturing*, Bedford: IFS Publications.

Hiromoto, T. (1988) 'Japanese management accounting', *Harvard Business Review* (July–August 22–26).

Imai, M. (1986) *Kaizen*, New York: Random House.

JETRO, International Economic and Trade Information Centre (1990) *Current Situation of Business Operations of Japanese Manufacturing Enterprises in Europe*, Sixth Survey Report, Tokyo: JETRO.

Johnson, H. T. and Kaplan, R. (1987) *Relevance Lost*, Boston: Harvard Business School Press.

Kamata, S. (1983) *Japan in the Passing Lane*, London: Allen & Unwin.

Kato, T. and Steven, R. (1989) 'Is Japanese capitalism post-Fordist'?, mimeo, Hitotsubashi University.

Kenney, M. and Florida, R. (1988) 'Beyond mass production', *Politics and Society* 16, 1: 121–158.

Lawrence, P. (1980) *Managers and Management in West Germany*, London: Croom Helm.

Oliver, N. and Wilkinson, B. (1988) *The Japanization of British Industry*, Oxford: Blackwell.

Schonberger, R. J. (1982) *Japanese Manufacturing Techniques*, New York: Free Press.

—— (1987) *World Class Manufacturing*, New York: Free Press.

Shingo, S. (1985) *A Revolution in Manufacturing: the SMED System*, Cambridge: Productivity Press.

Williams, K. *et al.* (1987) *The Breakdown of Austin Rover*, Leamington Spa: Berg.

—— (1989a) 'Why take the stocks out', *International Journal of Operations and Production Management*, 9, 8: 91–105.

—— (1989b) 'Do labour costs really matter?', *Work, Employment and Society* 3, 1: 281–305.

Willman, P. and Winch, G. (1985) *Innovation and Management Control*, Cambridge: Cambridge UP.

Womack, J., Jones, D. and Roos, D. (1990) *The Machine that Changed the World*, New York: Rawson Associates.

3

'JAPANESE MANAGEMENT' AND THE 'LOANING' OF LABOUR

Restructuring in the Japanese iron and steel industry

Toshiko Kamada

EDITORIAL INTRODUCTION

Recent discussions of the organization of Japanese employment relations have moved away from a simple emphasis on the 'three pillars' of life-time employment, nenko wages and enterprise unionism enjoyed by the core workers in large enterprises. On the one hand they have given increasing attention to the tensions and changes which have characterized these institutions, with debates about the limits of enterprise unionism, the growth of ability-based wages and the direct recruitment of specialists (Whittaker 1990; Tokunaga 1984). On the other hand they have underlined that around two-thirds of the workforce, in the hierarchies of medium and small subcontracting enterprises, remain outside these arrangements, often in insecure, low-paid and unorganized work (Chalmers 1989; Tokunaga 1984).

Kamada's chapter extends this reappraisal of the 'three pillars' by providing a detailed discussion of the increasing practice of the loaning and transfer of core workers, often to smaller enterprises or subcontracting firms, a development which has ramifications for both core and peripheral workforces and which further complicates the stratification of the Japanese labour market. In using the steel industry as her case study she takes a sector which has often been regarded as an exemplar of those blue-collar employment relations which have helped to sustain quality consciousness and multi-skilled teamworking (Koike 1988), and an industry which for long played a leading role in the yearly round of institutionalized wage bargaining. In the last twenty years, however, such erstwhile leading sectors as steel and shipbuilding have been beset by particularly severe economic pressures as a result of both world over-

91

capacity and the appreciation of the yen. Indeed, in shipbuilding and steel the loaning and transfer of workers has often been both an accompaniment and a partial alternative to redundancy. Thus Koshiro (1992) reports that in 1987 one shipbuilding company settled for 1,300 redundancies and 400 workers dispatched to subsidiaries on terms negotiated with the union, while a steel combine which sought 19,000 redundancies eventually agreed to transfer 6,000 workers to jobs in new business areas, 1,000 to three modern steel plants, and 500 to subsidiaries.

It is in these sectors, then, that some of the strains and limitations in the institutionalized relationships of core employment and the ways in which those relationships are being attenuated have become most evident. The leading export oriented manufacturing sectors, such as motors and electricals, have so far proven less vulnerable, not least because more of the overall production process in these sectors already takes place within extensive networks and hierarchies of subcontractors or involves dispatched agency workers at the assembly plants (Tokunaga 1984). In these conditions, and against a background of continuing labour shortages, managements in these sectors have made more limited use of the dispatch, loaning and transfer of workers. Yet despite such sectoral differences, the developments discussed by Kamada are not confined to the most depressed sectors, and there is survey evidence of their widespread growth through both the 1970s and the 1980s (Shimada 1980: 26; Whittaker 1990: 334–335). Thus by examining an extreme case her study illuminates more general changes and tensions in management strategies, worker experiences and union responses in contemporary Japanese manufacturing.

MANAGEMENT STRATEGY DURING THE 1980S

The oil crisis of 1974 saw the beginning of a low growth period for the Japanese economy. The high value of the yen which settled in following the Plaza Accord of 1985 was particularly responsible for the growth of a sense of crisis in the business world. The new strategy formulated by the Government and the monopolistic enterprises of Japan was to accept US demands for market liberalization and the expansion of domestic demand, and to promote the relocation of production facilities overseas, converting domestic industry to a fully multinational status. On the domestic front this involved the promotion of restructuring by reducing unprofitable

sectors, seeking new business opportunities, diversifying management, and developing new products within the domestic market.

The slogan of 'efficient productivity' which prevailed throughout
the country in the 1960s has now been replaced by those of 'internationalization', 'diversification' and 'flexibility', and it is widely
accepted that those who fail to follow these policies will not survive.
However, it should be emphasized that these terms express the
perspective of management and capital. When examined from the
workers' point of view the same strategy creates the negative conditions of 'deindustrialization', 'employment instability' and 'extended
working hours', suggesting that workers should not join the chorus
chanting these capitalist slogans.

As a result of successful industrial restructuring, Japanese firms
achieved a record increase of 25.75 per cent in operating income for
the period ending in March 1989 (48.3 per cent for the manufacturing
sector), and Westerners are bound to be intrigued again with the secret
of 'Japanese management'. Admittedly, the monopolistic industries in
Japan are doing their utmost to achieve better management. But the
same system would not necessarily succeed in Western countries, since
conditions are not the same: the structure of employment relations is
different, and workers lack class consciousness.

This chapter discusses the example of the iron and steel industry
to demonstrate how industrial restructuring in a depressed industry
took place, and to examine the specific methods employed in some
detail. In the course of the discussion, we shall see how a new
multilayer workforce structure was created, how working conditions have changed, how family life was affected, and what impacts
the change in workers' awareness will have on the 'Japanese
management system'. Lastly, we shall delineate problems in the
reorganization of enterprise labour unions which result from
restructuring, and comment on the political significance of the
recent reorganization of labour's 'national centres' and other
political developments in the 1990s.

RESTRUCTURING IN THE IRON AND STEEL INDUSTRY

Japanese methods of rationalization

If business strategy demands the elimination of unprofitable
operations and advances into new business fields, the simplest

approach to personnel administration would be to dismiss those workers involved in the unprofitable sectors. Japanese enterprises, however, have always encouraged loyalty to the company on the part of workers through the promise of life-time employment, and have sought to stabilize the labour/management relationship on this basis. The world renowned 'Japanese management system' is characterized by three major features: (i) lifetime employment: hiring employees fresh out of school on a lifetime basis; (ii) seniority-based wages: promotions and wage raises are provided according to seniority as the employee accumulates skills and experience within the company, guaranteeing the livelihood of the worker's family; (iii) enterprise labour unions: all the clerks, engineers, and labourers of a company join the union together, thereby facilitating labour/management compromises. A worker does not conclude an employment contract with an employer; rather, he or she joins a business community and becomes linked to its destiny until the very end. This is referred to as 'family management'.

Within a labour/management relationship such as this, sudden dismissals create problems. Those managers of declining industries who underwent the bitter experience of mass dismissals in the 1950s, which resulted in large scale labour disputes, learned their lesson and are therefore trying to decrease the number of employees gradually rather than abruptly. This is evident in the 'Mid-term integrated plan' published by five steel companies in 1987, which projected a reduction in annual crude steel production from 120 million tons to 90 million tons. The total number of employees working in the steel making sections of the five major companies (119,750 employees) was to be reduced by 32 per cent (38,300 employees) over a period of three years. Taking the example of Company A, 4 out of 12 blast furnaces in their 8 domestic steel mills were to be shut down in order to lower the production quantity of crude steel from 34 million tons to 24 million tons. The plan includes a huge personnel cut of 40 per cent, from 47,450 to 28,450.

At steel mill C of Company A, where all of its blast furnaces were to be closed down, the following plan was to be carried out in reducing the numbers of employees from 4,000 to 2,000:

1 Transfer, 650 workers: in line with a plant 'scrap and build' policy, they were to be transferred to new and improved steel mills. Those aged 45 or over (30 per cent of the transferees) were to be loaned out to subsidiaries immediately after transfer.

2 Loaning or 'shukkoh', 700 workers: four newly established subsidiary companies were to receive 400 workers on loan, while
  300 were to be loaned to other companies.
3 Dispatch to other companies, 20 workers: these workers
  were to be dispatched to auto or related companies.
4 Training: training for career change is covered by government
  subsidies for declining industries. Some workers aged 58 or over
  were not to work on the basis or pretext that they were undergoing education/training.
5 Temporary leave: some of those workers aged 58 or over
  were to be given temporary leave.
6 Retirement: the retirement age was to be extended to 60 in 1991;
  until then, workers were to be requested to retire at 59.
7 Early retirement: those retiring before the mandatory retirement
  age were to receive a premium retirement allowance.

Since there were 700 workers who were reaching the retirement age as
a matter of course, the total of reduction amounts to 2,000 employees.

These methods of workforce reduction are characterized by
'shukkoh'. 'Shukkoh' is a Japanese term which refers to the Japanese
practice of transferring or loaning workers to subsidiaries from the
parent company. 'Shukkoh' is not the same as re-employment since
the workers maintain their formal status within the parent company,
but actually work in the subsidiary. Although they work under the
subsidiary's working conditions and management, they remain
employed by the parent company to the end. That is to say, they are
'pseudo-employees' of the subsidiary, and subsidiaries never act to
dismiss such workers on their own. Thus workers subjected to
'shukkoh' may be termed 'loaned workers'. The intention behind
this practice is to assure the life-time employment of under-utilized
key personnel. The subsidiaries must receive such loaned workers
due to their subordinate economic relationship with the parent
company. It is vitally important to understand the concept of
'shukkoh' in order to be able to grasp the reality of the current
Japanese economic system. We shall now discuss the concrete
circumstances surrounding the loaning of workers.

Loaning to new ventures outside the industry

Company A's restructuring strategy focused on evolving a conglomerate structure so that even the 60 per cent reduction in its steel-

making operations would not affect the overall profitability of the company. Thus, the company moved into the fields of new materials (titanium, ceramics, electronics-related materials), engineering, chemicals, and construction. Since the development of high technology requires top engineers, personnel are recruited widely both inside and outside the company.

However, new companies are not only created to advance into high technology industries, but also to create subsidiaries solely for receiving persons to be loaned out. The latter include companies in the fields of housing, construction and the service industries, such as computer software houses, all of which absorb excess workers. The reason steel companies diversified their business operations was that, partly as a consequence of both factory and office automation, they had a wide variety of differing types of surplus workers: from high technology engineers to maintenance personnel, from transportation engineers to unskilled workers.

The companies created to absorb workers may be wholly owned subsidiaries of the parent company, or they may be nominally independent firms which have been captitalized entirely by the large enterprise. Some are owned jointly with other enterprises. In many cases, the subsidiaries operate their businesses on the premises of steel mills, so while some workers are loaned out to companies located far away, most continue to work in the same location but do different jobs. The unions of which such workers are members do not dispute such job changes, but rather act to persuade the workers to accept their new circumstances. Although these workers are still employed by Company A, they work under the conditions of the newly established subsidiary, and since the new company is small, the work conditions are inferior. Therefore, those who are loaned to new companies which are separate entities are clearly climbing down the ladder of success and are understandably uneasy about the future.

Those who are loaned to software houses must work at a client's workplace. This means that they are loaned out on a three- or six-month basis. Supposing a security company places an order for a software job following the installation of new computer terminals, a new company X which is jointly owned by Company A and Company E is consigned the job. Company X further subcontracts the job to five outside companies. Therefore, there are people from the security company, from Companies A and E, and five subcontractors working side by side. This has important implications for social relations at work, as it is difficult to make friends and people with conflicting interests labour side by side in a bleak atmosphere. Furthermore overtime hours are a matter of course because of deadline pressures.

Loans to subcontractors

There are distinct differences in working conditions between big companies and smaller companies in Japan. The 'Japanese Management System' applies only to big companies, while smaller companies undergo repeated voluntary bankruptcies, their turnover rates are high and employees constantly face the threat of dismissal. Wage levels are only 60 to 70 per cent of those of large enterprises, there are no labour unions, and the work environment is quite inferior resulting in frequent accidents and disasters. This situation is often referred to as the 'dual economy', in which the high profitability of large firms is obtainable only through the use of smaller companies as subcontractors. If large enterprises hired more employees their labour costs would increase, and within such firms dismissals are not so easily accomplished. The subcontractors are useful because of their low wage scales and as buffers absorbing fluctuations in the size of the labour force. Company A, with 620 subcontractors, hires 40,983 of its own factory workers and uses 53,295 employees of subcontractors, constituting 56.5 per cent of its workforce. In turn these firms also practice subcontracting to yet a lower level of firms, which in turn may subcontract a share of their work, and so on. While information on the first tier of subcontractors is readily available, the number of workers employed below the subcontractor level is not accurately known.

Subcontractors may manufacture a part of certain products, they may take over auxiliary work within the plant, or they may carry out basic work in the plant along with the regular workers. The employment status of worker: working on the same line is distinguished by the colour of their helmets. As employees of sub-contractors receive orders from regular employees of the company and are discriminated against, they are considered one rank lower. The number of workers employed by the smaller companies which form the lower portion of the dual economy account for the majority – around 70 per cent – of the total number of employed workers.

Previously, when an employee was shifted to a subcontractor it was a step up the ladder and led to a management position.

However, when such large numbers of people are being loaned out as is occurring today, the situation is entirely different. They move as general workers. In turn the employees of the subcontractor are pushed out as in a domino game, loaned out to sub-subcontractors or other companies, or dismissed. Employees of the subcontractors are, therefore, hostile to the workers of big companies, and are unwilling to coach the latter lest they lose their own jobs, underlining the tragic implications of this domino effect of worker transferral.

Loans to companies having no relationship with the parent company

Whereas the above patterns involve recipient companies with some sort of relationship with the parent company, this involves the transfer of workers to an outside company, into a job such as hotel sales person, building superintendent or odd job person. Usually the employee has to go alone, leading to feelings of insecurity and helplessness. However, the recipient company expects him to increase sales by using the personal connections he must have in the big company. Therefore, if he fails to meet such expectations he finds himself in an unpleasant position.

Wages for workers who are on loan are paid by the following method. The recipient company pays the loaning company, such as Company A, the worker's wages according to its own wage scale. The difference between this amount and what the loaned person used to earn at Company A is made up by Company A. Since Company A is designated a member of a depressed industry and therefore receives a 'subsidy for employment adjustment' from the government, it does not have to bear the whole amount. As most workers on loan are aged 40 to 50 and earn high wages under the seniority system, the labour costs of Company A are thus decreased.

The formation of new enterprise groups and multilayer structures

The creation of subsidiaries independent of the parent company and the loaning of employees have brought about fundamental changes in the labour force organization of large companies. Streamlining or eliminating less profitable operations, and forming independent subsidiaries has resulted in a corporate structure such as that shown in Figure 3.1, in which the top of the traditional pyramid has been radically narrowed and has been joined by other lesser peaks. The new independent firms are organized in a group and thereby constitute an enterprise group. When the policy of loaning out personnel is pursued systematically, the result is a labour shortage in the parent company. The primary solution to this problem is the use of outside workers who are employed by subsidiaries. Thus, the use of subcontractors increases even further.

This use of part-timers and dispatched workers is not peculiar to the iron and steel sector but has spread in other manufacturing industries and in the tertiary sector. The decade of the 1980s was characterized by the widespread use of workers with unstable employment status across all industries. By using such personnel these companies have been able to adjust their labour force according to changes in business conditions and to economize on labour costs. The number of such workers, who are mostly housewives, increased radically after 1975. Japanese part-timers work 7 to 8 hours a day, which is the same as full-timers and yet are paid only half the average wages of males freshly graduated from junior high schools, and are not entitled to any of the fringe benefits of full-time workers since they are not covered by social security insurance. Thus an important feature of the growth of unstable employment status has been sex discrimination, a point returned to below.

There are two types of dispatched workers: regular workers and registered workers. The latter are called out only when jobs are available and their status is unstable. Both types of workers are dispatched to clients' workplaces and work there. Older persons mainly work for building maintenance companies and young persons work as clerks and in information processing. The government used to prohibit the dispatching of personnel as a business under the Employment Security Law, but decided to legalize the system in 1986 by enacting the Law Concerning Personnel Dispatch Businesses because of the huge number of personnel being dispatched. In some cases a person who retired before reaching the mandatory age limit or who was loaned to another company is dispatched to the company where he was previously employed. In short, this is a means for large enterprises to reduce their labour costs.

The use of such a multi-layered structuring of employment has been a distinctive feature of restructuring in Japan. In summary, first of all the big enterprises protected their employees as far as possible

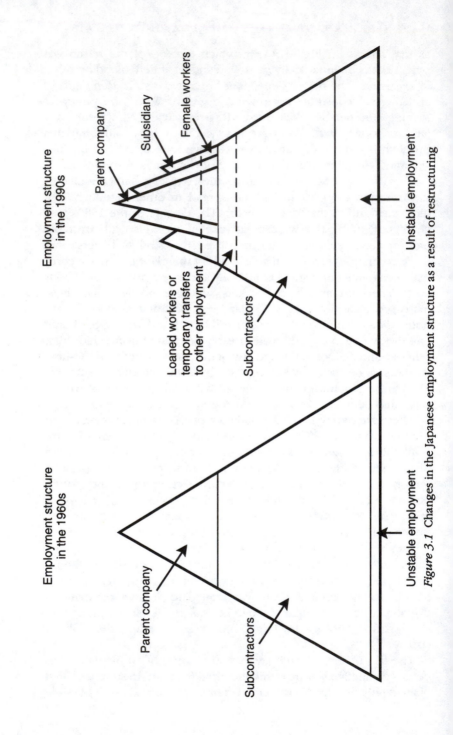

Employment structure in the 1960s

Parent company

Subcontractors

Unstable employment

Employment structure in the 1990s

Parent company

Subsidiary

Female workers

Loaned workers or temporary transfers to other employment

Subcontractors

Unstable employment

Figure 3.1 Changes in the Japanese employment structure as a result of restructuring

using this structure, and successfully avoided a rupture in Japanese labour management relationship. Secondly, the reason why big enterprises succeeded in obtaining agreement from their employees on virtually abolishing the long-standing and solid life-time employment system was that they guaranteed employment for the time being, although not for the future. Workers were persuaded because of the 'sense of crisis' emanating from the business world and the government. Thirdly, enterprise labour unions played the role of promoting the management strategies of their companies.

This resulted in diversified management groups and a new multi-layer structure, as in Figure 3.1. The connections within the multilayer employment structure are as follows: first, large companies create subsidiaries which advance into new business fields, shifting their employees into these subsidiaries; second, employees of large companies are shifted to subcontractors; and third, the employees of subcontractors are pushed into the stratum of unstably employed workers. Alongside such unstable employed workers, housewife part-timers and dispatched workers form a huge labour pool which is given temporary jobs by big enterprises according to the needs of the company. The significance of these developments lies in the fact that now almost all workers except for the handful of nucleus employees remaining in big enterprises are threatened with the possibility of losing their jobs. When the number of key-workers protected under the 'Japanese management system' decreases, and they are threatened by the possibility of being loaned as they become older, it seems likely that their loyalty to the company may begin to be threatened.

CHANGES IN LABOUR CONDITIONS

As a result of drastic personnel cuts, the annual working hours of the workers remaining in Company A increased. Contrary to the world-wide tendency toward fewer work hours, those in Japan alone increased, to 2,168 (in 1988), as a consequence of excessive reductions in the number of workers.

Following these cuts in company workforces the business climate suddenly took a favourable turn, but the companies are coping with the situation by increasing overtime work instead of the number of personnel. Since loaned employees are also working more overtime hours, the total amount of wages paid has also increased. In view of such circumstances, Company A conducted a review of the wage system in 1989. The major decisions which emerged from this review were to further modify the current seniority wage system by decreasing the seniority wage while increasing wages overall, and to decrease the amount of overtime allowance per hour. Table 3.1 charts the pattern of wages before, during and after the revision, and shows that the seniority component constituted 51.1 per cent of total wages before the revision, but only 41.7 per cent after. On the other hand, the proportion of wages attached to a given post increases from 42.2 per cent to 51.7 per cent. In short, the percentages of seniority- and position-based wages were reversed, significantly diluting the seniority based wage system. It also should be noted that the percentage of seniority-based wage is even less than these figures suggest, as the total amount of wages includes the overtime allowance as well as the midnight service allowance. The make-up of the wages of a 58 year old loaned worker is shown in Table 3.1: his allowances (including those for overtime and late night working and the shift premium) constitute as much as 37.3 per cent of the total wages, while wage-by-age is only 27.9 per cent. This is the reason why such a worker is willing to work overtime. The overtime during the month was 46 hours, but it sometimes goes up to as much as 80 hours. In the information processing industry, there are instances of 100–150 hours of overtime in a month.

Since the overtime allowance occupies a significant portion of the total wages many men tend to go home late at night, thus sacrificing their family life. Men are too fatigued with hard work and long commuting hours (2–4 hours per day) to attend to housework or their children, and this reinforces the gendered division of labour in Japanese homes. Burdened with keeping house and caring for the children single-handedly, women are unable to work full time and they inevitably choose part-time jobs which have flexible work hours, which they can quit at any time and which they can commute to within half an hour.[1]

Managers, unions and the consciousness of employees on loan

When a company proposes the loaning of an employee, he or she does not necessarily go without resistance. In the mills which were closing down blast furnaces, the employees were vehemently opposed to management policy, especially because they had faithfully cooperated with the company in improving productivity while avoiding strikes. They were angry with the way the company aban-

Table 3.1 Changes in an enterprise wage structure as a result of restructuring

	Before revision	During transition	After transition	58-year-old worker
Total wage, ¥en	319,974	319,974	325,880	412,186
Seniority based wage (%)	51.1	39.3	41.7	24.3
Tentative seniority based wage[1] (%)		10.3		3.6
Tentative wage attached to post (%)				4.6
Wage attached to post (%)	42.2	43.6	51.7	24.3
Performance wage[2] (%)	6.7	6.8	6.6	4.7
Overtime allowance (%)				24.4
Midnight service allowance (%)				8.5
Shift premium (%)				4.4
Temporary transfer allowance (%)				1.2

[1] The 'tentative wage' is the portion which changed during the transition, as the seniority based wage decreased and the wage for post increased step by step, a process completed in April 1991.
[2] The performance wage is the portion distributed in accordance with the total amount of production of the Company, and goes equally to all employees.

doned unneeded workers. The labour unions in big companies had, however, switched to a policy of cooperation and collaboration between management and labour during the high economic growth period of the 1960s, and they continued with conciliatory and accommodative policies when they were faced with restructuring.

The unions judged that the loaning of employees was basically unavoidable in view of the prevailing production conditions, and decided that, if the company guarantees life-time employment for loaned employees and prevents the personal sacrifices on the part of their members which accompany loaning as much as possible, then the unions would cooperate to achieve an efficient distribution of labour. In Japan, labour unions do not negotiate with management on equal ground since the latter is overwhelmingly stronger. Although there is a system of joint labour–management conferences, its basic structure is that the management explains or reports on rationalization plans and asks for the opinion of the union. Unions have lost the ability to mount effective collective strike action: the last strike by employees of major iron and steel manufacturers took place in 1965. Since then, there have been no labour/management confrontations; instead there have been typically Japanese 'adjustments of opinion' and 'mutual confidence relationships' between management and labour. The basis for maintaining such 'excellent' relationships between management and labour has been the 'loaning' of employees for indefinite periods. How long this ambiguous unwritten 'mutual confidence relationship' might continue will be the key issue for management/labour relationships in the future.

Against this background it is possible to explore the attitudes of workers by drawing on the results of a questionnaire survey of about 12,000 workers conducted by the labour union of Company A, and my own independent research on loaned employees which used interviews and questionnaires in order to probe patterns of consciousness. In summary, these sources revealed firstly that the workers consider the iron and steel industry to be a declining industry and resignedly accept the labour force reduction as inevitable. According to the union's investigation, the view that 'company management in the year 2000 will be diversified, and the weight of the iron and steel department will be substantially the same as the other departments within the company', was chosen by 43 per cent of respondents, and the view that 'other departments will play a more important role' was chosen by 19 per cent – and among this latter group there was a disproportionate number of loaned workers.

This degree of acceptance is partly attributable to the efforts of the Company, which, throughout the high economic growth period, frequently distributed employee magazines reporting changes in iron and steel production, current management policy, and domestic and foreign news. The workers were so stimulated to broaden their knowledge that many subscribed to a trade paper. Gradually, they took the viewpoint of the management and came to take a serious interest in domestic as well as foreign affairs. This is a clear example of success in labour/management reconciliation, and suggests that the reason why workers failed to read the management slogans of 'diversification', 'flexibility' and 'crisis' from the viewpoint of labour was that they had assimilated management's way of thinking. Thus, they readily agreed to the rationalization plans.

Among those surveyed it was, not surprisingly, lower management personnel who had most sympathy for the policy. Having experienced acting as union officers (becoming a key union officer is one path to success within the Company), and having acquired leadership skills, they were climbing the corporate ladder. They acted as steadfast advocates for the Company in persuading workers to accept the Company's offer of loaning. Loaned employees, by contrast, asserted that they were never convinced, but rather simply could not stand up to such persistence. In the face of what seemed inevitable, they felt they had better go before conditions deteriorated. They positively stated that it was not loyalty to the Company that brought about their concession. Ironically enough, lower management staff themselves were also to go out on loan following their subordinates. There are basically two responses among such lower managers: some wished to obtain better conditions for loaning, and others considered loaning to be atonement for what they did to their subordinates.

Once loaned, workers feel threatened by inferior labour conditions, hostility among the workers of the recipient company and anxiety over another possible move. As a result they come to resent their original company and deplore the inability of the labour union to oppose the policy. They are particularly angry over the broken promise of life-time employment, as well as over their reduced wages. According to the union's survey, a substantial number expressed negative views about the policy of loaning. Thus 12 per cent felt that 'in principle, loaning should not be implemented'; 22 per cent said 'loaning should be implemented prudently'; and 39 per cent emphasized that 'preferential consideration should be given to working conditions'. Among more positive views, 12 per cent felt 'loaning is inevitable for restructuring', while 14 per cent said 'loaning is an opportunity for a new life'.

When asked how their loyalty to the Company had changed, the loaned workers answered that it was absent from the beginning, and personal life was more important than the Company. Their supposedly strong loyalty to the Company was either a misunderstanding or has been lost. What, then, about the sense of belonging to the Company? All still feel attached to their original workplaces and have friendly feelings for their ex-colleagues. These feelings are often mistaken as loyalty to the Company, but what remains to the last is a sense of camaraderie, followed by a sense of belonging to a group. Even if loaned workers are stationed far from their original place of work, they do not become friendly with their new colleagues. Rather, they associate with their former colleagues and console each other. Even under miserable conditions they are supported by the pride of once belonging to a big company. In particular, those loaned to a subsidiary retain a strong sense of being the employee of a big company, since often those around such workers have been loaned from the same company. However, the differences in working conditions as well as the overall labour environment gradually let them down and increase their anxiety for the future. According to a survey by the labour union, the percentage of those who work with pride and a sense of responsibility is lowest among the loaned employees. Under such conditions it is questionable how long mutual confidence between management and labour can be maintained.

Alongside their criticisms and uncertainties about management, the loaned workers were also very critical of their union, with 60 per cent expressing disapproval of the union's role, 35 per cent 'disapproval to a certain degree', and only 3 per cent approval; results which prompted an expression of a sense of crisis in the union's own report. Why, then, had the union become so weak and ineffective? First, there had been a switch of political allegiance linked to changes in balloting procedures. In the past union officers were elected by a single ballot system in which each member cast a vote for a single candidate in an election for 6 posts. In this context the minority of workers who supported candidates allied to the Socialist Party could gain representation, as at least one such Socialist candidate used to be elected. However, after the 1968 revision of union election rules the system was changed to that of a plural ballot in which each member had to vote for 6 candidates; ballots without 6 names of candidates written on them are invalid. The only faction capable of nominating 6 candidates has been the 'unionist' or labour/management partnership faction, which is allied with the Democratic Socialist Party, and consequently Socialist candidates were unable to be elected at all.

Second, technical innovation decreased the numbers of workers, eliminated group work and created one-man work stations. Intensified Quality Circle activity at a workplace with fewer workers necessarily strengthens the leadership held by lower managerial staffers. Increasingly, a plant has become a pyramidal composite consisting of small workstations, with each strategic point fortified by lower managerial staff. In such a structure, the union officers who were elected (as president, vice president, chief secretary) were those recommended by both management and labour. One's criticism of the Company or the union is reported immediately to one's superiors. Wary of informers, the workers cease to talk. In other words, they are now under the dual control of the Company and the union. This process may not be completely clear to the reader, but it is linked to the fact that only after World War II was democracy introduced to Japan, and the concept of fundamental human rights has not yet taken root. In addition, people hate isolation and favour belonging to a group.

Problems facing labour unions in Japan

As the conciliatory labour/management relationship within the 'Japanese management system' was slowly deteriorating, the union was gradually losing its cohesive force. Under the long-established rules, a loaned employee lost the right to be a regular union member and was given the status of neutral member after one or two years. Neutral members were suspended from union membership; did not pay the union membership fee; did not have the right to go on strike; and could not stand as candidates for union office. The underlying reason may have been either that the Company feared rebellion among the great number of employees on loan, or that this was a hiatus between the Company's past policies and as yet undecided policies of the future.

However, the right to union membership was restored to loaned employees by the union in November 1987. Those loaned to subsidiaries were all reorganized into branches of the parent company's labour union. Those loaned to subcontractors or workplaces at distant locations were not organized into branches, but are treated as ex-members of their original workplaces. They receive the union news but are unable to actually exercise voting rights. Recent moves to reorganize them as union members may be due to a sense of crisis on the part of the union as it has become weak financially as well as socially after losing so many members because of loaning. In addition, if the existence of the union is valuable to the Company as a channel for instructing and communicating with the employees, the

107

bigger the union organization is, the more effective it can be. The union functions to mobilize voters during local or national elections. It is important that candidates jointly recommended by both management and labour be successfully elected to municipal assemblies where the Company's steel mills are located and that the Japan Democratic Socialist Party candidates recommended by the labour union are successful in general elections, to reinforce the policies of labour–capital conciliation.

The labour union of Company A once enjoyed a membership as large as 80,000, but this has dwindled to a mere 46,000. The number of loaned employees has increased to 9,090, nearly 20 per cent of the total. Organizational problems caused by restructuring are not limited to declining membership, but are compounded by potentially overlapping and clashing jurisdictions. Thus if a subsidiary, Company O, is established with the equity capital participation of Company A and Company X, union members of both A and X will be working together at O, making it impossible for them to take unified action as Company O workers. If subsidiary O is able to grow and hire new employees in the future, its union will consist of three groups of workers, those from Companies A, X, and O, a situation management will find intolerable. Finally, if one of the original Companies is in a more profitable industry than the other, there are likely to be wage and bonus differences among workers in Company O which are seen as unfair by the employees.

The simplest solution would be for the union of Company A to transfer its members to Subsidiary O. However, if it did this, the union's power would weaken. The union is faced with this dilemma of weakened organization because of its acceptance of the Company proposal on loaning. As a compromise, the union is considering treating loaned employees as associate members of Company A's union and collecting half of the union membership fee from them, but this has not as yet been finalized.

Such pressures and dilemmas helped to stimulate the reorganization of Japanese union centres which developed at the end of the 1980s in response to broader problems facing the labour movement. Currently only a quarter of the labour force is organized and the ratio of organized labour in Japan is decreasing annually. Restructuring is accelerating this shrinkage in several ways. First, the number of workers in big companies has decreased under the influence of technical innovation and restructuring, and it is these workers who have been most highly organized while union membership in small- or mid-size companies has been extremely low. Second, the number of workers with unstable status has increased, but they are rarely organized. Third, the unions have lost the confidence of workers, and increasingly existing members are leaving the unions while young workers lack interest in joining.

As restructuring has spread to all industries, the Federation of Labour Unions has experienced a sense of crisis over the declining levels of organization in the big companies, and in November 1989 it formed a new national centre, known as 'New Rengo', to strengthen national labour organizations. Labour unions of leading companies as well as government and other public offices have now united to organize 8 million out of their 12.2 million workers, or about 65 per cent, within New Rengo. However, some labour unions from both the private and public sectors oppose the conciliatory line of 'New Rengo' and did not participate. Of them, 1.4 million members joined the national centre 'Zenroren', and 500,000 another national centre 'Zenrokyo'. The remaining 2.3 million or 19 per cent are not associated with any national centres.

Against this background New Rengo claims that it will tackle the problems of the people within the framework of a democratic labour movement, as well as developing the political power able to win influence in the Diet. However, there exists a degree of mistrust in this regard. Although New Rengo accounts for the majority of organized workers, it is essentially not an organization formed by the spontaneous volition of its members. Furthermore, it is noteworthy that at 8 million New Rengo's membership covers only about 18 per cent of the total of 45.4 million employed workers in Japan. Thus 'New Rengo' has not really transcended the long-standing divisions and weaknesses within the Japanese labour movement, though it has shifted the centre of gravity of national organization more towards the private sector.[2] In particular, those core workers who suffer the most direct impact of rationalization, such as the loaned and transferred, are likely to become increasingly disillusioned, while the challenge presented by the unorganized workforce, who are often the least secure and well paid, remains acute. Meanwhile these weaknesses of union organization, combined with the divisions between the left political parties, have limited the effectiveness of any union and class-based political mobilization even in a period of crisis for the old machine politics of the Liberal Democrats, brought about by corruption scandals and the emergence of new political forces such as female community activists.

The conclusions to be drawn from this chapter are not straightforward. The experience of these workers underlines the growing need for a trade unionism more responsive to workers' interests, but there has been a further weakening of union organization within what is one of the most concentrated and centralized capitalist economies in the world. The threats to permanent employment appear to challenge the quid pro quo of labour–management co-operation which has characterized much of the post-1950s period in Japan, but a decline in union density and the differentiation of workers' attachments to their employers pose severe problems of unifying and improving the position of labour. Within the workplace new structural divisions between workers have been created, as loaned workers are seen as threatening the wages and security of 'permanent' workers. In consequence it appears that, for the moment, the workplace remains more divided and the working class weaker. But this situation could change if there is a further erosion of the class settlement based on job security for further sections of the working class. In these circumstances there may be stronger calls for more responsive and representative trade unions, from workers who want to share in the enormous wealth created by Japanese companies.

Acknowledgement

This chapter is a revised version of 'Labour and the restructuring of Japan's iron and steel industry: "Japanese management" and the dual economy', *Journal of Economy and Society* 18 (March 1990): 75–115, published by the Association of Sociology, Tokyo Women's Christian University.

NOTES

1 Women are a growing proportion of the workforce and by 1990 37 per cent of the employed workforce were women. This trend started after 1975, when industrial restructuring and the reduction of regular employees was taking place. The vacancies created by rationalization efforts and reductions in regular male employees were generally filled by housewife part-timers and dispatched workers earning lower wages, so that women often gained jobs as workers with unstable status rather than as regular employees. Furthermore traditional practices in the workplace as well as at home have made it difficult for married women to continue working in Japan. Childcare commitments and the long

hours of work reinforce retirement from the labour market to care for children, so women's employment peaks among young unmarried women and mothers with older children, and when women are ready to return to work they can only get part-time jobs. Nevertheless even a part-time job is an important source of income for family budgets, to cope with the expense of such things as education and housing, and this has enhanced the status and confidence of such women. At the same time, marginally more women than men have gained a higher education and this has also stimulated their aspirations, though only a small minority have gained promotion as a result of the Equal Employment Opportunity Law. These experiences, together with women's involvement in community-based campaigns, have meant that women have become increasingly critical of what they see as a distorted society built by men, and have become a significant independent force in society and politics. See Kamada (1990) for further discussion of these issues.

2 See Kamada (1990) for a fuller discussion of the political ramifications of union realignment (and for further English-language discussions of the dilemmas, strengths and limitations of contemporary Japanese unions, see also Kawanishi (1992) and Taylor (1989)).

REFERENCES

Chalmers, N. J. (1989) *Industrial Relations in Japan: the Peripheral Workforce*, London: Routledge.

Kamada, T. (1990) 'Labour and the restructuring of Japan's Iron and Steel Industry: "Japanese Management" and the dual economy', *Journal of Economy and Society* 18 (March): 75–115.

Kawanishi, H. (1992) *Enterprise Unionism in Japan*, London: Kegan Paul International.

Koike, K. (1988) *Understanding Industrial Relations in Modern Japan*, London: Macmillan.

Koshiro, K. (1992) 'The organisation of work and internal labour market flexibility in Japanese industrial relations', in OECD, *New Directions in Work Organisation: The Industrial Relations Response*, Paris: OECD.

Shimada, H. (1980) 'The Japanese employment system', *Japanese Industrial Relations Series* 6, The Japan Institute of Labour.

Taylor, A. J. (1989) *Trade Unions and Politics: a Comparative Introduction*, London: Macmillan.

Tokunaga, S. (1984) 'The Structure of the Japanese labour market', in S. Takunaga and J. Bergmann (eds) *Industrial Relations in Transition: the Cases of Japan and the Federal Republic of Germany*, Tokyo: Tokyo University Press.

Whittaker, D. H. (1990) 'The end of Japanese-style employment?', *Work, Employment and Society* 4, 3: 321–347.

Part II

TRANSPLANTS, TRANSFER AND ADAPTATION

PROLOGUE

There has been a long history of debates about the character of employment relations in the overseas plants of transnational firms. In Europe these have focused on the role of American companies, and have discussed the extent to which such plants seek to adapt to local labour markets and patterns of industrial relations, the circumstances under which they diverge from local practice and pursue global training and human resource policies, and the employment consequences of working for a branch-plant which is part of a global production process. These issues were also addressed in some of the early literature on Japanese branch-plants, but they have been increasingly subsumed into a more specific discussion couched in the contemporary terminology of the 'transplant' and focused on the effective transplantation of Japanese production management techniques overseas. The chapters in Part II provide a set of critical interventions into this discussion of transplantation, and in so doing also broaden the agenda of debate once again, both by qualifying claims about the novelty of work and employment practices in the transplants, and by underlining their varied and potentially contested character.

In Chapter 4 Laurie Graham provides the first insider's account of work in a Japanese auto transplant in the US, which as such has broad significance. Hitherto, ethnography of working for the Japanese has relied upon Kamata's (1983) account of his experience as a seasonal labourer on an auto assembly line in the early 1970s. But this is both dated and specifically about a Toyota factory in Japan, when critical discussion now centres on the diffusion and transfer of Japanese practices. Fucini and Fucini (1990) capture some of the texture of working life in Mazda's US transplant, and Garrahan and Stewart (1992) offer a glimpse of the experience of Nissan workers in the UK, but

Graham, drawing from her PhD thesis, offers the first full sociological participant-observation study of work in a transplant. The chapter is based on six months spent working at Subaru–Isuzu Automotive (SIA), one of the eight Japanese or joint-venture auto assemblers in the US. It questions the claims for transfer of Japanese practices made most strongly by Florida and Kenney (1991; Kenny and Florida 1993), by examining not just the transfer of 'structures', but workers consciousness within them.

Graham documents both compliance and resistance to management's technical and social control strategies. SIA management, in keeping with other auto transplants, attempted to gain worker adaptation through a series of techniques and strategies, which included lengthy pre-employment and selection procedures, careful administration of the orientation and training of new recruits, the team concept of working, the philosophy of continuous improvement or kaizen, and the direct shaping of shop floor culture, as well as the technical pacing and discipline of computerized assembly lines and JIT production. Graham describes the content and effect of these compliance practices, from the six month preselection procedures to the company rituals of song, celebration and team meetings. All are designed to integrate the individual worker into a company consciousness. But such practices are not received by passive workers, as the capital–labour relation reproduces, even within this most carefully managed form, reactions, resistance and conflicts which alter the practices. Thus the transfer of Japanese innovations is inevitably conditioned by workers' consciousness and conduct. Graham systematically documents types and instances of resistance, both individual and collective, and places these on a continuum of efficacy, recognizing that while some are insignificant for managerial control, others, especially collective resistance, actively force the modification of management action, and insert the voice of labour into the process. Finally it should be noted that elsewhere (Gottfried and Graham 1993) she has also explored the central importance of the active reconstitution of gendered subcultures in this workplace, both in relation to a management ethos which in some ways problematizes the conventional gendering of auto manufacture, and as a basis of both resistance and divisions among the workforce.

Her findings not only add weight to the management control interpretation of Japanese practices, but they also show that while the team concept utilizes the ideology of egalitarianism to mask capital–labour power inequalities, it does not suppress the sense of justice, solidarity and dignity of American labour which percolate into work in differing forms. While her account could be interpreted as overstating the degree and effect of worker resistance, this would be to misunderstand the need to carefully identify all instances of refusal and resistance under this kind of hegemonic managerial control, as well as compensate for the dearth of evidence about such experiences in the available accounts of work in Japanese transplants.

The chapter by Rinehart *et al.* complements that of Graham, for it also reports on workers' responses to new management techniques at a greenfield transplant, that of the Canadian General Motors–Suzuki joint venture (CAMI). This had most of the standard features of such transplants, such as highly selective recruitment and teamworking, but it is one of the few organized by a union, the progressive Canadian Automobile Workers (CAW), and this chapter arises from a rare venture in joint union–academic research. The access which this provided allowed the research team to follow the changing views and experiences of the workforce from the initial period of greenfield development through the consolidation of management policies and increased production. Elsewhere they have analysed the experience of teamworking (Robertson *et al.* 1992), but here they focus on the pivotal process of 'continuous improvement', which enthusiasts portray as an exercise in worker empowerment but sceptics portray as the selective appropriation of worker expertise to fulfil management priorities.

It is these issues which Rinehart *et al.* address by studying the evolving operation of suggestions schemes and quality control circles (QCCs) at CAMI. They show that CAMI management devotes substantial resources to these programmes, in such forms as training manuals, competitions and prizes, and has achieved high levels of participation, with widespread team and individual involvement. However, they also explore how, beneath this pattern of management commitment and worker involvement, the implementation of kaizen in practice has fed a growing scepticism and hostility among workers. Thus on the one hand managers appeared to gloss over the financial and engineering shortcomings of proposed improvements, to bolster a sense of worker participation. On the other hand, however, managers took advantage of worker initiatives to increase effort and work loads, as when they allowed teams to redeploy and reorganize their work routines to create a floating relief, only to relocate the erstwhile floater. Furthermore, Rinehart *et al.*

emphasize that kaizen operates on a transnational basis, as management selects those work standards and procedures which are to be generalized across the company's operations. The evidence from successive research visits suggests that such developments fueled a marked erosion of worker support for participation, and an increasing instrumentalism among those who did participate. By the time of their final survey the bulk of workers believed that kaizen and QCCs involved job reductions and more demanding work, and a majority regarded the outcome as working harder rather than working smarter.

On this account, then, management had not escaped the dilemmas of old-fashioned car production. They remain engaged in a complex balancing act, between motivating workers and capitalizing upon their expertise, and tightening up workloads and production schedules. Rinehart *et al.* acknowledge that workers may sometimes gain advantages through kaizen, if suggestions meet the immediate priorities of both managers and workers, but they suggest that in general the gains won by employees remain precarious, vulnerable to erosion by management, and protected only by active union organization and the forthright deployment of sanctions when necessary. They therefore underline the role played by the union, both in bargaining the implementation of JMS in ways which may limit the negative consequences for workers and by articulating a broader critique of the pretensions of these schemes. Of course, the research reported here is itself intended to inform both of these processes, and as such it is part of a distinctive union response to the challenges represented by the Japanese model of production management in such sectors as motors, pioneered by a union with a more radical agenda than those of the United Automobile Workers Union (UAW) in the USA or the Amalgamated Engineering and Electrical Union (AEEU) in Britain.

While Graham and Rinehart *et al.* develop sceptical accounts of the transformed character of work relations in those North American auto transplants which have often been seen as at the leading edge of innovation, the remaining two chapters in this part provide further critical leverage on the process of transplantation by examining the experience of transplants in Australia and Britain and by broadening the discussion to include the electricals sector. In Chapter 6 Dedoussis and Littler use the Australian experience to develop a novel interpretation of the operations of Japanese transplants, which identifies a rather different corporate logic to that generally ascribed to such operations. As noted in the introduction, Australia has received the lions' share of Oceania Japanese FDI, and although only 15 per cent of this has been in manufacturing, significant players, like Toyota, Sanyo and Matsushita have located in Australia, and the chapter draws on research from these and five other manufacturing companies.

The authors use the dual structure of employment in Japan, divided as it is between core large firms and peripheral small firms, as a vantage point from which to interpret the externalization of Japanese practices through FDI. Transplants, they argue, follow a logic typical of the peripheral enterprises, rather than the core-firm practices so widely assumed in the literature. They also suggest that Japanese overseas transplants, like other TNC subsidiaries, continue to be subordinate to the corporate strategies and interests of their parent companies in Japan, and since international operations follow cost minimization strategies, analysts should not expect the conditions operating in Japan to be transferred abroad. Even where the motives for the transplant are market and not cost driven, it is 'peripheral' and not 'core Japanization' which is exported, because the political, social and economic conditions that support core practices only exist in Japan.

This argument is explored through the eight case studies, which are drawn on to illustrate specific aspects of human resource management and industrial relations policies supposedly typical of Japanese companies. Practices such as seniority rules, recruitment of young workers, employment security, job rotation and extensive induction procedures are examined and divided according to the cost of their introduction. Evidence from the case studies is then utilized to explore the extent of transfer, and whether or not the low-cost strategies are the ones transferred. The authors' findings tend to support their theory, as many of the practices associated with 'core Japanization' were absent, while those associated with 'peripheral Japanization' were present. However, their findings are not totally consistent with their thesis, as size, the composition of labour and difference between the firms are all significant, and these seem to work against a simple paradigmatic differentiation of Japanese overseas practices. The authors then make some schematic comparisons of their findings with other research on Japanese transplants, though this is suggestive rather than definitive. In most cases transplant differences, where they can be ascertained – such as Toyota's preference for young workers elsewhere but older workers in Australia, or preferences for locating their factories in

119

non-auto towns in the US and Britain, but in an auto town in Australia – only suggest problems to be explained rather than answers.

The controversy around 'Japanization' in Britain has become increasingly preoccupied with Japanese car transplants and their ostensible imitators among other transnationals located in Britain, but over the longer term developments in the electrical engineering industry, the dominant sector in Europe in terms of Japanese manufacturing FDI, have been the centre of attention. It is therefore apposite that this sector should feature in Chapter 7, through interview-based case studies of both a prominent transplant – a Japanese consumer electronics transnational with a large Television factory in South Wales – and a domestic adopter – a British electricals transnational prominent in its advocacy of Japanese production methods.

The Japanese company can be regarded as a strong case against which to evaluate the diffusion of innovations in Britain, because the company has a regional level of management in Europe, as well as R&D facilities, and therefore does not conform to the 'screw-driver'/branch-plant model which is typical of most UK Japanese investments. If 'Japanese' practices are not found there, then it is feasible to assume that they will not be present in other transplants. Despite ostensible independence, the authors found that corporate management exercises considerable power over the plant, and the technology and designs used. They note, nevertheless, that product variability in the Welsh plant is greater than in Japan, and that Japanese managers come to the UK to study the plant. Interestingly, in terms of theories that link frequent product changes to enhanced worker involvement and enskilling, they find the stresses of frequent change more prominent in manager and worker assessments than any more positive evaluation. Moving into production, they observe that 80 per cent of the workforce is female and concentrated in unskilled assembly jobs, with males monopolizing more skilled operations in the factory. This is not typically Japanese, but is common to the industry. Japanese practices, such as JIT, are not in evidence on the shop floor and, moreover, involvement and commitment was found to be low, with high levels of absence. The single union agreement delivered a certain degree of compliance for management, but had different implications for production and skilled workers – suggesting that such forms of representation may not transcend the tradition of occupational and industrial relations sectionalism in Britain.

If the transplant example does not support Japanese diffusion, then the case of the adopter is also rather equivocal. Again, this company is something of a cause celebre for 'Japanization' in Britain, being guided by a central ideologue for Japanese manufacturing techniques among the engineering and management community and the subject of much research (Turnbull 1986; Oliver and Wilkinson 1988). A central feature of the adopters' work reorganization was the modularization of manufacturing – the grouping of resources and people in self-contained production units – an innovation with a pedigree older than more specifically Japanese models. The evidence of this study is that such innovations were diluted, not simply through union pressures, but through local management's rather sporadic commitment to fully resource the training necessary for modularization. Thus traditional features of British management practice – short-termism and underfunding of training – constrained the adoption of flexible working, and tasks remained routine and specialized. The greatest change to working practices was the abolition of pieceworking – hardly Japanese in inspiration. Appeals to Japanese practices facilitated the occupational advancement of engineering management inside the company, but provided more of an ideological referent than a concrete guide to the practice of restructuring.

The authors' overall conclusion is that in both the transplant and the adopter innovations associated with Japan were selective and variable, a significant finding given that each can be regarded as a strong test case. Moreover, it appears that sector conditions, rather than imported national practices prevailed in being the chief guides to work reorganization, with the gendering of tasks being especially important (and the gender hierarchy in both plants was more entrenched and 'settled' than in Graham's auto transplant, though not entirely stable or unchallenged). In these respects this chapter concurs with several pieces of research on US transplants (Abo 1990; Milkman 1991; Kenney and Florida 1993) in suggesting that we cannot generalize from the auto industry experience if we are to understand either the social organization of the work process or the employment relations (recruitment, participation, labour turnover) in other important sectors of transplant activity. Together with the other chapters in this part, they point the way towards a more differentiated analysis of the management of transplants and the experiences of their workforces, which gives systematic attention to the interplay between different corporate strategies and sectoral priorities and varied national and local labour markets, labour traditions and state policies.

REFERENCES

Abo, T. (1990) *Local Production of Japanese Automobile and Electronics Firms in the United States*, Research Report, Institute of Social Science, University of Tokyo, 23.

Florida, R. and Kenney, M. (1991) 'Organisation versus culture: Japanese automotive transplants in the US', *Industrial Relations Journal* 22, 3: 181–196.

Fucini, J. and Fucini, S. (1990) *Working for the Japanese: Inside Mazda's American Auto Plant*, New York: The Free Press/Macmillan.

Garrahan, P. and Stewart, P. (1992) *The Nissan Enigma*, London: Cassell.

Gottfried, H. and Graham, L. (1993) 'Constructing difference: the making of gendered subcultures in a Japanese automobile transplant', *Sociology* 27, 4: 611–628.

Kamata, S. (1983) *Japan in the Passing Lane*, London: Unwin.

Kenney, M. and Florida, R. (1993) *Beyond Mass Production: the Japanese System and its Transfer to the US*, Oxford: Oxford University Press.

Milkman, R. (1991) *Japan's California Factories: Labor Relations and Economic Globalisation*, Los Angeles: Institute of Industrial Relations, University of California.

Oliver, N. and Wilkinson, B. (1988) *The Japanization of British Industry*, Oxford: Blackwell.

Robertson, D., Rinehart, J. and Huxley, C. (1992) 'Team concept and kaizen: Japanese production management in a unionized Canadian auto plant', *Studies in Political Economy* 39 (Fall): 77–107.

Turnbull, P. (1986) 'The "Japanization" of production and industrial relations at Lucas Electrical', *Industrial Relations Journal* 17, 3: 193–206.

4

HOW DOES THE JAPANESE MODEL TRANSFER TO THE UNITED STATES?

A view from the line

Laurie Graham

INTRODUCTION

This chapter examines life inside a single Japanese auto transplant located in the Midwest corridor of the United States. Although it is a case study, management characteristics of this non-union transplant are typically found in other Japanese auto transplants including schemes such as workteams, systems of task rotation, a minimum number of job classifications, and worker involvement in quality control (Florida and Kenney 1991). Each transplant has a flat management structure, a single cafeteria, the same type of uniform is worn by top executives and workers, and all levels of management work together in a single, open office (with the exception of Nissan which has status distinctions such as private offices and no uniforms for top level management) (Florida and Kenney 1991). Beyond similar organizational arrangements and management schemes, with few exceptions, the auto transplants have located in areas with similar geographic and economic characteristics (Perrucci 1994). The majority have chosen to locate in the Midwest corridor where the economic context is sustained unemployment, factory closures, and a collapse of manufacturing (Perrucci 1994). Therefore, it is safe to say that this particular transplant is not exceptional and, on the whole, appears to be a fair representation of the Japanese auto transplant 'model'.

Research by Florida and Kenney (1991) suggests that management has been successful in transferring the Japanese model to the United States. They argue that large, resource-rich, powerful organizations have sufficient resources to transform their environments to suit the organization's needs. They maintain that the Japanese have successfully transferred the necessary organizational components for reconstructing the basic conditions unique to the Japanese model (i.e. workteams, task rotation, worker quality control, just-in-time inventory control). They assume that, once in place, these structures function as expected, proposing that the Japanese model is able to harness the collective intelligence of workers for continuous improvement and that managerial authority and responsibility is delegated to workers on the shop floor (Florida and Kenney 1991: 387). Their analysis measures the success of intraorganizational transference by the mere existence of structures. Because their analysis is one sided and top down, the dynamics of how those structures operate, when mediated by the workforce, is missing.

The present research, involving covert participant/observation in a Japanese automobile transplant, challenges Florida and Kenney's assessment. Emergent patterns of shop floor behaviour indicate that Japanese management practices can result in a range of individual and collective resistance among US workers. Workers participated in both spontaneous and planned resistance. Whether spontaneous or planned, only collective resistance produced the strength necessary to effectively challenge management's control on the shop floor.

The assumption that worker control is enhanced by the Japanese model through delegation of managerial authority does not hold true. In fact, these findings suggest the opposite. Ironically, kaizening[1] and decision making by consensus reinforced the unequal power relation between workers and management. During kaizening, management tightly controlled the agenda and decision making by consensus was simply a mirage. A legitimate consensus between management and workers, who are vulnerable to discipline or job loss, was simply impossible.

These findings support Fucini and Fucini's (1990) conclusion concerning adaptation problems at Mazda, another Japanese transplant located in the US. When a political dimension, measured through shop floor behaviour, is included in an examination of intraorganizational transference, these findings suggest that even though the structures of Japanese management are present, the way in which those structures are mediated by the workforce does not indicate the successful transference suggested by Florida and Kenney (1991).

In the present analysis seven components within the Japanese management structure are identified and examined as they relate to worker compliance and resistance. The findings are evaluated in light of labour process literature which addresses the nature of control at the point of production.

THEORETICAL BACKGROUND[2]

A clear definition of control at the point of production is difficult to pin down, because it involves a complex process of struggle between workers and management. Two aspects of control stand out in the literature. First, control is identified as possessing the technical knowledge of work, from conception through execution (Braverman 1974). Management systems aimed at gaining control over the technical aspects of work have been identified as Taylorism (Braverman 1974), despotic (Burawoy 1985), direct (Friedman 1977), and the technical component of hierarchical control (Edwards 1979).

The second aspect of production control is the social aspect, located in workers' culture and reflected in their behaviour toward the boss and each other at the point of production. The essence of this social aspect of control is described by Montgomery (1979) in the craft workers' ethos of brotherhood: a collective code in which the skilled worker was expected to assume a 'manly posture' toward the boss, to control his or her own output through working a certain stint each day, to control the use of his or her time, and to enforce the quota by stopping 'rate busters' (Montgomery 1979). Theorists have categorized management systems that attempt to interfere with workers' social behaviour as bureaucratic (Edwards 1979), responsible autonomy (Friedman 1977), and hegemonic (Burawoy 1985).

For the purposes of this study, control is multidimensional, grounded in the context of the production process, possessing both technical and social aspects. The struggle for control over the technical aspect emerges as a worker attains special knowledge about each job. Even management's fragmenting the most technical task will not necessarily uncover the tricks that workers learn from each other or from the act of doing a particular process (Manwaring and Wood 1985), tricks that often save the worker time and effort. According to labour process theory, this time becomes the focus of management's control.

The social aspect of worker control is found in the workers' culture which is reflected in behaviour and the day-to-day relationships at the point of production. Management focuses on controlling shop floor culture in order to win a worker's total allegiance in its competitive struggle.

RESEARCH SETTING AND DATA

The research focuses on the work experience within a single Japanese automobile transplant. From July 1989 through January 1990, I worked as a hidden participant/observer at Subaru–Isuzu Automotive (SIA) located near Lafayette, Indiana.[3] Both management and workers were unaware that they were under observation.

The intent of this research is to identify patterns of behaviour that reflect the relationship among workers and between workers and management in their day-to-day work experience. The analysis is based on extensive field notes involving informal discussions with numerous co-workers and team members,[4] on day-to-day observations of co-worker and worker/management interactions, and on formal documents distributed by the company.

The analysis has many limitations, the greatest of which is that evidence concerning the nature and effectiveness of management's control strategies are deduced from the position of a worker. There is no way of knowing management's intentions, they can only be inferred from observations and documents. Another limitation concerns the time period of the study. It is unique since it is during the company's initial months of production. People working in the plant today are experiencing a faster assembly line, a second shift now exists, and temporary workers work side by side with regular employees. Another unique aspect of the start-up period is that a certain amount of excitement over beginning production existed among many workers; this excitement may dissipate as the newness wears off. On the other hand, the start-up also provides an ideal setting for management to take advantage of workers' optimism and to attempt to induce a spirit of cooperation and 'pulling together' to beat the competition. Therefore, patterns that emerge contrary to this goal will serve as evidence of management's inability to gain control through cooperation and effectively transfer its intra-organizational environment.

A definite advantage of working during plant start-up was that it often allowed me free access to other areas within the plant. During start-up, there were problems getting the paint department up and running on a continuous basis. On several occasions, the line would be down for an entire day or, at least, for several hours at a time. When this occurred, we would find excuses to leave our area and investigate other parts of the plant. This enabled me to informally question workers from other areas and observe them at work. This was fortuitous, for when Chinoy (1955) worked on an assembly line as a participant/observer in an auto plant, he found that he was so tied to the line, that it was difficult to talk to other workers (Chinoy 1955).

The setting for the bulk of the observations is the trim and final department of the plant. Trim and final is the most labour-intensive area of the plant, where Subaru cars and Isuzu trucks are assembled. The car and truck bodies entered our department as empty shells and were driven off the line ready to be sold.

I worked on Team 1 in car assembly. There were 12 team members plus a team leader. Team 1 was part of a group of 4 teams under one group leader. The group leader was the lowest level salaried employee. A total of about 14 teams assembled the cars. Each worker was responsible for one station which, at that time, involved about 5 minutes of work on every car. We worked at a constant pace as the cars moved along the line, repeating the same set of tasks every 5 minutes.

Team 1 was the first team to work on the cars after they came out of paint (workers referred to the various departments, such as the paint department, simply as 'paint'). When the cars were finished in paint, they were held in one of the overhead conveyer systems. Once on our conveyer, the bodies (cars were referred to as 'bodies') were spaced about three or four feet apart.

There was a total of 67 workstations on both sides of the assembly line for assembling the cars. Team 1 was divided into 12 stations, 6 to a side. The stations and the people working them were referred to by their location on the line. In other words, when people referred to the work I performed, it was 'one left'. However, workers did not refer to one another by station location when away from the line.

The Japanese trainer organized Team 1 so that each person stayed on one side of the car and worked across from another team member. There was one exception. 'One right' finished the work at that station, before 'one left' began working, and each worked both sides of the car. Some of the parts were installed by two people, working across from one another, but most were installed by only one person.

On the line, each station (or person) had control of the car for a predetermined distance. Workers walked next to the moving car, installing parts as it moved through their area. Although the distance did not vary, the speed of the line could be changed so that the amount of time the team had to work on the car was increased or decreased. The takt time[5] was not supposed to vary from station to station. However, many of the processes did not work as smoothly as anticipated by the Team 1 trainer, so some stations took more time than others. In addition, most people simply did not work at exactly the same speed, so some workers just barely kept up. Also, after the start of production, the team was plagued by hand and wrist injuries (at one point seven out of the twelve team members had hand or wrist problems), which forced a change in the way certain parts were installed, usually involving more time. Finally, due to injuries, many workers were forced to work in wrist splints which also slowed team members down.

When designing the Team 1 stations, the Japanese trainer used standardized times based on how long it took workers in Japan to install each part. The times were recorded to the tenth of a second, and the timing for the installation of each part was broken down step by step. From this, he calculated the number of stations necessary for installing all of the parts designated for our area within a takt time of 3 minutes and 40 seconds (the goal time for full production). He jokingly told team members, 'we could each have an armchair at our station for resting between cars.' The 5-minute takt time was a hectic pace for some and a reasonable pace for others.

'One left' was the station I became most familiar with, as it was the last station I was assigned. The following is a step-by-step account of that process.

1 Go to the car and take the token card (a metal plate which contained specific information for each vehicle) off a wire on the front of the car.
2 Pick up the two VIN (vehicle identification number) plates from the embosser and check the plates to see that they have the same number.
3 Insert the token card into the token card reader. This will cause the specifications for that car to be printed out on a broadcast sheet and a 'spec' sheet.
4 While waiting for the computer output, break down the key kit for the car by pulling the three lock cylinders and the lock code from the bag.
5 Copy the vehicle control number (this number is the computer system number, which keeps track of the location of the car) and colour number on to the appearance check sheet.
6 Inspect the car for damage sustained while in the paint department. Look over the outside of the car and open each door and

128

inspect all areas that are not later covered up by some part. Mark down any scratches, chips, dents, or any other damage on a sketch of the car which is located on the appearance check sheet.

7   Go to a rack and pick up a hood stay, the workbasket (which contains plugs and grease), the hood jig (which holds up the hood while you install the hood stay), and lay them in the empty engine compartment.

8   Lift the hood and put the hood jig in place so it will remain open while installing the hood stay.

9   Insert the rubber hood stay grommet.

10 Insert the hood stay into the grommet, lift the hood, and prop it open with the hood stay. Insert a rubber hose at the top of the hood stay to insure that the hood will not fall while people work in the engine compartment.

11 Go to the printer and get the broadcast sheet (this alerts everyone down the line as to what options that particular vehicle will need). Check the VIN numbers on the sheet to the plates and verify that the plates match the coding for front or four-wheel drive.

12 Attach the broadcast sheet to the front edge of the hood with masking tape.

13 Check the VIN number from the broadcast sheet to the number engraved on the car body at the back of the engine compartment.

14 From the workbasket, pick up two rubber hood buffers and slide them on to the two hooks on either side of the engine compartment, so that the hood will rest on them when closed.

15 Pick up a right side fender cover from the right side of the line and attach it over the right fender.

16 Pick up two screw grommets and the fender top grommet from the basket and insert them in the proper holes under the left front fender.

17 Attach the front left fender cover (located on the left side of the line) and remove the hood jig and the basket from the car.

18 Tear off the specification sheet from second printer, attach it to the clip board with the appearance sheet, and put the key lock code on the specification sheet.

19 Collect the clip board, the trunk lock cylinder, token card, and small black VIN plate. Put everything except the clip board in the box on the car carrier and insert the clipboard into the slot underneath the car on the carrier.

20 Get the riveter, the two door lock cylinders, pick up two rivets and the large VIN plate. Carry them to the car.
21 Toss the yellow cylinder to the passenger side, and place the white cylinder on the floor of the driver's side.
22 Rivet the large VIN plate to the left hand centre pillar of the car.
23 Begin with step one on the next car.

In addition to the duties directly related to working on the line, each worker was responsible for keeping the stations neat and clean, recording the level of the 'oilers' and pressure gauges on the air lines located above the stations, recording each car number, and keeping tools in good condition. The number of tasks that 'one left' performed was typical of that at other stations. At the goal takt time, these tasks were to be completed in 3 minutes 40 seconds.

Before 'one left' finished with the car, 'two left' and 'two right' would have already begun. Whenever possible, each person tried to work ahead by beginning his or her station before the car actually crossed the line to enter his or her area. This gave the team an edge against breakdowns and parts shortages – the things that brought great emotional and physical stress because they caused the team to fall behind. Once behind, the team had to work intensely to catch up. Once the line speed began to increase toward goal takt time, the opportunity to work ahead steadily decreased and the Team 1 trainer ordered us to stop working ahead. Eventually, it became a moot point, there was no extra time. If someone on the team could see that another worker needed help, he or she would help if possible. It was, however, clearly a matter of pride to keep one's station under control and operating at the goal time.

As both the truck and car lines ran the length of trim and final and then back again in a 'U' shape, Team 1 was located between the final line on the truck side and the final line on the car side. Team 1 was the first team to work on the cars and, at the same time, could see the finished product driven off the line.

In trim and final a typical day began at 6.25 a.m. (five minutes before the scheduled start of work) when music was played over the loudspeaker signalling morning exercises. After five minutes of exercises, the team members would stand in a circle for a meeting. When the paint department worked out its problems, and the line was moving throughout the day, the team meeting lasted no longer than five minutes, because the line started moving at 6.35 a.m. At the end of the meeting, the team performed a daily ritual. Each person extended his or her left arm into the centre of the circle, with the hand clenched into a fist. The team leader then called on one of the members to deliver an inspirational message to the team. The usual message was, 'lets have a safe and productive day'. A few of the team members sometimes told a good-natured joke, making light of the ritual. After the message, all of the team members brought their right arms around into the circle with everyone's hands meeting in the centre in clenched fists. While doing this, the members shouted 'Yosh!' (a long 'o' sound) and then broke up and went to work.[6]

At exactly 6.35 a.m. a buzzer sounded, and the assembly line began to move. At 8.30 a.m. it stopped for a 10-minute break. At 10.30 a.m. the line stopped for a half hour, unpaid lunch. At 1.00 p.m. it stopped for another 10-minute break and at 3.00 p.m. the work day was over.

The type of work each team member performed varied as to its physical demands, its potential for injury, the speed in which it could be performed, and whether or not he or she was able to speak to other team members. For the most part, however, working on the line required a worker's undivided attention. During plant start-up, workers had time for conversation between each car and even while working the stations. As line speed increased, time for interactions between workers and periods of rest continually decreased. Increased line speed was also accompanied by the emergence of injuries. Once the speed-up began, the workers experienced constant pressure from the assembly line. Everyone was forced to work at a continuous, rapid pace.

FINDINGS

Of primary significance in the Japanese management scheme is its multidimensional structure. This multidimensional approach is most consistent with Burawoy's (1979) concept of hegemonic control, providing the qualification that Burawoy misses the resistance that is present in workers' adaptations in production (Thompson 1989). Its goal is to gain workers' total cooperation in the company's competitive struggle.

Each component in this system of control does not seem very powerful when examined separately. When combined, however, they form a formidable obstacle to the individual worker. When workers failed to resist collectively, practices such as speed-up and working off the clock were common. Some workers could be seen working during their breaks to get caught up, and others came in early to setup their stations. At the same time, however, this system of control gave rise to resistance by many workers. In general, it was only through collective action that workers were able to effect any balance in control on the shop floor.

In order to describe the full range of worker response and the dynamic nature of worker reaction to this system, the findings are divided into two sections: compliance and resistance. The first section connects examples of worker compliance to each component in management's scheme. For this analysis the management scheme at SIA is separated into seven components. Although many of the components combined both social and technical aspects of control, they are categorized according to their main effects. Five components focused on controlling social aspects of production:

1 Pre-employment selection process
2 Orientation and training for new workers
3 The team concept
4 A philosophy of kaizen
5 Attempts at shaping shop floor culture

Two components comprised technical aspects of control:

6 The computerized assembly line
7 Just-in-time production

The second section analyses the range and effectiveness of resistance to this management scheme.

Compliance to management's scheme

Selection process

The first component in SIA's system of control began before a worker was hired with a pre-employment selection process. All applicants underwent a battery of tests and observed exercises. I began my attempt to gain employment at the Company in February 1989, and six months later I was finally hired.

The selection process focused on eliminating potential workers. Applicants were evaluated after each step of the process and, if successful, were invited to participate in the next level of testing. The first step involved a four-hour general aptitude test (GAT). Anyone who scored a certain percentile (when I applied it was above 85 per cent) was invited to participate in Phase I, a four-hour exercise involving twenty applicants.

During Phase I the participants were divided into groups of five and each group participated in team scenarios involving problem-solving exercises. If an applicant passed the Phase I evaluation, then he or she would be invited to participate in Phase II. Phase II involved approximately eight hours of written attitude tests and timed exercises assembling parts. Following Phase II, the successful applicants were scheduled for a physical examination and drug screening at a local clinic. The final step in the hiring process was an interview with three team leaders at the plant. Even though team leaders were hourly workers, they made the ultimate decision on hiring.

After I was hired, I discussed the selection process with other workers. The more cynical view was that most people had succeeded in being selected because they were smart and had figured out the process, not because they were team players. There was a general sentiment that SIA used the selection process to get rid of anyone the Company considered undesirable. One person thought the process was an effort to screen out anyone who wasn't willing to be co-operative. Another said that the GAT was given to cut out anyone who wasn't fairly intelligent. One worker was almost certain the whole selection process was aimed at exposing any union supporters.

Two workers responded positively when asked about the selection process. One person, in particular, believed that the selection process was fantastic. When describing how he felt, he said that, for once, it gave him the chance to be fairly evaluated because the process involved much more than simply filling out an application and hoping for an interview. 'It gave guys like me, who didn't know the right people, a chance.' He felt that SIA had actually 'tapped into his potential,' that the examiners had 'really gotten to know him through the tests.'

Based on their statements, it appears that many workers complied with the perceived terms and conditions of employment at SIA by involving themselves in a kind of charade. Even those who expressed apprehension about working in a team setting said that they had made an effort to appear cooperative and enthusiastic when interacting with other applicants during team scenarios. When questioned, several people stated that they really were not team players, that they'd rather work alone if given the choice. Other workers stated that, right from the start, they knew what type of behaviour the company was looking for. There were many sources from which potential employees could deduce the requisite qualities of the successful SIA worker. A booklet explaining the Company's team philosophy was made available when applicants first filled out applications. Area newspapers ran several articles focusing on the company's 'new style' of management based on a team concept which stressed cooperation and quality.

In addition to giving the company ample time for selecting what it perceived as the most qualified workers, the selection process has the potential to effect behaviour on the shop floor. Since it was not necessary that an inherent liking for team participation be part of one's personality, the goal of the process is to select workers who outwardly adapt to management's efforts at structuring behaviour. To get the job in the first place, one had to be willing to play by the rules.

Orientation and training

Management's second mechanism, aimed at social control on the shop floor, emerged through the company's orientation and training programme. Every worker underwent one week of orientation and a minimum of two weeks of classroom training. The instruction fell into three general areas. The first area included 'nuts and bolts' information concerning such items as benefits, pay schedules, work rules, uniform fittings and tours of the plant. Within this area were basic lessons in reading blueprints, using statistical process control and structuring time studies. The second area involved lessons on the Company's history and philosophy, including testimonials from instructors and management. Also within this category were instructions in the concept of kaizening (a philosophy of continuous improvement) and lectures designed to demonstrate SIA's egalitarian nature. The third area of instruction involved an attempt to socialize workers as to their expected behaviour at SIA. This took place through formal, video-driven behaviour training sessions and also through facilitating informal interactions with other classmates. Generally, the 'nuts and bolt' area of instruction involved practical training while the second and third components worked toward shaping attitudes and values.

If the amount of time spent within an area of instruction is any indication of its value to the company, then practical training was not the priority of the orientation and training process. Out of 127.5 hours of orientation and training, approximately 56 hours were actually spent in practical training. The remaining 71.5 were concentrated on attitude and behaviour.

The weeks in orientation and training worked as part of the Company's overall scheme by providing a bridge between the worker's experience in the selection process and working in the plant. Workers at SIA often formed stronger bonds with their orientation and training class members than they did with their team members. For example, even though classmates were scattered in different departments throughout the plant, they often met for lunch on a daily basis and socially after work. This continued for at least several months after workers were separated in the plant.

The bond of friendship that formed between classmates was a useful tool in the company's overall attempt at shaping a cooperative workforce. First, it laid the groundwork for a smooth transition into the plant. As a new worker in a factory environment, I experienced less alienation and fear than I had when beginning work in previous factory jobs. A primary reason for this was that I had already formed connections with other workers, the training experience was often the first topic of conversation when a new worker joined the team.

Team concept

Perhaps the most powerful aspect of SIA's scheme was located in the team concept and its reorganization of work. Organizing work around the team could control workers in three ways. First, a form of self-discipline emerged from the responsibilities of team membership. Workers often pushed themselves to the limit in order to keep up their 'end of the bargain'. Second, peer pressure 'clicked in' if self-discipline failed. For example, when a worker fell behind or made mistakes, others on the team suffered because they were forced to correct those errors before the vehicle left the area. It was highly likely that, if the team member did not solve the problem, he or she would experience resentment from the others. For example, a worker from another team told me that he was training one of his team members on a station and that the team member was very slow. In reference to that worker's speed he said, 'you know, it kind of makes me mad'. A third level of direct control was exerted through the team leader and the Japanese trainers.

Self-discipline emerged as a part of the team structure. I found that I quickly internalized the responsibilities of team membership. I went to extreme measures to 'hold up my end of the bargain'. An example of this occurred during a period of time when management began altering my station. Each change increased the time it took to complete my series of tasks, forcing me to change other areas of the station in order to keep up. At one point, it simply became impossible to do the amount of work required, and I kept falling behind. Even though I knew the team leader had set unrealistic goals for my station, I felt guilty and feared the other team members would resent me for falling behind.

The following example illustrates the type of peer pressure that could be exerted by team mates. One member of our team 'Joe' regularly made mistakes and fell behind. We were understaffed, and each of us was working at least two and sometimes three stations. 'Joe' was covering two stations. Because he was having problems, the rest of us observed him and found that he was not following any prescribed order when doing his stations. One simply could not predict which part he would pick up first. In turn, this meant that we never knew which part or parts he might forget. Because our responsibilities included checking the work already completed and correcting any mistakes, Joe's unpredictability increased the level of stress for the team members that followed him. The team leader and team members tried to get Joe to use a system, but he refused.

The team leader decided that Joe was simply pretending to be slow and confused in order to get out of working those particular stations. Finally, the team leader devised a scheme to correct the situation. The team leader informed the rest of the team of the plan. None of the team members told Joe of the potentially humiliating plan. Team members cooperated with the team leader in an attempt to put pressure on another team member concerning his job performance.

Direct control was exerted through the team concept by the team leader. There was a team leader for about every seven workers, so a worker's behaviour was constantly monitored. Workers' actions were under close scrutiny, and if inappropriate behaviour occurred, workers were pressured to change. At times this meant a 'friendly' visit from the group leader. At other times, the attention of a department manager was engaged.

Additional pressure came from our Japanese trainer. He inspected each car as it left our team and reported on our defects (any missed or improperly attached parts). In some cases, he found as many as thirty defects. Even though the majority could be attributed to Joe, the problem worker, the other team members were upset. It was important to each one to gain and keep the respect of the Japanese trainer, not only because he was the boss, but because team members liked him and had great respect for his knowledge of work and assembling the car.

136

Another aspect of the team structure was that it gave the company technical control over job assignments. Team members were cross-trained to perform one another's jobs, so management was able to move workers around freely within the team or between similar teams. This not only increased flexibility, it allowed the company to hire fewer workers, because covering for absent or injured workers was handled by other team members.

Philosophy of kaizen

The fourth element of SIA's system of control was epitomized in the phrase, 'Always searching for a better way'. This was how one vice president described the philosophy of kaizen during orientation and training. What it meant was that everyone was expected to continually make his or her job more efficient, striving to work to maximum capacity. Kaizening could be directly enforced through periodically decreasing the takt time by speeding up the line. This forced workers to find ways of shaving additional seconds from work tasks. Indirectly, it had a 'domino effect' on the workforce. Making one person's job more efficient often meant shifting part of that process to another worker or team, thereby intensifying someone else's job.

A large part of kaizening involved time study. During training, workers were taught to perform time studies on each other and to check against the established standard for each task. This practice continued on the shop floor and was used to speed up each person's work process. If any time was left after the completion of a process, other tasks or subassemblies could be added, intensifying the job. For example, when 'two right' got his station under control and was able to work ahead, he was given additional duties. He performed rework such as taping wiring harnesses. The goal was for workers to be working every second of every minute.[7] Although the Japanese system is most consistent with the concept of hegemonic control, not every aspect of Burawoy's theory is applicable. 'Making out' – the idea that workers play games to create spare time and still make quotas, and by doing so, develop a consensual relationship within production – took on a different form in the present case. Instead of a consensual relationship developing through workers' games, kaizening attempted to block workers from making out in two ways. First, it threatened a worker with constant disruption by suddenly introducing changes in the workstation, directly interfering with the making out process. Just when a worker had a station under control, with a few seconds to spare, he or she ran the risk of having it kaizened – intensifying the job. Second, through the kaizen philosophy of continual improvement, management attempts to gain control over workers' creative knowledge and to use it to its own advantage. Kaizening is not only designed to capture a worker's secrets for gaining spare time, once management appropriates that knowledge, it controls when, where and how those ideas are implemented. Kaizening, therefore, is an extremely effective procedure. It essentially convolutes the making out process, which under other management systems benefits the worker, into a process that puts continuous stress on the worker and forces workers' compliance.

Shop floor culture [8]

The fifth element, cultural control, was two-tiered. First, at the level of the shop floor, there was an attempt to shape workers' culture through the team structure. Organizing work around the team circumvented the natural formation of small informal work groups, a traditional mechanism of worker solidarity and support (Roy 1983). By formalising work groups, management created a structure in which team members worked together to meet company goals. If the company could successfully appropriate workers' solidarity and support, then they would identify their interests with the Company's. Daily quotas and speed-up placed increased demands on workers and created resentment toward management. The culture of the team was one mechanism of dissipating resistance to those demands. Quite simply, when helping other team members keep up, workers supported the speed-up.

The second level of cultural control was the organizational level. There was an active campaign to create a Company-wide team culture at SIA, premised on the concept of egalitarianism. This was an attempt to elevate the responsibilities of team membership and identification to the level of the company.

Attempts to create an egalitarian culture occurred through specialized symbols, ideology, language and rituals. For example, everyone from the Company president on down wore the same uniforms, parked in the same parking lot, and used the same cafeteria. Workers were never referred to as employees or workers. Instead everyone, including management, was an associate. In addition, the Company president and vice presidents were often seen on the shop floor.

The team metaphor was used at all levels of the company. Company documents compared team leaders to basketball captains and group leaders to coaches (Subaru–Isuzu Facts and Information 1989: 2). The team metaphor was further extended to embrace the Company's struggle in the market place. When defining its corporate character in the Associate Handbook, the second principle was 'Together, we must beat the competition'. The Company song was 'Team up for tomorrow'. At one department meeting right before the start of official production (when we began building cars that would be sold in this country), the trim and final manager gave a speech that was reminiscent of a coach's 'go get 'em' right before the big game. In a very solemn tone he told the workers: 'We are finally entering into the competition. The company has done everything to prepare us for this moment. Now it is up to us to beat the competition.'

Company rituals included morning exercises, team meetings, department meetings, and company celebrations. These rituals brought workers in contact with management in a relaxed and casual atmosphere. At department meetings the teams sat together in the cafeteria, smoking and drinking pop while the trim and final manager delivered a 'pep talk'.

Company celebrations not only included workers, but workers were often the focus of the celebration. At the ceremony commemorating the official start of production, state dignitaries, community leaders, and top management from Fuji Heavy and Isuzu were present. The ceremony was laden with images of nationalism, the marching band from the local university played and baton twirlers performed. The climax of the celebration occurred when all of the employees from the plant marched across the stage through a haze of smoke as the company song 'Team Up for Tomorrow' played over the speaker system. An associate from Team 2 said, 'It seems kind of like graduation'. One might argue that it is odd for a Japanese company to appropriate all of these American symbols. However, if the company's goal is control through enlisting workers' cooperation as team members, then appropriating American symbols seems quite natural.

Computerized assembly line

The most direct form of control at SIA was the computerized assembly line. It not only set the pace of work, but the mainframe computer system had the ability to focus everyone's attention on any team that fell behind. For example, when a worker fell behind, he or she pulled a yellow cord located above the line. At that instant, the team's music (each team was assigned a few bars of music) would be heard throughout the area occupied by the fourteen teams that assembled the cars in trim and final via the loud speaker system. The computerized music was played repeatedly until the cord was pulled again by the team leader, signalling that things were under control. If the line actually stopped, the music continued until the line began moving again. This had the effect of focusing department-wide attention on the team with the problem.

In addition to playing music, the computer system kept track of the number of times each team pulled the cord and how long the line was stopped. Such a system of 'bookkeeping' allowed management to put tremendous pressure on specific team and group leaders. This pressure was passed on to team members. For example, at the morning team meetings, in addition to receiving a defect report, other teams' problems were often topics of discussion. Problems arising within the team were a definite focus of conversation. During start-up our group leader attended one morning meeting to inform us that we were 'the only team in trim and final that was still having trouble making takt time'.

Just-in-time production

The final mechanism of control, that had the effect of directly intensifying and speeding up our work, was just-in-time production. This is a method of inventory control in which the company keeps parts stocked on the line for only a few hours of work. This put severe time constraints on the material handlers who stocked the line and on the workers assembling the cars and trucks. Because the line was only stopped when absolutely necessary, the vehicles often continued moving, even when parts were missing. This meant that when the missing part arrived, the team had to work down the line installing that part after other parts had been attached, a difficult and time-consuming job. Even if the missing part arrived only a few seconds late, it was often enough to put that worker behind. Once behind, a worker often could not catch up and, therefore, the rest of his or her day was affected. No one wanted to fall behind and experience this pressure, thus workers often made extreme efforts to see that their parts were stocked. Sometimes workers left the moving line and, literally, ran down the aisle in search of a material handler to warn him or her that the line was becoming dangerously low on a part. Such actions could also put workers behind and increased the intensity of the jobs.

In summary, the points outlined above indicate that the combination of these components of control was quite powerful in controlling the individual worker. Only through collective action were workers able to effect any balance of power on the shop floor. The next section analyses the nature and success of worker resistance.

The nature of resistance

Evidence of worker resistance to SIA's system of management emerged in various collective and individual forms. Collective resistance emerged as sabotage when workers surreptitiously stopped the assembly line. Resistance emerged when workers collectively protested and refused to participate in Company rituals. Collective resistance emerged in the form of direct confrontation when workers refused management requests, and in the form of sustained, organized agitation at team and department meetings.

Individual resistance was expressed through silent protest when workers, on an individual basis, refused to participate in Company rituals and in the form of complaints through anonymous letters written to the Company as part of the company's programme of rumour control.

Collective resistance

Sabotage occurred when workers on one of the trim and final teams discovered how to stop the assembly line without management tracing their location. Whenever one of their team members fell behind and the 'coast was clear' they stopped the line. This not only allowed people on their team to catch up, it gave everyone time away from the line. In addition, it provided entertainment as workers watched management scramble around trying to find the source of the line stoppage. At one morning team meeting, our team leader reported that the line had stopped for a total of twenty minutes the day before, and the Company was unable to account for the time. Clearly, that team was taking a chance. However, the workers who were aware of the sabotage, never told management. Whether the reason for the complicity was selfish, because of the appreciated breaks, or was loyalty to other workers, their silence was a direct act of resistance and evidence of a lack of commitment to the Company.

Collective resistance also emerged in the form of protest. For example, in response to what they considered an unfair action by

141

the Company, Team 1 refused to participate in company rituals such as exercises and team meetings. This occurred in response to the company unilaterally taking away a five-minute clean-up period at the end of the day.

Collective resistance emerged in the form of direct confrontation with management. When the clean-up period was no longer allowed, workers refused management's request to work 'after the buzzer' (the end of the shift) in order to clean up and put away tools. For example, even when management directly requested workers' assistance in this matter, they were met with direct resistance at meetings and on the line. The group leader for our area called a special meeting of Team 1 and Team 2 to enlist help in cleaning up after the buzzer. At the meeting several workers from both teams directly confronted the group leader. A worker from Team 1 said, 'This is the kind of bullshit that brings in a union.' A second remarked, 'This place is getting too Japanese around here, pretty soon you will be asking us to donate our Saturdays.' A worker from Team 2 assured the group leader that he was 'not a volunteer'. As a group, they were adamant that they would not work after the buzzer.

On the following day, the line continued moving until the buzzer sounded, and as it happened, I was so far behind that when the line stopped, I did not realise the buzzer had sounded and I kept working. As two team mates walked by, they called to me 'Laurie, don't do it!' I put down my tools. As I was leaving, I overheard our team leader ask another team member a question concerning work. He replied, 'Look, it's after 3.00. I don't know', and he walked on by. From that day on, whenever the line ran up to quitting time, everyone on the team dropped whatever they were doing and immediately walked out, leaving the team leader to lock up the tools and clean the area. At a team meeting the team leader complained that she had stayed almost an hour after work cleaning up and putting away our tools. One team member said 'She was crazy to do it, and we weren't going to'.

Another form of collective resistance which emerged was jokes. Workers made light of company rituals and the philosophy of kaizen. For example, as mentioned above, some workers told jokes at the team meeting when called upon for an inspirational message during the 'yosh' ritual. They were making light of what was presented to us as a fairly solemn ritual. Another example of making light of rituals occurred at morning exercises when workers would jump around and act silly. Kaizening, the company's philosophy of continuous improvement, was also the brunt of workers' jokes. When the line stopped, someone would say 'Lets kaizen that chair', or if something really went wrong, they would say, 'I guess they kaizened that'.

Several examples of resistance emerged in response to management's unilateral scheduling and unscheduling of overtime. Resistance to overtime became resistance to the Company's philosophy of cooperation. In December, both Isuzu and Subaru were trying to meet the end of the year production quota. Within one week the following happened. On a Tuesday we were told that we would work Saturday. The following morning the car manager informed us that we would work nine hours that day and the next two days, so we would not have to work Saturday. At the same time, however, he assured us that if there were too many unscheduled line stoppages, we would end up working Saturday after all. One team member said the company was 'just trying to screw us out of eight hours of overtime'. Then, Friday morning they informed us that we would only work our regular eight-hour shift. However, when the 3.00 p.m. bell sounded, the line continued to move. Instead of staying with the line, nearly everyone on the car line put down their tools and walked out. As it turned out, the line only moved for another minute or so, but no one in trim and final knew this. To leave a moving line was a direct act of resistance and just cause for dismissed.

On the truck line, overtime scheduling was an even bigger issue because they had to meet larger monthly production quotas (ours were reduced because of the problems in paint). In the middle of December, I talked to a truck line worker I knew from my training class. Overtime scheduling was the subject of our conversation. On the previous day, her group leader told her team at 2.50 p.m. that the truck line would work until 4.00 p.m. At 3.00 p.m. they were given no break (even though stated company policy provided for a five-minute break at 3.00 p.m. when working overtime), so they were unable to call home. She was particularly upset because her young son came home from school to an empty house. At 4.00 p.m. the line was not stopped. It did not stop until 4.50 p.m. She said that several members of her team started leaving at 4.00 p.m., even though the line was still moving. The group leader literally chased them down and got them back to work by threatening them with their jobs.

Another act of resistance, triggered by overtime scheduling and the Company's response to workers exercising their rights according to Company policy, occurred on Team 1. Two days before

December vacation, the car manager decided to work the team overtime without sufficient notice. Our team leader asked us individually whether or not we were willing to stay over. I declined and so did another woman on my team. Previously, the Company had handed down a policy concerning overtime stating that 'scheduled' and 'emergency' overtime were mandatory, but 'unscheduled' was not. Scheduled was defined as having been announced by the end of the shift on the previous day. Therefore, in this case, the overtime was unscheduled, and we had the right to refuse.

That afternoon, the group leader approached me and asked why I was not willing to work. I, of course, had not expected to work and had a medical appointment I wanted to keep. Shortly after that, our team leader informed us that, 'According to human resources, if we left at 3.00, it would be an unexcused absence.' The company was instituting this policy on the spot. This caused a third woman on our team to also refuse the overtime. She said that it was obvious to her that the Company was simply fabricating the policy to force us to work. On principle, she decided to leave with us to protest the Company's method of assigning unexcused absences. Now three team members were leaving. When the group leader learned this, he informed the car manager that there would not be enough people to keep the line moving. At this point, the car manager approached me with the group leader by his side. He said: 'Look, here at SIA we are trying to be different. If this was any other place, I wouldn't bother to talk to you. I'd just tell the group leader to tell you to work or else. I don't want to get into a position where I am talking discipline with an employee, because I know you are a good worker. I've seen you work.' I replied: 'This wasn't scheduled overtime and you yourself have said it wasn't an emergency, so how could you discipline me?' He said, 'Anyone who leaves the line while it is moving is in jeopardy of being fired.'

At this juncture, our team leader made a surprising announcement. She told the car manager that she was also leaving. He put immediate pressure on her, in front of the team, informing her that she was putting her job in jeopardy if she left. Finally, when faced with the intended departure of four team members, and the fact that this would shut the line down, management backed down. I suggested to the manager that if he agreed that no one would get an unexcused absence for leaving, both the team leader and the other protester would agree to stay. They accepted those terms, myself and the other worker who needed to leave left. The next day our team mates informed us that only three cars were built after we left. They described the demands made on us as a 'power play by management'.

Finally, collective resistance emerged through organized agitation at team and department meetings. This occurred as workers attempted to stop the company from instituting a policy of shift rotation. Management announced the policy and stated that it was 'not up for discussion'. All workers would have to rotate when the second shift was added. This infuriated many workers. Several people stated that it was typical of the kinds of decisions workers were not allowed to participate in. Many things that had a direct effect on workers' lives, such as overtime, line speed, and shift rotation were not up for discussion. The essence of the participation workers were granted involved, at best, improving quality, at worst, and more commonly, speeding up the job. Workers used an informal communication network, which had emerged as part of a shop floor subculture (Gottfried and Graham 1993) to pass the word around the plant to 'keep the pressure on by bringing it up at meetings'. After that, the issue of shift rotation was brought up almost daily at the morning team meetings. Department meetings were regularly disrupted when various workers would state how 'unfair' it was that we had no input into the shift rotation decision. The issue continually surfaced. Eventually, management changed its ruling, and an announcement was made that there would be no shift rotation.

Individual resistance

Silent protest was a common form of individual resistance and an easy target was morning exercises. For example, workers arrived late for work in order to avoid morning exercises or else they remained sitting while others participated. The exercises were a relatively safe target of protest because they occurred before the start of the shift. Legally, workers had the right to refuse. A second form of individual resistance emerged in anonymous letters to the company.

The anonymous letter was a weak form of resistance because it involved little risk to the individual and it utilized a formal procedure instituted by the company. As part of their 'fair treatment policy', the company distributed prestamped, self-addressed envelopes for people to write in anonymously with questions or comments. The comments were posted throughout the plant on special bulletin boards with both the worker's comment and the Company's reply. Between 26 October, when the first batch was posted, and 5 January, 150 comments, questions, and complaints were aired. At first they were optimistic, containing questions concerning the future. For example, people asked if there would be a credit union, a car purchase programme, day care facility, or a fitness gym. Later it became a sounding board for complaints and dissatisfaction. Concerns emerged over scheduling overtime without notification. Parents complained that scheduling meetings after work and long hours of overtime conflicted with their childrens' hours at day care. Workers also expressed concern that favouritism existed in parking, lunch hours, bonus plans, scheduling of overtime, and the loaning out of Company cars. Repeated complaints emerged that group leaders and team leaders were being chosen without any job postings. Trim and final associates wanted to know why maintenance associates were paid $2 more per hour. There were repeated concerns that quality was being sacrificed in order to meet daily quotas. Workers questioned why seniority was used for some things such as enrolment in the pension plan but not for transfers and promotions. One worker wanted to know why security checks were unequally applied as people with lunch boxes were searched when leaving through the front door while those with brief cases were not checked. Another worker quoted state law concerning overtime pay, stressing that it was illegal for the company to require workers to clean their areas and put their tools away after the shift had ended. There were also the more predictable complaints concerning the food and long lines in the cafeteria, uniforms, gloves and plant temperature. Many complaints revealed that the company was not totally successful in instituting a spirit of cooperation and a culture of egalitarianism.

Table 4.1 provides a summary of the forms of worker resistance. Strength of resistance is measured by workers' success at gaining a desired change in company policy or action. In general, the weakest forms of resistance were individual and called for no action by the company. The most effective forms tended to be collective, involved some risk to the individuals involved, were goal directed, and challenged the company's claim to fairness and equality. Planned, collective action was not necessarily more effective for achieving desired results than was spontaneous, collective action. Possibly this was because spontaneous action could be interpreted as a direct indication of the importance that workers placed on a particular issue. Spontaneous, collective action was not only a show of worker solidarity, it indicated a certain level of militancy, as it reflected a

Table 4.1 Dimensions of worker resistance at SIA

	Weak ←———		———→ *Strong*	
	1 *Veiled protest*	**2** *Symbolic protest*	**3** *Dispersed agitation*	**4** *Direct confrontation*
Examples of individual resistance:	Refusal to exercise Sabotage	Anonymous letters		
Examples of collective resistance:	Jokes making light of company philosophy or rituals	Not exercising as a team protest	Conflict over shift rotation	Leaving a moving line Refusal to cooperate and work without pay
	Sabotage with group knowledge and approval			Overtime confrontation

[1]Evidence of a 'spirit' of resistance with no direct request for change, resulting in no apparent change by management.
[2]Acts of resistance with a low level of risk which had a goal of changing a specific management policy or action but resulted in no apparent change by management.
[3]Actions which were organized, sustained over a period of time, dispersed throughout the company, and directed at a specific goal. This resistance resulted in management changing its policy after a period of time.
[4]Actions which involved a threat to the job security of the individual worker. They tended to be spontaneous, collective, and goal oriented. Workers usually expressed that they were acting on 'principle', and invoked management's policy of fairness. This type of resistance resulted in immediate capitulation from management.

worker's willingness to engage in risky behaviour without knowing if others would join in. In either case, both planned and spontaneous actions expressed a collective will in direct opposition to management's authority.

CONCLUSION

Data collected by means of covert participant/observation does not support Florida and Kenney's (1991) contention that the Japanese model delegates managerial authority to the shop floor, increases worker control. Workers were seldom allowed to make even the most inconsequential decision on their own. Kaizening provided a mechanism for keeping decision making under the tight control of management. Additionally, the company's use of consensus in decision making assured management's control over the outcomes. The unequal relationship between worker and management made it nearly impossible to reach a consensus involving little more than token input from workers.

Although the Japanese model does not rely on traditional Fordist management schemes such as deskilling and task fragmentation to increase technical control over the workforce, workers were not given greater technical control through this system. Instead of deskilling, job enrichment or enlargement more accurately described the assignment of tasks. The number of tasks tended to be expanded rather than narrowed, as expected in a deskilling process. However, even though workers performed a wider range of tasks, they were not 'reskilled'. Jobs were fragmented and rationalized to the tenth of a second. Additionally, even though workers were trained to perform others' stations, this cross training did not increase worker control over the technical aspect of work. The opposite was true. Flexibility increased management's control by making workers more vulnerable to job intensification and speed-up.

The Japanese model did attempt to harness workers' collective intelligence for continuous improvement. However, this did not benefit the worker. The kaizen process had the opposite effect. Management controlled the parameters of what was within the realm of consideration and also how, when, and where a job was altered.

Concerning the social aspect of production, at SIA, control was decentralized through the team leader and the management structure was flat, not the hierarchical structure found in traditional factory systems which use bureaucratic control. The lack of a burdensome bureaucracy may, on the surface, seem to be a reason for arguing that the team structure is a winning situation for both parties. However, decentralized authority within the plant created a situation where workers had very little autonomy. On the average, every seven workers were under the direct supervision and close scrutiny of the team leader. The concept of team participation in a decentralized structure hid the capitalist–worker relationship through an ideology of egalitarianism. This calls into question Edwards's (1979) contention that bureaucratic structures are required to mask the capitalist–worker relationship. While bureaucratic structures can do what Edwards says, so can other structures.

Unlike the traditional management schemes found in the automobile industry, the Japanese model focuses on gaining control over the social aspects of production. Socialization takes place informally through the team culture and formally through orientation and training. Through its focus on the social aspects of production, the Japanese model attempts to invade territory in which the worker has historically maintained control. The success of collective resistance at SIA provides evidence that management has every right to fear worker solidarity. It is the workers' greatest weapon. It was through this social aspect of production that workers effectively won concessions from management.

Concerning the issue of transference, the resistance by workers at SIA provides additional evidence that intraorganizational transference of Japanese management practices may not be as successful as research has indicated. This is particularly the case when including a political dimension of analysis, shop floor control. Examining overt structures provides only a partial understanding. It cannot get at the unintended consequences of those structures nor can it expose how those structures are mediated by workers. Mid-level examination, through means such as participant/observation, allows the social scientist to get at levels of understanding which are usually inaccessible. This research, with its emphasis on patterns of worker behaviour, suggests that successful transference at one level of measurement is not synonymous with successful adaptation of worker behaviour on the shop floor.

NOTES

1   Kaizening is a philosophy of continuous improvement. It is instituted by asking workers to continually find faster or more efficient ways of performing their jobs.
2   This chapter relies heavily upon an earlier paper, 'Inside a Japanese transplant: a critical perspective', *Work and Occupations* 20, 2: 147–173.
3   Gaining employment and working in the plant as a hidden participant/ observer is the method of choice for this particular study for several reasons. First, entry could not be gained with management's knowledge. Second, it has been used by other researchers when attempting to understand shop floor culture and experience (Linhart 1981; Pfeffer 1979; Kamata 1982; Cavendish 1982). Third, entering the plant without the knowledge of management or worker speeds up the process of

gaining acceptance and is least disruptive to the natural course of events – as people may attempt to modify their behaviour if aware that they are under observation. Finally, this type of methodology allows questions to be asked and observations to be made as events occur (Bollens and Marshall 1973).

4　Through the course of the pre-employment selection process and the six months working at SIA I talked with 150 employees, 46 were women, 3 were black.

5　Takt time is the amount of time a worker is given to complete a station, it was the same throughout the entire plant.

6　It was our understanding that 'Yosh!' was a cheer, meaning something similar to 'Lets go!'. Every team in trim and final performed this daily ritual.

7　In a typical American auto plant workers maintain a 40- to 50-second-a-minute work pace, whereas Japanese auto plants tend to run close to 60 seconds a minute (Fucini and Fucini 1990: 37).

8　For an examination of the emergence of gendered subcultures at Subaru–Isuzu see Gottfried and Graham (1993).

REFERENCES

Bollens, J. and Marshall, D. (1973) *Guide to Participation*, Englewood Cliffs, N.J.: Prentice Hall.

Braverman, H. (1974) *Labor and Monopoly Capital*, New York, N.Y.: Monthly Review Press.

Burawoy, M. (1979) *Manufacturing Consent: Changes in the Labour Process under Monopoly Capitalism*, Chicago: University of Chicago Press.

—— (1985) *The Politics of Production*, New York, N.Y.: Verso.

Cavendish, R. (1982) *Women on the Line*, London: Routledge and Kegan Paul.

Chinoy, E. (1955) *The Automobile Workers and the American Dream*, Garden City, N.Y.: Doubleday.

Clawson, D. (1980) *Bureaucracy and the Labour Process: The Transformation of U.S. Industry, 1860–1920*, New York, N.Y.: Monthly Review Press.

Edwards, R. (1979) *Contested Terrain*, New York, N.Y.: Basic Books.

Florida, R. and Kenny M. (1991) 'Transplanted organizations: the transfer of Japanese industrial organization to the US', *American Sociological Review* 56: 381–398.

Friedman, A. (1977) *Industry and Labour: Class Struggle at Work and Monopoly Capitalism*, London: Macmillan.

Fucini, J. and Fucini S. (1990) *Working for the Japanese: Inside Mazda's American Auto Plant*, New York, N.Y.: The Free Press, Macmillan.

Gottfried, H. and Graham, L. (1993) 'Constructing difference: the making of gendered subcultures in a Japanese automobile transplant', *Sociology* 27, 4: 611–628.

Graham, L. (1993) 'Inside a Japanese transplant: a critical perspective', *Work and Occupations* 20, 2: 147–173.

Kamata, S. (1982) *Japan in the Passing Lane*, New York: Pantheon Books.

Linhart, R. (1981) *The Assembly Line*, London: John Calder.

Manwaring, T. and Wood, S. (1985) 'The ghost in the labour process', in D. Knights *et al.* (eds) *Job Redesign: Critical Perspectives on the Labour Process*, London: Gower.

Montgomery, D. (1979) *Worker's Control in America: Studies in the History of Work, Technology, and Labour Struggles*, Cambridge University Press.

Perrucci, R. (1994) 'Embedded corporatism: auto transplants, the local state, and community politics in the Midwest Corridor', *Sociological Quarterly* 35: 2.

Pfeffer, R. (1979) *Working for Capitalism*, New York, N.Y.: Columbia University Press.

Roy, D. F. (1983) '"Banana time": job satisfaction and informal interaction', in J. R. Hackman, *et al.* (eds) *Perspectives on Behaviour in Organizations*, New York, N.Y.: McGraw-Hill.

Thompson, P. (1989) *The Nature of Work: An Introduction to Debates on the Labour Process*, 2nd Edition, Atlantic Highlands, N.J.: Humanities Press International.

5

REUNIFYING CONCEPTION AND EXECUTION OF WORK UNDER JAPANESE PRODUCTION MANAGEMENT?

A Canadian case study

James Rinehart, David Robertson, Christopher Huxley and Jeff Wareham

The subject of this paper – workers' opportunities to conceptualize under a system of lean production – is one of many issues addressed in our longitudinal case study of CAMI, a unionized joint venture automobile assembly plant in Canada.[1] The project arose from concerns of the Canadian Automobile Workers (CAW) union over an emergent, rapidly spreading system of management and production about which the union had only second-hand knowledge and virtually no information on how this system recasts the labour process and relates to an independent union. The CAW research group on CAMI was interested in understanding not how Japanese production management (JPM) works in theory, but how it actually operates in a concrete setting. Research questions and methods were framed by union concerns, debates in the literature on JPM – particularly distinct views of how this system affects workers and unions – and our interest in examining the social relations of production on the shop floor.

From these starting points we formulated questions that guided the research. How are workers recruited and trained? What are the components of the CAMI production process and how does this process affect job content, workpace, workloads and labour intensification? Does the system entail empowered, multiskilled workers with opportunities for continuous learning and skills acquisition? Are workteams cohesive groups, and if so are they a source of resistance to and/or cooperation with CAMI? How do workers respond to aspects of JPM such as job rotation, kaizen and associated participatory programmes and the Company's efforts to cultivate a committed workforce? What is the relationship between CAMI and the union, and is it possible for an independent union to develop in a JPM workplace? While much of our data remain unanalysed, a number of these questions have been addressed in preliminary papers (Robertson, Rinehart and Huxley 1991, 1992) and in a report that provides a general overview of our findings (Robertson and CAW 1992).

INTRODUCTION

Proponents of JPM or lean production herald it as a system capable of efficiently, flexibly and humanely producing a wide variety of products. Where Taylor strove to remove all mental components from a workers' job and Ford's ideal was to have one worker perform one repetitive operation, the Japanese are credited with rediscovering intelligence on the shop floor and breaking down the separation of the conception of work from its execution. Florida and Kenney (1991: 388) view JPM as 'a new and potential successor model [to Fordist mass production] based on harnessing workers' intellectual and physical capabilities'. So taken by the possibilities offered by lean production is the MIT group that they contemplate a workplace of 'highly skilled problem solvers whose task will be to think continuously of ways to make the system run smoothly and productively'. (Womack, Jones and Roos 1990: 102) The re-unification of mental and manual labour is realized through the development of multiskilled workers who perform challenging jobs and who take responsibility for the continuous improvement of operations (kaizen).

These sanguine pronouncements are contested by those who view JPM as a kind of super-Taylorism built around fast-paced, standardized jobs and managements whose prerogatives are virtually unrestricted. Under JPM workers' capacity to conceptualize work and make decisions is limited, leaving them only free enough to participate in escalating their own exploitation (cf. Berggen, Bjorkman and Hollander 1991; Dohse, Jurgens and Malsch 1985; Parker and Slaughter 1988; Turnbull 1988).

Our entry to this debate is through the front door of CAMI, a General Motors–Suzuki joint venture whose operations are patterned after Japanese principles. Our concern in this paper is to evaluate shop floor conceptualization and participation by examining the kaizen process and responses to it by workers and the union.

JAPANESE PRODUCTION MANAGEMENT AT CAMI

Located in Ingersoll, Ontario, midway between Detroit and Toronto, CAMI is a greenfield operation that makes the Geo Metro sub-compact car and GM Tracker and Suzuki Sidekick 4-wheel drive utility vehicles. It is one of four transplants in Canada and the only one to involve Japanese and North American partners. The plant began production in April 1989 and is now operating two-shifts with a workforce of about 2,300. Production workers were selected in a six-stage, 13-hour screening process from among some 45,000 applicants. Workers at CAMI are members of the Canadian Auto Workers union (CAW), making this the only unionized transplant or joint venture car factory in Canada, and one of only four such organized plants in North America.

The physical environment of CAMI marks it as distinct from traditional auto plants. There are no reserved parking spaces (with the lone exception of the Company president). All employees eat in the same cafeteria and wear similar uniforms with first name labels above the pocket. This ostensible egalitarianism is reflected in the absence of a category of employees called workers. Those who work on the shop floor and who are union members are known as production associates, team leaders (all workers are members of teams) or maintenance associates.

That the Japanese own half of this company is obvious. Japanese words spelled out in English are used and posted throughout the plant. The nagare production system is driven by the principles of just-in-time. Staffing levels are lean and there is no corps of relief workers to cover for the absent and injured. Andon cords which enable workers to call for help or stop the line are found at most work stations. Pokayokes (devices insuring fail-safe operations) are located throughout the plant, and CAMI recently instituted a kanban system to move operations closer to stockless or pull production. The manual used to train recruits has its origin in Japan, and at the bottom of each page the English words in the text are translated into Japanese. In the training area each room has a Japanese name on the door. The 5Ss, 3Ms and 3Gs refer to Japanese words that establish rules of conduct and a production philosophy. One M – muda – for example, refers to the sin of waste. Workers are expected to do pre-shift calisthenics called taiso. Employee suggestions go by the name of teians. And one of CAMI's four central values (in addition to open communication, empowerment and team spirit) is kaizen.

KAIZEN OBJECTIVES

The CAMI training manual makes the point that the only way to secure profits in the competitive world of automobile manufacturing is to cut production costs (as opposed to raising car prices or increasing market share). According to the manual, 'The primary source of profits at CAMI is through the elimination of waste.' Kaizen is defined as the 'process of searching out waste, eliminating it, then deploying the resources made available to a more productive task'. Waste is anything not essential to an operation: unnecessary inspection, transport or human movement, excessive inventory, producing defective parts. Any activity that does not directly add value to the product is waste. Installing a bumper is value added, but walking to pick up the bumper is waste.

In contrast to traditional factories, CAMI does not rely on an industrial engineering department. As one manager observed:

> We have 26 different competitors and the only way we can get better than them is that we need the ideas of every individual on the floor. Otherwise, we're just not going to be able to make it down the road.

While kaizen is characterized by the Company as a benign, win-win process built on the technical common sense and innovative capacity of workers, the ultimate goal of kaizen is to produce with the absolute minimum of workers. The continuous reduction of cycle time via time study and line rebalancing is emphasized, for example, in the kaizen report book – kept by team leaders (unionized), area leaders (first-level management) and production managers. The book describes a hypothetical five-person team in which each worker needs a slightly different amount of time to complete his/her job. The team leader repeatedly times the jobs, discusses the results with and gets input from the team and then evens out the workloads of four persons, leaving the fifth with little to do. The lesson continues:

> Then, as a next step, improve E's [the fifth person] operation so his man-hour is eliminated [i.e. drop him from the team]. If not eliminated, he should be given additional jobs. What is important in assigning operations, each associate should be given jobs up to 100 per cent cycle time.

There is more to kaizen than reducing necessary labour time. Kaizen is at the heart of CAMI's campaign to convince workers that they have the capacity to make important workplace decisions. Ideally, the kaizen process is a means of instilling in the workforce a sense of empowerment, an attitude that can reduce workers' likelihood of resisting, stimulate their initiative and effort and commit them to the company. A manager characterized the participatory programmes CAMI has instituted to realize kaizen as 'part of the empowerment process'.

> We've hired people for their brains as well as their brawn. Nowadays the workforce is not going to feel fulfilled if you just come in and tell them what to do. Our philosophy is that the engineers can't possibly know as much about the jobs as the people that are doing them. . . . If you feel you really are empowered, you have some ability to control what you do and how you do it, you're going to walk out of this place feeling a lot better about yourself at the end of the day.[2]

In training, recruits are continually reminded of the necessity for kaizen. Trainees are taught that it is not the dramatic innovations but incremental improvements on which CAMI counts. As an instructor told the trainees, 'base hits win ballgames'. One can get a sense of kaizen training from the following description of a classroom exercise representing a die change in a stamping press.

There are three brick-sized blocks of wood stacked and fastened together with two long bolts and topped with washers and nuts. The bolts are inset from each end of the blocks, and they extend about two inches beyond the top surface of the blocks. The middle block represents a die. Although this block can be put in place in a variety of ways (i.e. left to right, top to bottom), there is only one correct way that allows all the blocks to be properly aligned. The task is to dismantle the blocks, take the middle one out and then reassemble them.

The group of twelve is divided into teams of two, with the exception of one person who is identified as a quality auditor to determine if the blocks are properly aligned and another with a stop watch to time each team. Each team comes to the front of the room and is given a few minutes to decide how to do the job. There are different ways to do it. A person from the first team initially unlocks both nuts with the wrench, then holds the assembly while the other worker uses both hands to spin the nuts off the bolts. The other teams watch, incorporate the good techniques, avoid the pitfalls and add their own innovations. Team 1 comes in at 69.5 centiminutes. There is a round of applause. Team 2 has a good time but there is a quality adjustment – a penalty of 15 centiminutes is imposed. Another round of applause and some good-natured jibes. Team 3 registers 77.25 centiminutes. The competition continues. The best time is 59 centiminutes. It is a good time that, under the circumstances, is probably impossible to beat.

But now comes the punchline. Their best was not good enough. The goal is to get the time down to 15 centiminutes. Around the room there are expressions of disbelief and some dismay. Their best time was four times that! This is the message of kaizen. No matter how well they did, they can, and must, do better.

KAIZEN AND STANDARDIZATION

Work standardization is a key component of production at CAMI. The original standards were brought into CAMI from Suzuki headquarters in Japan. Japanese advisors, along with area leaders and team leaders, set up and refined the jobs, which were then codified on standard operation sheets (SOSs). The key elements of the SOSs appear on CAMI operating standard (COS) sheets. These sheets specify the procedures to be followed in the performance of a job and are posted at virtually every work station in the plant. Standardized operations are not fixed and absolute. It is the essence of the kaizen process to constantly revise standards as more efficient ways are found to perform jobs. The ongoing setting of standards is not the responsibility of industrial engineers. In theory, each team serves as a mini industrial engineering department. Area leaders and team leaders are trained in time study and job analysis. 'Standardized operations,' the CAMI manual states, 'are the basis of continuous kaizen in process operations. If everyone performs the operations in the same way, potential problems or waste will be easily identified so that kaizen can be readily made.' So in addition to workers being required to follow the 'one best way', they are instructed to constantly ask 'is there a better way?'. A manager expressed the relationship between standards and their revision:

> The whole secret of it is to do the operation the same way every time, exactly the same way every time. And you'll notice even the COSs on the line are made in pencil so that if you change it you just erase parts and add to it. And that's from Japan.

REALIZING KAIZEN THROUGH WORKERS' PARTICIPATION

Elaborate suggestion (teian) and quality control circle (QCC) programmes are the most important vehicles for the realization of kaizen at CAMI. As a manager observed: 'Fundamentally, what is going to make us [CAMI] different, I think, is the QCC programme and the teian programme.' Despite the cost-down thrust of kaizen, these participatory programmes are portrayed by management as issuing in outcomes that benefit both workers and the company. Management's rationale for this goes beyond the obvious claim that job security is linked to company profitability; kaizen also entails outcomes like making jobs easier and safer. Perhaps to drive home this point, CAMI has placed no rigid boundaries around the types of teians that may be submitted or the themes that may be taken up in QCCs. A manager declared:

> One thing we said right at the beginning was that we did not want to recognize that some themes are better than other themes. So we're not going to say that a cost theme is better than a safety theme. What we appreciate is people working together on problems on their own.

CAMI sponsors an annual rally in which QCCs throughout the plant compete for prizes. The winning group gets a free trip to Japan, where it competes with QCCs from Suzuki's plants around the world. In 1990 the second place circle received $2,000 and third place was worth $1,000. The seven runners-up each received $500.

At the 1991 rally nine QCCs gave presentations accompanied by documents describing their themes, problems, goals, proposed solutions and projected results. Included were calculations of percentage improvements in quality and yearly cost-savings. The documents contained written descriptions and rationales, elaborate fishbone diagrams analysing the potential causes of the problems, bar and pie graphs and precision drawings of tools, dies, jigs, components and pallets. Several documents concluded with the words, 'We are CAMI. Yosh!'.[3] A few examples of the presentations will suffice to illustrate their character.

A QCC from assembly set their problem as accommodating to an impending increase in line speed. A series of modifications – movement of jigs, replacement of components, tool changes, transfer of some tasks to another team, etc. – enabled the team to handle the new line speed. According to the circle's calculations, these changes would save CAMI $368,000 in the following year and would reduce defects by 72 per cent. Another circle reduced paint usage and eliminated two of four paint sprayers (i.e. workers), for projected savings of about $150,000 a year. The solution involved splicing the air line into four pieces and then attaching air lines and guns to them. The winning circle from stamping solved the problem of metal slivers (produced by trim die cutting action) marring metal finishes and causing press stoppages to clear dies. A combination of improvements, including a technique to air-blow the slivers away, new modes of metal cutting (recommended by engineers) and a revised method of greasing dies was projected to save the company annually nearly a quarter of a million dollars.

CAMI goes to great lengths to cultivate the individual submission of suggestions. While the programme is voluntary, every employee below the level of assistant manager is expected to submit five teians a month. On CAMI suggestion forms employees state the nature of the problem (what, when, where), the recommended change and its effects (including cost to implement). There are spaces on the form for the signatures of the team leader, area leader, manager and other managers who may be affected by the change. Potentially valuable teians ($1,000 or more a month in savings) must be approved by high-level managers, but minor (i.e. cost-free, small alterations in work sequence) suggestions can be quickly reviewed by low-level management and implemented by workteams. This fast-track implementation of teians distinguishes CAMI's system from standard suggestion programmes.

A person submitting a teian gets 50 cents (or a coupon worth this amount) and if the teian is approved (but not necessarily implemented) the submitter receives an additional 50 cents or a coupon. Coupons can be exchanged for cash or used in the company cafeteria. Teians that save CAMI money fall into ten classes, ranging from monthly savings of $5,000 or more down to less than $100. For each of the ten classes there are specific cash awards for the team, ranging from $500 to nothing, and teian points for the individual suggestor ranging from 500 to 5. For teians that are implemented but do not save money, the team receives no prize money, but the individual submitter receives 50 points for an 'outstanding' idea, 25 points for an 'excellent' teian and 5 points for a 'good' one. Teian points can be accumulated and traded in for products listed in a popular retail store catalogue. For 186 points – the equivalent of 37 'good' suggestions – one can, for example, purchase a Bulova wall clock. If a person amasses 10,000 points, they can be turned in for a CAMI car.

Each month the Company president personally awards some department the teian cup on the basis of the number of suggestions submitted. At the end of each year individuals with the highest teian (implemented) point totals receive plaques and cash awards: 375 points gets a bronze plaque and $100; 525 points is good for a silver award and $300; 700 points is worth gold and $500. The year's top ten teian submitters receive a platinum plaque and $1,000. Five of these people are selected for a two-week study trip to Japan.[4]

New incentives for handing in teians continue to appear, giving the programme the appearance of a workplace lottery. Teams with excellent teian records are treated to free pizza at the end of the month. Team recognition dinners are awarded. At the end of each month in the stamping department the person with the most teians gets the use of a Tracker for a weekend. Teian points can now be exchanged for a microwave oven which is placed in a team rest area.[5]

EVALUATION OF THE PROGRAMMES: COMPANY STATISTICS

The reports of finalists in the QCC competition were remarkable for their technical acuity, thoroughness and projected results. These outstanding presentations, however, were not typical. Managers told us that the great majority of suggestions (from both programmes) do not have cost-reduction implications, many dealing with safety issues or making the workplace more comfortable. Moreover, it is undoubtedly true that of the cost-reducing suggestions, only a handful have any significant impact on costs. Despite this, the Company claimed the approval rate was in the high 90s, and in 1990 CAMI reported it saved $10,840,121 from the ideas of its employees.

Local union activists expressed scepticism about CAMI's reported savings from suggestions. For example, they told us the prize winning QCC suggestion from stamping described above turned out to be a dud. Central to this proposal was a modified cutting edge of the trim die. Initially, the adjustment worked, but when the operation reached the required speed the cutting edge broke repeatedly. We were also told that CAMI's announcements of cost savings arising from suggestions are based on projections rather than on calculations of savings after a period of time, say a year.

CAMI claims it does not measure the success of the suggestion programmes by their economic return. When asked about calculating the effectiveness of the programme, one manager said there is no cost or quality measure of success; the only criterion is the degree of participation. He explained:

> This comes from the president, and I think it's pretty good counsel . . . you want to try to get people to feel that their ideas are worth something, and it's very easy to say 'no' all the time. So when you get a suggestion that might not be acceptable, what is a way that you can find so that you can make it acceptable, because that way a person will continue to participate and feel good about that.

If we use the company's criterion of effectiveness – degree of employee participation – the programmes appear as an unqualified success. There were 149 QCCs and 1,230 employees registered as circle members between May, 1990 and April, 1991. In 1990, 106,451 suggestions were submitted for an average of 68 teians per person per year (a monthly average of over 5 per person). Management claimed to have implemented about three-quarters of these teians and another one-fifth were approved or under evaluation.

KAIZEN OUTCOMES

At CAMI kaizen aims at a moving target (continuous improvement) and one that is firmly fixed in Japan. On our first visit a manager boasted that staffing levels of his area were approaching the lean levels of Suzuki's plant in Kosai, and he was determined to surpass them. A team leader described the emulation process:

> We know how many people it takes in Japan. Say we've got four and everything is working well. They [management] come to me and say: 'This time we're going to try it with three.' We [the team] talk about how to do it with three, and if the team says that's okay, then it's okay.

Another team leader discussed the relationship between kaizen, line speed and peoples' jobs:

> We pretty well have an outline of how many people are supposed to be at each work station and how many people are supposed to be on each team. Sometimes we might try and

reduce steps in a particular job . . . because over an entire day production will be higher if your steps are less and in some cases the production associates won't have to go through so much, they won't get as tired in a full day. Everybody in the team is interested in that. If they create less steps and make the job easier, then your time is more productive. Let's say they were to speed the line up or speed the process up – if you had fewer steps it's going to even out.

In the early stages of our research, before production reached its peak and as new lines and systems were being developed, there were a series of 'leaning' or kaizen periods when teams were involved in industrial engineering tasks – reducing idle time, re-balancing jobs and sending redundant workers to other teams. On our third and fourth visits we learned of intense kaizening and workload increases accompanying the introduction of the 1992 models. This was especially true with the addition of the so-called 'soft shifts' on the truck line. There wasn't enough production demand for two full shifts working at full staffing levels, and there was too much demand to allow for only one shift. This prompted a reassessment of job standards and staffing levels. It was decided to reduce the number of workers per shift and to increase the work-loads of each worker. A time study expert was hired to evaluate the jobs for the soft-shift change. This individual timed jobs throughout the plant, resulting in a further 'leaning' of the work process. A team leader described, with some consternation, the activities of this industrial engineer:

> He actually came to the floor and he did a time study of all the teams. . . . He does it with a stop watch . . . they already have figured out how much time it takes for a movement, so all he does is write down the part and then he'll circle a little number on his sheet for degree of difficulty of moving that part. And then all he does is he consults a chart and tells you how much time it takes for a human being to go like that.

This development and others suggest the kaizen process cannot, and never was intended to, rely entirely on ideas emerging from the shop floor. QCC agendas theoretically are set by workers, but we learned of substantial management involvement in the themes pursued by the circles. And during our second visit to CAMI we were told of roving kaizen teams comprised of non-union personnel. One such team tried and failed to eliminate one person from a workteam in assembly, but they did manage to increase the workloads on most of the jobs. According to one member of the workteam, 'they kaizened everybody'. This 'left a bad taste in everybody's mouth' and caused morale problems. The team complained there was no time at all between one job and the next and insisted they needed another person. Of the 14 workers on the team, 4 victims of repetitive strain injuries (RSIs) were going for ice and 1 was off on Workers' Compensation.

In the above cases the objectives of the kaizen process were realized. In other instances the outcomes were not so one-sided. Some teams have been able to use kaizen to make work easier and less stressful. On our first visit to CAMI we observed a work station in welding that was particularly heavy. On our return the team, operating as a QCC, had eliminated the job and saved an extra thirty seconds for themselves. Workteams, especially in the assembly area, have used QCCs to achieve increases in the rate at which they rotate jobs. As a result, it is now common in assembly for workers to rotate jobs within the teams every two hours. A team in assembly formed a QCC and managed to unburden some of their jobs. They also proposed that their workloads be further reduced and one person added to the team when an impending line speed increase is implemented. Five team leaders from the truck line 'kaizened one job per team' to create an off-line sub-assembly area to allow workers to periodically rotate off the more physically demanding main line. These cases indicate that kaizen, which has the company defined goal of cost-down, can be appropriated by workers to achieve workers' objectives.

But there were developments that exposed the vulnerability of gains made by workers through kaizen and clearly expressed the conflict between empowerment building and the economic objectives of the kaizen process. On our third visit to CAMI we discovered that management had unilaterally eliminated the off-line sub-assembly positions and incorporated the jobs back into the teams on the main truck line.

Another setback involved what had become a common practice at CAMI – teams redistributing their work tasks between jobs to free up a position to carry out off-line duties. The jobs, known as floaters, were incorporated into the team's rotation schedule and were intended to offer workers a break from the main line. But increasingly the practice at CAMI is that management transfers workers from teams with floater positions to other teams or areas in response to staff shortages. So workers on teams that took on added work to create off-line positions got stuck in their line jobs, risking further injury, with little else to show for their kaizen efforts. A local union leader related an incident on the car line.

They kaizened their area . . . to create a floater among the team. The guy was moving around, helping everybody, un-packaging stuff, and then the company turned around and started taking the person away when there were headcount problems. The team busted their ass to create the position within the team to make it a little easier for themselves. And then as soon as they did it the company started fucking them by taking it away all the time. And the team exercised its right to refuse unsafe work a couple of times as a result of that.

In this instance the work refusals succeeded in getting the floater returned to the team.

EVALUATION OF KAIZEN ACTIVITIES: VIEWS FROM THE SHOP FLOOR

When we probe beneath the surface of the Company statistics on kaizen involvement by listening to voices from the shop floor, a more sobering picture of the participation programmes emerges. Only a minority of team leaders we talked to wholeheartedly endorsed the suggestion programmes. One enthusiast reported his team had 40 circle meetings over a 12-month period. He proudly described how a QCC transformed an operation that once took two workers one hour and now takes one person 30 or 40 minutes. Another team leader said: 'Speaking for my team, we know where the true sense of security lies and that's in how this place runs. If we're going to compete with Ford and Chrysler that's how you do it [by eliminating waste through QCCs and teians].'

Some team leaders appear to be sold on the idea of suggestion programmes but believe CAMI's are poorly conceived. A common criticism is that there is too much emphasis on quantity and not enough on quality. As one team leader complained, 'We have people who hand in 50 teians a month, and once you start looking at them closely they're ridiculous, stupid.' This sentiment was echoed by a team leader who said: 'I write maybe one every three months. There's other people who write 80 a month, but they're stupid ones. . . . It's always been like that. If you say, "put the

164

garbage pail over there" you get 50 cents, so they do it, right?' The following exchange between this team leader and the interviewer sheds light on what happens at some circle meetings and workers' reasons for participating.

Q. What do you do with the QCCs?
A. Mickey Mouse things.
Q. Only Mickey Mouse? Why do you have them then?
A. It's the money [$1 per person per meeting]. It's like the teians.
Q. So what do you talk about at QCCs?
A. Like I said, we do stupid ones, like changing team names. That's to up the morale.
Q. Who sets the agenda in QCCs?
A. We don't. They have an agenda that's already set. But we don't follow it. We have a meeting, write the meeting up and that's what they get for their QCC.

This individual revealed that his team holds circle meetings on company time but management is told the meetings take place during lunch hour.

Another team leader denied that anything gets accomplished with QCCs:

> To tell you the truth, if we had to go through QCCs to solve everything, we'd be back in the Dark Ages. It just takes too long. People aren't willing to give up their lunch periods, you know, more than once a month. You don't get much accomplished in a half an hour.

In the union newsletter CAMI was criticized for buying pizzas each month for teams whose members turn in five teians apiece. This, the article maintained, only generates absurd suggestions:

> The buck for these teian and pizza extravaganzas must stop. We are all familiar with the outrageous management-approved teians, such as rotating a garbage pail, removing the dead fish from an aquarium, or everyone's favourite: If it's a hazard, tape it. This has driven our fellow workers to write dozens upon dozens of the most stupid teians imaginable in an effort to milk the system.

The solution: greater monetary rewards for good ideas. 'Any idea that really reduces costs or prevents accidents is surely worth more than a slice of pizza.'

The majority of team leaders and local union leaders were critical of, or uninterested in, the suggestion programmes. One viewed the QCC programme and particularly the contest for the teian cup as creating divisions within the workforce. One disillusioned team leader told us that a suggestion to remedy a problem with an assembly component took two years to be acted on. Another team leader expressed concern only with production. In his opinion, teians make no contribution to this task:

> Three-quarters of them [his team] are from assembly, and I think they came up here with a bad attitude. They won't hand in teians. They won't do exercises. . . . Nothing's said to them as long as they do their jobs.

When asked about QCCs, one team leader remarked:

> We don't do any because we hated them. It's like exercising in the morning. We stopped. We said, 'Sorry, no more unless you're going to pay us for it'. They [management] tried to kick up a bit of a stink about it, but we just kept saying, 'You're not paying us for it. It's our free time.'

A local union official viewed the outcomes of the suggestion programmes as beneficial only to the Company:

> This empowerment, when it's cost saving or quality problems, okay, but when it's human problems, a comfort issue, whatever, there's no empowerment. It's one-sided. That's the bottom line.

The union local has stepped up its criticism of CAMI management and the company's failure to live up to the enlightened values it professes. In the union newsletter the president of the local wrote: 'We've all heard about those who kaizen out a job from their teams, and then find they are overworked.' He warned the membership:

> to be wary of how easy it is for management to fill up the time we save with our improvements. This sort of continuous redistribution of work costs us jobs, and eventually puts such a burden on us that we risk injury from trying to work too quickly, forgetting about safety. . . . If you can figure out a way to do something in less time, keep your secret within the team. This is your time, you've earned it.[6]

In an issue of the union newsletter there appeared a poem warning that teians only benefit the Company and can eliminate jobs. The poem ends with the following message:

Every time we write a teian,
We only do their work.
Smarten up I say
Don't accept their JUDAS PAY!

How do production workers relate to the suggestion programmes? In round 1, 56 per cent of workers in our sample said that they belonged to a QCC and a remarkably high 82 per cent reported involvement in the teian programme. By our second visit people had less time to spend writing up teians or attending meetings because the plant was running at full capacity. In round 2, participation in the QCC and teian programmes dropped to 41 per cent and 69 per cent respectively. Since round 2, circle involvement has remained fairly constant at around 40 per cent, but there has been a continuous erosion of support for the teian programme (only 45 per cent by round 4).

Growing disenchantment with teians was also shown by answers to the question, 'Do you think everyone should (participate in the suggestion programme)?' In the first round 56 per cent of the respondents thought everyone should hand in teians. This percentage dropped sharply to 27 per cent in round 2, and by the final interview only 17 per cent felt everyone should participate.

There is little doubt that by comparison with participation rates in North American auto plants, including transplants, CAMI could legitimately boast, even by round four standards, that its suggestion programmes were an overwhelming success (cf. Florida and Kenney 1991). However, statistics on sheer numbers of participants do not reveal workers' motivations for their involvement. Is participation related to a sense of empowerment and commitment to CAMI or is it reluctant, half-hearted or cynical?

When asked in the first round, 'Is there any pressure to participate in QCCs?', 40 per cent replied 'yes'. One worker said her team was paid $1 for attending QCC meetings during lunch, and 'if you're not there, there is trouble'. Participation, workers told us, was considered in personal appraisal sessions. A worker said that when the line goes down you have a choice – attend QCC meetings or clean the area. Team leaders and area leaders were cited as the source of the pressure.

The above question was changed in round 2 to ask only *those who participated* in QCCs why they did so. By round 2 and thereafter reports of pressure declined substantially; only 11 per cent in round 4 attributed their QCC involvement to pressure. The decline in pressure to submit teians reflects local union and union newsletter assurances that participation is purely voluntary and that the union will stand behind those who refuse. In addition, the union's clarification of the team leader role and its insistence that team leaders not assume managerial duties, which would include pressing participation among workers, undoubtedly contributed to an easing of pressure.[7]

In rounds 2 and 3 roughly one half of the respondents *who participated* in QCCs said they did so because 'they are a good idea' and just over one third chose 'other reasons'. In the final round QCC participants were less likely to attribute their involvement to the circles being a 'good idea' (35 per cent) and more likely to choose 'other reasons' (over one half). We asked these *participants* what they had in mind when they said QCCs were a 'good idea' or what their 'other reasons' were. In round 2, 54 per cent said QCCs solve real problems, like rotating or rebalancing jobs or making them easier or safer. In round 4 only 31 per cent provided this rationale. In round 2 slightly under one third said they participated because there was nothing else to do or just to go along with the team. As one worker said, 'I'm sitting at the table playing cards and it [circle meeting] happens to go on around me.' In the last two rounds no more than 15 per cent gave this 'just happens around me' type of explanation. In round 2, 15 per cent of participants attributed their QCC involvement to the cash and prizes of the programme. In the final interview, these extrinsic rewards were the most frequent reason advanced for QCC involvement (56 per cent). There was, then, a clear shift in workers' rationale for participating from one based on the conviction that QCCs solve real problems to one that implies calculation rather than commitment or, as one worker put it, 'using the system'.[8]

That nearly one third of QCC participants in round 4 said the circles solve real problems reflects that at times QCCs were being used to achieve objectives important to workers, like balancing workloads and frequent job rotation. Rebalancing and rotating jobs are accommodations to increasing line speed and workloads, but CAMI's goals were not uppermost in the mind of the worker who said, 'we used it (QCC) to force the Company to rotate us'. Workers, then, were using a participatory programme ordinarily employed by firms to increase production and cut costs to implement changes that have no direct cost implications and make work less onerous.

This raises the question whether such results are departures from, or consistent with, the purposes for which participation was established. The rate at which line jobs are being rotated may not have been anticipated by the Company, but it appears that CAMI is prepared to implement suggestions that benefit workers as long as they do not conflict with cost and production goals. Job rotation facilitates production by reducing monotony (hence greater alertness and care) and perhaps repetitive strain injuries (RSIs). This is a win-win outcome. However, there is reason to believe that involving workers in balancing workloads is part of CAMI's game plan – a dimension of the kaizen process. Consider the previously mentioned example from the kaizen report book, which suggests that workers' participation in line re-balancing is orchestrated from the top, part of a strategy to continuously reduce necessary labour time. Workers, then, are drawn into a pre-planned exercise, the goals of which, they are led to believe, they have had a hand in formulating.

However, workers' participation in, and consent to, the reduction of necessary labour time are being undermined by the Company's policy of operating with a lean, bare-bones workforce, one example of which is the removal of floaters. This leaves CAMI the sole beneficiary of the revamped work practices and produces more cynical attitudes toward participation, kaizen and the Company.[9]

The marked decline in workers' commitment to CAMI revealed by our surveys, is reflected not only by the erosion of support for the suggestion programmes but also by increasing scepticism of the overall kaizen process. During our first visit to CAMI kaizen did not seem to be an issue. On return visits there were increasing signs of concern. One worker defined kaizen as 'a polite way to get more out of us'. Another worker said she regretted kaizening (eliminating) a job from her line. And in our final visit when we asked workers in the sample, 'which best describes CAMI's efforts at reducing waste and increasing efficiency?' 61 per cent chose 'working harder' over 'working smarter', 92 per cent chose 'reducing' over 'increasing' jobs, and 90 per cent said 'a more demanding' rather than 'a more comfortable' workpace. These figures reveal workers have few illusions about kaizen.

CONCLUSION

While kaizen and the suggestion programmes have enlisted a high but declining level of involvement, workers' reasons for participating are not, for the most part, grounded in a commitment to CAMI. If workers do not regard participation in teian and QCC programmes as empowering experiences, these programmes can hardly be expected to commit workers to CAMI and its objectives.[10] The limited sense of control associated with CAMI participatory mechanisms is based on a realistic assessment by workers. QCC and suggestion programmes are implemented by management for management's purposes. Even though CAMI's programmes appear to be more flexible than most, they remain firmly under management control. Like other participatory programmes in North America and Japan, CAMI's give workers a voice but not a vote. Workers can make suggestions, but the disposition of these suggestions is entirely in the hands of management.[11] Of course, workers can join together to pressure management to accept their recommendations, as has sometimes been the case at CAMI, but this is a manifestation of informal power that takes determination, solidarity and organization to put into effect. Management's capacity to determine the disposition of suggestions, in contrast, ordinarily is taken for granted, automatic and effortless.

CAMI can claim to have been partially successful in enlisting workers' cooperation in the participatory programmes, but kaizen is a contested process fraught with contradictions. Workers have on occasion shaped their participation in ways that facilitate the achievement of workers' ends. The continued viability of kaizen and the suggestion programmes may depend on CAMI remaining flexible enough to permit the programmes to operate in this fashion. To delimit the themes that can be legitimately taken up by workers would in all likelihood render the management-defined purposes of the programmes so transparent that only the most enthusiastic yoshers would continue to participate. And if suggestions beneficial to workers are repeatedly negated by CAMI's bare-bones staffing policy, more graffiti like that on a whiteboard in the assembly area – 'GET OFF YOUR KNEES. THIS IS A TEIAN-FREE ZONE' – is likely to appear, and current participation levels will in all likelihood continue to decline.

What, then, can we say about JPM's contribution to reunifying conceptualization and execution? CAMI does encourage workers to use their brains and knowledge to reduce costs and raise productivity, but workers have always possessed such production wisdom or 'trade secrets'. What distinguishes CAMI from traditional auto plants is not the intelligence of its workforce but its systematic efforts to appropriate this knowledge to realise the company's objectives. The type of worker involvement afforded by the kaizen process at CAMI (not to mention standardized work and 'multi-skilling' that takes the form of rotating easily learned, repetitive jobs) allows for only limited modes of conceptualization. Cost reduction, not human development, is the goal of kaizen. This and the absence of opportunities for continuous training, learning and skills development, in conjunction with a hierarchical control apparatus (thinly veiled by an egalitarian facade), marks CAMI as a company that has made no genuine movement toward the reunification of mental and manual labour. To generalize from the results of a case study is always risky, but we have seen no hard evidence in the JPM literature that contradicts our conclusions on this point.

Acknowledgements

This project was funded by Labour Canada and the Canadian Auto Workers Union (CAW). The research was conducted by a team of two CAW researchers from the national office, three local CAW officials and two academics. In addition to the authors of this paper, the research group consists of Steve Benedict (CAW local 112), Alan McGough (CAW local 27) and Herman Rosenfeld (CAW local 303).

NOTES

1   We spent one full week at the plant at four regular intervals between March 1990 (prior to full production) and December 1991. At each of the four visits we interviewed a randomly drawn sample of 100 workers, 10–15 team leaders and 10–15 managers. Schedules consisting of both fixed-choice and open-ended questions were administered to the workers. Interviews with team leaders and managers were open-ended and most were taped. While the same workers were interviewed each time, the team leaders and managers often changed. All employees were interviewed on Company premises and in Company time. Another major component of our study was the repeated observation of work stations on the shop floor. This allowed us to track changes in the labour process over the two-year period. As far as we can determine, this is the first study of a Japanese or joint venture plant in North America to systematically draw information from a

randomly selected sample of workers and to have such unrestricted access to the shop floor.

2   Monden (1983: 126), chronicler of the Toyota production system, believes the real purpose of many suggestion programmes is to cultivate company loyalty and pride among employees. He maintains that the primary goal of Toyota's suggestion programmes, however, is to tap shop floor knowledge, although the Company, Monden says, is not oblivious to the psychological import of these programmes. Employers' attempts to cultivate committed workforces, of course, are not peculiar to the Japanese. This was an objective of the North American corporate welfare schemes and employee representation plans which appeared in the late nineteenth and early twentieth centuries, as well as of the human relations studies conducted by Elton Mayo in the 1920s and 1930s at the Hawthorne Works in Chicago. In 1948 an influential experimental study by Coch and French helped persuade 'progressive' executives of the link between worker participation and commitment. The study found that prior consultation with workers muted their resistance and committed them to heavier work loads. The manipulative thrust of the study is suggested by its title, 'Overcoming resistance to change.'

3   The term 'yosh', the equivalent of the hoorays of a high school cheerleader, could occasionally be heard being shouted by teams during pre-shift calisthenics. At CAMI Company oriented workers are known as 'yoshers'.

4   The individual in charge of CAMI's teian programme recently was sent to Germany to set up a similar programme at GM's Opal plant.

5   Using microwaves as an incentive was inspired by skilled tradesmen, who brought their own oven into the plant. Management objected, but the workers persisted. Instead of continuing to contest this issue, management appropriated the idea and incorporated microwaves into the teian incentive system.

6   To advise workers to keep their ideas to themselves is an explicit violation of the CAMI–CAW contract, which commits the union to supporting continuous improvement activities (kaizen).

7   The role of team leader is a contentious one, the target of a tug of war between the company and the union. After heated discussion of this position at a well attended union meeting, the local produced a union handbook for team leaders which was 'intended to be used as a guide by all team members' and which was designed to help team leaders in performing their functions and be 'good union members'. The handbook stresses that the team leader is a unionized worker who is 'a technical adviser', not 'a personnel manager'. The great majority of workers want to replace the current practice of managerial selection of team leaders with elections by team members. The local plans to push this issue through collective bargaining when the current contract expires. It is important to note that the CAMI local, a unit of a national union that has publicly questioned JPM, is building on the shop floor a collective force that can defend and advance workers' interests. The union presence is viewed by workers as necessary, and the union culture has already influenced the

manner in which JPM operates at CAMI. Whether it is helping to shape the role of team leader or assuring workers that they can with impunity refrain from engaging in activities like kaizen and suggestion programmes, the union has made a difference.

8   Michael Burawoy (1979) would interpret playing the system in this manner as having the effect of generating consent among workers. Workers who perceive they are making decisions, however limited, acquire a sense of empowerment that obscures their subordinate position in the workplace, and this binds them to the Company and its objectives. It is our impression that workers who used the system to achieve their ends were under no illusions about their subordinate position, and they expressed little or no commitment to CAMI.

9   Over the two-year research period we witnessed growing worker disillusionment with CAMI. Confirmation of this came from a 'commitment scale' constructed from seven items of the worker interview schedule. In round 1 the percentages of workers whose scale responses indicated 'high', 'medium' and 'low' commitment to CAMI were 28, 32 and 41, compared with 1, 9 and 80 in round 4. This sharp decline took place in spite of the Company's aggressive efforts to develop in workers an enterprise consciousness through selective recruitment, ideologically loaded training, participatory programmes, and an egalitarian exterior.

10 Our surveys revealed that most workers' sense of empowerment is limited or non-existent. When there is some degree of felt empowerment, it takes the form of being able to make small-scale adjustments to one's immediate job or work area or to perform a job in one's own way. Only a handful of workers who felt empowered to some degree attributed this to the teian or QCC programmes.

11 Even Lincoln and Kalleberg (1990: 14), who are advocates of participation and JPM, admit that QCCs 'diffuse responsibility and commit workers to organizational decisions without producing significant alterations in the governance structure of the firm'.

REFERENCES

Berggen, C., Bjorkman, T. and Hollander, E. (1991) *Are They Unbeatable? Field Trip to Study Transplants in North America*, University of New South Wales, Australia.

Burawoy, M. (1979) *Manufacturing Consent: Changes in the Labour Process Under Monopoly Capitalism*, Chicago: University of Chicago Press.

Coch, L. and French, J. R. P. (1948) 'Overcoming resistance to change', *Human Relations* 1 (August): 512–532.

Dohse, K., Jurgens, U. and Malsch, T. (1985) 'The social organization of the labour process in the Japanese automobile industry', *Politics and Society* 14: 115–146.

Florida, R. and Kenney, M. (1991) 'Transplanted organizations: the transfer of Japanese industrial organization to the US', *American Sociological Review* 56 (June): 381–398.

Lincoln, J. R. and Kalleberg, A. (1990) *Culture, Control and Commitment: A Study of Work Organization and Work Attitudes in the United States and Japan*, New York: Cambridge University Press.

Monden, Y. (1983) *Toyota Production System*, Norcross, Georgia: Industrial Engineering and Management Press.

Parker, M. and Slaughter J. (1988) *Choosing Sides: Unions and the Team Concept*, Boston: South End Press.

Robertson, D. and CAW Research Group on CAMI (1992) *Japanese Production Management in a Unionized Auto Plant. Final Report to Labour Canada*, North York, Ontario: CAMI Research Department.

Robertson, D., Rinehart, J. and Huxley, C. (1991) 'Team concept: a case study of Japanese production management in a unionized Canadian plant', Paper presented to the Annual International Labour Process Conference, Manchester, England.

Robertson, D., Rinehart, J. and Hickley, C. (1992) 'Team concept and kaizen: Japanese production management in a unionized Canadian auto plant', *Studies in Political Economy* 39 (Fall): 77–107.

Turnbull, P. J. (1988) 'The limits of 'Japanization' – just-in-time, labour relations and the UK automotive industry', *New Technology, Work and Employment* 3 (Autumn): 7–20.

Womack, J., Jones, D. and Roos, D. (1990) *The Machine that Changed the World*, New York: Rawson & Associates.

6

UNDERSTANDING THE TRANSFER OF JAPANESE MANAGEMENT PRACTICES

The Australian case

Vagelis Dedoussis and Craig R. Littler

INTRODUCTION

The literature on Japanese management has tended to focus on core employees in Japan's primary-sector enterprises. Consistent with this research focus, is the adoption of a unified model of Japanese management and the implicit assumption about its applicability to all segments of the workforce. However, the Australian data suggests that the practice of human resource management in over-seas Japanese firms involves substantial variations from the above-mentioned model. For instance, welfare practices are poorly developed, remuneration is based on prevailing market rates rather than seniority, semi-annual bonuses are practically absent and the involvement of local employees in the decision making process is minimal. This is in sharp contrast with the development of company welfarism, seniority-based remuneration including substantial bonuses and an emphasis on employee involvement in decision making in the standard, core model of Japanese management.

In the light of these research findings, it can be argued that the relationship between local employees and overseas Japanese firms is defined by a different model of management. This model is characterized by the limited internalization of labour markets which is especially evident in the case of smaller size firms and white-collar employees. The limited internalization of labour markets may be partly attributed to the small size of many overseas Japanese enter-prises – though this is only part of the story. The development of internal labour market procedures by smaller firms in Japan does not take place to any appreciable extent. Thus, the behaviour of smaller size overseas firms appears to be consistent with the broader, home country pattern, except that these organizations are multiunit multinationals. The limited internalisation of labour markets for non-Japanese, white-collar employees reflects the underutilization of their skills and expertise in Japanese multinational corporations. That is, there is very little need for the implementation of internal labour market procedures among local white-collars as they are hired in order to perform specific tasks and not as generalists like their Japanese counterparts.

The limited internalization of labour markets in overseas Japanese firms does not, however, preclude the introduction of certain human resource management practices which can offer advantages to the organization. For example, job rotation, internal training and lack of demarcations, practices associated with the model of Japanese management defining the relationship between core employees and large-scale corporations, are found in many bigger size Japanese manufacturing subsidiaries. This suggests that management aims at a cost-minimization utilization of the overseas workforce, precluding the introduction of certain high cost practices such as seniority wages, company welfarism and tenured employment which would increase costs and reduce organizational flexibility.

Thus, we argue that the relationship between local employees and overseas Japanese firms can be defined by a peripheral model of Japanese management. Underlying the peripheral model is the lack of long-term commitment to the host country by Japanese multinationals. Japanese corporations hive off labour-intensive activities to subsidiaries and subcontracting firms. In the context of the globalization of production and the overseas expansion of Japanese subcontracting networks it may be anticipated that production activities in any one host country will continue to be carried out as long as conditions remain favourable from the viewpoint of the parent corporation. This however means that the commitment of the subsidiary firm to the host country is substantially lower compared with the parent company in Japan which is subject to the dual influence of ownership and employees' interests (Aoki 1990).[1]

The lack of long-term commitment to the host country, where labour-intensive activities are carried out, is associated with the decentralization of human resource management. In this way the management of heterogeneous segments of the workforce in the multinational corporation becomes easier while a more privileged employment structure can be maintained in the parent companies. The decentralization of human resource management leads to the exclusion of the local workforce from human resource management

(HRM) practices such as the development of an internal labour market and the development of an intensive socialization process which underlie the standard core model of Japanese management. This, in turn, means that human resource management practices among local employees in overseas Japanese firms differ significantly compared with human resource management practices which are known to prevail among core employees in parent companies. This conclusion changes the nature of the transferability argument.

METHODOLOGY

The research reported in this paper was based on an intensive set of case studies, eight in number, conducted over the period 1986 to 1990. The firms were Canobolas, Hoya, Lachlan, Matsushita, NEC, Nippondenso, Sanyo and Toyota operating in Australia. All of the firms were in the manufacturing sector: there was no attempt to deal with the services sector. Complete details of the methods of investigation can be found in Dedoussis's PhD thesis (Griffith University 1991; see especially chapter 5).

The focus of the research was HRM and industrial relations practices in the case study firms. As a consequence, it was not the intention to examine just-in-time systems, accounting practices or inter-firm relations. We are aware that a complete description of the Japanese model of management would involve a consideration of these factors. In addition, this paper focuses on structural characteristics given our concern to elucidate an ideal type. There is no attempt to deal with the level of social action.

The peripheral model of Japanese management

The differences in human resource management practices between Japanese firms in the home country and overseas, as suggested above, reflect differences in the nature of parent companies and overseas subsidiaries. That is, parent companies are subject to the dual influences of ownership and the interests of core employees. However, the interests of employees do not exercise any critical influence in the case of overseas subsidiaries, given the absence of long-term commitment to host countries. In other words, overseas subsidiaries can be considered simple profit maximizers rather than entities seeking the fulfilment of the interests of a variety of stakeholders as in the Aoki model. Consequently, human resource management in overseas subsidiaries will be characterized by the introduction of low cost practices which can offer immediate and distinct advantages to the organization. High cost labour practices, such as tenured employment and seniority based remuneration which aim at securing the long-term presence of a loyal and committed workforce, need not be introduced to subsidiaries. A basic rationale for the peripheral model of Japanese management is cost minimization in the context of well-developed external labour markets. It is a fallacy to suppose that Japanese managers wish to totally transfer 'Japanese management practices', even assuming that they have a clear conception of such a model. The rhetoric is very useful (it produces a long line of good recruits), but the practice can be expensive.

The key elements of the peripheral model of Japanese management defining the relationship between local employees and overseas Japanese firms are indicated in points 1–12 below. It is divided into two sets of factors: first employment practices which entail high administrative and labour costs. Many of these factors are commonly emphasized elements of a Japanese model of management. Our argument is that they are either absent in a peripheral model or very limited. Second, there are a set of employment practices which entail low administrative and labour costs: these are central to a peripheral model.

High cost practices (if present)

1 Few welfare benefits.
2 Limited or non-existent bonuses offered to local employees. This may imply that seniority is not important in the direct remuneration system.
3 Extensive induction programmes absent or minimal, especially for white-collar staff.
4 Job security is highly variable and is more rhetoric than substance. Security of employment depends on the market performance of each firm and is generally higher in large-scale firms and in firms experiencing growth. Reductions in employment levels take place whenever adverse economic and business conditions exist.
5 Direct recruitment of young, manual workers, because socialization benefits outweigh training costs. External labour market recruitment of experienced, white-collar and technical workers, because training costs are too high, especially given unpredictable labour turnover rates.

6 Following from 5, internal training for blue-collar workers. Internal training for white-collar and technical workers will be less well developed or absent.

Low cost practices

7 Job rotation. This will vary with scale: in smaller firms there is less scope for job rotation. Job rotation may be less frequent among white-collar personnel, because it is associated with increased training costs.

8 Internal promotion systems. However, internal promotion may become less evident whenever firms experience rapid growth. Seniority is important in internal promotion.

9 Flexible job assignments and work allocated to groups. However, flexible assignments and work allocated to groups may be less evident among white-collar employees.

10 Decision making by consensus and open lines of communications is a common rhetoric. However, as the decision making process is dominated by Japanese managers in contact with Tokyo or Osaka, the actual involvement of local staff is likely to be minimal.

11 Extensive screening processes associated with recruitment as a managerial control process.

12 Small group activities, such as quality control circles and suggestion schemes, are low cost and should be widespread.

As can be seen above, the elements of the Japanese model of management are divided into low cost practices and high cost practices. We would expect that the high cost practices would be minimal or absent whilst the low cost practices would be present and widespread.

The balance of features mentioned above are part of the peripheral model of Japanese management, defining the relationship between local employees and overseas Japanese firms. In the first part of this paper the peripheral model will be assessed against data from the Australian case study material. This will be followed by an assessment of the model against data from other countries as presented in the literature. The issue involved in the latter comparison is whether the Australian data indicate a novel pattern. We anticipated that the Australian data would not be unique, but would be indicative of a specific pattern (perhaps common to East Asia), whilst Western Europe and North America may reflect a different pattern according to the factor characteristics of particular economies.

ASSESSMENT OF THE PERIPHERAL MODEL: THE AUSTRALIAN DATA

This section of the paper considers the Australian case study data in terms of the twelve factors discussed above. For reasons of space we have not attempted to deal with individual cases.

1 Welfare benefits

We constructed an index of thirteen items (from Christmas party to subsidized education) as a measure of the provision of welfare benefits. The data showed that very few welfare benefits (only two or three items) are provided by smaller firms. Employees at one firm expressed the view that the organization offered 'nothing above the minimum' compared to other, Australian-owned firms in the area. By contrast, an extensive range of welfare and fringe benefits has been developed by larger size firms (range of 6–10 items). Nevertheless, high cost benefits, such as non-contributory superannuation schemes or loans at below market interest rates, were not offered by more than one or two firms. Some benefits were confined to managers. Most benefits had been introduced on the initiative of management rather than after pressure or requests by employees and unions. It is possible that the provision of benefits is linked to local labour markets and labour turnover rates, however our data is swamped by the size effect.

2 Seniority-based remuneration

The marginal role of seniority in remuneration is evidenced by the absence of seniority based increments in six firms while such increments are offered on a symbolic basis in the remaining two firms. Toyota is a typical example: in 1986 it had a marginal blue-collar seniority increment consisting of 1 per cent of the commencing wage of apprentices. This was phased out and by 1990 had been abolished. Earlier plans to introduce seniority increments to the salaries of administrative and managerial personnel were scrapped. The bonus system was found in only two firms, although unsuccessful attempts for the introduction of productivity-linked bonus have taken place in several firms. The amount of bonus paid does not exceed a few hundred dollars a year (approximately £90). Allowances in most firms do not exceed the legally required levels. In conjunction with the absence of above award level wages in almost all firms,[2] this suggests that remuneration policies are guided by a cost minimization approach.

3 Induction

Induction programmes are absent in the three smaller size firms. In bigger firms induction programmes exist, but they are brief (2 or 3 days; 4 days at Toyota) and narrow in scope: the focus is on work related issues (e.g. procedures and safety requirements) rather than company history and philosophy. Familiarization of employees with the philosophy and objectives of the organization as part of the induction programme was found at Matsushita only. There was no evidence for continuing induction associated with the development of interpersonal relationships and the socialisation of employees.

4 Security of employment

Improvement in market position at NEC, Toyota and Nippondenso has been accompanied by increase in employment levels while no redundancies have taken place in these three firms. On the other hand, decreased employment levels and redundancies have taken place at Hoya, Matsushita and Sanyo, which experienced deterioration in market position. Redundancies have been widely used to reduce employment levels in several firms. The percentage of regular employees is generally higher among the five bigger size firms. The highest percentage of regular employees was found at NEC followed by Toyota while the lowest was reported by two smaller size firms. There were formal commitments to job security at only two firms (NEC and Sanyo), though one of these (Sanyo) had decreased its labour force by 46 per cent over five years primarily through redundancies.

5 Recruitment

Mid-career recruitment, focusing on the 35–40 age group, is the dominant type of recruitment for both shop floor and white-collar positions in most firms researched. Previous work experience is highly valued by all firms, while formal educational qualifications are mostly unimportant with the exception of candidates for managerial positions in bigger size firms. Blue-collar employees are recruited directly in all firms, while the direct recruitment of white-collar employees takes place in most firms. Recruitment is almost always conducted on a non-periodic basis.

Significant variations from the above pattern exist in the recruitment practices of NEC and, to a lesser extent, Toyota. Recruitment at NEC focuses on the 25–30 age group. Moreover, periodic recruitment on a limited scale has been introduced in the two firms in anticipation of further expansion in business and employment level. Both firms rely on direct recruitment for all levels of employees while the services of professional recruiting agencies are used only in exceptional circumstances such as the hiring of senior managers. Mid-career recruitment is used only when vacancies cannot be filled internally.

6 Internal training

Internal, on-the-job training of employees by personnel dispatched from parent companies in the early stages of operations was reported by all firms. Upon the completion of training programmes Japanese personnel returned home. In all firms, internal, on-the-job training takes place for employees up to the level of leading hand. Although figures were not available in all firms, it appears that a higher percentage of wages/salaries is spent on training by bigger rather than smaller firms. In addition to on-the-job training, which exists in all firms, off-the-job training programmes are found in bigger size firms only. Internal training receives more attention in the two bigger firms, that is NEC and Toyota, as evidenced by the establishment of training sections and the presence of training officers in these firms only. The introduction of new technology as well as changes in production methods and in organizational structure are accompanied by renewed emphasis on internal training. For instance, the continuous training of employees by personnel from the parent company at NEC is made necessary by the frequent introduction of new technology. On the other hand, the shift to small batch production at Matsushita and Sanyo was accompanied by intensive cross-training programmes.

In addition to internal training provided by the firms the existence of training programmes conducted by parent companies was reported. Participation in these programmes is normally open to employees from the level of leading hand and above. The frequency and duration of training trips to Japan vary with the size of firms, with longer and more frequent trips offered by bigger size firms. The percentage of Japan-trained employees is the highest at NEC and Toyota but quite low in smaller firms. Australian managers, hired as specialists, receive little or no training at all. The only exception is a few lectures on Japanese management provided to Australian personnel managers during their visits to parent companies.

7 Job rotation

No formal policies on job rotation exist in smaller firms. Job rotation in smaller firms, left to the discretion of supervisors, is limited as it is usually conducted within the boundaries of the same section/department in an unplanned manner. By contrast, formal policies on job rotation have been established in bigger size firms. Job rotation in larger firms takes place in a planned manner although its frequency varies depending upon the needs of production. The importance attached to the ability to rotate the workforce is evidenced by the emphasis placed by bigger firms on the selection of employees who would not be likely to object to job rotation. Job rotation for white-collar personnel is practically absent with the exception of NEC where limited rotation for younger white-collars was reported.

8 Internal promotion

In all firms the policy is to rely on internal promotion for shop floor vacancies. In bigger size firms the policy is to rely mostly on internal promotion for administrative and managerial vacancies while smaller firms follow a dual policy of relying both on internal promotion and external recruitment for white-collar vacancies. The implementation of policies on internal promotion is significantly affected by the rate of employee turnover. Thus the extent to which vacancies are actually filled internally tends to be lower in firms experiencing high rates of employee turnover. Internal promotion is affected by the trend in employment levels as well. Substantial increases in employment levels are generally associated with lower rates of internal promotion, especially in the case of white-collar vacancies, while higher rates of internal promotion are found among firms where employment levels have stabilized or declined. Some firms reported being under pressure from parent companies to reduce rates of employee turnover as a matter of policy.

The length of service record plays a crucial role in the promotion of both blue-collar and white-collar employees. Internally promoted leading hands and supervisors have an above average length of service record in all but two firms. This is also the case for internally promoted managers whose length of service record is above average with the exception of two firms. Length of service record affects promotion in an additional way. That is, long-serving employees have often received training in parent companies, which enhances their opportunity for promotion. In other words, Japan-trained, long-serving employees have a better chance for promotion than employees with shorter length of service record who are not usually selected for overseas training.

9 Flexible assignments and workgroups

In most firms job descriptions for blue-collar employees are absent, while there is emphasis on the performance of tasks as required by the demands of production. Job descriptions, when in use, serve only as broad guidelines which can help new employees to become familiar with their major function, rather than as limits restricting employees' performance of tasks. In conjunction with the absence of job descriptions there is little regard for functional, and sometimes even hier-archical, demarcations in most firms. Higher wage rates and oppor-tunities for career development are offered to employees who are prepared to become multiskilled and willing to perform a variety of duties. Workgroups are used in larger size firms while tasks are allo-cated to individual employees in smaller firms. Although instances of shop floor duties being performed by managers during periods of busy production schedules were reported in some firms, there was no evidence that either the multiskilling of white-collar personnel had been attempted or that tasks had been allocated to groups rather than individual white-collar employees.

10 Open communications and consultative decision making

Information is disseminated to employees in bigger size firms by means of newspapers/newsletters, regular addresses by senior managers as well as pre-/after-work meetings. The objective of making information available to employees is to enable them to perform their duties more effectively rather than to allow them to have any significant involvement in the decision making process. The involvement of Australian managers, who account for over half of all managers in most firms, in the decision making process is very restricted. Australian managers are mostly involved in the imple-mentation of decisions which are often made without much input on their part.

The actual responsibility for decision making is in most cases in the hands of Japanese advisors who must endorse decisions made by Australian managers. Japanese advisors with the status of manager have the power to block the implementation of decisions taken by Australian managers. This translates into the marginal involvement of Australian managers in the decision making process. Regular management committee meetings, in which issues of a wider scope are discussed, take place in a few firms, while such meetings are infrequent and of limited scope in most firms. Australian managers are excluded from informal after-work meetings where decisions are made by their Japanese counterparts. Bottom-up, consultative type of decision making was found in three firms only. However, it should be noted that proposals submitted by Australian managers are restricted in their scope, referring mostly to operational aspects of decision making. Bottom-up decision making aims primarily at enlisting the support of Australian managers in the decision making process rather than delegating authority to them. In general, the flow of communications tended to be one-way only, that is top-down. There was no evidence that either an 'open door' policy allowing employees direct access to senior management or channels facilitating the multi-directional flow of information had been established.

11 Selection

A distinction in the importance of different selection criteria may be made between small and bigger size firms. While the ability to perform specific jobs is almost the sole selection criterion in smaller firms, adaptability and teamwork ability feature as prominent selection criteria for blue-collars in the two bigger firms, that is NEC and Toyota. Experience in the same or similar type of industry and/or position is important in the selection of managers in bigger firms. This can be evidenced by the hiring of former staff from competitors. In the light of high employee turnover rates in most firms it is unsurprising that the background of candidates is extensively scrutinized by means of reference checks and interviews. The prospect for commitment features as an important selection criterion in most firms.

12 Small group activities

All firms had attempted to introduce quality control circles and most had attempted to introduce suggestion schemes. By the time of the research, such initiatives had collapsed in all three smaller firms. In two of the five bigger firms, Matsushita and Sanyo, small group activities were close to collapse. At Matsushita the participation rate in QCCs was 5 per cent of employees. At Sanyo, QCCs had been suspended indefinitely since 1986. Both Matsushita and Sanyo had been affected by redundancies and reorganization of production. Small group activities were in operation in only three firms although several problems, such as low employee participation rates, short life span of circles, opposition by supervisors and low number of suggestions per employee, were reported. Small group activities were also disrupted by high employee turnover rates.

It is clear from the Australian data that the peripheral model of Japanese management based on the adaption of high cost practices to an environment of well-developed external labour markets is a useful, but not a total, explanation of the situation. Welfare benefits vary by size of the organization; job rotation practices vary by size and blue-collar/white-collar; such practices as QCCs encounter the same problems as they do in other Australian (and British) firms – high rates of labour turnover and lack of commitment.

Data from the Australian case studies summarized above suggest that the size of the subsidiary is a crucial variable affecting HRM practices. In addition, differences in employment practices exist between blue-collar and white-collar employees.

ASSESSMENT OF PERIPHERAL MODEL AGAINST DATA FROM OTHER COUNTRIES

Given that the ideal type of a peripheral model of Japanese management appears to provide some explanation of the Australian pattern, to what extent is this replicated in other countries? Do the data from other countries suggest a pattern which has not been discerned because of the focus on the problematic of transferability and culture? We were not in a position to conduct an international study, so the existing studies were surveyed in order to see what could be gleaned. The existing studies constitute a mixed bunch and our results can only be treated as provisional. In Table 6.1 the peripheral model of Japanese management is assessed against data from other countries. Some of the major sources are listed at the end of Table 6.1.

The survey of existing studies of Japanese owned subsidiaries indicates greater similarities with the Australian data than we anticipated. In a number of areas there is a lack of data and this is indicated above; in other areas there were significant differences indicated in relation to human resource management practices: these are discussed below.

First, the recruitment of experienced, mature-age blue-collars takes place in Japanese firms in Australia. This appears to contrast

Table 6.1 Assessment of the peripheral model of Japanese management against data from other countries

Peripheral model of Japanese management	Data from other countries	Differences/similarities with Australia
Welfare system		
Generally poorly developed	Generally poorly developed	Several welfare benefits in bigger firms. Practically non-existent welfare system in smaller firms
Remuneration		
Seniority unimportant	Seniority unimportant	No difference
Small bonus and few allowances only	Bonus practically absent and few allowances	No difference. Legally required allowances only
Induction		
Absent	Generally absent except few bigger firms	No difference
Security of employment		
Depends on market performance	Sufficient data not available	Depends on market performance
Higher in bigger firms and in firms experiencing growth	'No lay-off' policies in bigger firms	Higher in bigger firms and in firms experiencing growth
Retrenchments in adverse conditions	Sufficient data not available	Retrenchments in adverse conditions
Recruitment		
Non-periodic, direct recruitment of inexperienced young blue-collars	Non-periodic, direct recruitment of inexperienced young blue-collars	Recruitment of experienced mature age blue-collars
Non-periodic, indirect recruitment of experienced mature age white-collars	Non-periodic, indirect recruitment of experienced mature age white-collars	Direct recruitment of white-collars

Table 6.1 Continued

Peripheral model of Japanese management	Data from other countries	Differences/similarities with Australia
Internal training		
Internal training developed for blue-collars in bigger firms	Internal training developed for blue-collars in bigger firms	No difference
Less developed in smaller firms and among white-collars	Less developed in smaller firms	No difference
Emphasized when new technology is introduced	Sufficient data not available	Emphasized when operations and new technology is introduced
Job rotation		
Practiced among blue-collars in bigger firms	Practiced among blue-collars in bigger firms	No difference
Less developed in smaller firms	Less developed in smaller firms	No difference
Less developed among white-collars	Sufficient data not available	Absent among white-collars
Internal promotion		
Generally practiced	Generally practiced	No difference
Seniority important	Seniority unimportant	Seniority important
Less evident when firms experience rapid growth	Sufficient data not available	Compromised when firms experienced rapid growth
Flexible assignments and workgroups		
Practiced among blue-collars	Practiced among blue-collars	Practiced among blue-collars in bigger firms
Absent among white-collars	Absent among white-collars	No difference

Table 6.1 Continued

Peripheral model of Japanese management	Data from other countries	Differences/similarities with Australia
Open communications and consultative decision making		
Common practices in many firms	Developed in many firms	Developed in bigger firms
Minimal involvement of local employees	Little involvement of local managers	No difference; top down flow of communications
Selection		
Applicants' background thoroughly scrutinized	Rigorous selection process. Careful screening of applicants	No difference
Adaptability and teamwork ability important for blue-collars	Adaptability and teamwork ability important for blue-collars	Important in bigger firms only
Specialist knowledge important for white-collars	Specialist knowledge important for white-collars	No difference
Small group activities		
Developed in most firms though some variations with task structure	Generally absent or poorly developed	Developed in bigger firms. Absent in smaller firms and those experiencing difficulties

Sources: The second column, 'Data from other countries', draws on Dedoussis (1991, chapter 4). The major sources used include: White and Trevor (1983), Sethi *et al.* (1984), Takamiya and Thurley (eds) (1985), Kujawa (1986), Fukuda (1988), Oliver and Wilkinson (1988), Shibagaki *et al.* (eds) (1991), Abo (1990), Weiermair (1990), Egon Zehnder (1991), Amante *et al.* (1992).

with recruitment practices in Japanese firms in other countries. In the latter case the focus is on young candidates with no previous work experience. Second, while white-collar employees are recruited directly by most of the firms surveyed, Japanese firms established elsewhere recruit white-collars indirectly. Third, seniority was found to play an important role in internal promotion in the firms surveyed, evidenced by the above average length of service record of internally promoted employees. By contrast, the findings of other studies suggest that seniority is less important in promotion. Finally, there was no evidence for the existence of 'open door' policies allowing employees direct access to senior management as suggested by other studies. Lines of communications may be formally open in the bigger firms surveyed, however the flow is from the top down, while the involvement of local employees in the much vaunted consultative decision making is minimal.

In attempting to explain the differences in recruitment, promotion and communications between the firms surveyed and Japanese companies established in other countries, it is necessary to take into account several factors such as size and sector of firms examined, nature of the local labour market as well as the human resource management strategies of parent corporations. However, details on these factors are in most cases not provided in the literature on the transfer of Japanese management. This in turn imposes limitations in drawing conclusions regarding differences between the firms surveyed and Japanese firms in other countries.

Occasionally it is possible to compare aspects of human resource management in subsidiaries of the same parent corporation operating in different countries. For example, recruitment at Toyota plants in the US and Canada focuses on high school graduates in their early 30s with no record of work in the automobile industry (Wilkinson *et al.* 1989: 18). On the other hand, experienced employees in their late 30s are recruited by Toyota in Australia. Toyota's plants in North America and the new plant in Britain have been established in areas without vehicle assembly traditions; in contrast Toyota Australia (established in 1979) operates on the outskirts of Melbourne where several other auto makers are also established. It may therefore be suggested that Toyota Australia takes advantage of locally available skills by recruiting experienced personnel. This is not, however, possible in the North American plants of Toyota. In the above example differences in recruitment practices may be attributed to the nature of local labour markets.

The assessment of the peripheral model of Japanese management against data from the Australian case studies and data from other countries suggests that there may be a specific pattern of human resource management in overseas Japanese firms – the parameters of which are not yet clear. The transfer of Japanese management practices will not take place in a uniform way across national borders; in particular the relative factor endowments of economies will affect the processes of Japanese foreign direct investment. For example, Australia is not a core manufacturing economy nor a major centre for R&D. Secondly, HRM practices will be the outcome of managerial strategies, and whilst strategy will vary with size, industrial sector and local labour markets, it cannot be reduced to these factors.

CONCLUSIONS

Much of the existing literature on Japanese management sets up a problematic, that of transferability and culture, which closes off basic issues. Management strategies are not oriented to the pursuit of specific models in all and every circumstance. There are costs involved in transferring certain management practices. Consequently the requirements of profit maximization, or adequate returns, imply that high cost practices will not be implemented without clear pay-offs. This argument has been clearly noted in the East Asian literature (e.g. Ofreneo in Amante 1992: 36–7, 55).

If this argument is accepted, then it changes the nature of the transferability debate. Many researchers have noted the apparent 'incomplete' transfer of Japanese management practices to other Western or Asian economies: this has been interpreted as the outcome of cultural barriers, or structural, especially labour market, barriers. Our argument is that subsidiaries in many Western economies should be seen as relatively peripheral, on a par with some subcontractors in Japan, and that a different model of management is applicable. Japanese senior managers transfer as much as they wish, and as little – high cost HRM practices are left at home and low cost practices are put in place over time. It is the peripheral nature of the production system which is key. The transfer of Japanese management cannot be expected to entail complete 'Japanization' – that is, the full scale reproduction of HRM practices which prevail amongst core employees in large scale, Japanese plants. Rather, a different kind of 'Japanization', entailing the reproduction of a core-peripheral dichotomy across national boundaries is more likely to take place.

Thus our next step in the argument was to setup an ideal type – a peripheral model of Japanese management practices – which incorporates the likely balance of managerial strategy. We attempted to do this by establishing a difference between high cost and low cost employment practices. In drawing up the peripheral model of Japanese management we were influenced by the

Japanese literature on large firm/small firm relations in Japan. Clearly, we are not suggesting identical patterns of structuring; Japanese subsidiaries are not necessarily operating as sub-contractors to home firms. Many like Toyota in the USA, will be setup to supply the home market. However, many subsidiaries in the Philippines, Indonesia, Thailand, etc. are acting as sub-contractors, and this may explain why the Asian literature looks at the problem differently.

Discussion in this paper suggests that the findings of the Australian case studies are generally consistent with the peripheral model of Japanese management. But have we just isolated a peculiar Australian adaptation? The overview of research presented in Table 6.1 suggests that the peripheral model may help to explain a wider range of cases.

Significant differences exist between the peripheral model of Japanese management, characterizing practices among the local workforce in many overseas Japanese firms, and the stereotypical model of Japanese management which defines the core workforce/large-scale corporations relationship in Japan. The differences in the practice of human resource management become more pro-nounced when smaller size Japanese firms in Australia are com-pared with large-scale enterprises in Japan. On the other hand, several similarities in the practice of human resource management can be observed when comparing larger size Japanese firms in Australia with large-scale enterprises in Japan. Besides the variable of size, the practice of human resource management in the firms surveyed depends upon the task structure and the type of the workforce, that is, whether reference is made to blue-collar or white-collar employees. Several 'Japanese' practices, such as internal training, internal promotion and job rotation, are found among blue-collar employees in bigger size overseas firms. By contrast, few, if any, Japanese practices exist among white-collar personnel. This higher degree of 'Japanization' of human resource management practices among blue-collar than white-collar employees in the firms studied is consistent with findings on Japanese firms in other countries (White and Trevor 1983; Weiermair 1990). This is, however, in sharp contrast with practices in the home country enterprises where 'Japanese' practices are more prevalent among white-collar personnel than blue-collars.[3]

Comparative methodology is a process of successive contrasts and elimination. What about Australian firms generally? Is there any

Japanese effect or does the local culture swamp the situation? Does ownership matter? A review of the Australian literature suggests the existence of similarities in the practice of human resource management between Australian firms and Japanese subsidiaries of a comparable size. Thus, the internalization of labour markets is negligible or even non-existent in smaller size Australian firms and Japanese subsidiaries. By contrast, features of internal labour markets are present among bigger size Japanese subsidiaries and, to some extent, Australian firms. However, several qualifying remarks are due before the answer to the question whether ownership is a significant variable in the practice of human resource management can be provided.

Looking at smaller size Japanese subsidiaries there is very little evidence of distinctiveness in human resource management practices. Smaller size Japanese subsidiaries and smaller size Australian firms behave in much the same way as far as the practice of human resource management is concerned. Equally, the internalization of labour markets in bigger Australian companies and large-scale Japanese subsidiaries is more extensive compared with smaller size firms. So far, size seems more important than ownership. Wait – let's dig deeper. The limited evidence available suggests the existence of several significant differences in the practice of human resource management between larger Australian companies and large size Japanese subsidiaries. For example, internal training appears to be far more developed in bigger Japanese subsidiaries compared to the largely unsystematic approach to training, characteristic of many Australian companies.[4] Similarly, job rotation in Australian companies, subject to several barriers, is conducted mostly on an *ad hoc* basis. By contrast, the conduct of planned job rotation, made possible by the existence of relevant formal policies, was found in bigger size Japanese subsidiaries. Furthermore, internal promotion, especially for blue-collar employees, is well developed in Japanese subsidiaries. However, internal promotion appears to be the exception rather than the rule in Australian companies associated with high turnover rates for both blue-collar and white-collar staff.

The preceding discussion suggests that features of internal labour markets are probably more pronounced in large size Japanese subsidiaries than in Australian firms of a comparable size. In other words, large size Japanese subsidiaries are characterized by higher internalization of labour markets than large size Australian companies. Therefore, we can conclude that ownership can be considered a significant variable since it is associated with distinct human resource management practices in relation to larger Japanese subsidiaries. Nevertheless, the pattern is not that of stereotypical 'Japanization' and we hope that we have punched a few holes in the conventional Japanization problematic.

NOTES

1 The Aoki model of the Japanese firm (the so-called J-model) is summarized in the three duality principles (Aoki 1990: 22). These are contrasted with the implications of agency theory in relation to the structure of the firm. Whereas agency theory implies the hierarchical decomposition of control, market-oriented incentive contracts and value maximization, the J-model implies lateral coordination, status hierarchies and (and this is the key point here) dual control involving the influence of financial interests and 'employee' interests. 'Employees' in this context refers to core employees. The Aoki model has become very influential in the past few years. However, there are serious problems with the model, though there is not space in this paper to discuss it systematically.

2 An 'award' is a legally binding document setting out the wages and conditions for workers in a particular occupation, company or industry. Awards are set by industrial commissions, either state or federal. Most awards set minimum pay rates and most large, Australian companies pay above award rates in order to attract and keep labour.

3 Koike's work and his notion of 'white collarization' of blue-collar wage systems has led to some misinterpretations. The idea of white collarization was used to refer to the diffusion of some white-collar HRM practices and that this was distinctive from Western practice (e.g. Koike 1988: 24). It did not imply the localization of Japanese management practices to blue-collar workers.

4 This statement relates to pre-1991. During 1991 new training legislation came into force, though the effects are subject to debate.

REFERENCES

Abo, T. (1988) *Nihon Kigyo no America Genchi Seisan* (Local Production of Japanese Enterprises in the US), Tokyo: Toyo Keizai Shimposha.
—— (1990) 'Overseas production activities of Nissan Motor Co.', Paper presented to the Symposium on 'Perspectives for Asian and European enterprises in the 90s: cooperation or competition?', Japan–German Center Berlin/ Euro–Asia Management Studies Association, Berlin, December 18.
Amante, M. S. V., Aganon, M. E. and Ofreneo, R. E. (1992) *Japanese Industrial Relations Interface in the Philippines*, Quezon City, University of the Philippines, Solair UP.
Aoki, M. (1990) 'Toward an economic model of the Japanese firm', *Journal of Economic Literature* 27 (March): 1–27.

Dedoussis, V. (1991) 'Human resource management practices in Japanese firms in Australia', Ph.D. Griffith University.

Fukuda, J. (1988) *Japanese-style Management Transferred: The Experience of East Asia*, London: Routledge.

Iida, T. (1983) 'Transferability of Japanese management systems and practices into Australian companies', *Human Resource Management Australia* 21, 3: 23–27.

Koike, K. (1988) *Understanding Industrial Relations in Modern Japan*, London: Macmillan.

Kujawa, D. (1986) *Japanese Multinationals in the United States: Case Studies*, New York: Praeger.

Oliver, N. and Wilkinson, B. (1988) *The Japanization of British Industry*, London: Basil Blackwell.

Sethi, P. S., Namiki, N. and Swanson, C. L. (1984) *The False Promise of the Japanese Miracle: Illusions and Realities of the Japanese Management System*, Massachusetts, Mass.: Pitman Publishing.

Shibagaki, K., Trevor, M. and Tetsuo, A. (1991) *Japanese and European Management: Their International Adaptability*, Tokyo: University of Tokyo Press.

Takamiya, S. and Thurley, K. (eds) (1985) *Japan's Emerging Multinationals*, Tokyo: University of Tokyo Press.

Weiermair, K. (1990) 'On the transferability of management systems: the case of Japan', in P. Buckley and J. Clegg (eds) *Multinational Enterprises in Less Developed Countries*, London: Macmillan, 1990.

White, M. and Trevor, M. (1983) *Under Japanese Management: The Experience of British Workers*, London: Heinemann Educational Books.

Wilkinson, B. *et al.* (1989) *Japanizing the World: The Case of Toyota*, Paper presented to the APROS Conference, 13–15 December, Australian National University, Canberra.

Zehnder, Egon International (1991) 'US research study of Japanese subsidiaries', mimeo, New York.

7

TRANSPLANTS AND EMULATORS

The fate of the Japanese model in British electronics

Bill Taylor, Tony Elger and Peter Fairbrother

INTRODUCTION

Two rather different assessments are evident in the discussion of the so-called 'Japanization' of British industry. The first, most clearly articulated by Oliver and Wilkinson (1988; 1992), emphasizes substantial moves towards the adoption of Japanese-inspired innovations in work organization, which promise substantial competitive advantages but also involve a much greater dependency of management upon a committed and cooperative workforce. This dependency in turn requires new and increasingly sophisticated personnel and industrial relations strategies designed to achieve and sustain such cooperation. Thus there is a logic of 'Japanization' which runs from competitive pressures, through the recasting of the labour process, to the development of personnel policies designed to minimize the risks arising from such enhanced dependency.

The second assessment, reflected in several commentaries on the notion of Japanization (Ackroyd *et al.* 1988; Elger 1990; Wood 1992), emphasizes the necessarily selective character of any borrowing from Japan, as specific corporate managements, in different social and economic conditions to those faced by the Japanese innovators, seek to adapt elements of the model to match their circumstances. Furthermore, this sensitivity to the selective character of such innovations is reinforced by an appreciation of the varied and changing features of the policies and practices of Japanese enterprises even within the distinctive matrix of the Japanese political economy (Tsuda 1981; Kikuno 1985), and by an increasing awareness of differences in the innovative repertoires of Japanese transplants in such different sectors as motors and electronics (Abo 1990; Milkman 1991; Kenney and Florida 1993).

In this paper we seek to address the issues raised by these contrasting assessments in the light of case studies of two enterprises which must be regarded as central to any process of British 'Japanization': one a Japanese electronics transplant and the other a subsidiary of a British electricals firm strongly influenced by the Japanese example. In examining each of these cases we have sought to assess the character and dynamics of any selective appropriation of Japanese production and management techniques, and in particular to assess how far the relationships between competitive pressures, work organization and attempts to orchestrate worker cooperation correspond to or diverge from those highlighted by Oliver and Wilkinson. The experience of each of these companies will be discussed in turn, drawing on research conducted by Taylor (1993) at Orki's Terebi manufacturing plant in South Wales and by Elger and Fairbrother (1992) at the Central Rebuild factory of Electricals plc in the West Midlands.

ORKI: A LEADING JAPANESE ELECTRONICS FIRM IN BRITAIN

The owner of the transplant, Orki, is a huge Japanese consumer electronics corporation, a long established company who's founding owner is often seen as a folk hero in Japan. Like other Japanese companies which are now well known in the West, Orki had already undertaken considerable overseas investment in materials and parts manufacture in East Asia in the 1960s, in advance of its investment during the 1970s and 1980s in production in the West. As a result, it now has many final assembly manufacturing plants all over the world, and Terebi is one of several in Europe, though the only one making televisions. Thus Orki is a leading Japanese inward investor, and from the vantage point of Taylor's (1993) wider research on such firms, the Terebi site may be regarded as typical of many features of Japanese electrical manufacturing operations in the UK.

Orki, as a Japanese plant located in the UK, exemplified the way in which even a Japanese firm only selectively utilized and drew upon production practices identified with the Japanese model. Not only were they selective, but pivotal components of the model were absent, for there was little evidence of just-in-time (JIT) or of new forms of flexibility at the plant. At the same time, the management sought workforce cooperation in a variety of ways, some of which are associated with the Japanese model.

Changes in the mass market for televisions

As a TV manufacturer, Orki operates in a mass market in which there is only slight differentiation between fairly standard products. Ten years ago this market was characterized by competition between domestic, European and East Asian producers, but now the local producers have disappeared and competition is focused among foreign-owned TNCs slugging it out in the fiercely competitive UK market and increasingly the European market. During the period of the research Orki held 6 per cent of the British and 4 per cent of the European market, and Terebi produced 99 per cent of the TVs for these markets, the other 1 per cent being specialist sets sourced from East Asia. While it remains a mass market, there have, however, been two important changes in this market over the last fifteen years: first, there has been an increased emphasis on customer perceptions of reliability; and second, there has been a proliferation of variants of the basic set. Perceived quality differences have allowed some price differentiation between competitors, as those seen to be of low quality can only compete by lower pricing. Since the Japanese manufacturers have been seen as introducing 'quality as standard' this has allowed them to carry a quality premium, but among themselves they have had to remain price competitive. For this reason those controlling the UK transplants have struggled hard to extend the premium of 'made in Japan' to include 'Japanese made in the UK'.

The product life-cycle of the basic TV set has been extended by introducing a larger range of screen sizes and adding further features such as teletext. The small screen set has become oversupplied and price competition has squeezed profit margins, stimulating companies like Orki to look for more profitable niches, though these markets are themselves becoming very competitive as each company tries to cover all parts of the market. Thus currently TV production is not a profitable business, and Terebi is operated to secure market share rather than high returns, though the parent company hopes for higher returns from some of its future product innovations.

Corporate organization and management control

Orki, like those companies studied by Trevor (1983), had internationalized its production operations largely to overcome state policies of economic protectionism in the West. It is clear from interviews undertaken in Japan that, in line with this, the local plant was not an independent profit centre but formed part of a global strategy under centralized control. Thus Orki has adopted a policy of very close contact between the centre and the local plant, although the exact relationship between them is quite complex. On the one hand, there is less communication between the centre and local plant than there had been in the past, because a new tier in the management structure has been added – a European HQ for all Orki's products in Europe. On the other hand, however, as a manufacturer of TVs the Welsh plant has much more in common in many respects with its parent plant in Japan, and the Japanese managers are in constant touch with their counterparts in that plant. Furthermore, these contacts appear to be reinforced by the career structure of the global enterprise. Few of the Japanese will be permanently located or see their career progression within the European operation, they may feel their careers are threatened by being out of the normal social networking which characterizes the Japanese management development/promotion system, and thus they are likely to be trying to maintain a foothold in Japan.

Alongside the operation of this powerful informal network, within which it is unclear who the individual Japanese manager sees as his overall boss, there is also an explicit structure with defined areas of responsibility. One British manager said of this division of responsibility between Japan and the plant managers: 'targets are set by the Japanese but how we get there is up to UK management', implying significant local discretion; and indeed local managers regard Terebi as essentially British. However a Japanese manager thought of it somewhat differently, for he felt 'generally it is managed here [in Wales] but contact is needed for Japanese know-how, materials etc.', implying a far more ambiguous relationship, though with operational responsibility devolved to the branch plant – and it is notable that workers and supervisors also saw the plant as a Japanese one, controlled and directed from Japan.

These differences of perception highlight the issue of the power relations between British and Japanese managers at the local plant. One manager reported that in the original plans for the UK plant there were only supposed to be ten Japanese managers on site, but there were actually still seventy there, partly because plans changed with an expanded view of the European market. At the same time, the type of expatriate manager had changed, with a shift from those skilled in production matters to those involved in administration.

Another local manager explained that all the Japanese were there as part of their training, learning from the Welsh plant before being given jobs back in Japan.

As for the Japanese managers, both those at Terebi and at the Japanese HQ were deeply critical of British managers. British management was seen as a problem, while workers and even supervisors were seen as being no different from those in Japan. Thus a senior Japanese manager believed that local managers 'have flexible ideas because they do not have to have a loyalty like in Japan', reflecting the widespread perception that local managers called in at Japanese plants to improve their career prospects as they moved between companies, and they were off home to their families at 6.00 p.m. in the evenings rather than socializing with colleagues – though a few of the younger Japanese engineers noted with regret that they could not do likewise. This suggests that corporate HQ preferred to confer the power to control the local plant on the expatriates rather than the locals. However, some local managers were trusted and seemed to be included in the control process. The result was that local managers did much of the work of keeping the plant running but their work was studied and controlled in detail by the Japanese expatriates and the local semi-insiders.

The implications of this allocation of control may be more clearly identified by considering specific areas of responsibility. For example, product design for the European countries is delegated to the local plant, but the overall and basic design – which determines the basis of the production process and is thus a fundamental constraint on any potential local autonomy – is undertaken in Japan because of the high cost of R&D; though there are plans for more of the basic design work to move to Europe. Managers and engineers certainly look to Japan for advice, not only because of the contribution of basic R&D but also because many production innovations are pioneered in the home plants.

However, while it is often assumed that innovation and flexibility is greater in Japan than in Britain, the Welsh plant is in important respects *more* flexible than the Japanese. In the Japanese plant they have more capability for automation under conditions of market and production stability and make 5,000 of exactly the same TV before changing to another type, while Terebi, which serves between fifteen and twenty countries with different designs and sizes of TV, seeks to achieve batches of 1,000. The result is more change than in the parent plant, which requires more flexibility.

About ten years ago, when Japanese plants were exporting TVs all over the world, they had to organize work as Terebi does now, but they now concentrate on their own domestic market. Thus, while some of the techniques developed earlier in Japan are now used in the Welsh plant, the younger generation of Japanese managers also come to the UK to study operations here. It should also be noted, that the change and flexibility of the British plant was not experienced as a positive feature by those who worked there. Workers found it stressful, while managers found that it was detrimental to quality and required more work from them.

The organization of production at Terebi

Of all the major components of a TV – speakers, tube/screen and associated electronics, transformer, case/chassis, tuner and various circuit boards – the Welsh plant manufactured only the printed circuit boards (pcbs), and bought in all the rest which were then assembled into complete TV sets on site. While the final assembly process was primarily labour-intensive, the production of pcbs was substantially automated, though around 25 per cent of the insertion remained manual, in part because some components were awkward to automate but also because new specifications could be handled manually while waiting to be automated. Thus manual insertion also contributed to production flexibility.

The process of automated insertion involved two stages: the automated 'sequencing' of components in preparation for insertion and then the process of insertion itself accomplished by 'pick and place' machines. This involved two main groups of workers, highly skilled programmers who prepared the programmes controlling sequencing and the machine minders who did the more routinized tasks of loading, monitoring the machines and checking the products. The latter usually monitored several machines and found themselves cross-pressured between these different tasks. Manual insertion was organized on the flow line principle long used in the electricals sector (Kelly 1982; Cavendish 1982). This started with a line of operators, generally women, completing a sequence of tightly defined short-cycle tasks along a conveyor operated by the workgroup, and also involves a mechanized soldering process supervised by a technician; manual cleaning and checking at different stages; and final semi-automated checks and adjustments. The final assembly process also involved flow line assembly, though with a variety of bigger components and a

different sequence of quality checks, before final inspection and packing, another conveyor belt task.

Overall, 80 per cent of the shop floor workers were women, and
there was an explicit and visible sexual division of labour, with
manual tasks divided between 'male' and 'female' jobs, and related
distinctions in terms of acknowledged skill. Men tended to do
non-dextrous but skilled work in the assembly areas, while women
were in dextrous and 'unskilled' jobs, and there was also an
historical link between 'men's' work and heavy work, although men
and women worked alongside each other on the lines and some
ostensibly heavy work, such as the final packing using hoists, was
actually relatively light. Within this overall pattern of segregation,
there were quite distinct promotion paths for men and women. In
general, men were more likely to receive rapid promotion to less
monotonous and more skilled jobs. Even where women workers
were promoted, it tended to be at a much slower rate than for the
men. In summary, this pattern of gender divisions was not distinctively Japanese but rather was fairly typical of the sector (Kelly
1982; Cavendish 1982).

Complementing and overlapping with the sexual division of
labour, jobs were graded in terms of the supposed skills attached to
them. The most highly skilled jobs – maintenance of the automated
machines and computers – were undertaken by outside contractors.
Other skilled jobs were done by the established workforce, principally men. This included the maintenance work for other
machines and the lines. Two important jobs which involved a range
of competences were the floaters and reworkers, both done mainly
by women. The floaters covered for the workforce during breaks,
and had to be quite experienced and capable of doing most of the
jobs on their sections, while the reworkers mended complex pcbs
and were familiar with the logics of these boards.

Changing batches

As mentioned earlier, the work at the factory was, in part, organized
around the frequency of batch runs. Supervisors were responsible
for overseeing batch changeovers, ordering components from
stores and arranging the preparation of machines and lines. This
required considerable planning and foresight. To illustrate, the most
common changeover in assembly was the switch from one board to
another. The sequencer, in this case, would be stopped and new
sequencer ribbons prepared and fed into the machine. This was

then followed by a test and preparation period with the production of a few boards, followed by careful checking of both the ribbons and the boards to ensure that everything was in order for a batch run. Not only was supervision heavily involved in this process but so too were the parts feeders and quality checkers.

When there was a model changeover, the parts feeder was also responsible for obtaining new components from the stores and preparing the line for the new model. As with board changeovers, the parts feeders and quality checkers had the responsibility for ensuring the lines were ready for the production of the new model. It was also not uncommon for the supervisors to stay behind during breaks to organize the preparation for these new runs.

The lines were generally kept running during changeovers, but this resulted in periods of high reject rates, sometimes approaching 80 per cent. Thus continuity of production was achieved, but in a way very different from that envisaged in JIT, because poor quality production was allowed through, hopefully to be screened out at one or another of the quality inspection sub-routines. Furthermore, these changes were particularly stressful for some sections of the workforce, especially the supervisors and the quality checkers. Such a pattern of production required both a flexible workforce and a closely supervised production line, again long established features in this sector and elsewhere (Cavendish 1982; Pollert 1981).

Stock control and JIT

Batch production under the circumstances just described required a ready availability of stock, to facilitate smooth changeovers and a more or less continuous production flow, and this meant a variety of stock-holding policies for different components and stages in the production process. There were two contrasting policies in relation to the supply of goods to the factory. For expensive and bulky items, usually ordered from European suppliers, 3 days' stock was held, though given the cost of some of these items (such as tubes) even 3 days' holdings incurred substantial costs which a radical JIT policy would have avoided. For smaller parts, often sourced from South East Asia, 25 days' stock was held in case there were problems with the supply lines, and for some of these parts there was over 6 months lead time between ordering from suppliers and delivery. Such parts rarely vary much from one model to another and are quite cheap, despite the transportation costs, and management sacrificed the flexibility of local supply in favour of cheapness and reliability.

Within the factory, management sought to keep a buffer stock of 3 days between the automated assembly process and the next stage of manual assembly, and 1 to 2 days stock (work in progress) between the various sub-assemblies and the main lines, to cope with uncertainties. Finally they aimed to maintain at least one month's supply of finished packed sets, amounting to 25,000 units, with additional stock in transit to customers. In all these respects this clearly was not a JIT procedure, as it had been intended in Toyota and had been claimed elsewhere.

At the same time Terebi management's relations with British suppliers were considered close and they displayed features of the linkages common in Japan. A European TNC had co-developed a new tube exclusively for Terebi, even though it also made televisions, and almost all of Terebi's tubes came from this single supplier. Though this is not evidence of, or even a move towards JIT, it showed a level of trust, technical cooperation and mutual dependency often flagged up in JIT (Wilkinson and Oliver 1989), and exceptional even among Japanese electricals transplants (cf. Taylor 1993 for comparisons).

Quality

Quality targets set in Teribi seem poor compared to those in the parent plant in Japan. The Japanese manager explained that this was because there were many more parts of the process subcontracted in Japan than in the UK plant. All managers and supervisors agreed that a balance had to be struck between quality and output. These, they claimed, were mutually exclusive objectives, such that almost 100 per cent quality could be assured if one set an hour was produced but not with 100 sets an hour. Nevertheless the plant appeared to be gaining an image of quality among consumers; management were proud of this and attributed similar pride to their workforce. The actual process by which this reputation was achieved was a form of 'management of detail', with daily reject charts for individual workers and a management preoccupation with engineering and monitoring (compare Sewell and Wilkinson 1992, though the regime at Orki was somewhat less draconian).

Nevertheless, there were 'blips' when quality rejects increased, especially with major changeovers from one model to another. Managers and engineers consistently agreed that change was the main cause of quality problems. In order to minimize poor quality it was necessary to first minimize change and second control those points when change was unavoidable. For example, toilet breaks for line workers were arranged in rotation so that the line did not stop. Moreover, the worker had to finish the operation she was doing before being excused. Finally, the supervisor or deputy would keep a special watch on the quality standards of the returned worker.

Flexible employment patterns

The Teribi management sought to cope with fluctuating demand and production requirements in very conventional and traditional ways, through the use of overtime, accepting seasonal patterns of employment and developing strategies to cope with absenteeism. In these various ways the management further qualified the principles of JIT working.

Overtime working was usual at the plant and was allied to seasonal fluctuations in demand. At the end of the season there was some Saturday working which involved repairing faults as well as preparation for the coming week. On average, a third of the workforce worked overtime at any one time. In the busy season the usual pattern was one and a half hours overtime a night, except on Friday, and two hours on Saturday mornings, though levels of overtime in the auto-insertion section were higher to cover expanded output in advance of investment in new machines. The production manager in Terebi commented that volunteers for overtime were assigned to jobs or lines similar to these during the day to avoid time in training. This, however, had a rather drastic implication for production flows: lines did not run where management was unable to obtain sufficient volunteers to staff them.

Terebi's management relies on labour turnover as a form of numerical flexibility. In the slack season leavers were not replaced and in the busy season more were employed. This was a very unsophisticated method of coping with seasonal demand but it had been made possible because there had been more or less continuous expansion of production facilities at the factory. At Terebi some seasonal labour was used as a way of meeting fluctuating demand, with an extra 6.00 to 10.00 p.m. shift – employing mainly mothers and often called 'the baby shift' or 'twilight' shift – introduced for part of the busy season. Again this has been part of the standard repertoire of employment practices in electricals since the war (Beechey and Perkins 1987: 48–56).

Absenteeism was a major problem at the Teribi plant, averaging around 28 per cent, with about 35 per cent among women shop floor workers. Management coped with this difficulty by splitting jobs between fewer workers or by moving people between lines to prioritize certain products. This movement was not liked by either workers or supervisors as it created considerable disruption, both for the workgroup which received the new worker and for that which lost a worker.

Orchestrating worker cooperation at Terebi

Whilst one major strand in the discussion of Japanese enterprises has focused on new production concepts, and especially JIT, another has emphasized the harmonious character of employment relations, underpinned by cooperative decision making, single status and life-time employment. As we have seen, there is little evidence that markedly innovative and distinctively disruption-prone manufacturing arrangements characterized the Terebi site. Indeed, in many respects the factory conformed to a long-standing sector pattern of work routines and employment practices. It was against this background that managers sought worker cooperation and compliance, sometimes in innovative ways.

One method for enhancing worker compliance is to determine the conditions for unionism at the workplace. As with several other Japanese firms, union recognition on the site took the form of a single union agreement, somewhat similar to that developed by Toshiba and the EETPU (Bassett 1987). The single union agreement at Teribi was mainly concerned with issues related to 'total flexibility' and harmonization, and had been signed with the GMB. Since the consumer electronics sector has not been particularly militant the insistence on such an agreement by Japanese management appears to reflect somewhat irrational fears of the poor state of industrial relations in the UK.

Despite the concern to gain worker cooperation, personnel policies had a rather equivocal impact. One Japanese manager emphasized that the object was to recruit locals who had the same loyalty to the Company as themselves, while other managers stressed the permanence of the plant, alluding to the opportunity for life-time employment. Certainly there was no obvious 'frontier of control' governing day-to-day relations in the factory, and little overt expression of conflict. However the contrast between the power and position of the expatriate management and the bulk of the over 1,000 employees makes the generation of any sustained corporate loyalty problematical, and indeed the plant was characterized by high labour turnover. This not only undermined any pattern of life-time employment but also hints at a latent dissatisfaction among workers.

A rather more plausible starting point in explaining this pattern of relative harmony may be sought in the interplay of the sexual division of labour and trade unionism within the plant. The strongly gendered character of the division of labour involved in the manufacture of televisions in this factory has already been underlined, whilst other commentators have also highlighted this feature of both the new and the old electrical industries (Cavendish 1982; Morgan and Sayer 1985).

Management certainly sought to utilize many other channels of communication alongside the union, through such arrangements as periodic management briefings, quality circles, and daily supervisory briefings. Such procedures were generally experienced by workers as information rather than participation exercises, but at the same time many workers felt distant from the union, and saw it as of little importance as a channel of communication. Nevertheless the union had gained what were felt to be good pay increases, a sick pay scheme and other benefits.

Against this background there was a clear difference in the responses of male and female union members. The men, technical workers and operators of the automatic machines, saw the union as marginalized and ineffective, but the women workers, almost all of whom worked on the line, saw it as giving them worthwhile benefits. In part this difference of judgement may have reflected long-standing differences in the expectations which men and women have of this sort of trade union, and in part it appeared rooted in contrasting patterns of job involvement, similar to those documented in some other studies of women workers (e.g. Pollert 1981), since most of the women saw their jobs as of less importance than those of the men.

In a real sense, then, management benefited from the divergent expectations and responses of male and female union constituencies. This pattern reinforced, and was in turn reinforced by, the extent to which the union on site shared the perspectives on the plant projected by Orki management, expressing an understanding of the need for high output and good quality in the face of a competitive market. Unsurprisingly, then, the convener and the personnel department seemed to have close ties, with regular meetings and an open-door policy on the part of the personnel department. However, relations with senior production managers were strained, not least because the convener suspected that he was being discriminated against in job allocation. Paradoxically, the close links with personnel meant that the union accepted the strong discipline imposed on the young female workforce (the average age of the whole plant being 25) over such matters as lateness and toilet breaks.

Finally, both management and workers shared a common perception that Terebi would continue to grow in South Wales, despite modest market penetration, intensifying competition and squeezed margins. This meant that plant closure was not a fear, but that there was something of a premium on retaining such a job. There was a clear sense that this depends on obedience to management and avoidance of appearing to be a trouble maker. Given this, the union ensures fair play, and the personnel department, with its own interests in maintaining a role for itself, responds positively.

Terebi and the problematical realities of 'Japanization'

A central feature of much contemporary discussion of the 'Japanization' of manufacturing in the UK has been the emphasis placed on flexibility and particularly upon JIT. However, the organization of work at this plant suggests that such features cannot be treated as fundamental to the successful operation of Japanese inward investors, let alone their UK imitators. It is true that at Teribi there was a complete flexibility agreement but, except for limited use amongst maintenance technicians, this was implemented in a minimalist and *ad hoc* fashion. The balancing of quality, output and the need for constant change constituted persistent problems for site management. Finally, there is no real evidence of JIT at this or other similar sites, either in the UK or in Japan.

Though these routines of production do not suggest any abnormal dependency of management upon their employees, it is evident that managers have succeeded in maintaining a relatively docile workforce and peaceful industrial relations, despite the latent dissatisfaction (and problems created for management) indicated by high levels of both worker absenteeism and labour turnover. The distinctive features of personnel and industrial relations policies which have been embraced by this and other Japanese owned British electrical manufacturing sites have clearly contributed to this pattern. However, it was not the case that managers were simply able to select a loyal and cooperative workforce, since high levels of labour turnover also necessitated high levels of recruitment. Rather, such high turnover, coupled with the relative acquiescence of the union, meant that management could usually depend on a fairly quiet and compliant workforce.

ELECTRICALS PLC: 'JAPANIZATION' WITHIN A BRITISH MULTINATIONAL

In comparing the operations of Japanese inward investors with any so-called 'Japanization' within UK companies it appears especially appropriate to focus on the experience of workers in an Electricals plc factory, Central Rebuild, since this firm has become identified as an influential exponent of such change. A key figure in the processes of reorganization within Electricals plc has been the group director for manufacturing technology and a notable feature of his proselytizing has been his advocacy of a Japanese influenced approach to manufacturing systems engineering. In particular, he explicitly contests claims that Japanese competitiveness is grounded in cultural peculiarities, more automation or low wages, and thus underlines the relevance of JIT, Total Quality Management (TQM) and other aspects of Japanese manufacturing practice for work reorganization at Electricals (Parnaby 1987c). It is not surprising, then, that this firm has also figured among the key examples discussed by commentators on 'Japanization' in UK manufacturing: it featured in the study by Turnbull (1986, 1988) which gave initial currency to this notion, whilst Oliver and Wilkinson cite it as 'a comprehensive example of the process and nature of "Japanization"' (1988: 44).

Central Rebuild, a wholly owned subsidiary of Electricals plc, presented a very different picture to that at Orki. At this plant there has been a carefully orchestrated attempt to introduce key features of the Japanese model of production. However, this became an ideological justification for change at the plant rather than a basis for the comprehensive introduction of JIT, Total Quality Control (TQC) or kanban. Further, although union relations were recast at the plant in the course of these changes, these were in ways that have not been anticipated in the debates about 'Japanization'.

Corporate restructuring and rationalization

Electricals plc is a large transnational firm based in a major UK city, but with companies in many parts of the world. It has for long been one of the major producers of electrical accessories and components for the motor industry, and during the 1960s it also gained a substantial share of aerospace component production (Wainwright and Elliott 1982: 18–20). Despite a long-term trend towards overseas production and the selling off of several UK plants during the 1980s, Electricals remains a dominant manufacturer of electrical systems for both these sectors. The 1980s saw a major reorientation of Electricals management in the wake of a crisis of profitability which was particularly acute across the automotive component divisions; a result of the increasing vulnerability of both the British car market and the European component supply market to international competition (Vliet 1986: 40–41).

A central feature of the reorientation of corporate management at Electricals was the competitiveness achievement plan (CAP). This procedure was developed from the earlier experience of the restructuring of the aerospace business, and required each division to assess its performance and develop its strategic plans against the yardstick of its most efficient competitor. According to one director, 'the threshold of tolerance of failures was lowered' (quoted in Vliet 1986: 43), and around a quarter of the business units were disposed of during a five-year period.

This tightening of strategic financial control from the centre was accompanied by the development of a more interventionist approach regarding manufacturing methods. The motor manufacturers had responded to tighter competition in the car market by extending product variety and purchasing components for a given model from a wider range of suppliers. As a result of these developments 'the demand was shifting towards small volumes and high variety' (Vliet 1986: 44) while there was overcapacity in high volume flow line production. This was the context in which John Parnaby was appointed group director and allocated a central staff of systems and engineering project managers, with the specific remit of stimulating changes in manufacturing methods. It is reported that direct comparisons were made with Japanese production procedures, and these highlighted shorter lead times, more rapid turnover of stock and above all far fewer indirect staff (Vliet 1986: 44; Parnaby 1987a, 1987b, 1987c).

In the light of such comparisons, corporate level plans for changes in manufacturing management emphasized the reduction of indirect staff and the modularization of production – to 'group people, machinery and processes around materials flows in natural cellular self-contained product units' (Parnaby 1987c: 6) – with the application of a mixed regime of performance measures and control systems combining Western and Japanese variants tailored to the requirements of specific modules. As such the centrally endorsed manufacturing strategy represented a reworking of ideas about modular production, which gave a Japanese gloss or edge to notions of group technology or unit assembly which have had quite widespread currency in batch production engineering since at least the 1960s (cf. Kelly 1982, chapter 5; Littler 1985: 22–24). These ideas were carried into operating units through task forces of consultants and engineering specialists, which had the potential to bypass un-enthusiastic managers whilst coopting local expertise.

Flow-line production and rationalization at the workplace

Before the recent rounds of reorganization, work at the site we studied ('Central Rebuild') had been characterized by quite different priorities to those emphasized by Parnaby. Production had long been organized as a flow of rectification work through a series of specialized production areas, each dedicated to a particular stage of production which involved a sequence of fairly standardized tasks performed under a piecework regime. These stages included the stripping down, cleaning and reclamation of parts; casting, pressing, machining, winding and welding to produce replacement parts; and repair, wiring and reassembly of units. The dominant forms of work organization were clusters of similar machines in the machine shops and flow lines of up to around fifteen operators for assembly work. There was a complex routing of work around different sections and parts of the plant, with priority given to the maximization of machine utilization, whilst a large range of reclaimed and replace-ment parts were held in stock, but stocking levels were only loosely related to demand for specific assemblies. This pattern of work organization also applied to a recent innovation on the site: an experiment in the development and manufacture of a new rather than reconditioned product. Finally a characteristic feature of these long-standing patterns of work organization and work relations in the factory was that the direct production workers on the sections, significant numbers of whom were female, were paralleled by sub-stantial groupings of indirect craft and technical workers, concerned with such service functions as production scheduling and machine maintenance, and these workers were virtually all men.

Nevertheless, corporate rationalization had impinged on the Central Rebuild site well before the full apparatus of competitiveness achievement plans and task forces was brought to bear, most particularly through reallocation of the plant within the corporate divisional structure; through replacements and reorganization among senior management; through the relocation of processes and employees which followed from the closure of other sites in the locality; and finally through a variety of changes in working arrangements. During the early 1980s such modifications in working practices had included the allocation of inspection tasks to operators; the subcontracting of tasks both on and off site; the redrawing of job boundaries to extend overlapping duties; attempts to establish quality circles; and the implementation of a new computerized stock control system.

The wider reorganization of the Electricals Group, coupled with the general manufacturing recession of the early 1980s, engendered considerable anxiety among those working at Central Rebuild, regarding both the vulnerability of specific jobs and the possible sale or closure of the whole business. While the site unions sought to gather information on, and respond to, the range of changes occurring at this and other sites, this climate also afforded some scope for the divisional manager to present himself as the potential saviour of the Central Rebuild works. During this period the joint shop stewards committee (JSSC) at the factory quite successfully resisted non-negotiated changes, boycotting and undermining such proposals as quality circles, tightly policing an unusual agreement to allow a temporary three-month redeployment of workers between sites, and pursuing prolonged negotiations to reach agreements on such issues as new technology. Overall their stance was one of wary cooperation informed by an awareness of the pressures for change across the Electricals empire (union records).

It was against this background that senior management at the factory became increasingly receptive to the centrally promulgated project of modularization. This receptiveness reflected a combination of corporate level pressures and the practical experience of managing the site. The pressures exerted by head office monitoring were coupled with an awareness that other plants, guided by task forces drawn primarily from Parnaby's cadre of engineering managers, had already embarked on work reorganization. Alongside this, management were aware of a continuing shift in the character of production on the site itself, involving the processing of

212

smaller batches of more varied components. Though a trend towards increased variety and smaller volumes was a common experience of automotive component factories in this period (cf. Turnbull 1989), it took a particular form for the business unit we studied. This was because reconditioning, which was the major activity at Central Rebuild, increasingly embraced the stripping and reassembly of a diverse range of equipment initially manufactured by competitor firms, while work involving longer production runs had been lost as it was concentrated at another site. In the words of one of the conveners: 'We were a very high volume factory, but we are not a high volume factory now.'

The practical implementation of modules

The proposals for modularization implied major changes to the established divisions of labour and patterns of job specialization associated with the older production methods, even when, as at Central Rebuild, they were unaccompanied by any systematic implementation of TQM or JIT. In particular a radical reduction in the numbers of indirect workers was envisaged, as some of their functions were virtually abolished (e.g. rate fixing consequent on the dismantling of piecework payment), some were reallocated to direct production workers (inspection), and some were relocated through the deployment of ex-indirect workers into the modules (e.g. machine maintenance). In turn this reorganization involved a change in supervisory responsibilities, signalled by the title 'module controller', while the parallel rationalization and relocation of stock holding involved the reorganization of stores and materials handling with the creation of module based materials controllers.

At Central Rebuild, as elsewhere, the plans for modularization were initially formulated by a task force which began work well in advance of formal discussions with the trade unions. Against the wider background of crisis, management were then able to gain union consent for a pilot project in one area whilst engaged in longer negotiations on proposals for another key area. In this context senior management lavished considerable symbolic attention (e.g. cream buns) and practical resources (especially extended training) on the first module. This enabled them to cultivate a parochial elitism among the pilot workforce which both threatened the cohesion of union organization and allowed management to project this module as an exemplar for other groups. At one stage workers in the experimental module threatened to ignore a JSSC organized overtime ban, but they were pulled into line as a result of a mass meeting (McDivitt 1987: 75). As management policy and union bargaining evolved, however, the spread of modularization across the site also involved a dilution of the original model, though it continued to result in a substantial reduction in the numbers of indirect workers, both through job losses and through the eventual redeployment of some ex-indirect workers into module teams.

The reorganization of inspection and stock control

Given the logic of modularization, a crucial arena of negotiation concerned the reorganization of such hitherto indirect functions as stores, maintenance and inspection. On inspection, for example, site management had made initial proposals to reallocate certain inspection tasks to setters and operators nearly a year before the modularization task force arrived on site. Since such plans were also being pushed at other factories, the responses of the occupational groups involved were coordinated by group-wide union sub-committees for inspectors and for setters, with the latter, less vulnerable, group the more strongly in opposition. Nevertheless, management gained agreement to several pilot projects in the use of statistical process control (SPC) by setters, including one at Central Rebuild, and also threatened to short-circuit negotiations on the training and pay of a new grade of inspector by filling the positions from among apprentices. Against this background negotiations at both group and site level on each of these developments focused on training and payment, and eventually led to a substantial reallocation of inspection duties which meshed in with the process of modularization (union records).

The reorganization of stores was also central to the savings sought by management, and again this was the subject of prolonged negotiations which eventually resulted in an upgrading of materials handlers but also job losses and the relocation of such workers within the modules. The growing diversity of products both to be dismantled and rebuilt had combined with the traditional separation of different stages of the production process to generate an escalating surplus stock of little used parts. In the words of one informant the reorganization of production 'only caught this in a nick of time', as modularization allowed the storage of parts alongside the work area and thus greater visibility of stock holding and a tighter control of stock by the newly defined 'materials controllers'. This development, combined with the computerization of stock control which had been undertaken several years earlier, certainly reduced the levels of stock held, though in the remanufacturing areas these levels continued to be driven by the push of the dismantling process and the variety of products which might need to be rebuilt as well as the pull of rebuilding for warranties and other customer orders. Only in the small new build area which formed the experimental module could the imperative of stock reduction be pursued more systematically, though even here its initial label as the 'kanban' cell could only be justified in terms of a very inclusive rather than strict interpretation of that term.

The impact of competing management priorities

The varied and often somewhat diluted implementation of modularization noted above (and detailed in Elger and Fairbrother 1992) resulted not only from union pressures but also from qualifications to management's own priorities and commitments in the face of persistent cross-pressures and resource limitations. For example, our interviewees suggested that the resources devoted to the training of the pilot groups proved to be deceptive, as management increasingly sought to gain flexibility without off-the-job training by reliance upon workers to coach one another. Furthermore quality control was reported to have remained a source of difficulties: the devolution of inspection to the shop floor did not readily reconcile competing pressures for throughput and quality, and in consequence engineering management found themselves rebuilding a quality department. There was also evidence that the reorganization of work by no means eliminated problems of materials supply, and according to stewards' reports some of the initial experiments exacerbated rather than resolved such problems. Finally a striking feature of the experience of modularization at Central Rebuild was a continuing reorganization of the relationship between management control and responsibility: according to one respondent 'the module leaders never had the autonomy they thought they would have', and a later designation of business units involved a further redefinition of the role of the module leader.

As a result of such contingencies, the biggest change for most production workers was not the reorganization of work tasks but the abolition of piecework. This had significant ramifications for working arrangements since it removed the anxieties about loss of earnings which had previously accompanied movement between machines, and it ended the wrangling over job times and waiting time which had earlier distorted the visible pace of work. Despite this, the work process in many modules remained quite specialized and routine with job rotation confined to adjacent tasks shared by a small group of workers, for such limited flexibilities appeared to meet management's production requirements. As one union activist remarked: 'what we thought was that it would be flexibility within the module [but] somewhere along the line it got lost and it became flexibility in the module within the cell you work in.' Nevertheless it was widely agreed that the somewhat increased task flexibility and focused expertise which was associated with modularization facilitated the processing of a diverse range of reconditioned product lines (there were 110 different types of heavy duty starter motors for example) and was generally welcomed by workers. One respondent described the change as 'a shift from theoretical bulk build to the reality of batch to batch production'.

Workplace unionism and industrial relations

Against this background union initiatives also influenced the uneven pattern and process of change. In part such union responses were aimed directly at protecting workers' earnings and expertise through the negotiation of change, and in part they represented efforts to rebuild and sustain workplace union organization and thus retain some effective leverage as modules were implemented. The union agenda in the lengthy negotiations which surrounded the implementation of the first remanufacturing module at Central Rebuild covered rates for the job, methods of job selection, job specifications, manning levels, training and negotiating spheres of influence; and the first three issues proved particularly contentious, especially in regard to materials handlers and remanufacturing craftworkers. The materials handlers eventually resorted to an overtime ban and successfully gained skilled status, whilst accepting redesignation as materials controllers. The opposition of skilled maintenance workers was more prolonged and of particular importance in modifying the early development of modular production, as this group initially effectively refused to be redeployed into the modules as manufacturing craftworkers. However, job losses amongst works engineers eroded the leverage of this group, and eventually agreement was reached on the relocation of most craft workers, though a residual group was retained outside the modules whilst a depleted tool room was constituted as a discrete module.

As for union organization, the leading convener described how they 'went through a period when the unions took a right dive', partly as a result of losing experienced stewards, partly because of the reduced significance of the craftworkers who had earlier played a pivotal role, and partly because it took time for the stewards to adapt their operations to the new modular arrangements. Nevertheless, steward representation was rebuilt within the modules through the joint efforts of the manual unions, working relationships between manual and white-collar unions were extended, and the JSSC was reorganized as a smaller but still effective body.

Overall, then, the pattern of industrial relations at Central Rebuild during the 1980s was characterized by substantial continuities. There was no dramatic recasting of the relationships between management and trade unions or management and workers, as workplace union organization continued to constitute the key channel of communication and negotiation. Rather, there was a more subtle reorientation of relationships which was primarily a response to an increasingly hostile commercial environment (a compound product of general recession and growing unemployment, intensified sectoral competition and ruthless corporate restructuring), though it was also influenced by the changed centre of gravity of trade unionism on the site which resulted from the process of modular reorganization.

Throughout the 1980s site management sought to maintain an effective working relationship with the unions, despite a widely perceived tendency towards 'management by edict' and occasional instances of acting tough, usually in dealing with staff rather than the shop floor. Whereas at some other Electricals plants the JSSC was effectively marginalized at critical moments during the programme of corporate restructuring and work reorganization (cf. Turnbull 1986, 1988), at Central Rebuild the pressures on the unions were more oblique. The translation of central corporate priorities into CAPs, the visible erosion of job security which accompanied the relocation of work and plant closures elsewhere in the city, and the pursuit of voluntary redundancy and redeployment coupled with spasmodic short-time working at Central Rebuild itself, all heightened the uncertainties and insecurities of workers and unions at the factory, and this formed the background to any discussions of the survival and restructuring of the site. Nevertheless site management remained in prolonged negotiations over the implementation of some aspects of the main task force recommendations, and under pressure made concessions on the grading of certain jobs. At the same time managers utilized several opportunities to emphasize the attractions of the new working arrangements and to establish precedents for later changes. Thus they began to reorganize production arrangements and to test out some of the possibilities for task reallocation in advance of any detailed agreements; they self-consciously utilized outline agreement to a pilot project to dramatize their commitment to change and their appreciation of worker cooperation; and once modules were being introduced they sought to buttress their credibility by improving the working environment and encouraging the module controllers to 'communicate with' their workers.

In this context union activists were often appreciative of the efforts of plant management to strengthen the commercial viability of the factory, while remaining sceptical about many of management's claims and hence wary about the specific impacts of restructuring on their members. They also remained sensitive to the importance of rebuilding effective workplace union organization where it had been weakened, whether by job losses among hitherto key occupational groups or by complacency among some of the more favoured modules. The signs of such reorientation and union revival were most evident among the manual workers while remaining much more provisional among supervisory and technical staff. Among the manual workers the JSSC had evidently made quite effective efforts to ensure steward representation in each of the modules, and furthermore leading stewards were consciously giving their own distinctive inflection to management's new rhetoric about the central importance of the 'direct producers' which, in the context of modularization and a sexually and ethnically diverse workforce, underlined the potential for an increasingly inclusive and cohesive shop floor unionism. Such an orientation will evidently be of increasing importance since Electricals plc has now devolved wage bargaining to workplace level.

In what sense 'Japanization'?

A critical assessment of the strategic policy of the top management of Electricals plc could portray the Japanese referents of their centrally orchestrated programme of work reorganization as primarily a presentational gloss on established tenets of manufacturing systems engineering, especially those associated with

group technology or cellular batch production. This would, however, be an incomplete account, in that the Parnaby proposals also
represented an organizationally more far reaching extension of
those tenets in a form which meshed in with the comparisons being
made through the CAPs.

From the vantage point of Central Rebuild, however, any emphasis
on the Japanese model appears more significant as an ideological
legitimation than in providing a repertoire of organizational innovations, and this is true in three related respects. First, the main thrust
of organizational change at this workplace focused on modularization
and the reduction of indirect staff, in ways which owed relatively little
to the specific methodologies of JIT, TQC and kanban extolled by
Parnaby. Second, the results of such work reorganization have generally been rather more mundane than those celebrated by exponents
of 'Japanization'. Finally, though these ideas appear to have been
of considerable importance in consolidating a mission for the cadre of
engineering managers within Electricals plc in the circumstances of
corporate crisis, their role in the 'politics of the factory' is less clear. At
Central Rebuild they were only one facet of a wider argument about
competitive survival and plant viability, and the changes in industrial
relations which have characterized this site are broadly comparable
with those reported for other manufacturing concerns during the
recessions of the 1980s (Jones and Rose 1986; Terry 1989; Elger 1990)
rather than being marked by a distinctive dynamic of 'Japanization'.

This is not to suggest that management–worker relations and
workplace trade unionism are being remade on precisely the same
organizational and occupational terrain that they occupied in the
1960s. Indeed, we would highlight increased job rotation and task
enlargement and, more crucially, the redivisions of labour between
direct and indirect workers as aspects of modularization which will
have a continuing impact on employment relations and forms of
workplace trade unionism at Central Rebuild. There is, however,
little sign so far that modularization at this plant has dramatically
changed the character of management dependency upon the workforce, or given birth to anything resembling enterprise unionism.

It will have been evident from our account that, as a primarily
remanufacturing site Central Rebuild occupies a distinctive market
and production niche even within the Electricals plc automotive
division. In this sense we cannot claim any simple typicality for the
site. In some respects, particularly the extent of variety and small
production runs, it might be regarded as a particularly appropriate

test case for notions of Japanese forms of adaptable production organization. In other respects, especially the competing pressures of cost effective recovery of parts and production to order, it may be regarded as a more difficult terrain for 'Japanization'. Nevertheless it remains an apt example of some of the practical ramifications of a process of restructuring influenced by the rhetoric and some selected components of the practice of Japanese management techniques, and their implications for middle management, for office and shop floor workers, and not least for workplace trade unionism.

CONCLUSIONS: ARRIVALS AND DEPARTURES FROM THE JAPANESE MODEL IN BRITISH ELECTRONICS

The first conclusion which we draw from our case studies concerns the highly selective and uneven character of the practical implementation of such new production concepts as JIT and TQM in manufacturing in Britain. At Electricals plc, a well known exponent and exemplar of 'Japanization' among British electrical companies, innovations at site level have been very variable and selective, with most of the changes at Central Rebuild more intelligible in terms of longer standing approaches to work reorganization, such as unit assembly and group technology. More importantly, the pattern of work organization at the Terebi plant of the Japanese multinational Orki reveals little evidence of many of the ostensibly key components of the Japanese model of production. In particular there is no JIT at Terebi (or at any of the other Japanese TV plants studied by Taylor), suggesting that this aspect of the organization of production cannot be treated as an invariable feature of the way in which successful Japanese manufacturers operate or, hence, as a core component of the 'Japanization' of manufacturing.

We have, of course, only discussed two specific case studies, whereas Oliver and Wilkinson based their positive assessment of the late 1980s (1988, now mildly qualified in 1992), primarily on survey evidence. Nevertheless, despite the specificity of our case study examples, we believe that our findings suggest the need for considerable circumspection in drawing strong conclusions from such surveys. As a preliminary point it should be noted that the response rates for the questionnaire surveys reported by Oliver and Wilkinson were understandably very low, especially for the emulators (for whom it was 18 per cent in 1986 and 14 per cent in 1991), severely compromising the representativeness of the responses. Our case study findings also highlight the problematical relationship between the accounts provided by enthusiasts at plant or corporate level and the specific character of the real changes taking place on the ground. At Terebi and other similar plants it was commonplace for initial management contacts to claim that such features as JIT operated on the site, only to find that in practice this was not the case. Similarly at Electricals plc the extremely coherent programmatic strategy for manufacturing change developed at the centre had a distinctly Japanese gloss, but the practice at site level was a good deal more varied and mundane.

It should also be noted that in the 'Japanization' debate various facets of flexibility have become subsumed as elements of JIT. Although some form of work based flexibility is a prerequisite for the effective operation of JIT, pressures for enhanced flexibility often take a quite conventional form. In the case studies it was clear that elements of changing job content and structure were being undertaken within Electricals plc and some parts of Terebi. However, whether this constituted a move towards practices commonly witnessed in Japan remains doubtful. Certainly in Terebi, British engineers and Japanese managers agreed that such flexible practices were not new but were standard long before the Japanese made televisions in Britain. At Electricals plc, meanwhile, management had negotiated modest increments in flexibility, both in relation to the modules and other aspects of employment relations, but it would be difficult to argue that any radical changes were involved.

This underlines the importance of established repertoires of work organization and restructuring, both within national economies and internationally within sectors, as influences on the ways managers select ideological themes and practical techniques from the wider management discourse about Japanese models. At the same time it points towards the role of this discourse in lending some coherence and legitimacy to management initiatives, particularly among managers themselves, though less obviously among employees. The Electricals case study underlines the complexity of the relationship between ideological threats and appeals and the practical restructuring of production, for the apparent fusion of these aspects at the level of corporate policy formation coexisted with rather more separation at site level. At corporate level the apparently Japanese-inspired programme of work reorganization helped to mobilize a distinctive role for engineering management in the wider process of corporate rationalization and restructuring. However, in what we observed at plant level Japanese models played only a subsidiary role, both in the practicalities of work reorganization and in ideological appeals for commitment and cooperation. In the latter context it was a relatively minor component of a forceful claim that the survival of the workplace depended upon radical restructuring which necessarily involved job losses and low pay increases as well as modularization.

The shallowness of much of the rhetoric of Japanization is revealed particularly sharply when it is recognized that the transplants are not necessarily more innovative than the so-called emulators. Not only did Terebi, the UK site of our inward investing Japanese Company, reveal little evidence of the new production concepts which have often been identified with 'Japanization', but Orki's Japanese factories were likewise bereft of such features. This clearly raises profound questions about the benchmarks against which any processes of transnational transmission of management approaches might be measured.

Furthermore, the actual pattern and range of work organization at our research sites suggests that we should give renewed attention to the persistent dilemmas which beset the organization and reorganization of production, without being beguiled into accepting the argument that the competing imperatives of throughput, cost and quality are on the brink of reconciliation. In addition we need to look more closely at the specific market relations and sectoral conditions which have influenced the very uneven selection and adaptation of new management models and initiatives.

Another implication of our analyses is that, while the Japanese example is widely used as a metaphor for the orchestration of organizational loyalty and commitment, the manufacturing of a (problematical) consent in these particular workplaces was more directly facilitated by rather different and more widespread features of employment relations. At Terebi the gendered division of labour constituted a crucial point of departure for the institutionalization of a rather passive form of trade unionism, and the entrenchment of an ethos in which any dissatisfactions could be represented as an individual failure to deserve employment on the site. At Central Rebuild, by way of contrast, the orchestration of a qualified cooperation depended heavily on a sense of the continuing precariousness of the whole factory against a background of marked sectoral and regional recession. Thus even the specific ideological role of the Japanese model must be carefully contextualized, as for example Garrahan and Stewart (1992) seek to do in their case study of Nissan.

Finally, these reflections on the logics of production organization and reorganization and the dynamics of employee and industrial relations in our two case study plants lead us to question the influential model of dependency relations and the organization of consent developed by Oliver and Wilkinson. In our research we have found little evidence of profound changes in the organization of production and resultant patterns of dependency, but instead we have identified rather mundane variations on longer standing patterns of dependency and control. This also implies that, whatever limited contribution Japanese-inspired organizational devices and rhetorical appeals do make to the organization of compliance and consent, they should not be understood primarily as responses to a peculiarly heightened dependency of management upon their workforces.

Acknowledgements

Taylor's research on Orki was conducted as part of wider research for his Science and Engineering Research Council funded PhD, and additional findings come from his two-year period studying industrial relations in Japan, funded by the Japanese Ministry of Education (Monbushō). The study of Electricals plc forms part of wider research into the restructuring of employment and union renewal in the West Midlands linked to an Economic and Social Research Council financed project on workplace management and local trade unionism conducted by Fairbrother (Ref. ROOO 23 2006).

REFERENCES

Abo, T. (1990) *Local Production of Japanese Automobile and Electronics Firms in the United States*, Research Report of the Institute of Social Sciences 23, University of Tokyo.

Ackroyd, S., Burrell, G., Hughes, M. and Whitacker, A. (1988) 'The Japanization of British industry', *Industrial Relations Journal* 19, 1: 11–23.

Bassett, P. (1987) *Strike Free: New Industrial Relations in Britain*, London: Macmillan.

Beechey, V. and Perkins, T. (1987) *A Matter of Hours: Women, Part-time Work and the Labour Market*, Cambridge: Polity.

Cavendish, R. (1982) *Women on the Line*, London: Routledge and Kegan Paul.

Elger, T. (1990) 'Technical innovation and work reorganisation in British manufacturing in the 1980s: continuity, intensification or transformation?', *Work, Employment and Society*, Special Issue 67–101.

Elger, T. and Fairbrother, P. (1992) 'Inflexible flexibility: a case study of modularisation', in N. Gilbert *et al.* (eds), *Fordism and Flexibility: Continuity and Change*, London: Macmillan.

Garrahan, P. and Stewart, P. (1992) *The Nissan Enigma*, London: Cassell.

Jones, B. and Rose, M. (1986) 'Re-dividing labour: factory politics and work reorganization in the current industrial transition', in K. Purcell *et al.* (eds) *The Changing Experience of Work*, London: Macmillan.

Kelly, J. (1982) *Scientific Management, Job Redesign and Work Performance*, London: Academic Press.

Kenney, M. and Florida, R. (1993) *Beyond Mass Production*, Oxford: Oxford UP.

Kikuno, K. (1985) 'Changing environmental conditions and the new look of Japanese personnel management and industrial relations', *Rikkyo Keizaigaku Kenkyu* 39, 2: 1–36.

Littler, C. (1985) 'Taylorism, Fordism and job redesign', in D. Knights *et al.* (eds) *Job Redesign: Critical Perspectives on the Labour Process*, Aldershot: Gower.

McDivitt, W., (1987) 'Module production: Lucas Electrical', in P. Fairbrother (ed.) *From Productivity Deals to Flexibility at Work*, Monograph in Labour Studies, Department of Sociology, University of Warwick, mimeo.

Milkman, R. (1991) *Japan's California Factories: Labor Relations and Economic Globalization*, Los Angeles: Institute of Industrial Relations, University of California.

Morgan, K. and Sayer, A. (1985) 'A "modern" industry in a "mature" region: the remaking of management–labour relations', *International Journal of Urban and Regional Research* 9: 383–403.

Oliver, N. and Wilkinson, B. (1988) *The Japanization of British Industry*, Oxford: Basil Blackwell.

—— (1992) *The Japanization of British Industry: New Developments in the 1990s*, Oxford: Basil Blackwell.

Parnaby, J. (1987a) 'Competitiveness via total quality of performance', *Progress in Rubber and Plastics Technology* 3, 1: 42–51.

—— (1987b) 'Practical just-in-time – inside and outside the factory', The Fifth *Financial Times* Manufacturing Forum, London, mimeo.

—— (1987c) 'The need for fundamental changes in UK manufacturing systems engineering', Advanced Manufacturing Summit 87, Birmingham, mimeo.

Pollert, A. (1981) *Girls, Wives, Factory Lives*, London: Macmillan.

Sewell, G., and Wilkinson, B. (1992) 'Someone to watch over me: surveillance, discipline and the JIT labour process' *Sociology* 26, 2: 271–289.

Taylor, B. (1993) 'Work organisation and management strategy in consumer electronics', Ph.D. Department of Sociology, University of Warwick.

Terry, M. (1989) 'Recontextualizing shop floor industrial relations: some case study evidence', in S. Tailby and C. Whitson (eds) *Manufacturing Change: Industrial Relations and Restructuring*, Oxford: Basil Blackwell.

Trevor, M. (1983) *Japan's Reluctant Multinationals*, New York: St Martin's.

Tsuda, M. (1981) 'Perspectives of life-time employment security practice in the Japanese enterprise', in V. Rus, A. Ishikawa and T. Woodhouse,

Employment and Participation: Industrial Democracy in Crisis, Tokyo: Chuo University.

Turnbull, P. (1986) 'The "Japanization" of production and industrial relations at Lucas Electrical', *Industrial Relations Journal* 17, 3: 193–206.

—— (1988) 'The limits to "Japanization" – just-in-time, labour relations and the UK automotive industry', *New Technology, Work and Employment* 3, 1: 7–20.

—— (ed.) (1989) 'Industrial restructuring and labour relations in the automotive components industry: "just-in-time" or "just-too-late"?', in S. Tailby and C. Whitson (eds) *Manufacturing Change: Industrial Relations and Restructuring*, Oxford: Basil Blackwell.

Vliet, A. van de (1986), 'Where Lucas sees the light', *Management Today* (June): 39–45, 92.

Wainwright, H. and Elliott, D. (1982) *The Lucas Plan: A New Trade Unionism in the Making?*, London: Allison & Busby.

Wilkinson, B. and Oliver, N. (1989) 'Power control and the kanban', *Journal of Management Studies* 26, 1: 47–58.

Wood, S. (1992) 'Japanization and/or Toyotaism?', *Work, Employment and Society* 5, 4: 567–600.

Part III

ADOPTERS, ADAPTERS AND ALTERNATIVES

PROLOGUE

In this part we turn to the activities of non-Japanese companies, and consider the influence of the Japanese model on their production procedures and employment practices in a variety of national settings. Much of the contemporary discussion of Japanization focuses on the extent to which elements of this model have been taken up outside the Japanese transplants, and on the circumstances which have influenced the selection and adaptation of those elements. However, it is important to recognize that the Japanese model (or rather the variant versions of it which have been deployed in the management literature) must contend not only with established ways of doing things but also with alternative models of work organization and employment, themselves drawing inspiration from distinctive patterns of innovation in particular regional or national arenas. Prominent examples would be those drawn from manufacturing in Germany or Sweden, or the model of flexible specialization inspired by developments in the 'third' Italy. Thus the debate about the adoption or adaptation of Japanese-inspired innovations is also a debate about alternative forms of work and employment relations; a debate which concerns both their competitive viability in changing economic conditions, and their attractions for employers, managers and different categories of workers.

The 'Swedish model' has had pervasive and celebrated currency in discussions of national variants of work organization. Anti-Taylorist job design experiments at Saab and Volvo, and strong welfarism and corporatism based on historic class compromises are all part of this distinctive 'model'. In labour process terms, one writer has recently suggested that the more experimental human centred group working patterns at Volvo provide a model, which could potentially be united with certain Japanese technical innovations, to

229

create a hybrid production system which is both efficient and kind to workers (Berggren 1992). Indeed, when the business school world appears to be falling over itself promoting the 'Japanese model', the most telling criticism of Japanese transplant operations from a workers' perspective has come from a Swede, confident in the possibility of an alternative way (Berggren 1993).

But how far are the practices of the experimental plants at Volvo embedded in the company or Swedish society, and how far are they being transferred as 'best practice' by Swedish TNCs? Does the 'Swedish model' represent more of a moment in Swedish history which is now past than an enduring societally specific set of practices? Or does it offer a rival way of organizing work within capitalist relations of production which enhances workers' skills and contributions, combining efficiency with humanity? In Chapter 8 Thompson and Sederblad examine these issues, and especially the stability and diffusion potential of this model under new conditions of global production, which are opening Sweden to international capital and increasing the rate of export of Swedish capital overseas.

The authors explore the origins of the Swedish model and the crisis in Swedish society, as the centralized and internationalized sections of Swedish industry have attempted to escape high costs and other problems by exporting production abroad. What the authors are interested in exploring is the effect of globalization on Sweden, and whether the acceleration in moves abroad, mergers and joint ventures facilitates the diffusion of certain Swedish work organization practices, or rather exposes these international companies to more conventional methods of production. First, they examine the extent to which practices associated with Volvo, especially group working, have spread to other sectors in Sweden and therefore whether we are examining a national or a company model of distinctiveness. This they do through company studies in the chemical and food sectors, which support the case for societal diffusion. They next examine the auto sector or more properly the heavy goods sector, and Volvo's international takeover of Leyland DAF in the UK, and whether any noticeable work organization changes were transferred through this network into British production facilities.

What they conclude is that in Sweden there are currently simultaneous and contradictory processes of transfer of certain Swedish work organization practices, such as group working, through Swedish TNC networks, and the incorporation of dominant Japanese and other

Taylorist practices into Swedish companies through greater international exposure. Berggren (1992: 257) noted how in the case of some Swedish TNCs – Electrolux, for example – conformity to local conditions rather than retention of national practice was the norm. But Thompson and Sederblad, from their case studies, suggest that some of the distinctive aspects of work organization are considered both to give a comparative advantage to Swedish capital and to dovetail into dominant thinking about work, as with group rather than individual systems of work. Nevertheless, through links with international capital – Saab with GM and Volvo with Renault – closure of the more radical experimental factories has occurred, and more conventional labour process control strategies are entering Sweden through these ownership networks. Therefore they conclude that far from the 'Swedish model' acting, in some paradigmatic way, as a systemic alternative to the 'Japanese case', the integrity of the model and the context of its retention and diffusion are moving in contested and contradictory ways. This supports our overall argument against 'national' work organization paradigms in the age of increasing capitalist globalization.

The next two chapters, Bonazzi's on Fiat's Italian auto plants and that by Black and Ackers on a GM auto-components plant in the US, each consider the ways in which work organization and employment relations are currently being recast in specific non-Japanese transnationals, against the background of the increasingly dominant position of the Japanese producers in the international motor industry. They differ in terms of types of enterprise and national setting, and also focus on somewhat different features of management policy, but they share two central concerns. First, they both seek to trace the evolution of management policies against the background of tightening market pressures, and to consider the relationship between the internal dynamics of corporate policies and any 'learning from the Japanese'. Second, they each discuss the extent and the basis of increasing worker and union commitment to the teamworking initiatives which were, in different ways, central to developments in both Fiat and GM.

In Chapter 9 Bonazzi acknowledges the 'cultural influence of the Japanese model' for developments at Fiat, but also seeks to show that these developments followed a distinctive logic and trajectory which must be understood in its own terms. Thus the innovations of the early 1980s involved southern greenfield sites, but were primarily built around a drive for advanced technical sophistication in production, as Fiat management sought to overcome and distance themselves from the conflictual relations which had characterized the older mass production facilities around Turin during the 1970s. Bonazzi argues that the moves towards new forms of teamworking and worker involvement at Fiat were primarily responses to the difficulties encountered in simultaneously achieving the quality and productivity targets set for these high-tech production facilities. In this context managers were undoubtedly influenced by existing debates about a variety of organizational innovations, though the Japanese model was only one of several associated with cellular production, but Bonazzi also stresses management's direct awareness of the limits and potentials of the new plant. Furthermore, the relative freedom to experiment at the greenfield sites led to few *organizational* innovations until pushed by a tightening of market conditions.

Bonazzi also documents a continuing process of experimentation with organizational innovation at Fiat. This involved the development of more general corporate policies, drawing lessons from the experience of the greenfield sites, but also cautious implementation of such policies at the northern brownfield sites. At those sites it was primarily the power of supervisory management rather than union strength which prompted caution, for the position of supervisors had been strengthened after their pivotal role in the defeat of militant workplace trade unionism in the bitter 1980 strike.

Against this background Bonazzi considers shop floor responses to the uneven but widespread implementation of work reorganization at Fiat. First, he emphasizes that workers generally accepted the changes, though they mixed caution with enthusiasm, and increasingly cooperated in suggestion schemes and quality circles which feed their knowledge of the production process into continuing work reorganization. Second, though, he rejects one popular explanation for such developments, namely that cooperation flows from an enhancement of worker autonomy and empowerment, because Fiat workers remain tied to limited, and increasingly closely monitored, work routines. Instead he draws on earlier analyses of work effort and tacit skills to develop the provocative argument that the crucial bases of cooperation and consent were a relaxation of work effort and less authoritarian supervision, as the technical innovations of the 1980s made work 'easier, lighter, more comfortable' as well as 'more accurate, repetitive and restraining'. Where earlier workers would have concealed those tacit skills which allowed them to cope with heavy loads and tightly paced work, they can now share their expertise without fear of loss.

In developing this argument Bonazzi also recognizes that it raises several unresolved questions. Will the experience of lighter and easier work which remains highly fragmented and routinized remain sufficient to sustain worker cooperation? And how far is the relaxation of work effort a permanent result of technical and organizational innovations, or how far might it be compromised by more intense market pressures and the tighter specification of workloads, for instance by reducing buffer stocks? In considering these questions it should also be noted that the recent trend towards increased workplace consultation in Italian industry remains both varied and unstable, while Fiat's moves in this direction have been particularly hesitant, piecemeal and instrumental (Ferner and Hyman 1992: 583–590).

In Chapter 10 Black and Ackers use a case study of the recasting of work organization and industrial relations within one substantial GM components plant to explore the implications of the emergence of management sponsored employee involvement programmes and the resulting spread of joint management–union cooperation in the American auto industry. The innovations in this and other GM plants have taken place against the background of plant closures and concession bargaining, and in this context the UAW has shifted from a relatively combative arms-length relationship with management to commitment to cooperative participation in 'the relaxation of contract enforcement' and productivity building, through what came to be called the joint process (a markedly more cooperative stance than that adopted by the CAW, discussed in Chapter 5).

The case study focuses on the collaborative establishment of new working practices associated with the installation of highly automated equipment in one area of the factory. It highlights the role of joint management–union working parties and team building sessions in the design of new working arrangements; the dismantling of demarcations and job ladders among production workers to facilitate flexible teamworking (though it is also noted that workers often continued to specialize); moves towards cross-craft maintenance in the new area; an emphasis on the flexibility of short runs and quick tool changes, facilitated by automation as well as flexible working; and a reorganization of management control. The latter involved focused financial monitoring, replacement of several layers of management by team leaders, and supervisory oversight of job rotation.

Black and Ackers suggest that such developments have had mixed consequences for workers, but pose major dilemmas for the union. Workers have often gained job security, they have valued being consulted, and some have experienced enhanced job satisfaction. But work intensification has been widespread (driven by a mix of team discipline, low buffer stocks, reduced manning and machine pacing), and the protections offered by the older seniority systems and job demarcations have been eroded. The joint process (JP) has drawn union representatives into the cooperative relaxation of negotiated contract arrangements in the interests of productivity. However, this undermines their traditional sources of leverage over management (via contract compliance), and increases the scope for managers to play off one plant against another. Thus in the US involvement in the pursuit of joint gains further threatens the independent mobilizing capacity of the union, in circumstances where workers may well face new pressures and insecurities.

Chapters 9 and 10 focus on different aspects of work reorganization, for Bonazzi is primarily concerned with the evolution of management initiatives while Black and Ackers address the changing dynamics of collective bargaining, and the influence of Japanese techniques appears more pressing in the American case. But despite these differences there are also significant parallels, for both studies stress that teamworking and suggestion schemes held some real attractions for workers, but also that these were much more mundane than many of the optimists imply. Furthermore, they both recognize that any gains were interwoven with new pressures and constraints, and that trajectories of change remained somewhat provisional and precarious, open to fresh twists in response to both bargaining capacities and wider market conditions.

The final two chapters, by Humphrey and Postuma, turn to a rather different setting in which to investigate the influence of the Japanese model – that of Brazil, a large developing economy with a substantial manufacturing and export sector, which has been characterized by authoritarian management, employment insecurity, low levels of literacy and training and conflictual labour relations (Humphrey 1982). Humphrey begins by laying out a paradigmatic contrast between older forms of mass production and the new Japanese management techniques, and highlights the manner in which the principles, if not the variagated practice, of the latter involve a model of active upskilling and workforce involvement, through the development of workers' capabilities and responsibilities for quality, smoothing the workflow and continuous improvement. It would appear, then, that Brazilian enterprises would find great difficulty in adopting these practices.

However, Humphrey argues that, while earlier experience with quality circles, for example, lent some support to this diagnosis, more recent evidence points to major corporate initiatives in response to the pressures of trade liberalization and state sponsored quality and productivity drives. There has been 'an impressive catalogue of innovations inspired by Japanese management practice', which has resulted in significant productivity and quality gains. Indeed, in some respects Brazilian conditions may have facilitated such moves, through established patterns of worker flexibility and the absence of craft demarcations. At least in some firms this has involved a real commitment to training and to the development of a more secure and involved workforce, though more often the moves have been more partial and selective, sometimes with limited training and little involvement – differences which appear rooted in differing management strategies and the exigencies of corporate size and sector.

Humphrey suggests that in some enterprises this has meant a substantial transformation in management–worker relations, involving an 'implicit exchange' of enhanced skills and job security for greater commitment and cooperation, though on occasion this has been underpinned by initial redundancies or the victimization of labour activists. At the same time such developments have remained markedly uneven, even exceptional, and also vulnerable to economic conditions – the downturn of the early 1990s meant substantial redundancies which compromised this 'exchange' in some firms.

Finally Humphrey considers the wider implications of these changes for the role of the unions and the character of management control in the workplace. He is sceptical of the view that a strengthened union movement has had a direct impact on the development of these policies, for they have been adopted in areas of union weakness and only in a few union strongholds have they been actively negotiated. Instead he suggests that the implementation of these techniques has been informed by management concerns to marginalize unions and pre-empt their adversarial potential. Against this background he notes that, while the implicit contract holds real attractions for workers, there are also signs of an increasingly sophisticated management use of teamwork performance targets, to intensify work and to mobilize peer pressure to discipline workers. Such threats, together with the precarious character of some of the advantages, underline the continuing need for more effective union organization, but perhaps also fresh union strategies, in the future.

In the final chapter Posthuma examines some of these developments in more detail, with particular reference to the activities of the auto-components suppliers. Her evidence emphasizes the uneven process of selective adoption and adaptation of elements from the Japanese model even more strongly than Humphrey. Thus she documents near universal use of statistical process control (SPC), less extensive and more qualified use of QCCs, and only a limited commitment to JIT focused on internal inventories rather than inter-firm relations. This selectivity of innovation reflected a continuing management emphasis on fault rectification rather than the mobilization of worker initiative to ensure zero defects, an emphasis which was reinforced by illiteracy among production workers and by established patterns of mutual mistrust between managers and workers. Such features meant that even where QCCs survived, half had a membership restricted to managerial and technical staff. Finally, management continued to see advantages in retaining substantial inventories, especially in an inflationary economy and as a protection against unreliable suppliers, hence sharply qualifying the modest moves towards JIT.

Thus Posthuma documents a wider pattern of uneven and selective adaptation of specific management techniques, to be set against the more radical and strategic changes of some leading firms. She also emphasizes, however, that within the specific social relations of manufacturing in Brazil, which sustain a supply of cheap and insecure labour while making it difficult to generate positive worker commitment, this piecemeal adaptation of Japanese production methods nevertheless provides significant gains for management. In pointing towards the possible emergence of a distinctive, 'Brazilianized', hybrid of management techniques with its particular ramifications for workers, the labour market and union organization, she once more emphasizes the need to go beyond the ideal typologies of production paradigms if we are to understand the dynamics of work reorganization in different national, sectoral and local settings (see also Humphrey 1993).

REFERENCES

Berggren, C. (1992) *The Volvo Experience – Alternatives to Lean Production*, London: Macmillan.

—— (1993) 'Lean production – the end of history?', *Work, Employment and Society* 7, 2: 163–188.

Ferner, A. and Hyman, R. (1992) 'Italy: between political exchange and micro-corporatism', in A. Ferner and R. Hyman (eds), *Industrial Relations in the New Europe*, Oxford: Blackwell.

Humphrey, J. (1982) *Capitalist Control and Workers' Struggles in the Brazilian Auto Industry*, Princeton: Princeton University Press.

—— (ed.) (1993) 'Quality and productivity in industry: new strategies in developing countries', *IDS Bulletin* 24, 2.

8

THE SWEDISH MODEL OF WORK ORGANIZATION IN TRANSITION

Paul Thompson and Per Sederblad

INTRODUCTION

The 'Swedish model' has been described in different ways by academics and other commentators: as a distinctive system of politics, welfare, industrial relations, labour market regulation or work organization. Whatever dimension is emphasized, it has to be located within the historical development of capital–labour relations. In this sense the formalization of the model is often seen to have been the Saltsjöbads agreement between the central blue-collar union (LO) and the employers' organization (SAF) in 1938. This created an industrial and political settlement between capital and labour which led to a long period of stability under Social Democratic hegemony that lasted until the middle of the 1970s. We will return to the nature and development of the model later, but two points are important for explaining the purposes of this chapter. First, though the model is associated primarily with general social organization, we will argue that it has important work organization dimensions, which become central to its current reconstruction.

If the focus of the model is narrowed down to work organization, then current Swedish practices such as those focused on group working can be seen as a source of competitive advantage. Riegler and Auer (1990: 232) argue that recent changes 'seem to us to be a feature of technological progress where the Swedish automobile industry is clearly in advance of other countries'. This debate sums up the main theme of this chapter with great relevance for the whole volume. To what extent are Swedish patterns of work organization both distinctive and an alternative to Japanese and other practices in the global economy?

Second, Sweden has functioned as a wider workplace and societal model for academics and politicians on the Left in other countries. For example, Clegg (1990) sees it as the major alternative to Japan in a postmodern age. Whereas 'global Japanization' would be based on a core of privileged skilled workers locked into exclusivist patterns of gender, ethnicity and age, Clegg states that Swedish experience offers enhanced skill formation, and a modified workplace division of labour within a wider economic citizenship and encroachment on the rights of private capital. He argues: 'The "Swedish Model" is not culturally specific but institutionally produced. Such developments are institutionally feasible at national levels, despite the increasing interdependence of national economies and their susceptibility to economic factors outside their control' (1990: 233).

This language of national roots, yet international replication strongly reflects a societal effect approach which has emerged through the work of institutionalists (Maurice, Sorge and Warner 1980; Lane 1991). For such writers institutional logics are embedded in societally specific processes which produce stable organizational and employment patterns at national level. Such logics are particularly located in education, training, labour market and industrial relations structures.

Though avoiding determinism and 'one best way' fallacies by stressing the principle of the functional equivalence of organizing logics, comparison is accompanied implicitly or explicitly by evaluation. For example, the comparisons of France, Britain and Germany in the work of Lane consistently favour the latter. The perspective therefore continues to identify 'best ways' in a manner consistent with the search for competitive advantage. This returns us to the arguments of Auer and Riegler, and that of Clegg detailed earlier. However, the weakness of the latter position is that the corporatist arrangements underpinning the traditional Swedish model have, as we show later, been under severe attack at home for over a decade; while internationally the prospects for their replication are clearly very limited.

A 'global' perspective is important. For the great deficiency of the distinctiveness-diffusion framework is that it has tended to consider the workplace solely in a context of national economies and institutions. While work organization and any other feature of the industrial order will always differ from others at a national level, societal institutions are subject to 'external' pressures for change. As Smith and Meiksins observe: 'Institutionalizts seem to forget that capitalist countries are part of a global system' (1991: 12). It is therefore worth spelling out at this stage what might be involved in globalization, using the Swedish economy and organizations as illustrative examples.

GLOBALIZATION

It is widely held that globalization has been a major strategic response of large firms since the 1980s (Ohmae 1985; Bartlett and Goshal 1989; Dicken 1992); reshaping key sectors such as engineering (Edquist and Jacobsson 1988) and high technology (Henderson 1992). Globalization consists of a number of inter-related processes amongst the productive, commodity and financial circuits of capital. Foreign direct investment and industrial reloca-tion have obviously been long-term factors in the international-ization of production. What is newer is the organization and coordination of activities by transnational companies at a global level. Multi-domestic companies and competition with portfolio management of largely autonomous subsidiaries become global when 'rivals compete against each other on a truly worldwide basis, drawing on competitive advantages that grow out of their entire network of worldwide activities' (Porter 1991).

Swedish capitalism has always been export oriented. In recent years there has been a qualitative leap in the shift abroad of Swedish capital in the form of new direct investment such as the rapidly expanding Scandic Hotel group (Thompson *et al.* 1993) and acquisitions that include Zanussi (Italy), White Consolidated (USA), Feldmuhle (Germany) and the UK companies Sealink, Reedpack and Crown Berger. Even in the earlier period of 1970–1976, 3,700 mergers took place (Olsen 1991: 117), and Sweden now ranks as the tenth largest foreign investor and fifth most multinational country in the world, if foreign investment is related to GNP (Blomström 1990: 93).

With a very high concentration of capital, this internationalization has been led by the twenty or so firms who have 2,000–60,000 employees abroad and had 86 per cent of foreign employment in 1985 (Forsgren 1990). Such companies in Sweden and elsewhere are increasingly 'stateless'. Shifts take place away from mere expan-sion of home base through sales and subsidiaries and corporate structures based on centre–periphery relations, to global firms which have foreign based units with group-wide functions in manu-facturing, marketing and other areas. Capital is increasingly mobile and may even move company headquarters from the country of origin, particularly after a series of mergers and acquisitions, pursuing global strategies that owe little loyalty to any spatial location. The year 1990 marked the first time that Swedish firms invested more capital outside than inside the country, with a number of companies such as IKEA moving their head offices abroad (Olsen 1991: 138). At the same time, as the Swedish economy opens up, inward investment begins to match outward capital flows, a process we discuss in more detail later with reference to the motor industry.

Transnationals have not merely led the rapid growth of world trade, but promoted its integration. This includes the erosion of protected national enclaves and acceleration of movement out of mainly domestic markets by particular national capitals. Sweden is a prime example of the latter tendency, a process of course shaped by the small size of that market.

Internationalization also involves financial markets. Not only has the general circuit of finance become truly global in the recent and more deregulated past; there has been a closer integration with the circuit of productive capital. Transnational banks offer new services to multinationals, such as financing acquisitions, management of liquid assets and leasing arrangements. At the same time increasing numbers of banks are subsidiaries of multinationals. It is therefore possible to speak of transnational finance capital in which the two actors, 'are organically linked in their internationalization' (Andreff 1984: 66). In Sweden powerful ownership groups overlap banking interests, notably the Wallenberg sphere whose SEB bank 'holds sway over a federation of more than twenty very large, world class, export-orientated industries' (Olsen 1991: 117). Meanwhile strict exchange controls were relaxed in a general deregulation, resulting in an increased role for the stock exchange and significant outflows of capital. Swedish entry into the EC will accelerate tendencies towards economic, financial and social convergence, even allowing for the uneven progress towards monetary and other forms of union.

At the firm level, mergers, acquisitions, collaboration and joint ventures produce greater internal standardization and enforced compliance of external forces, such as supplier companies. As Haspeslagh and Jemison comment with respect to acquisitions: 'Increasingly long-term competitiveness on a global scale is driven as much by the ability to transfer learning as by economies of scale or scope' (1992: 278).

The latter is part of the important trend towards the more rapid diffusion of 'best practice'. Diffusion of leading management methods has always taken place, for example that of Taylorism. But Smith and Meiksins argue that the more extensive integration of corporate structures noted above, allied to factors such as the internationalization of consultancy, business schools and the market for management literature, are enabling more rapid learning processes. In a global economic and political order part of this process may include 'dominance effects' which result 'in a transformation of particular national patterns of work organization, management and labour relations into universal standards of best practice' (1991: 20). The most obvious example is the spread of lean production techniques associated with Japanese manufacturing, promoted in books such as *The Machine that Changed the World* (Womack *et al.* 1990).

However, as we shall show later, it would be wrong to talk of globalization following single paths such as a transition from Fordism to post-Fordism, or necessarily involving standardization and convergence. Corporate and firm strategies continue to provide sources of economic divergence as well as convergence. The sectoral level must also be considered when establishing patterns of development within globalization. Mainstream business analysis (Kitschelt 1992; Porter 1991) provide useful insights into how there are important variations by sector in processes of industrial innovation and competitive advantage.

In addition, inherent constraints and limits remain at a societal level. These include: organizations using the comparative advantage given by particular national environments; companies attempting to export models and coming up against the constraints of alternative industrial relations systems; different organizing logics within countries and sectors; and firms having to adapt against their will to political and economic environments. It is obvious from these instances that globalization does not preclude a strong role for the state in providing a supportive framework for capital accumulation or bargaining over production and investment decisions. (Jessop 1992)

This section of the chapter has attempted to outline a conceptual framework within which we can understand the development of work organization in Swedish firms in the context of a changing political economy. Our argument has been that globalization is producing significant changes at the level of company and state. What we want to explore is whether the two-way internationalization process is encouraging Swedish firms to 'escape' the traditional institutional conditions, or whether those firms are seeking competitive advantage through exporting societally specific practices. To answer this, we need to focus in more detail on changes in Sweden, utilizing a general analysis of the transformation of the 'Swedish model', as well as case studies of firms at home and abroad.

THE 'SWEDISH MODEL'

The characteristics of the 'Swedish model' can be seen in terms of dimensions and (pre)conditions[1]. There are, as we see it, three central dimensions: work organization, industrial relations and state policies, while the main preconditions involve particular capital formation, economic development, union structuring and political situation. Our focus is on work organization.

Work organization

This can be divided into work design, control structures and employment relationships (Littler 1990). The work design in many Swedish companies in the 1950s was increasingly built on Taylorist principles, with detailed division of labour and degradation of work. Unions in the 1950s and 1960s took a largely uncritical attitude towards technological and organizational issues (Johansson 1993). As a consequence, piece-rate wage systems based on Method–Time–Measurement spread rapidly (Berggren 1981; Berner 1981). In fact, one purpose of the Saltsjöbads agreement was to gain technical development and rationalization in industry, which was expressed in a separate agreement (Söderpalm 1980). With this Taylorist dominated bargain, the 'model' was not built on any unique qualities compared to other capitalist societies. A similar argument can be made concerning control structures. The development of line production meant that technical control was becoming important. In the big export companies this was combined with administrative control, paralleling developments in other societies (Edwards 1979).

What is specific to Swedish work organization is the employment relationship. These relations have to a very large extent been regulated through negotiations and agreements between unions and employers. The negotiations have been conducted on the company level, but they have been based on central or industry agreements concerning wage increases, working hours and many other working conditions, as well as the 'solidaristic' policy of gradually eroding differentials between groups. Such a system presupposed organizations on both sides with a high density and centralized negotiating structures.

As a social settlement the 'model' rested on employer's right to determine the nature of the workplace in return for recognition of unions as a partner in industrial relations and a power in the labour market. The latter was underpinned by a welfare corporatism based on state directed full employment and universal social provisions. Arrangements of this nature created the basis for a cooperative and self-regulated industrial relations system.

Preconditions for the successful operation of the model included an economy sustained by high productivity and export growth; continuity of state policy under Social Democratic government; hegemony and homogeneity of manufacturing unions (LO) on the labour market; and the dominance within capital of domestic firms or Swedish based export companies. It is on the last factor we wish to dwell, as it is important to our analysis of the model in a changing global context.

Originally there had been a conflict in the employer organization SAF before the decision was made to take part in the Saltsjöbad negotiations. The large export companies were against this, seeing their interests in lower wage costs to compete on broader markets. But in spite of the economic importance of the export companies, they were not able to control SAF at this time. In contrast, the dominant home market sector had an interest in economic policies of domestic reflation and protectionism, backed up by labour co-operation and compromise.

Despite the differences, export capital adapted and made effective use of the emergent model. An example is the solidaristic wages policy which favoured the big, successful companies and tended to accelerate the structural rationalization of the economy, since firms with financial problems were thrown out of the market at an early stage. In this respect it can be seen that it also favoured the dual development of mass production in the big companies and a relatively egalitarian distribution of incomes that has facilitated mass consumption. This favourable adaptation was, however, eventually to be challenged by internal contradictions and external pressures.

Crisis

In the late 1960s and then more extensively in the 1970s, the model came under pressure, with work organization a central feature. The Tayloristic division of work was reaching a point when the disadvantages of the system became clear and the resistance against it was increasing. Miners, woodworkers and cleaners struck to protest against an increased division of labour; standardized work operations and piecerate systems based on time and motion studies. Swedish trade unions began to show 'a marked interest in questions of work organization' (Johansson 1993: 2). On an individual level, the discontent with the work organization took the form of absenteeism and labour turnover. Problems of recruitment to industry, especially among the youth, became a problem and has, to varying degrees, continued ever since. Employers felt that problems such as absenteeism and labour turnover were exacerbated by the de-commodifying effects of Sweden's extensive and generous welfare system.

The changed climate between the employers and the unions also became apparent in industrial relations, where the bargaining system was subject to increased crisis tendencies. In the wage bargaining round of 1980 the tensions led to an open conflict between LO and SAF. Conflicts with white-collar workers and private and state employers also erupted during this period. The capacity of the formal system to manage such problems was made more difficult by the rise of new union blocs outside LO.

Employers responded on the work and pay terrains. Experiments began with new forms of work organization, often based on group working or 'semi-autonomous groups'. The ideas behind the experiments came mainly from the socio-technical school which had its roots in the Tavistock Institute before transferring to Sweden via Norway. The most well known were in the car industry (Volvo and SAAB), but were present in many other sectors. The employers usually took the initiative in the experiments, but a number of them were conducted in collaboration with the unions (Sandberg 1982). Moves were also made to break with the centralized bargaining system, a process we will pick up again in the next section.

What changed conditions lay behind the crisis? The Swedish economy certainly experienced lower increases in productivity and GNP in the 1970s, and there was a deterioration in international competitiveness. But a shift in the structure of capital was also influential. During the crisis period Swedish multinationals increasingly tried to escape rising costs and other problems by exporting facilities to their affiliates abroad, thus accelerating the internationalization process (Blomström 1990: 96). The importance of these companies in the economy, manifested in share of GDP, had further increased and their greater foreign penetration meant that 'capital would now be more willing to reject at least parts of the Swedish model which had been premised upon capital's dependence on the domestic labour force and market' (Olsen 1991: 120). But the nature and costs of the settlement meant that employers were also willing to take initiatives at home. For example it was mainly the big export companies that took part in work organization experiments. The balance of power, leadership positions and policies of SAF and other employer organizations also shifted. Such firms were less interested in continuing to support the negotiating system as they felt they were able to handle their own bargaining and needed to compete on criteria of international costs.

Beyond industrial relations, changing conditions also affected the labour market, with marked increases in white-collar workers and women, especially in state and local government sectors, upsetting the old balance of power. It was no longer unquestionable that the private blue-collar workers should give the norm for the wage increases (Bengtsson *et al.* 1985). Finally the state context also changed. The fiscal crisis affecting all capitalist countries had its echoes in Sweden and on public expenditure. During the 1980s unemployment figures began to rise, though they remained low compared to other countries. Of equal importance, the political conditions for the model altered as the Social Democrats (SAP) lost governmental power in the election of 1976 as the crisis in the model intensified.

Reconstruction

It had become clear to the major actors by the early 1970s that the crises were not of a temporary character. At that time, attempts at reconstruction of the 'Swedish model' began. The substantial programme of legislation to regulate the enterprise, notably the law of codetermination, introduced by SAP, was a first step towards increased state intervention. This law prescribes duties to inform and negotiate with the unions before any substantial decisions are taken by the management. The effects were limited by being a 'framing' law without specific compulsion at local level. The complementary central agreement, the development agreement on codetermination (UVA) between the LO and the SAF, was not concluded until 1982, when SAP after six years returned to office. However, the significance of the law was a break from the previous agreement to allow the enterprise to be governed solely through managerial prerogative.

At the same time, the crises in the 'model' and pressures from below gave some of the strategists of the labour movement an opportunity to realize a long-standing perspective of extending democracy. The well known proposal by the LO for wage earner funds was a tool for fulfilling this. Another development was the attempt by the SAP to produce centrally determined income policies from 1982 onwards. Though the process zig-zagged according to competing pressures, once again the effect was to break with the previous pattern of self-regulation of bargaining by the labour market actors. Taken together, these policies constitute a strategy, particularly from the SAP, to find new forms of corporatist regulation.

A significant part of capital's response also emphasized new wage formation policies. SAF, and especially the engineering employers organization and big export companies, began to propose a decentralization of the bargaining system to the industry and later to company level (Rehn and Viklund 1990: 318–319). The other major sphere of employer action has been that of work organization. The background was continuing problems with recruitment to industry and high absenteeism, but also the need for flexibility caused by changes in technology and product markets. More group working and job rotation have been introduced. Referring to the engineering industry, Bengtsson comments: 'The new approach is in forms such as reduced work division, work integration and a transition to a group-based production' (1992: 40). When combined with firm-specific wage policies, this has been read by some writers as constituting a shift from societal to managerial corporatism, which mean that 'regulation between work and capital, employees and employers takes place at the firm level' (Brulin and Nilsson 1991: 330).

Unions had little choice but to engage with employers on the terrain of work organization, given the failure of wage earner fund proposals; the gradual, if uneven, success of employers in eroding the old system of centralized bargaining; and the strengthened power of the large internationally orientated firms. Nevertheless, consistent with the proactive traditions of the Swedish trade union movement, they also developed their own strategy encapsulated in the term 'solidaristic work'. This strategy was developed by the Metalworkers union, but has also been partly adopted by LO. The aim is to integrate the solidaristic wage policy with solidaristic work:

> Through continuous training and a gradual expansion of tasks, the individual worker will benefit from enlarged job

content as well as economic rewards. Thus pay differentials are to be used as incentives to encourage workers to climb a skills 'ladder', developing their competence in the performance of an increasing number of tasks within a more flexible and democratic work organisation. Work groups in which tasks are horizontally and vertically integrated are recommended as a way of achieving 'rewarding jobs'.

(Kjellberg 1992: 53; see also Mahon 1991: 306–11)

The general attitude of the unions to flexible forms of work organization is positive, providing it is compatible with work enrichment and codetermination (Rehn and Viklund 1990: 319, 323).

Many commentators would see those conditions as being met:

Swedish companies enjoy a good reputation for being at the forefront of work organisation design and experimentation, and a common strand in most of the experiments conducted is the participation of local unions in the planning and implementation of new forms of work organisation.

(Hart 1992: 8)

These developments provide a basis for some to argue that there is an opportunity for a post-Fordist historic compromise focused on the sphere of work organization between capital and labour. Though they do accept that several conditions have to be fulfilled, notably national coordination of wages directly or by some job evaluation system (Mahon 1991; Brulin and Nilsson 1991). Auer and Riegler (1990; Riegler and Auer 1991) contrast the recent developments to Volvo's well known experiments in the 1970s at Kalmar and elsewhere. Whereas these were rather isolated experiments concerned with a humanization of work and problems of declining job satisfaction, newer and more systematic developments using semi-autonomous groups are justified in terms of functional goals of greater flexibility and quality to cope with new products, technologies, and markets.

Talk of post-Fordism, let alone historic compromises between capital and labour have understandably been greeted with considerable scepticism in Britain and other European countries. The special conditions that have generated and reshaped the 'Swedish model' have propelled the major labour markets actors into initiatives in the sphere of work organization. But, as elsewhere, the reality in many companies is one of multiskilling and interchangeability of tasks, as Mahon (1991: 305) herself admits. Union proposals for 'good jobs' and solidaristic work haven't resulted in a new stage of a historic compromise, with capital and unions themselves remaining somewhat sceptical whether the initiatives, positive though they may be, remain anything more than isolated experiments (Janerus 1992).

There are, as will be shown in the next sections, considerable variations within and between Swedish firms on the extent and character of new forms of organization. There is evidence that Volvo maintain a commitment to advanced work group organization, flexible teams and flatter management hierarchies in some of its divisions (Lansbury *et al.* 1992). But in an earlier paper that this chapter draws from (Thompson, Sederblad and Ahlstrand 1992), we argued against Auer and Riegler's (1990: 296) claim that every new work organization form introduced in the company is some kind of team model. For us, new initiatives had to be set against the considerable variations in the 'stock' of Volvo's work organization methods. The massive Torslanda plant in Gothenberg, using traditional assembly methods, still dominated Swedish car production, and this qualification was multiplied in importance in the context of the even greater variations in vehicle production within and between the domestic and foreign plants of Volvo and Saab (Kjellberg: 1992).

This judgement has been confirmed by recent developments. The recession in the 1990s has meant that work organization experiments have been more limited and some of the most well known plants have been earmarked for closure, notably at Volvo's Uddevalla and Kalmar. We also have a new political context with a centre–right coalition gaining office in 1991. The new political conditions and economic circumstances combining a more open economy and recession means that the unions have been forced largely on the defensive, concentrating on saving their member's jobs. We shall return to these developments later, but now turn to our own case studies and other empirical work to deepen an understanding of recent trends. A common theme is that of the extent and character of group working, as this fits into a broader Swedish debate about rival models of work organization.

For example, Berggren compares new Swedish production concepts in the car industry with Japanese concepts, such as 'Toyotism' and others used in transplants in USA and Britain. As these concepts are also based on 'teamwork', Berggren compares the meaning of this to the Swedish forms of group working (Berggren 1990: 395–397). In the 'Swedish model' organization based on groups should be seen as linked to the production design, as a condition for extended worker influence. There are parallel assembly and docks with buffers between the stations. An important difference to the Japanese forms of teamworking is the possibility for worker autonomy. The supervisors are reduced or even eliminated in the Swedish system and are regarded mainly as a planning and support function. The unions have a bargaining position not only on wages but on issues such as classifications and work intensity. In this sense then, Swedish production concepts are related to the industrial relations system.

WORK ORGANIZATION IN SWEDISH INDUSTRY

The empirical work in this section is based on two research projects. One of the authors made an investigation of the organization of work in six Swedish companies in the late 1980s (Sederblad 1990). Two companies, divisions or other units, were selected from the food, chemical-technical (pharmaceuticals, plastics, paint, etc.) and petro-chemical industries.[2]

The other research project focuses on foreign acquisitions and the consequences for work organization and industrial relations, particularly the merger between SAAB–Scania automobile division and General Motors in 1990.[3]

Food, chemical-technical and petro-chemical industries

Work design and working groups

In the petro-chemical companies, the organization of work was based on groups consisting of a shift team or parts of it. The plant at Petro-chem 1 was divided into five areas, which corresponded to the operations in the continuous production process. These areas were the basis for the organization of groups and contained a maximum of four people. Production at Petro-chem 2 was based on a discontinuous process in separate units not directly linked to each other and the shift team at each unit functioned as a working group. Shift working meant that the working groups at the petro-chemical companies were also of considerable social importance to the workers. Group working was also in evidence in the maintenance department.

Table 8.1 Research sites in the Swedish food and chemicals sectors

	Food 1 (division)	Food 2 (two units)	Chem-tech 1 (division)	Chem-tech 2 (unit of div.)	Petro-chem 1 (company)	Petro-chem 2 (company)
Number of employees	520	300	320	540	380	490
Workforce	Male/female	Female/male	Male/female	Male/female	Male	Male
Products	Consumer products	Consumer products	Transformation of raw materials	Components in complex	Transformation of raw materials	Intermediate/ consumer product
Production process	Continuous process/batch	Batch/ discontinuous process	Discontinuous process	Discontinuous process/batch	Continuous process	Discontinuous process
Technical level	Automation/ high/medium	Low/ medium	Low/ medium	High/ medium	High/ automation	High/ automation
Ownership	Swedish combine	Swedish combine	Swedish combine	Swedish combine	Scandinavian combine	State/Swedish combine
Locality/ population	Small community of 15,000 near city	Small town of 27,000	Medium town of 35,000	Medium town of 71,000	New community of 18,000 near industrial complex	New community of 18,000 near industrial complex

Work organization in the food and chemical-technical industries was primarily based on a detailed division of work and working groups were less common. Those that did exist were often working at parts of the production process that had been automated, or at computer controlled machines. A trend towards an increase in the number of working groups was detectable by retrospective questions in the interviews and when two of the companies were revisited a couple of years later.

Group working is often combined with job rotation, the latter defined as a systematic change of work tasks after specified time periods. Job rotation was common in the petro-chemical industries, particulary at Petro-chem 1 where it included about 90 per cent of the workers. At this company, a sophisticated system for a daily job rotation between indoor and outdoor work existed, which also included changes between the different areas after about a year. As a result workers have a broad competence after some years. The rotation system at Petro-chem 2 was not quite so general (about 70 per cent of the workers were included), and it was limited to job changes within the groups. On the other hand, this system included a supervisory position as 'coordinator' in each group. About half of the workers were willing and permitted to have this position. Changes between positions took place after about three months.

Job rotation was quite common at Chem-tech 2, and comprised about 40 per cent of the workers, but this was mainly in the form of short intervals between changes of non-mechanized tasks, performed by women. Changes between tasks took place after short intervals of between 30 and 60 minutes and the system was intended to reduce monotony, fatigue and injury. In the other three companies studied, job rotation was limited to approximately 20 per cent of employees and was similar to the system at Chem-tech 2. The wage systems usually increased the differences between the companies as far as job rotation was concerned. There was increased pay at the petro-chemical companies for multi-task competence. In order to increase job rotation, a bonus of this kind had recently been introduced at Chem-tech 1, but had only been given to a small number of the workers.

To summarize: the petro-chemical companies were to a lesser degree based on Tayloristic principles. This has been described as a sector 'where Taylorism hasn't reached' (Bergman 1988). Although this is an exaggeration, it puts the spotlight on the specific conditions in this kind of process industry. In the companies group working is a central aspect of the work design. The work design in the chemical-technical and food industries were mainly built on Tayloristic principles, and group working was quite restricted. The company Chem-tech 2 was partly different, which will be demonstrated in the discussion of control structures.

Control

Supervisors traditionally exercise direct control over both machinery and workers. The number of supervisors had declined during the last five years at four of the companies. The number of supervisors at one of the other two companies, Petro-chem 1, had been low to begin with and had further decreased in relation to the number of production workers. At Food 2 this was reversed, and a new position of shift leader (superior to the supervisor) had been introduced, but in the follow-up study two years later, this level again had been eliminated. The work tasks for the supervisors had generally changed in the direction of long-term planning and financial control. When, in the follow-up study, group work was introduced more broadly in Chem-tech 2, a revival of the supervisor as responsible for the workforce was noticeable.

In all of the companies in the first study, the function of 'assistant supervisor' had been created. The name of the function varied – first man, contact man, production group leader or co-ordinator. The position included production work, but also a supervisory function as group leader, consisting of such things as daily planning and distribution of unusual work tasks to the group members. In some of the companies the holder of this position also deputizes for the supervisor when he is absent. The person appointed to assistant supervisor generally has worked in production prior to his appointment. In consequence, with the changed role for the supervisors in Chem-tech 2, the 'first men' disappeared almost totally in the beginning of the 1990s.

'Workplace meetings' have become common in Sweden in recent years and these were occurring at the companies, except for Chem-tech 2 and Petro-chem 1. At the latter company, there were similar meetings, but these had a different name. Workplace meetings are usually held every month for a couple of hours and all of the employees in a department or the entire factory participate. The idea is to keep the employees informed and a supervisor or even plant manager might talk about company results or coming activities, with subsequent questions and discussion. Unions at local and national level have a positive attitude.

Employment and gender relationships

The petro-chemical companies form part of an industrial complex consisting of five similar factories in the neighbourhood of Gothenburg. The complex is located outside a small community which has grown rapidly since the building of the complex in the 1960s. Usually, the employees had been fishermen or seamen. These occupations often involve teamwork. Petro-chem 1 was the first factory to be built in the complex and was then owned by an American multinational company. These factors, combined with Scandinavian traditions of industrial relations, can be assumed to have influenced the organization of work in the petro-chemical factories in the study. Other high-technology companies, such as precision welding and computer programming, have also been founded in the community.

The other companies in the first study, except for Chem-tech 2, are older industrial factories. In Sweden, this type of enterprise was previously common in small communities dominated by one company, and resulted in a rigid social stratification. In the communities where the three companies are located, there has been considerable immigration recently, and many of the immigrants work at the factories. The local traditions and the mixture of nationalities have obstructed organizational changes. Chem-tech 2, on the other hand, was established relatively recently. It was previously located outside Stockholm, but was taken over by a large multinational Swedish combine with high-technology production. Rapid technical rationalization is also under way at this factory, resulting in a division of the employees between centre and periphery: those who can cope with the new technology and those who cannot. This company is also practising Japanese production methods, notably just-in-time.

The division between centre and periphery at Chem-tech 2 is almost totally linked to the sex of the employees. The technical development has primarily affected women since some of their work tasks have disappeared and the remaining tasks are monotonous (cf. Furst 1985). Some of them are working in groups which practise job rotation, but this does not generally result in any increased competence.

The differences between the companies in the study, as far as technical level and the prevalence of group work is concerned, is generally closely related to the proportion of male workers among the employees. This can been seen as an indicator of an increasing gender polarization on the labour market. However, there are some examples in the study of women who have organized working groups on their own initiatives and changed worktasks. This has sometimes been followed by demands for training in how to control and repair the machines, but these demands have met with male resistance.

Vehicles and other industries

Motors is a sector where the most well known experiments of work organization in Sweden have been conducted. However, from a Swedish perspective, the production of trucks and buses is of considerable importance and the market position for Volvo and SAAB is very strong; in total 20 per cent of the world market for heavy trucks and buses. The production of trucks and especially buses is done in small series, which opens up forms of work organization that diverge from line production. Accordingly, new forms of work organization have been introduced and established in several of the plants for production of trucks and buses in Sweden, for example the Volvo bus plant at Borås.

The experiments started in the beginning of the 1970s with the Kalmar plant and its dock assembly and group working system. The development of this plant has, like several others, followed an uneven path. Volvo and SAAB's main plants are large, older production units with line production, though even here minor changes towards a break with this kind of production have been taken. The plant in Uddevalla meant a clear shift towards dock assembly and integrated forms of group working. SAAB's plant in Malmö also partly had this form of work organization, though combined with line assembly.

In the Swedish automotive industry, market conditions in the 1990s have been problematic. This has forced both SAAB and Volvo to engage in an extended collaboration with foreign car producers; GM and Renault respectively. In 1991, only one year after the SAAB–GM merger, the decision was taken by the GM-dominated company to close down the Malmö plant, a process influenced by clashes on work organization. At Trollhällan, the main plant, the number of employees has been cut down dramatically. The work design has become more totally based on assembly line systems.

There has been a concentration of production and of the control structure in SAAB Automobile. The management of the head plant in Trollhällan now controls all the production units in the company. Another change in the control structure has been a standardization of white-collar jobs. The Japanese influence in the Company has gradually became more and more obvious, with GM as the conduit, partly via its transplants in the US. The employment relations have been changed and the tensions between the Company and the unions have increased. This means also that the industrial relations on the Company and sector levels no longer can be characterized by cooperation and negotiations in all situations. SAAB Automobile has been in the forefront of this development.

It is not only the automotive industry in Sweden that have had problems in the last years. In other sectors as well mergers and acquisitions with foreign companies have opened the economy up to more external influences which clearly have an impact on the possibilities of forming a reconstructed 'Swedish model' based on new forms of work organization.

In the last few years, a noticeable increased influence of Japanese management practises in Sweden has occurred. The prime example for this has been ABB, the merged company between ASEA and the Swiss, Brown Boveri. Teamwork and JIT principles have been two of the pillars. In the Swedish car industry, the Japanese influence has taken the form of a specific concept: QLE – quality, delivery, economy. The concept was first developed in SAAB, before the entrance of GM, but after that the Japanese influence has increased. In one of the companies in the first study, Chem-Tech 2, the Japanese ideas were adopted already in the late 1980s.

But the most important event has been the previously mentioned decision to close the plants in Uddevalla and the following year, Kalmar. This means that two of the most famous examples of new forms of work organization will disappear. Today, the unions in Sweden must fight for the jobs of their members and defend the wages. Even in Volvo, union representatives have been ambivalent and divided about the closures.

DIFFUSION OF SWEDISH WORK ORGANIZATION

If group working, however problematic, has been an important aspect of the recasting of Swedish work organization, then the question arises of whether this will or can be exported. In turn this raises the question of how 'special' the Swedish institutional conditions are. As we saw earlier, Swedish goods have always had a high export penetration. In conventional business terminology of competitive advantage, we might expect a diffusion of work organization patterns. However, the conditions which influence the necessity for technical and organizational innovations may still be country specific. Other writers are indeed sceptical about the likelihood of diffusion of work organization. Berggren has argued that there is 'no Volvism' across national frontiers, with 'small scale manual technologies being concentrated in Sweden'.[4]

The Volvo case

Volvo has historically been less internationalized than many of the other representatives of large capital and remains a mixture of multi-domestic and global firm. Nevertheless the trend away from the home base is clear. By 1990 the previous percentage of 22 per cent had increased by 10 per cent. Company strategy is clearly based on a move into EC markets in its central vehicle manufacturing area. Acquisitions such as Leyland Bus in the UK, the extensive link-up with Renault to create the world's biggest truck and bus manufacturer, are part of this trend. Volvo has had a presence in the UK since the mid-1970s with the truck plant in Irvine, Scotland. The purchase of Leyland Bus took place in 1988. After locating in Workington, in a relatively short time all but one of Leyland's product range (the Olympian double decker) had been eliminated, due to the existence of parallel products in a shrinking market.

It quickly became apparent that Volvo management wanted to reorganize production on the lines of its bus manufacturing plant in Sweden: 'They said to us that "you will adopt the teamwork approach, we are convinced that Borås is the right way to work so what we want you to do is transport Borås"' (interview: training manager, Workington). This required a shift from the traditional assembly methods at Workington to cell assembly and team build or group working. Such methods were begun in a small island in the chassis area, based on a team trained at Borås, with the aim of spreading gradually to the rest of the plant. If there were limits to the spread of the new methods, it can be accounted for by the restricted volumes dictated by the market and by resistance from some sections of workforce and management, rather than by Volvo's intentions or the efficiency and quality of the teams. What, then, accounts for this diffusion?

Taking a wider perspective influenced by theories of post-Fordism or flexible specialization, it is possible to argue that new production arrangements are part of a more general trend dictated primarily by organizational adaptations to requirements for more flexible production. Though this is consistent with the facts of the largely low-volume, non-standard bus production, it seems to us that the above perspective neglects a more crucial factor deriving from the internationalization of Volvo's production chain. Declining bus markets accelerated the company strategy of 'global' or at least European coordination. Plants can no longer stand alone. In particular, in an integrated network work design has to converge in order to facilitate coordination of manufacture of an increasingly common product range.

> We had the intention with the UK capacity, if I may call it so, that it should be used for the expansion of the Volvo line or products in the future. To make that possible, to be flexible when we take it to this factory or that factory, we have to have the same kind of system. That we in one week or three months could change from producing the orders in Sweden, to take the Italian orders, for example, to the UK instead. That meant we must have similar production facilities or at least work organization.
>
> (interview: financial director, Volvo Bus, Sweden)

Therefore the system and the workers themselves have to be flexible enough to respond to shifts in the use of that capacity along the points of the chain.[5]

Employment relations

Employment relations, however, manifest different tendencies. As we saw earlier Volvo has developed very close relations with unions in Sweden, most recently in cooperation in design and operation of the new working arrangements at Uddevalla (Brulin and Nilsson 1991: 339). But such employment relations are deeply embedded in an industrial relations system which has been a key part of the 'Swedish model'. Relationships with unions and employees at Workington have also been largely consensual, but there the similarity ends. Cooperation in work organization is more a function of a traditionally moderate unionism and acquiescent membership, than any active involvement and interest in such issues. This can be seen from two angles, the AUEW convenor commenting to us that 'there has never been any resistance at Workington to any kind of method of work'; while from the management side: 'the history is that they have not trusted the manager and that has been their problem. They are not used to doing things themselves and taking responsibility for change. They are used to meeting once a year to talk about pay' (interview: Swedish senior manager in UK).

Any changes in bargaining arrangements or remuneration have been purely localized or driven by internal considerations. Yet there were some early expectations that Swedish-style employment practices would be imported:

> There was a view initially that it would change considerably, that Swedish philosophy would be introduced or imposed or whatever. There was a view from initial contact that everything in the garden would be rosy. That in time has proved to be false. We have had to resolve our problems in the traditional way by getting round the table and thrashing out painful solutions.
>
> (interview with UK industrial relations manager)

Similarly expectations that those trained at Boras would receive comparable pay and conditions have remained unfulfilled, a fact which caused considerable resentment.

Control

If the focus is on the control of labour (direction of work tasks, supervision, evaluation, discipline and reward), the evidence on diffusion is mixed. There is no indication of any intent concerning general strategies towards labour deriving from Volvo's Swedish experience. Nor has there been any significant alteration in the effort bargain, as we saw in the previous section. Nevertheless, group working requires some alteration in methods of task allocation and direction, as well as supervisory arrangements, broadly consistent with notions of responsible autonomy. Workington has not gone as far as Borås where supervisors and teams have responsibility for their own mini-budgets; nevertheless there was a gradual transition towards delegated powers.

If, however, we focus on control of management, there are more important change processes. Central to this is a concern for standardized management systems, which as with work organization, have the function of facilitating coordination, common strategies and processes over dispersed spatial locations. This is not to say that Volvo's structure is incompatible with a measure of devolved responsibility, or local adaptations; something that senior management constantly stress. Indeed the purpose of a strong managerial culture is to allow that. That culture does, however, appear to be strongly policed by Swedes. As one senior manager remarked: 'I am not saying that Swedes are better than the others, but to implement Swedish behaviour and to make it closer to the model of organization, it is normal, also in Volvo, to have top management coming from there.'

To summarize: we argue that the need for flexibility along the production chain puts a premium on an integrated work design and in this case encouraged the Company to export a successful domestic model. That model cannot be described as unambiguously 'Swedish' or even of an homogeneous Volvo company, though it draws on the repertoire of practices within both frameworks. When management talks of 'Swedish behaviour' it is overlaying national characteristics to the requirement for a management system that is sufficiently standardized to allow effective control and coordination. In that sense it is little different from the policy of Japanese or German transnationals. However, that is less of a requirement for other factors, notably employment relations. Not only that, even were it desirable for the domestic pattern to be diffused, it would be difficult given the embeddedness of such relations.

CONCLUSION

In the previous section we made a largely contingent case for the diffusion of innovative work organization within a part of Volvo's operations. Is it possible, then, to identify any general tendencies? Is there anything distinctive about Swedish work organization despite the double process of internationalization?

The earlier case studies did identify the extension of group working, a decrease in the number of supervisors and a shift in their functions. This is reasonably consistent with other evidence, notably that of Berggren (1990). Although an overall evaluation of Sweden's vehicle sector revealed only 'flexible Taylorism', the more advanced had group working as the main organizing principle. Teamworking is, of course, not unique to Sweden. But Berggren and other writers (Cole 1989; Sandberg *et al.* 1992; Ramsay 1992) are keen to distinguish the content, particularly from Japanese practices. Two crucial differences are highlighted. Whereas Japanese factory regimes are authoritarian and based on work intensification, Swedish group work 'is characterized by sociotechnical principles of design and union ideas of "good work", which may also be productive. Job cycles are long and horizontal integration is supplemented by some degree of vertical integration, which gives a certain autonomy' (Sandberg *et al.* 1992: 94). This potential for autonomy is combined with genuine possibilities for union inputs on a range of work and job issues.

Regardless of how distinctive the practices, they have not evolved to the point were they are considered a substantial alternative in the global battle of 'best practice'. In fact the death knell of such influence has been sounded with the closures of the 'model' plants Uddevalla and Kalmar. Despite the symbolic and practical importance to those in Sweden, these events should not be over-estimated. Just as Kalmar in the 1970s became a symbol which distorted a more complex reality, so there are now still important and distinctive forms of work organization in other plants such as ABB (Karlsson 1992).

It is also important not to neglect the socio-political context. In both Japan and Sweden 'new forms of work organisation were placed firmly in their wider social setting' (Ramsay 1992: 38). As we have argued, work design initiatives were informed by the industrial relations system and the wider social settlement that underpinned it. Joint labour–management influence was a key facet, but its form is changing. With the breakdown of Social Democratic hegemony and the retreat of union strategies to reconstruct the 'Swedish model', the more politicized SAF have declared that model dead (Whyman and Burkitt 1993: 4). It is widely accepted by all the labour market actors that the focus of employee participation has become more driven by production-driven than by a perspective of economic democracy. Nevertheless it is wise to remember that new initiatives are built on the back of old practices and that past labour movement gains such as the Codetermination Act have not yet been rolled back. The future will depend in part on the preferences and power of those actors. In this respect there is every indication that directions are being contested within management and unions as well as between capital and labour (Forslin 1992; Sandberg 1993).

There is, however, no going back to the old, more homogeneous 'Swedish model'. Diversity of practices 'on the ground' is being increased by a less unitary labour market; more decentralized industrial relations and devolution of operational responsibilities within corporate structures. It is also accentuated by the acceleration of Sweden's integration into international markets. Any transformed elements of Swedish work organization have to compete with other models of best practice at home as well as abroad. Being a global company does make a difference. It is no longer a question of internationalization in which there is a tension between the need for standardized methods to keep diverse networks together and the processes of adjustment to new national and local contexts. Global operations require the integration of increasingly diverse activities within complex corporate structures that combine different companies. The cooperation between Volvo and Renault is a case in point, with the latter questioning both the capacity and culture of the former's production (Sandberg *et al*. 1992).

But these tendencies don't mean total convergence or conformity. It is true that in locating abroad, Swedish capital has sought to escape what they perceive to be the constraints of the domestic social settlement. But in escape they carry with them parts of the baggage, differing according to the actor's choices and circumstances. Flight from the nest and diffusion are not mutually exclusive. Messy, but reality is like that.

Acknowledgements

The authors would like to acknowledge the important role played by our colleagues Terry Wallace and Roland Ahlstrand in contributing to the research which underpins some sections of this chapter.

NOTES

1 This discussion of the model is obviously highly compressed. A longer version of the argument can be found in Thompson, Sederblad and Ahlstrand (1992). Some other prominent accounts include Korpi (1978, 1983), Esping-Anderson (1985), and Kjellberg (1992).

2 The main method used was interviews with a sample of nearly one tenth of both blue-collar and white-collar workers in the companies. Managers, supervisors and union representatives were also interviewed. Three of the companies, Food 2, Chem-tech 2 and Petro-chem 1 were revisited in the beginning of the 1990s. Observations of the production during about two weeks in each company and informal interviews with the workers were made.

3 The project started in 1992 and is supported by the Swedish Work Environment Fund. The methods used are interviews with managers and union representatives, also formerly employed, and analysis of written documents as reports and bargaining agreements. It is part of a comparative project involving the other author and colleagues from the Universities of Central Lancashire and Lund.

4 He particularly emphasizes the lack of travel to the expanding plant in Ghent, Belgium, but he does, however, notice the export of group working to Workington (1990: 438–439).

5 Workington has now closed due to the drastic collapse of the market in the recent period. The stated intention of the company is to transfer the working methods, along with the production, to the Irvine plant in Scotland. We are still in the process of researching these developments.

REFERENCES

Andreff, W. (1984) 'The international centralisation of capital and the reordering of world capitalism', *Capital and Class* 22: 58–80.

Auer, P. and Riegler, C. (1990) 'The Swedish version of group work – the future model of work organisation in the engineering sector', *Economic and Industrial Democracy* 11: 291–299.

Bartlett, C. and Goshal, S. (1989) *Managing Across Borders*, Boston: Harvard University Press.

Bengtsson, L. (1992) 'Work organisation and occupational development in CIM: the case of Swedish NC machine shops', *New Technology, Work and Employment* 7, 1: 29–43.

Bengtsson, L., Eriksson, A.-C. and Sederblad, P. (1985) 'The Swedish Employers Confederation and centralized bargaining in 1980, 1981 and 1983', Discussion Paper IIM/LMP 84-24, Berlin, Wissenschaftszentrum.

Berggren, C. (1981) 'Slog Taylorism aldrig igenom i sverige?', *Arkiv* 19–20.

—— (1990) 'Det nya Bilarbetet', *Arkiv Dissertation Series* 32, Lund University.

Bergman, P. (1988) 'Grupper som objekt fökunskap och manipulation', *Arkiv* 40.

Berner, B. (1981) 'Teknikens värld. Teknisk förändring och ingenjörsarbete i svensk industri', *Arkiv Dissertation Series* 11, Lund University.

Blomström, M. (1990) 'Competitiveness of firms and countries', in J. H. Dunning, B. Kogut and M. Blomström, *Globalisation of Firms and Competitiveness of Nations*, Lund: Lund University Press.

Brulin, G. and Nilsson, T. (1991) 'From societal to managerial corporatism: new forms of work organization as a transformation vehicle', *Economic and Industrial Democracy* 12: 327–346.

Clegg, S. (1990) *Modern Organisations*, London: Sage.

Cole, R. E. (1989) *Strategies for Learning: Small Group Activities in American, Japanese and Swedish Industry*, Berkeley, CA: University of California Press.

Dicken, P. (1992, 2nd edn) *Global Shift*, London: Paul Chapman.

Edquist, C. and Jacobsson, S. (1988) *Flexible Automation: The Global Diffusion of New Technology in the Engineering Industry*, Oxford: Basil Blackwell.

Edwards, R. (1979) *Contested Terrain: The Transformation of Workplace in the Twentieth Century*, New York: Basic Books.

Esping-Andersen, G. (1985) *Politics Against Markets*, Princeton: Princeton University Press.

Forsgren, M. (1990) *Managing the Internationalization Process: The Swedish Case*, London: Routledge.

Forslin, J. (1992) 'Towards integration: the case of Volvo engine division', *European Participation Monitor* Issue 3 (first edn): 19–23.

Furst, G. (1985) 'Reträtten från mansjobben', Dissertation, Department of Sociology, University of Golthenburg.

Hart, H. (1992) 'Employee participation and workplace development in Sweden', *European Participation Monitor* Issue 3 (first edn): 8–11.

Haspeslagh, P. C. and Jemison, D. B. (1992) 'Industry restructuring, acquisitions and the value creating process', in K. Cool, D. J. Neven and I. Walter (eds) *European Industrial Restructuring in the 1990s*, London: Macmillan.

Henderson, J. (1992) *The Globalisation of High Technology Industry*, London: Macmillan.

Janerus, I. (1992) 'Participation, diffusion and control – comments from LO', *European Participation Monitor* Issue 3 (first edn): 24–27.

Jessop, B. (1992) 'Towards the Schumpetarian workfare state: global capitalism and structural competitiveness', Unpublished paper.

Johansson, J. (1993) 'The Swedish trade union movement and new organisation of work', Paper to the 11th Annual Labour Process Conference, University of Central Lancashire.

Karlsson, K. (1992) 'New industrial work methods at ABB distribution', *European Participation Monitor*, Issue 3 (first edn): 12–18.

Kitschelt, H. (1992) 'Industrial governance structures, innovation strategies, and the case of Japan: sectoral or cross-national comparative analysis?', Unpublished Paper.

Kjellberg, A. (1992) 'Sweden: can the model survive?', in R. Hyman and A. Ferner (eds), *Industrial Relations in the New Europe*, Oxford: Basil Blackwell.

Korpi, W. (1978) *The Working Class in Welfare Capitalism*, London: Routledge & Kegan Paul.

—— (1983) *The Democratic Class Struggle*, London: Routledge & Kegan Paul.

Lane, C. (1991) 'Industrial reorganization in Europe', *Work, Employment and Society* 5, 4: 515–539.

Lansbury, R. D., Sandkull, B. and Hammarström, O. (1992) 'Industrial relations and productivity: evidence from Sweden and Australia', *Economic and Industrial Democracy* 13: 295–329.

Littler, C. R. (1990) 'The labour process debate: a theoretical review 1974–1988', in D. Knights and H. Willmott (eds) *Labour Process Theory*, London: Macmillan.

Mahon, R. (1991) 'From solidaristic wages to solidaristic work: a post-Fordist historic compromise for Sweden?', *Economic and Industrial Democracy* 12: 295–325.

Maurice, M., Sorge, A. and Warner, M. (1980) 'Societal differences in organising manufacturing units', *Organisation Studies* 1: 69–91.

Ohmae, K. (1985) *Triad Power: The Coming Shape of Global Competition*, New York: Free Press.

Olsen, G. (1991) 'Labour mobilisation and the strength of capital: the rise and stall of economic democracy in Sweden', *Studies in Political Economy* 34: 109–145.

Porter, M. (1991) *The Competitive Advantage of Nations*, London: Macmillan.

Ramsay, H. (1992) 'Swedish and Japanese work methods – comparisons and contrasts', *European Participation Monitor,* Issue 3 (1st edn): 37–40.

Rehn, G. and Viklund, B. (1990) 'Changes in the Swedish model', in G. Baglioni and C. Crouch (eds) *European Industrial Relations: The Challenge of Flexibility,* London: Sage.

Riegler, C. and Auer, P. (1990) 'Workforce adjustment and labour market policy: Sweden', in P. Auer (ed.) *Workforce Adjustment Patterns in Four Countries: Experiences in the Steel and Automobile Industry in France, Germany, Sweden and the United Kingdom,* Discussion Paper FS 1: 91–94, Berlin, Wissenschaftszentrum.

Sandberg, T. (1982) *Work Organisations and Autonomous Groups,* Lund: Liber.

—— (1993) 'The end of the road?', Arbetslivcentrum, Stockholm.

Sandberg, T. *et al.* (1992) *Technological Change and Co-Determination in Sweden,* Philadelphia: Temple University Press.

Sederblad, P. (1990) 'Work organisation, technology and culture in Swedish industry', Paper to the 8th Annual Labour Process Conference, Aston University.

Smith, C. and Meiksins, P. (1991) 'Theories of cross-national organisational analysis: a new explanatory model', Paper for the 10th EGOS Colloquium, Vienna.

Söderpalm, S. A. (1980) *Arbetsgivarna och Saltsjöbadspolitiken,* SAF, Stockholm.

Stephens, J. (1979) *The Transition from Capitalism to Socialism,* London: Macmillan.

Thompson, P. and Smith, C. (1992) 'Socialism and the labour process in theory and practice', in C. Smith and P. Thompson (eds) *Labour in Transition: The Labour Process in Eastern Europe and China,* London: Routledge.

Thompson, P., Jones, C., Nickson, D., Wallace, T. and Kewell, B. (1993) 'Transnationals, globalisation and transfer of knowledge', Paper for the 11th EGOS Colloquium, Paris.

Thompson, P., Sederblad, P. and Ahlstrand, R. (1992) 'Labour processes in an age of globalisation', Paper for the 10th International Labour Process Conference, Aston University.

Whyman, P. and Burkitt, B. (1993) 'Restructuring the labour process in Sweden: the offensive of the SAF and the LO response', Paper for the 11th International Labour Process, University of Central Lancashire.

Womack, J. P., Jones, D. T. and Roos, D. (1990) *The Machine that Changed the World,* New York: Macmillan.

9

A GENTLER WAY TO TOTAL QUALITY?

The case of the 'integrated factory' at Fiat Auto

Giuseppe Bonazzi

BACKGROUND: IS THERE A WESTERN WAY TO LEAN PRODUCTION?

The starting point for this chapter is a peculiar contradiction in the current debate on the Japanese model. On the one hand, widespread fears exist that the Japanization of the labour process entails a dramatic worsening in working conditions: intensified work rhythms, increased working hours, a tamed or annihilated trade union and a climate of subtle and insidious pressures aimed at obtaining the employees' total acceptance of company demands. Some research on Japanese transplants in the American automotive industry, on the Mazda plant at Flat Rock and on the NUMMI joint venture in California, seem to reinforce these pessimistic expectations (Fucini and Fucini 1990; Greiner 1988; Parker and Slaughter 1988; Klein 1989, 1991; Rehder 1990; Berggren *et al.* 1991).

On the other hand, the small amount of research currently available on European companies which have initiated 'lean production' processes presents the reader with a situation which seems on the whole less alarming (Oliver and Wilkinson 1988; Starkey and MacKinlay 1989; Turnbull, 1989). This is also true of the Fiat plants where the research reported below was conducted. No apparent fears of imminent work intensification seemed to exist there and, furthermore, agreements with the trade unions have helped guarantee the success of various initiatives linked to Fiat's total quality programme.

These contrasting results raise a number of questions:

1 Is it possible that the Fiat workers' lack of fear and the unions' agreement result from a misperception? Might this favourable climate simply reflect some initial phases of a transformation

process, which may become bitter and bleak once the process begins to manifest its true colours? Will the trade unions therefore soon find themselves faced by the dilemma of either accepting work intensification or risking job losses due to Fiat's decreasing international competitiveness?

2 Is it possible that Fiat management is succeeding in refining the Japanese model and removing its most traumatic effects? Is it being diluted or adapted so that its implementation proves virtually painless; and if this is the case, what effectiveness remains in the face of foreign (and principally Japanese) competition?

3 Or finally, is it possible that the Japanese model is only a catch-all concept which embraces a mix of heterogeneous, Japanese-like elements able to guarantee substantial improvements in productivity and quality and, at the same time, avoid the traumatic effects of a total Japanization?

Official declarations at Fiat emphasize that many convergent paths lead to the goal of total quality and contrast this with any simple necessity to 'do like the Japanese'. This could be read as an indication that the third and final hypothesis is most appropriate. However, both the methods and the timing used by Fiat management suggest that we are dealing with a rather specific scenario in which two elements appear to be particularly relevant. The first is Fiat's way of achieving its goal of an 'integrated factory' (IF); the second concerns the specific reasons for the high degree of worker consent to Fiat's innovations. The first and the second parts of this chapter deal, respectively, with these two elements.

The chapter presents and discusses the main results of two distinct phases of research at Fiat. The first part considers the implementation of the integrated factory. The information was gathered in the second half of 1991 during in-depth visits to the factories at Mirafiori, Rivalta, Chivasso, Verrone, Termoli and Cassino. Recorded interviews lasting from one to three hours were conducted in each factory, with management, technicians, workers and shop stewards, covering about thirty people in all. In addition interviews were conducted with all the engineers belonging to Fiat Auto Production's top management. The second part of the chapter analyses the main results of an earlier phase of research, from summer 1990, on the evolution of manual work at Fiat Mirafiori. This fieldwork was based on direct and prolonged observation of workplaces as well as in-depth interviews with more than thirty managers, technicians and workers. Further visits to the same factory were carried out in autumn 1991 and winter 1992.

THE FIAT APPROACH: A LONG ROUTE TOWARDS THE INTEGRATED FACTORY

Cellular manufacturing and its impact on work conditions

There is no doubt that Fiat's most important decision in the last few years has been to implement the so-called integrated factory, viewed as the main tool for achieving the objective of total quality. Both from official documents and informal statements, one gains the impression that Fiat Auto management sees the transition to the IF as the most important organizational revolution in the Company's recent history.

The IF can be considered as a variant of cellular manufacture (CM) and the latter, as can be seen in what is now a vast literature on the subject (Wemmerlöw and Hyer 1987, 1989; Parnaby 1987; Oliver and Wilkinson 1988; Turnbull 1986, 1989; Dawson 1991) has the following main features:

1 the production process moves from an organization based on the grouping of analogous operations to one based on the group- ing of heterogeneous and consecutive operations constituting a complete segment of the productive process;
2 self-contained workcells are setup, equipped with all the technical and cognitive tools required to deal with any production anomalies;
3 the hierarchical structure is flattened and decisions regarding the control or resetting of the standard state of the production process are delegated to lower levels having immediate contact with production.

The totality of these changes has also been termed the 'focused factory', and the workcells are often described as 'minifactories'. The advantages offered by CM are reputed to be significant reduction in lead times and setup times, in time lost due to production defects, in inventories and in handling of materials. These advantages are also integral to lean production objectives and, more generally, the JIT production model. In particular, CM prospers most efficiently when implemented in the context of the U layout recommended by Toyota (Wemmerlöw and Hyer 1987). However, if the available literature contains fairly precise ideas on the managerial advantages brought about by CM, little research has so far been carried out on the effects on shop floor work and, moreover, the results obtained by existing research appear to be controversial.

In research at an Australian GM plant, Dawson (1991) presents a generally optimistic picture, which seems to support the thesis of Piore and Sabel (1984) regarding flexible specialization. According to Dawson, CM has favoured an increase in responsible autonomy, group work and worker involvement in the processes of production improvement. However, he notes that the union's agreement does not reflect a real commitment to the new production model, but that such consensus is rather due to improvements in the material working conditions which are part of the new model: less effort, less noise, and a more comfortable and cleaner environment.

On the other hand, research in Britain (Turnbull 1989) presents a much more critical picture. In this case, CM seems to have implied a net increase in managerial control of the workers, the end of old informal skills, the elimination of traditional labour porosity, increases in responsibility without a real increase in the exercise of capabilities, and a loss of power on the part of the union. Turnbull (1989: 150) admits, however, that the general working conditions remain much better than the 'pure' Japanese ones, and a real worsening would occur only if 'true' JIT systems were introduced.

These controversial results pose the question: is the situation resulting from the advent of the IF at Fiat closer to that described by Dawson or by Turnbull? We can anticipate that, although Fiat shows some elements which resemble each analysis, the overall scenario differs decidedly from both of them. The climate of consent, the importance given to the improvement of environmental working conditions, the long preliminary phase of transition to CM – all recall Dawson's results. Dawson's central thesis, however, is that labour is moving towards a combination of responsible autonomy and group work, and this does not appear to be confirmed by our findings in Fiat. In this respect our results seem closer to those of Turnbull – especially with regard to increased management control through monitoring; decreases in tacit skills used by workers to control their workspace; and the irrelevance of the concept of professional upgrading as a key to understanding the changes in shop floor work.

It is appropriate to ask how these elements, in appearance so contrasting, coexist within a coherent context. To answer this we must first admit that CM is not a given technical and organizational structure which would allow us to forecast either its consequences for human labour or the character of worker responses. On the contrary, it seems reasonable to assume that such consequences and responses will depend to a large extent upon the nature of management's previous decisions about technology, industrial relations and worker commitment. That is, they will depend on the history of the company and on the management strategy within which CM is located. Adopting this approach to Fiat leads us to focus on three aspects. First, the significance of the IF in the wider post-Fordist reconversion of the Company; second, the way in which Fiat has achieved the IF; and third the reasons for the employees' agreement to the implementation of the IF and the changes this involves on the shop floor, for both workers and supervisors. These three elements are not unrelated, for the answers to the first two provide us with a background for addressing the third.

The integrated factory and post-Fordism

In contrast to what has occurred in other companies, such as Ford UK and British Leyland, the IF at Fiat was chosen towards the end of the 1980s by the same management corps that had already successfully overcome the Fordist crisis by pursuing the 'hyper-technological' route known in Fiat as the higly automated factory phase (HAF) between 1982 and 1988.

Thus, the IF was not a response to the rigidities of Fordist production, since these had already been overcome by earlier technological innovations. Rather, it was developed to overcome certain technical and organizational limits encountered in the implementation of HAF: limits essentially concerning the lack of coherence between an extremely sophisticated technology and a rather traditional management and organizational structure.

A key to understanding the path taken by Fiat is given in Figure 9.1 where 'low' or 'high' technological levels are matched with lean or what might be referred to as 'fat' production (large inventories in keeping with a just-in-case logic). Phase I corresponds to the traditional Fordist factory with mechanization and/or rigid automation. When flexible automation is introduced but production still remains 'fat', we are in the phase which in Fiat corresponds to the HAF (phase II). Here technological innovation allows a significant increase both in productivity and in flexibility of the production mix. It also involves an important evolution in manual work: a reduction

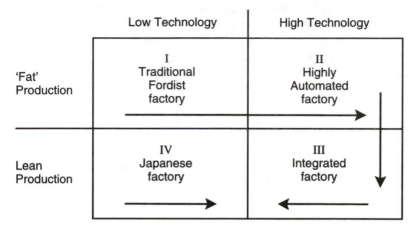

Figure 9.1 Trajectories of factory reorganization at Fiat

in physical effort and widespread ergonomic and environmental improvements. Nevertheless, production still operates with the traditional criterion of accumulating inventories in order to cope with emergencies, and both an 'administrative Taylorism', with a rigid hierarchy and subdivision determined by competence, and a firm belief that product quality can be completely guaranteed by technological innovation, remain typical.

The IF is achieved only when we reach phase III, where high automation is matched with lean production. In this phase production flexibility combines with efficiency parameters (reduction of lead times and inventories) and quality is defined as 'total' because it is now clearly understood that quality is not the result of high technology alone, but also of intelligent and responsible human work. Finally, phase IV – lean production with 'low' technology – corresponds to the 'pure' Japanese model (note that in this context 'low' refers to a frugal rather than to backward technology). This kind of factory does not exhibit paths between the various boxes because the improvements have grown spirally from the very beginning of that model, though the small arrow inside phase IV indicates the recent trend to acquire further automation, even in Japanese factories. In the same way the arrow in phase III indicates the more recent trend at Fiat to build new plants with less automation than at Termoli and Cassino. We can therefore claim that the arrows represent a potential convergence in the mix of technology and production systems.

For a clearer understanding of the specificity of the path pursued by Fiat, the high automation phase can also be interpreted as a phase of 'naive flexibility', in which flexibility is conceived as a value in itself, an intrinsic sign of excellence, to be pursued despite its high cost or even on the basis of a tacit assumption that beyond a certain technological threshold flexibility is free. This was a real organizational myth (Meyer and Rowan 1977) which in the mid-1980s was encouraged by the production boom enjoyed by Fiat.[1] It was only when the market started to cool, around 1987–1988, that Fiat management felt the need to reconsider the myth of flexibility at any cost, and started to match production flexibility with the efficiency parameters suggested by lean production, thus laying the bases for their transition to phase III. In this sense the IF was seen as an organizational tool and was introduced by Fiat as an attempt to improve the relationship between quality, productivity and flexibility objectives.

Greenfields and brownfields

The second point to be emphasized here is that the various Fiat plants are not homogeneous from a technological point of view. The mode of implementation of the IF in the different plants reflects this lack of homogeneity, and appears to be the result of a learning process in which cognitive and strategic aspects intertwine. The process began in the greenfields of Termoli and Cassino – the two plants with the most advanced technology – and was implemented only later, and with slightly different objectives, in the older, less automated plants.

During the 1980s, Fiat setup one of the most automated automotive factories in the world at Termoli, dedicated to the production of the 'Fire' engine. Fiat's selection of this hyper-technological option has been much debated (Bechis 1986). Dina *et al.* (1988) suggest that Comau, the Fiat owned technology supplier, acted as a pressure group within Fiat Holdings in order to sell its products to Fiat Auto, thereby testing their effectiveness before making them available to other markets. It is also likely that such lobbying actively encouraged the conviction that only integral automation would be capable of guaranteeing regular production coupled with perfect quality. What is more, the technological option was supported by a desire to exorcise the memory of the turbulent Turin brownfields during the 1970s, with their masses of unskilled and angry workers.

Given these premises, one might assume that Fiat management, for a while at least, toyed with the idea of the ummanned factory, to be located, moreover, in an absolutely calm and tranquil social environment like that of the Molise.

As part of the objective of maximum technological efficiency, a 'monoline' was built with restrained workflow, high and preset rhythms, qualitative standards integrated into the production process, and a widespread use of information technology. The most common worker role was that of machine setter, whose task was to guarantee the regularity of the production flow by operating the complex machines, diagnosing problems and re-establishing standard running. Besides a large maintenance staff, 'line technologists' were also trained to look after homogeneous groups of machinery. The new roles, however, were introduced into a traditional organization with a multilayered hierarchy and functional divisions based upon competence.

This configuration started to collapse towards the end of 1986 when production went from one to three kinds of engine. Even though a system of integrated computer information was quickly installed, an increasing number of backlogs developed for a whole variety of reasons: faults in the computerized management of inventories, machinery faults, defective materials. Since the quality incorporated in the production process was zero-defect, as soon as the smallest problem arose everything came to a halt. During the worst period, out of 2,700 engines programmed per day, only 1,800–2,000 were being produced whilst hundreds of other engines lay on the ground waiting to be completed.

Fiat's production management came to realise that resorting to even the very best technology was not enough. They had to overcome an organization that was still based upon an assumption that breakdowns are rare occurrences, to create an organization capable of promptly and efficiently tackling the continual risk of faults and breakdowns. Without realizing that they were moving in the same direction as CM, the team of engineers assigned to restructure Termoli reviewed the organization from top to bottom. They moved the technical department from the offices to the shop floor, and setup self-contained technological elementary units (UTEs), each one of which was responsible for a complete phase of the production process (driving shaft, basement, piston rods). As head of each unit they appointed a 'plenipotentiary' with the tools required for interventions across the whole range of problems, and flanking him was a technological team with a staff function over all the possible process and product synergies. Lastly, it was decided that the workers would not be confined to running the machinery, but should be actively involved in a constant improvement programme. Around the end of 1987 the first experimental IF came into being, and within a year production at the Termoli plant was again under control.

In the history of Fiat the recovery at Termoli can be seen as a typical process of learning by doing and it highlights several considerations. First, the IF was perceived as a solution imposed upon Fiat by its new technology. Those people who participated in the recovery operation openly describe it as an extreme case of technological determinism, which they believe explains why the transition from HAF to IF was relatively short. One engineer observed that the HAF already contained the IF in a latent form which only needed to be brought to the surface.

Second, the objective was not to improve the quality of the product – given that the optimum standards were already incorporated in the production process – but rather to normalize the process itself. It was only after the phase of acute backlogs was overcome that it was decided to institutionalize constant improvement in order to make the workflow increasingly fluent and synchronized.

Third, the transition to the IF did not involve changes in the layout, which was already optimal for an automated production process. Thus it was a purely organizational endeavour. Manual work remained individual even though interaction with the members of the technological team increased. In this regard it must be noted that the team is not a working group in the usual sense of the term, but rather a structure comprising technicians who focus their attention on specific problems (Cattero 1991).

Fourth, those most affected by the change have been supervisory staff who were charged with managerial responsibilities, and 'enriched' by an increase in required competence and the novelty of consultations with other specialists. The repercussions for workers have been relatively bland, as they were already doing a job mediated by technology. What did change, though, was their social role, as they are now openly encouraged to communicate their practical knowledge by way of rewarded suggestions or by taking part in meetings of the technological teams, which under these circumstances act as real quality circles.

Finally, although the IF is the fruit of pioneering research and carried out virtually in isolation, the cultural influence of the

Japanese model is undeniable. Particularly interesting in this regard are changes in the ratio between direct and indirect workers. Until 1985 the philosophy behind the HAF suggested that work would increasingly be carried out by indirect workers. In line with that assumption the number of indirect workers gradually increased to 57 per cent of the total. After that year though, the curve was reversed in line with the Japanese teaching that indirect work produces no added value and should be, as far as possible, eliminated. This reverse trend manifested itself most clearly in the transformation of many 'pure' maintenance personnel into machine setters also entrusted with plant maintenance.

The positive results at Termoli prompted the Company to extend the principles of the IF to the bodyshop at Cassino (1988). Here too, the major difficulty was the contrast between the plant's high level of automation and its traditional organization. In this case, slightly different solutions were required because of the particular complexity of the process and because much more human work was involved than had been the case at Termoli, especially in final assembly. Thus some 'excessively' automated phases were simplified by reintroducing human work, and the solution involved not only process improvements (as at Termoli) but also product improvements.

This widening of objectives encouraged a serious re-evaluation of manual labour. Nervi, general director of bodyshops in Fiat Auto says:

during the HAF phase we were all obsessed with technology . . . first, pursuing the chimera of automation, we neglected the fact that the worker has not just a pair of arms but also has a head. For us their arms were enough because we wanted to manage their heads with computers and automation. Today we have abandoned that idea because we need human intelligence and the employees' cerebral activity. . . . Taylorism, if I may reinterpret this historic word, was very much the Highly Automated Factory.

It is noteworthy that a top Fiat manager is aware of the fact that even with high automation, manual work will remain Tayloristic if there is no involvement of human intelligence. At the same time his comments suggest that this transition to late Taylorism offers a basis upon which workers can agree to cooperate using their intelligence.

From a technological necessity to a strategic opportunity: Fiat brownfields towards the integrated factory

Towards the end of 1989, while all of this was going on, Fiat's general manager, Romiti, delivered a now famous speech which launched the battle cry of total quality. In the brownfields in and around Turin (Miraflori, Rivalta, Verrone, Chivasso) there was a mobilization to promote quality circles, and to introduce the CEDAC (cause-efficiency diagnosis and control) method, the flag system, Ishikawa diagrams and so on. The effect of all of this was a widespread and at times anxiety-fraught awareness of the Company's new goals on the shop floor, but with rather limited practical results. Some managers openly admitted that significant advances in the 'battle for quality' could only be achieved through radical organizational change. Documents compiled by various brownfield plant managements in 1990–1991 stated that the old organizational model had resulted in the fragmentation of operational tools amongst the various units and poor interaction between them; extremely long hierarchical chains of command with delayed decisions; segmented and at times contradictory objectives; and human resources with little commitment to the required improvements. Company documents declared the need to move to a new organization based on a bottom-up integration of all the formerly divided functions (production, maintenance, logistics, quality); the creation of self-contained UTEs dedicated to complete segments of the production process; and shorter chains of command. However, until around the middle of 1991 the implementation of the IF formula in Fiat Auto was still limited to Termoli and Cassino.

There are many reasons for the delay in the brownfields' move to the IF. The first is that at these sites there was no urgent need to correct a highly sophisticated system of machinery which was constantly jamming. Although important, the innovations in the 1980s had not led to a fully automated 'pipeline' in these factories and the general running of the process there remained largely in human hands. Thus the IF was not perceived as a technical necessity, but came to be conceived of as a strategic opportunity for a progressive reduction in those inconveniences which led to defective products.

The second reason is that the transition to the IF has proved to be more complicated with a traditional technology than with the high automation present in the greenfields. Unlike the high automation situation, the more traditional technology does not contain the latent potential of an organization by process. This led one engineer to say: 'defining the UTE at Termoli was simple, at Mirafori it needs a lot of thinking through'. This difficulty is linked to the fact that in the brownfields both layout and workteams follow criteria of operational homogeneity rather than those of the product. Furthermore, economic and spatial constraints have prevented almost any changes to the layout, so the engineers have had to redesign the boundaries of the new UTEs without taking the physical proximity of the operations into account. The result is that in the Fiat brownfields many UTEs have enclaves in the territory of others. In principle this is not a serious inconvenience, but it has not eased the transformation process.

Another and more serious reason for the delay arose from the need to prepare the employees, both supervisory staff and workers. Fiat management realized that it had to overcome a handicap unknown to the historyless 'greenfields': it was seeking a radical transformation of the plants, dominated both by a Fordist culture and by collective memories. As far as supervisors were concerned, they had to overcome the retaliation syndrome that had characterized the 1980s following the famous 'march of 40,000' of October 1980. They had been the main protagonists in the re-establishment of 'order' in the factories after the turbulence of the 1970s, and they knew they could count on the gratitude of the Company. Although the technological innovations which followed this re-establishment of 'order' provided the material support to relax their direct control over workers, the majority of supervisors persisted in the belief that the most natural way to make a workshop run lay in hierarchical bureaucratic power. Top management understood that it had to modify that system of beliefs, to make it clear that in the factory of the future there would be fewer supervisors and those left would have higher managerial responsibilities than before, with hierarchical levels reduced from eight to five. So, supervisors needed intensive retraining courses, and a 'gentle' selection of the most suitable individuals, aimed at eliminating around half the existing supervisors, was also necessary. A strategic and cultural operation such as this obviously required time.

Meanwhile Fiat management also had to overcome obstacles represented by the low per centage of qualified workers, which made it impossible to consider creating anything like autonomous working groups such as those in the German factories, where 'professional workers' (Facharbeiter) make up the core of employees.

Consequently Fiat management had to devise another formula to obtain the highest qualitative performance and involvement from a majority of unskilled and semiskilled workers, for the most part trained in individual tasks or at best in tasks carried out in pairs

A solution to the problem was only found in the autumn of 1991 with the creation of the role of the 'integrated process operator' (*conduttore di processo integrato*: CPI). Unlike the machine setter who works on automated complex machines, the CPI is a skilled worker introduced in a ratio of 1 for every 10–12 unskilled or semiskilled workers. They are not involved in production but concentrate exclusively on control, monitoring, quick diagnosis and assistance to other workers regarding quality problems. In terms of Company strategy the CPI should become the UTE leader's closest collaborator and at the same time a natural consultant for other workers. They have been given the delicate job of acting as a link person between the horizontal flow and the first level in the hierarchical structure, with tasks that recall the moniteur in some French factories or even the 'first class worker' in many Japanese factories. This role still lacks precise definition, however, and particularly at Mirafiori this has contributed to delays in implementing the IF programme.

Finally, a detailed 'remapping' was required, team by team, of all the technical and logistical operations of production and the available human resources, and this too has contributed to prolonging the transition as management sought to eliminate disparities between the real production flow at team level and the often insufficient information available to workshop management. Fiat viewed this remapping as a necessary premise to initiating a total quality programme, and when it was finished 'homologous teams' were setup, equipped with all the cognitive and technical tools to identify and gradually eliminate the faults present in their field of competence. These homologous teams can therefore be considered as a transition phase from the traditional shop floor organization to the IF, where the teams themselves are gradually transformed into UTEs.

The programme requires that within a supplier–customer framework there is:

1 visibility of production and faults (up-to-date statistics on notice board) so that teams can immediately point out any machinery anomalies or defects found in material coming from the suppliers (external subcontractors included);

2 a complete and 'public' listing of all operations undertaken by the team, in order to obtain both a higher standardization in the production process and a better understanding of the process among workers;

3 the rearrangement of workflows and work positions with the elimination of any informal 'banks' of work;

4 a record on notice boards of all skills possessed by the workers, in order to define training programmes to increase the capabilities within the team.

These teams have been setup, but their gradual transition to UTEs is taking place in a differentiated way. In the smaller plants it has generally lasted a few weeks and has not given rise to particular problems. In several Mirafiori plants it is still going on, due to the complexity of the operations. In the plant at Rivalta the creation of homologous teams has been the subject of an agreement between shop stewards and local management, which in turn has led to the creation of a joint committee for implementing the programme.

Varied patterns of consent in post-Fordism

The changes described so far seem not to have evoked hostility among Fiat's employees. Rather, their attitude has ranged from prudent observation to open support. These attitudes are in line with other indications, including the development of active union cooperation to improve both process and product quality. This cooperation is particularly evident at Termoli, Cassino and Rivalta where, at the beginning of 1991, the union signed agreements with plant management covering financial awards for every improvement proposal put forward by individual workers and accepted by a technical board specifically setup to assess them. Over a ten-month period (February–November 1991) the percentage of workers whose proposals were accepted by the Board was 12 per cent at Rivalta, 15 per cent at Termoli and 17 per cent at Cassino.

In other plants, particularly Mirafiori, cooperation, though more cautious, has been especially evident in the growth of CEDACs. CEDACs are an instrument for reducing specific defects identified by the Company within defined time frames. From conversations with shop stewards at Mirafiori we gained the impression of a cautious though positive disposition towards this innovation, while they seem particularly to look forward to the day when rewarded individual suggestions will be introduced at Mirafiori as well. Finally, it is interesting to note that in all Fiat Auto factories quality circles have increased from 339 in 1989 to 562 in 1990 and more than 900 in November 1991.

The Union justifies this policy of cooperation with various arguments: the end of the era of conflict; the presence of a new generation of workers who are less ideological and more pragmatic; the need for the Company to meet the challenge posed by international competition; to defend jobs; the progressive rejection of Taylorism; the fact that for the first time the Company is recognizing and paying for intelligent suggestions from the workers (Cerruti and Rieser 1991).

The fact that workers are prepared to make suggestions and cooperate in improving process and product quality raises the problem of correctly interpreting the meaning of this consensus. Worker consent to new production methods is the leitmotif characterizing two well known approaches in the post-Fordist literature: flexible specialization (Piore and Sabel 1984) and new production concepts (Kern and Schumann 1984). Both support the argument that worker consent is related to growth in the professional workers' sphere of responsible autonomy. However, this explanation cannot be applied to Fiat. What one observes there is not the growth of 'black boxes' within the labour process which are entrusted to the workers, but a very different phenomenon.

What is more intriguing is the fact that in Fiat workers' consent is expressed mainly through their willingness to render their own knowledge explicit, and through their acceptance that the Company will use their knowledge to rationalize the production process and improve the product. Fiat's appeal for greater responsibility on the job has led, ultimately, to cooperation, and this in turn has meant the production process has become more transparent.

From a sociological viewpoint, these issues are of great theoretical importance. They involve nothing less than explaining why workers accept withdrawal from traditional work practices like that of concealing information regarding gaps between formal and informal aspects of the labour process. From Gouldner to Crozier, from Roy to Burawoy, workshop studies have described how attempts by firms to eliminate the hidden aspects of manual work have always met with opposition. To what extent can such an operation be successful in Fiat today? Can monetary rewards alone explain workers' willingness to offer their suggestions, or is some wider explanation of this phenomenon required?

The processes which are rendering production progressively more transparent have become the object of much recent debate, especially in response to the growing importance of the Japanese model. Rather schematically, one can identify three main positions which emerge from studies in this area of research. First, there is a pessimistic position which emphasizes the negative effects of the radical application of JIT (Klein 1989). Some authors outline an almost Orwellian scenario in which workers are at the mercy of an electronic panopticon which controls every aspect of the labour process (Delbridge *et al.* 1991; Sewell and Wilkinson 1992). From this viewpoint every increase in the transparency of manual work can only be interpreted as an increase in the company's control and a significant loss in workers' autonomy. In such circumstances, any consent that might exist can only be interpreted as the result of manipulation. At the other extreme is a more reassuring inter-pretation that explains the harnessing of tacit skills as the effect of consensual mechanisms and the internalization of company needs (Wood 1989). Finally, there is an intermediary position which inter-prets the cooperation of employees as being due to structural causes rather than to ideological manipulation. These causes are identified in the relationship between the absence of other local job oppor-tunities and the effectiveness of kaizen mechanisms (Garrahan and Stewart 1991).

Which of these positions is most relevant to the phenomena observed in Fiat? In our opinion none exactly fits our findings at Fiat, although the last seems to come closest. Our hypothesis is that the reasons for the Fiat workers' consent reside primarily in certain transformations of manual work in the 1980s – during the so-called high automation phase. It should also be noted that the most remarkable innovations in work organization associated with the IF involve supervisors rather than workers. Thus the implementation of the IF – which seems to complete the transformations begun during the high automation phase – involves manual work only marginally and without traumatic effects

The second part of this paper, which draws on research on developments at Fiat Mirafiori over the last decade, is devoted to supporting this hypothesis. The research began in summer, 1990, when the campaign to increase awareness regarding total quality had already begun but there was yet no mention of the IF. Subse-quent visits in autumn 1991 and winter 1992 allowed us to trace the movement towards the IF.

IN SEARCH OF THE REASONS FOR WORKERS' CONSENT

Ten years of work transformations at Fiat Mirafiori (1980–1990)

Compared to the early 1980s, the most obvious innovation to be seen at Mirafiori plants is the remarkable improvement in environmental and ergonomic conditions. Today work goes on in conditions which are less noisy, better lit, cleaner, more spacious and safer, with more comfort in general. Most jobs now require less physical effort, the reduction being as much as 80 per cent in some cases. The improvements came about because (a) robots took over most of the most tiring and unpleasant tasks; (b) machinery was placed more rationally with big savings of space and movement; (c) buffers were increased by about five times; (d) the overhead conveyors were mostly replaced by transport on electric trucks; (e) parts are now available immediately on mobile supports, without workers having to pick them up and carry them by hand; (f) workers use equipment which is easier and lighter to handle; and (g) the ergonomics of physical posture are improved. A further aspect of the change is the increased regularity of the labour process. This arises because the new technologies make it less dependent on human variations in both quantity and quality. It is not by chance that the word 'objectivation' is widely used in the technical jargon at Mirafiori. Today monitoring devices make it possible to detect hidden defects in real time and to discover their origin.

These trends can be seen in both maintenance and production. In routine maintenance flexible automation involves greater technical complexity, but procedures have become more routine. It is now possible to programme frequent changes of equipment. Consequently, professionalism in routine maintenance means, above all, speed of operations, requiring a thorough knowledge of tried and tested procedures. In emergency maintenance, however, the need to avoid interrupting production means the most important skill is not the quick repair of breakdowns with the machine stopped, but rather the ability to make temporary repairs without stopping production. This requires a knowledge of predetermined schemes, as well as considerable ingenuity.

On production work there is a general reduction and simplification of the various operations, but the job now includes small-scale maintenance which used to be carried out by special teams. There also tends to be a progressive split between direct production jobs and those involving inspection. In production jobs human intervention is reduced to simply loading the pieces onto transfer machines and pushing a button to start up the automatic process, generally reducing average working times. In inspection, work has been transformed qualitatively. The worker no longer carries out the various operations himself, as his job is limited to ensuring that the operations performed by the machine have no defects. For occasional defects the operator uses manual tools to complete and correct the job, and for systematic imperfections he contacts the setup man.

A third aspect of the transformation during the 1980s is the changed relationship between supervisors and workers. The firm has setup training programmes to sensitize supervisors in their relationship with workers, aimed at less authoritarian, more formal relations paying more attention to 'psychology'. Moreover, regular relationships between supervisors and personnel officers have been institutionalized. In consequence supervisors feel less alone in taking decisions in the workshop, and advice from their superiors tends to make their conduct more consistent with centralized regulations. This uniformity is especially useful in relations with newly hired workers, who usually have a better formal education than their foremen.

A key consequence of the innovations described above is that work in production has become easier, lighter, more comfortable, but also more accurate, repetitive and restraining. The situation is ambiguous: the advantage afforded by the reduction of physical effort seems to be counterbalanced by the loss of autonomy and the chance to use one's discretion. But the two dimensions can only be distinguished at the analytical level, because in workshop life they fade into a change which is experienced as totalizing, homogeneous and univocal: that of a technical progress which increases the volume, regularity and quality of production, while at the same time affording the operator greater comfort. A foreman in charge of assembling doors onto car bodies describes the change like this:

> We used to have a mobile line, about two feet overhead, and the car bodies travelled on this. You had to pick up the door by hand, with no tool to help you, and with one hand you held the door still while with the other you put the first bolt in, then still with one hand you took hold of the screwdriver and

screwed up the bolt so as to hold the door still for a moment. Then you got the other bolts and put them in, then when the door was tacked on you tightened up the other bolts. Then you had to adjust it. It was five times the amount of work it is now. If today we have one minute to put on a door, at that time it took us five or six minutes . . . And then you were moving as you worked, following the body, and you had to move about twenty metres, then go back and start again with another body, and so on. The work was heavier and more complex, if you like, not because of the difficulty of the work itself, but because of the difficulty of how you had to do it. . . . The work is more fragmented today, but before the operation was longer but much more tiring.

And a steel body-work checker remembers how he used to work before the automatic welders were introduced:

We used to have to get into the body while it was moving, two of us, one on each side, and with the welders we had to weld eighty to a hundred spots each, before getting out and leaving the body to the next pair of workers. We had to try not to get in each other's way, and we had to hurry, too . . . we used to call it the belly dance . . . welding the spots and at the same time keeping the door open with your hip, put down one welder and pick up another, while the line kept going. . . . Today I work standing still, and in peace. The car bodies go by in front of me and I check that the PAC (automatic welder) has welded the spots properly. If something's wrong, I use the hand welder to do the missing spots. Compared to the past, I save 90 per cent of the effort, and the work is better, more dignified.

In both of these accounts there is an ironical touch about a 'past' which is only five years ago but no one would like to go back to. There is astonishment about a time which was so recent, but which would now be so intolerable.

Work content, procedures and effort

As mentioned above, the evolution of manual work at Fiat Mirafiori poses problems of no small importance concerning recent debate. On the one hand, the increased importance of maintenance and of checking and inspection functions among jobs in production seems to support an optimistic position – in particular the Kern and Schumann theses (1984) on the growing importance of qualitative aspects of work in the new production models. On the other hand, the further simplification of many production jobs and their reduction to simple operations of loading and unloading onto automatic machinery appears to confirm Braverman's theses (1974) on the inevitable degradation of manual work.

One way of reconciling these features would be in terms of a split between those jobs which have tended to become more skilled and those which have been impoverished, but our evidence suggests the main changes in manual work at Fiat are less to do with upgrading or deskilling of jobs, and more to do with the connections between technological progress, reductions of effort and the dynamics of consent. In the first place, the reduction of effort and greater comfort of work appear integral to the development of technical procedures, the diminishing of idiosyncratic irregularities and the greater possibility of monitoring operations. Increased ease and increased regularity seem to be two sides of a single phenomenon induced by technological innovation, though they are also related to changes in relationships between workers and supervisors.

Second, workers' subjective attitudes to these changes are crucial. Supervisors, trade unionists and workers themselves all tell the same story. In many jobs in direct production, the fact that workers no longer have to use their old skills is seen as a negligible price to pay for the improvements. Indeed, it is seen as an advantage which helps to make the job less tiring, less uncomfortable and less harassing. In many cases workers did not like having to use these working skills, even though they were very good at them, and their loss is not mourned or protested, especially when the skills in question were of no value on the job market, but simply 'survival techniques' to achieve quotas, to keep the job, to avoid being told off by the foreman or made fun of by your mates[2].

To understand these features it is useful to link the old work of Baldamus (1961) written at the height of the Fordist era and the influential contribution by Hirschhorn (1986) that reflects upon the consequences of high automation for work. Baldamus argues that the central object of industrial sociology is the control system which regulates the quantity, quality and distribution of human effort. Accepting this enables us to admit that the analytical centrality of effort remains even if and when its intensity is reduced to the point of allowing potentially positive aspects of comfort to appear in work. Twenty-five years later, Hirschhorn gives a post-industrial twist to Baldamus's thesis when he argues that new technologies allow the separation of output from effort, thereby making increasingly irrelevant both Taylorism and its critique.

Linking Hirschhorn to Baldamus helps us to interpret recent developments at Fiat which would otherwise remain enigmatic: namely the extensive processes of simplification and standardization of tasks, and the contemporaneous reduction in the fatigue and heaviness of the work. The coexistence of these trends suggests that Taylorization processes admit a variable degree of sophistication in their implementation. We can suggest that from a crude and authoritarian tool of exploitation and control in the first decades of this century, Taylorism has evolved into an increasingly elaborate, impersonal instrument for time and method analysis, and in the extreme, is sublimated into a mere framework for cost calculation (cf. Littler 1982 on the evolution of variants of Taylorism). This suggests that during the 1980s HAF at Fiat led to the overcoming of Taylorism through its dilution and attenuation, rather than its transcendence.

These considerations lead us to the crucial thesis of our analysis, that the roots of worker consent are to be found in the reduction of effort. Some might object that workers' consent founded on a simple decrease of effort is a weak form of consent, but there are two answers to this objection. First, consent arises not only from immediate material improvements, but also from their symbolic significance; that is, from a widespread recognition that improvements in the quality of work in the factory are in line with wider improvements of the quality of life which are taking place in industrialized countries. In the workers' perception of the quality of his life, the use of the same standards of comfort inside and outside the factory is a concrete demonstration that in the factory he is considered as a citizen and not only as a worker.[3] Second, we must distinguish between passive consent based on the elimination of sources of conflict, and active consent to prolonged and reliable service.

The status of skills and the traditional pre-eminence of quantity

To understand the basis for active consent at Fiat we must consider the functions of tacit skills in the production process. Critics of the degradation thesis have emphasized the indispensability of a variety of forms of tacit skills in the production process (Kusterer 1978; Jones and

Wood 1984; Manwaring and Wood 1985) and the working skill needed in microelectronic technology (de Tersacc and Coriat 1984; Bernoux *et al.* 1987). Cavestro (1989) has also observed that automation encourages the tendency to formalize workers' tacit skills – probably the observation closest to my thesis. To understand the current phenomena at Fiat, however, emphasizing that tacit skills are coming into the open is not enough, for it is necessary to recognize that tacit skills have widely differing functions in the production process, some legitimate and others opportunistic.

The best way to distinguish between the various types of skill is to look at how they are judged under the implicit or explicit factory rules. In this way we can define three large classes of tacit skills. First there are assumed or legitimate skills, the informal skills or operations which are useful and often indispensable for the production process since they compensate for technological limits. In this class of skills we include the workers' practice of cutting the corners of the formal system, such as taking urgent action based on experience when the person formally responsible is absent. On the opposite side there is the class of deviant or forbidden skills – all those opportunistic but skilful tricks and practices aimed at making the work easier and quicker, but which compromise the quality of the product or the safety of the working process.

In between these good and bad skills are the ambiguous or tolerated skills.

> This class is very wide and originates from the overlapping of explicit prohibition and tacit permission. It includes almost 'innocent' practices, typically aimed at accumulating informal rest time (little tricks to increase the rhythm of the work, preparing ready machined pieces in advance), but it also includes more questionable practices, such as taking over another's job, repairing breakdowns without waiting for the technician or getting material directly from the store.
>
> (Bensman and Gerver 1963).

The wide range of tolerated tacit skills takes on particular importance. These are not only a convenience for workers but are historically tied to a production orientation which places greater emphasis on quantity than on quality. When supervisors have only approximate and bureaucratic criteria available for judging quality, and know that their work is evaluated primarily on the basis of the quantity produced, they are understandably likely to ignore irregular practices, provided they meet production schedules. Thus the wider the area in which ambiguously tolerated tacit skills abound, the greater the probability that quality is subordinated to quantity criteria. As a result the diffusion of ambiguous tacit skills can be considered as an index of poor quality.

Another aspect to be borne in mind when analysing tacit skill is that the worker's inclination to keep information to himself is not a constant but a variable that depends on the prevailing technological conditions and management policies. In the traditional production regime the fact that this was directly connected to a certain degree of continued human effort made it necessary for the company to control and discipline the forms in which effort was expressed. From this point of view Taylorism can be seen as the scientific aggravation of an existing management imperative. This was a 'zero-sum' situation: all the work which management succeeded in bringing to the surface – that it brought under control – fell from the workers' control, and vice versa.

The consequence was that a large share of labour was carried out in a sort of hidden arena, where workers sought to jealously guard their tacit skills. These skills served above all to protect workers from exploitation; but they were also niches of worker subjectivity and the informal basis for work satisfaction. On the one hand, work was performed in a situation of objective antagonism between a management which wanted to Taylorise and workers struggling against any such move; on the other hand the workers often manifested degrees of responsibility and silent cooperation (for example, the production games described by Roy (1953) and Burawoy (1979)).

The new production model is no longer like this. The fact that there is a less direct nexus between production and sustained physical effort means that control has increasingly been transformed from an external disciplinary fact into intelligent conformity with procedures. Such conformity is more technically analysable than in the past: it accompanies a reduction in effort and does not necessarily involve any impoverishment of work content. Above all, the zero-sum game, typical of the Tayloristic era, is disappearing, and with it a fundamental part of the factory workers' daily experience which nourished a dichotomous and conflict-ridden vision of society.

Total quality and new strategies on the job

The technological innovations which have occurred in Fiat during the 1980s have laid the basis for overcoming a production regime which favoured the 'opportunistic' guarding of information. Subsequently, the new situation has been exploited by Fiat to encourage workers' cooperation in achieving total quality.

In day-to-day life at work, what concrete forms does the mobilization towards quality take? Interviews with supervisors in 1990 repeatedly revealed an apparently contradictory attitude towards workers' skills. On the one hand these skills are condemned with 'Taylorian' arguments: 'If the firm has established a certain way of working, this is not by chance. The worker who insists on doing things his own way is obviously not working as he should.'

More than one supervisor, remembering the disorders of the 1970s, condemned illicit initiatives of this type: 'workers used to go back up the line, they did the work as quickly as they could and ran off to play cards.' But during the same interviews these supervisors emphasized that 'today the firm encourages suggestions coming from the workers' experience. If they are good then it adopts them and rewards the person who gave them' – a reference to the quality circles and the CEDACs which were first launched at Mirafiori in the summer of 1990.

The apparent contrast between these declarations can be interpreted as a sign of the desire to reduce the workers' skills to only two large categories: negative skills to be condemned and repressed and positive skills to be recognized and rewarded. The intermediate area of ambiguously tolerated skills is thus eliminated. The logical consequence of this dichotomy is that, in principle, there should not be any intentionally hidden skill. In the eyes of the supervisors, to hide a skill is in itself a good reason to suspect that it might compromise the quality of the product. If the skill is positive, there can be no reason to hide it, since the firm will recognize and reward it.

The potential reduction of skills to these two categories reflects the fact that the new technology offers the chance to eliminate so-called 'idiosyncratic relations' between man and machine. It is also an expression of the firm's intention, via supervision, to exploit that possibility to make manual work as transparent as possible. When we asked: 'What do you do when you find out that one of your workers is using tricks on the job?', one foreman answered, implying a purely negative understanding of such tricks:

For a long time I had to pretend I couldn't see what was going on, except in very extreme cases [referring to worker combativity at Mirafiori during the 1970s]. Now, apart from there being a different climate, the technology helps me, and the opportunities for tricks have been reduced by 70 per cent. But most of all, it is no longer worth their while.

Of course, ambiguously tolerated skills will never disappear completely, however severely they may be reduced. There will always be tiny margins. The worker who is in a hurry to finish a job so as to avoid having to queue at the canteen is unlikely to disappear. What counts, however, is not the residue of ambiguously tolerated skills, but their irrelevance to a theory of workers' behaviour at work today.

There have, then, been profound changes at Fiat over the last twelve years. Today there is, for workers, no sense in using the old skills in an antagonistic way, while a possible strategy might be to bring them out into the open, so that they may be used to improve quality. The end of the old state of conflict does not annul the workers' bargaining capacity. Rather it redefines it. To participate in a quality circle, to collaborate with a CEDAC, become instruments of negotiation in a subtle trade relation, where the counterpart is the occasional bonus, a merit raise, enhanced promotion opportunities, but also the symbolic reward for having participated: this last is not an insignificant factor.

Mirafiori one year later: some consequences of implementing the integrated factory

This was the situation in the summer of 1990, a few months into the mobilization for total quality at Mirafiori, when a somewhat astonished satisfaction at the favourable worker response was the prevailing atmosphere among managers. Our return visit a year later suggests that such cooperation has been extended and consolidated, but at the same time some new features and problems are emerging.

The most visible phenomenon is the consolidation of the use of CEDACs. At Mirafiori these grew from 205 at the end of 1990 to 314 at the end of 1991 (in Fiat Auto overall they increased from 1,135 to 1,890), and their use has become more systematic and rational. In the initial phase, before the IF had been created, responsibility for managing the CEDACs was entrusted to the team supervisors, but the administrative Taylorism in which the supervisors were still embroiled led them to maximize the local advantages to their team rather than seek any overall improvement in the product. The supervisors considered the CEDACs primarily as a 'preferential route' to obtain those operations and tools they had already requested, but had never obtained, from workshop management. Furthermore, as workers were not accustomed to provide written suggestions, it was not uncommon for supervisors to urge trusted workers to fill in the cards with proposals suggested by the supervisors themselves.

At the end of 1990 Fiat management tried to eliminate these teething problems with precise directives giving priority to product improvements, but real improvements only occurred when, with the passage towards the IF, the basis for overcoming the old localisms had been established. Today, the UTE supervisors get the necessary information for making decisions on what must be improved from the quality office. As a result the CEDACs setup in 1991 were approximately half those in 1990, but the positive results went from around 50 per cent to almost 90 per cent.

While the CEDACs in Mirafiori have become a consolidated routine, it is likely that they will lose their present monopoly position in gathering workers' knowledge as soon as the 'quality improvement suggestions' (QIS) channel, already adopted at Termoli, Cassino and Rivalta, is extended to Mirafiori (June 1992). Fiat's official position is that the CEDACs will remain in being to collect suggestions focused on eliminating specific defects pointed out by the Company – while the QIS will function as a channel for gathering suggestions of a more spontaneous and diffuse kind. In reality, many managers believe that the QIS will become the much preferred channel because it allows workers to offer suggestions more directly linked to their daily experience; it is less bureaucratic, and each 'valid' suggestion gains an immediate reward (whereas with CEDACs the reward comes at year-end and is left much more to supervisory discretion).

Running parallel to this development in suggestion giving, is the growing role played by literacy during worktime. On the one hand, there are fewer note books with standards in techno-bureaucratic jargon (which as a rule stopped with the team supervisor, the last person in the chain able to read and understand them). On the other hand, those standards are increasingly being replaced by graphs and sheets which are not restricted to the UTE supervisor or the CPIs, but which also circulate among workers so they can carry out self-certification of their work. An increasing number of workers use these sheets, ticking off the operations they have done or marking operations still unperformed or which must be returned to. In 1991 the Company decided that these self-certifications should no longer be considered an 'extra' with respect to 'real' work performed. Since these activities have been included in defined worktimes (with the consequent proportional reduction in the production material quota to be dealt with), the noting of defects by workers has doubled, from only 40 per cent of those discovered at inspection up to 80 per cent today. All this makes it legitimate to argue that reading and writing during worktime is becoming ever more a matter of habit, even among unskilled and semiskilled workers.

Within this substantially favourable picture, the greatest problems arise from the contrast between the invitation which the Company extends to employees to work using their intelligence, and the routine of a work regime which, although less laborious than in the past nonetheless remains monotonous and restrictive (for example, on the assembly line for the 'Uno' the work rate was 250 vehicles for every shift of 450 minutes, with an average rhythm of one vehicle in less than two minutes).

On the one hand, Fiat insists that unlike Japanese companies it will never utilize workers' suggestions to intensify work rhythms. As the director of the body workshop at Mirafiori said:

> We have so many areas of superfluous fat to get rid of, in the logistics, the warehouses, maintenance, in the procedures to be rationalized, that before thinking of reducing the workforce years will pass. But even then I don't think that we will aim at intensifying the workload. It would mean throwing the capital of trust which we are striving to build up with the workers out of the window; it would be suicidal. I can remove one individual if the technology allows me to do it, but even in that case caution is required.

On the other hand, however, the same director admits that there is a tendency under way to 'saturate' worktimes, to eliminate informal porosity within the prescribed 450 minutes. This tendency results partly from a desire to recover the loss of production volume caused by the creation of the CPI, because of the loss of workers who have been taken from production to be trained exclusively in monitoring quality on the line. In part the increase in 'saturation' is a direct consequence of the recent reduction in buffers: a reduction which, as we saw, is an integral part of implementing the IF, and which reversed the trend followed in the 1980s. As stocks are gradually reduced between one UTE and the others, the scope for workers to accumulate the work done ahead of time has been reduced, as has the possibility of informal pauses. As an assembly shop steward declared:

> It's not a question of increase in fatigue, but of a contrast between the Company's request that workers work with intelligence and the greater restrictions imposed on the work. The small pauses which we can take moving about the department become a moment for reading the cards along the line, for commenting on them with workmates and thinking about them, maybe coming up with a new idea. What is the point of it all if they put the cards up but then reduce the time we have to read them? There's a contradiction between the Company's desire that we become increasingly more aware and critical of the way we work and the increase in saturation.

This touches on what is currently probably the greatest limit to the IF in a brownfield site like Mirafiori. The technological innovations of the 1980s have allowed reductions in work fatigue. This has laid the basis for workers' consenting to provide suggestions, but its very success is now also laying the basis for a new tension. On the one hand workers are induced to provide conceptual contributions to the resolution of new problems which accompany the continual innovations in both process and product, and these contributions involve a qualitative leap with regard to suggesting simple, practical tacit skills which they alone possess. On the other hand the passage from HAF to IF (see Figure 9.1) requires work which, though less fatiguing and more intelligent than in the past, is much more saturated, and therefore creates mental and social conditions which are less conducive to thinking about innovations. This contrast is likely to produce forms of stress which have hitherto been unknown in the Fiat plants.

Acknowledgements

This chapter is an abridged version of the book *Il tubo di cristallo* (The Crystal Tube), Il Mulino, Bologna 1993. All the documentation – only a small part of which is given here – has been supplied by Dr Maurizio Magnabosco, head of Fiat Auto personnel and organization, and Dr Mairano, head of training and communication development, to whom I express my sincere thanks.

NOTES

1 Some managers revealed to us that when it was not possible to assemble all the car bodies demanded by the market at Mirafiori, the extra bodies were assembled at Cassino, more than 700 km away. Similarly, the more the number of models and their variants grew, the bigger the stocks had to be to guarantee immediate availability.

2 These trends are confirmed by the fact that where automatic and manual production lines coexist, supervisors generally put the older workers on the automatic lines and the younger ones on the old manual lines. This is because progress from the more tiring jobs to the easier ones is informally established on the basis of seniority. But there is also a hidden learning factor. One foreman explained:

> working on the manual line is a bit like driving a hundred miles on a narrow windy road in a runabout, whereas working on the automatic line is like driving five hundred miles on the motorway in a luxury car. It is only fair that the youngsters learn the skill needed to drive on a narrow road before going onto the motorway. That way they realise how much the machinery has changed over the years.

3 These rather optimistic observations nevertheless conceal a certain ambivalence, related to paradoxical features of the workers' contemporary condition: on one hand, the desire to smooth over all possible rough edges of the work, so as to forget that condition as fast as possible. On the other, the fact that just this desire betrays the peculiarity of being a worker today. At Fiat, low pay is without doubt the greatest impediment to any post-worker pretence.

REFERENCES

Baldamus, W. (1961) *Efficiency and Effort*, London: Tavistock.

Bechis E (ed.) (1986) *Indagine su di un caso di progettazione congiunta prodotto/processo: il mo tore Fiat Fire e lo stabilimento di Termoli,* Piemonte: Quaderni IRES.

Bensman, J. and Gerver, I. (1963) 'Crime and punishment in the factory', *American Sociological Review* 28: 588–598.

Berggren, C., Björman, T. and Hollander, E. (1991) *Are They Unbeatable?* Royal Institute of Technology, Stockholm, mimeo.

Bernoux, P., Cavestro, W., Lamotte, B. and Troussier, J.-F. (1987) *Technologies nouvelles, nouveau travail,* Paris: Fédération de l'Education nationale Ed.

Braverman, H. (1974) *Labour and Monopoly Capital,* New York: Monthly Review Press.

Burawoy, M. (1979) *Manufacturing Consent,* Chicago: Chicago UP.

Cattero, B. (1991) 'Automazione e integrazione. L'organizzazione del lavoro nello stabilimento Fiat di Termoli 3', in *Prospettive di ricerca neo-industriale in Europa,* Dept. di scienze sociali, Torino.

Cavestro, W. (1989) 'Automation, new technology and work content', in S. Wood (ed.) *The Transformation of Work?* London: Unwin Hyman.

Cerruti, C. and Rieser, V. (1991) *Fiat: qualità totale e fabbrica integrata*, Roma: Ediesse.

Dawson, P. (1991) 'Flexible workcells: teamwork and group technology on the shopfloor', 9th International Labour Process Conference, Manchester (April).

Delbridge, R., Turnbull, P. and Wilkinson, B. (1991) 'Pushing back the frontiers: management control and work intensification under JIT factory regimes', 9th International Labour Process Conference, Manchester (April).

Dina, A. *et al.* (1988) *Il robot fatto a mano*, Torino: Rosenberg and Sellier.

Fucini, J. and Fucini, S. (1990) *Working for the Japanese. Inside Mazda's American Auto Plant*, New York: Free Press.

Garrahan, P. and Stewart, P. (1991) 'Flexible systems and the international automobile industry: a case of lean or mean production?' 9th International Labour Process Conference, Manchester (April).

Greiner, G. J. (1988) *Inhuman Relations: Quality Circles and Antiunionism in American Industry*, Philadelphia: Temple University Press.

Hirschhorn, L. (1986) *Beyond Mechanization*, Cambridge, Mass.: MIT Press.

Jones, B. and Wood, S. (1984) 'Qualifications tacites, division du travail et nouvelles technologies', *Sociologie du Travail*, 4: 407–421.

Kern, H. and Schumann, M. (1984) *Das Ende der Arbeitsteilung?* Munich: Beck'sche Verlagsbuchhandlung.

Klein, J. (1989) 'The Human Cost of Manufacturing Reform', *Harvard Business Review* (March–April): 60–66.

—— (1991) 'A reexamination of autonomy in light of new manufacturing practices', *Human Relations* 44, 1: 21–38.

Kusterer, K. (1978) *Know-how on the Job: The Important Working Knowledge of Unskilled Workers*, Boulder Col.: Westview Press.

Littler, C. (1982) *The Development of the Labour Process in Capitalist Societies*, London: Gower.

Manwaring, T. and Wood, S. (1985) 'The ghost in the labour process', in D. Knights *et al.* (eds) *Job Redesign*, London: Gower.

Meyer, J. and Rowan, B. (1977) 'Institutionalized organizations: formal structure, myth and ceremony', *American Journal of Sociology* 83, 2: 340–363.

Oliver, N. and Wilkinson, B. (1988) *The Japanization of British Industry*, Oxford: Blackwell.

Parker, M. and Slaughter, J. (1988) 'Management by stress', *Technology Review* (October) 37–44.

Parnaby, J. (1987) 'Practical just-in-time: inside and outside the factory', Paper presented to the Fifth *Financial Times* Manufacturing Forum, mimeo, London, 6–7 May.

Piore M. and Sabel C. (1984) *The Second Industrial Divide*, New York: Basic Books.

Rehder, R. (1990) 'Japanese transplant: after the honeymoon', *Business Horizons* (January–February) 87–98.

Roy, D. (1953) 'Work satisfaction and social reward in quota achievement', *American Sociological Review* 18: 507–514.

Sewell, G. and Wilkinson, B. (1992) 'Someone to watch over me: surveillance, discipline and the JIT labour process', *Sociology* 26, 2: 271–289.

Starkey, K. and McKinlay, A. (1989) 'Beyond Fordism? Strategic choice and labour relations in Ford UK', *Industrial Relations Journal* 20, 2: 93–100.

Tersacc, G. de and Coriat, B. (1984) 'Micro-électronique et travail ouvrier dans les industries de procès', *Sociologie de travail* 4: 384–397.

Turnbull, P. (1986) 'The "Japanization" of production and industrial relations at Lucas Electrical', *Industrial Relations Journal* 17, 3: 193–206.

—— (1989) 'Industrial restructuring and labour relations in the automotive components industry: "just-in-time" or "just-too-late"?', in S. Tailby and C. Whitston (eds) *Manufacturing Change*, Oxford: Basil Blackwell.

Wemmerlöw, U. and Hyer, N. (1987) 'Research issues in cellular manufacturing', *Intern. Journ. of Prod. Research* 25, 3: 413–431.

—— (1989) 'Cellular Manufacturing in the US industry: a survey of users', *Intern. Journ. of Prod. Research* 27, 9: 1511–1530.

Wood, S. (1989) 'The Japanese management model: tacit skills and shop floor participation', *Work and Occupations* 16, 4: 446–460.

10

BETWEEN ADVERSARIAL RELATIONS AND INCORPORATION

A study of the 'joint process' in an American auto-components plant

John Black and Peter Ackers

This chapter explores new directions in labour relations in the US car industry by focusing on innovations in union–management cooperation and 'teamworking' at a General Motors (GM) components plant in upstate New York. It is concerned with the nature, origins and plant level implications of what has become known in the US auto industry as the 'joint process'. The focus of the chapter reflects an interest in the changing nature of management control and trade union responses. Rarely are changes in social behaviour completely new or revolutionary. Elements of labour–management cooperation have existed in the past (Brodie 1985). However, we argue that recent changes involve a qualitative leap in United Automobile Workers (UAW) ideology and practice.

We are seeing an increasing internationalization of managerial practice and ideology reflecting the economic pressures of recession, the globalization of product markets and the tendency to compete with Japanese corporations by emulating their management systems and structures. These developments have been associated with widespread pressure for the decentralization of bargaining to plant level, and in this context the potential undermining of national bargaining in the US has wider relevance.

It is a premise of this chapter that the nature of such changes at plant level is best understood in terms of the perceptions of the individuals participating in the changes. Accordingly we draw heavily upon statements from the participants at the components plant, on the basis of in-depth interviews with four committeemen (stewards), two joint organization development officers; the shop chair and the personnel director together with discussions with workers in this and other plants. Our objective is to provide an insight, not only into the changes which have taken place, but also into the process of psychological commitment to the joint process which has occurred.

The first section of the chapter sets the study in the US context and outlines the development of employee involvement (EI) in the motor industry. The second focuses on the case study, tracing the nature and origins of team organization and its relationship to flexible work patterns. Finally, our concluding discussion offers an assessment of the implications of such developments for job control and the centrality of collective bargaining, through an exploration of such issues as the reduced reliance upon contract language and the breakdown of national agreements. The central concern of the chapter is not so much whether particular changes in work practice are liberating or constraining – important as these questions are – but rather with the implications of the new processes of co-operation. Are we witnessing a phase of successful adaptation or the erosion of worker protection and union independence?

INTRODUCTION AND CONTEXT

Since 1955, when the AFL/CIO merger took place, the American trade union movement can be characterized by the epithet 'business unionism'. Thus their major rationale and focus has been the defence and enhancement of employees' employment rights in the workplace. In practice, it can be argued, the American unions, like the British, have acted pragmatically in order to achieve this, taking an adversarial stance, but compromising when it appeared expedient, whilst attempting not to go beyond the threshold which would detract from their ability to defend themselves in future battles.

A vital question to be addressed at this juncture, is whether some unions and groups of workers may be venturing beyond this indeterminate frontier. The context is one in which foreign competition in many markets conspires with economic depression, an unhelpful legislative framework, an increasingly antagonistic ideological climate, high (real) unemployment and a proliferation of low-paid and part-time employment. There has been an accompanying loss in union membership,[1] recourse by employers to union busting 'consultants', threats of plant closure and relocation of facilities to the US 'Sunbelt', Mexico and Puerto Rico. The proportion of total auto parts employment in the north-central states has decreased from 70 per cent in 1974 to 57 per cent in 1983 (US Department of

Labor 1987). Foreign imports and outsourcing have severely weakened the bargaining power of the automobile unions.

'As a result,' Luria (1986) comments, 'every plant siting decision and every sourcing change is a response to market pressures to reduce the costs of production.' Organizations working in this environment have sometimes had their traditional markets eroded by Far Eastern competitors, and are attempting to push back the frontier of control with labour so as to enhance product reliability, quality and lower unit costs. Much evidence suggests that by the end of the 1980s there were few companies in the US not attempting to introduce some form of work restructuring (Walton 1985). Debate focused on the nature, extent and implications of these changes (Klein 1989; Kochan *et al.* 1986; Parker and Slaughter 1988; Piore and Sabel 1984; Wells 1987). The innovations involved, although featuring such ostensibly technical changes as 'cell' manufacture,[2] are essentially new ways of perceiving and managing labour (Walton 1985). American industry, for so long relatively isolated from international competition, has been jolted into a reassessment of its methods since the late 1970s by substantial market penetration from overseas in key areas such as steel and automobiles. Hence the 1980s has seen widespread interest in JIT, SPC, 'parallel structures'[3] of work innovation such as quality circles, and a wide range of joint committees under the general banner of quality of working life (QWL). The automobile industry was among the hardest hit. In 1980–1981 the 'big three' showed a combined loss of $5.5 billion and Japanese imports, which had taken 10 per cent of the American market in 1977, were by 1987 in excess of 21 per cent (US Department of Labor 1987). This was the background to such labour relations developments in the auto industry as 'concession agreements', job losses, joint ventures with Japanese corporations, and more specifically the changed focus of GM on the 'joint process'.

Historically the UAW, although charged with engaging in business unionism, has pursued 'adversarial' labour relations to the extent that, when necessary, it would stand firm and demand its share of the cake.[4] Although not challenging management's right to manage, it rigorously defended the frontier of control by strict adherence to the contract language and enforcement of rigid demarcation and seniority rules. Although references to QWL were incorporated in the national agreement in the 1970s, they generally had little impact at plant level. However by 1981 the UAW leadership[5] was committed to a much more radical and penetrating form of involvement. The 1987 GM–UAW national agreement contains thirty pages (compared with two in 1973) devoted to the 'joint process'. Through this contract the union made a full commitment, under the notorious Attachment C, to wide-ranging joint union management activities and to produce, within six months, an 'operational improvement plan' (GM–UAW 1987: 217).

There is disagreement about the merits of the new cooperative workplace. Some stress the mutual benefits to be gained. 'Only lately,' writes Walton (1985), has management 'begun to see that workers respond best and most creatively, not when they are tightly controlled by management, placed in narrowly defined jobs and treated like an unwelcome necessity, but instead, when they are given broader responsibilities, encouraged to contribute, and helped to take satisfaction in their work.' On the other hand, Klein (1989) has argued that attacking waste by means of JIT 'inevitably means more and more strictures on a worker's time and action', while Parker and Slaughter (1988) employ the term 'management by stress' to describe the New United Motors Manufacturing Incorporated (NUMMI) system, which they argue has achieved its gains by greater regimentation of the workforce rather than any mythical worker involvement, control of the work process or increased satisfaction in work.

Among the plants most vulnerable to relocation or outsourcing strategies or 'whipsawing' tactics are the dedicated components facilities.[6] As Luria (1986) notes: 'these pressures affect US parts suppliers with special force because foreign import competition is greater in this segment'. Given the high proportion of value added in the components sector, these plants are both an obvious target and a soft underbelly for cost savings. Yet compared with the much visited assembly plants such sites have been under-researched.

In this context a major question concerns the extent to which EI and 'team concept' (TC) could be the means by which collective bargaining may be displaced from the centre stage of labour relations by a system of management–labour relations which, in conceding a greater degree of control over the labour process, undermines the traditional protective role of the trade union. Given the uncertainties which exist in the development of management policies (Wood 1988), and given that in the 1970s GM had attempted to setup non-union plants, it is not surprising that there are tensions and ambiguities in the UAW stance. The UAW, faced with

substantial job losses has, as a quid pro quo on EI, gained a measure
of job security through the JOBS (job opportunity bank, security
program) scheme, which guarantees against job loss for reasons
associated with increased efficiency in working methods or the
introduction of new technology. However, insofar as the new
systems replace or undermine the tried and trusted methods by
which workers have defended themselves and gained benefits, we
may ask: what are the implications for the future role of the union?
As Kochan *et al.* (1986) enquire: 'can labour union leaders . . .
achieve new roles that aid employers' competitive performance
without destroying the solidarity that traditionally gave unions . . .
the power to improve . . . living standards.'

Our data from the GM components plant allows us to consider
this question in relation to the introduction and operation of the
'joint process' (JP) and associated forms of restructuring. The leading edge of the work restructuring is known as 'team S' (T-S), a cell
based manufacturing unit operated by workers in a single 'universal'
classification (where previously seven grades existed) organized as
a multiskilled flexible group. T-S also initially incorporated two
combined 'craftsman' grades, for maintenance work beyond those
tasks which were the responsibility of the universal operator. Within
the team's enlarged area of responsibilities are: production start-up;
shift scheduling; inspection; SPC; machine loading and tool change.
The team area is established as a separate accounting base so as to
track the efficiency of the unit.

In this plant we see a high level of commitment by the UAW local
shop committee to the JP and the relaxation of contract enforcement. The national contract, traditionally the capstone of both the
generally peaceful labour relations climate and the defence of
workers' rights, is receding in importance. As the trade-off for job
security there has been a relaxation of work rules and increased
managerial freedom regarding job classifications, seniority ladders
and work specifications.

Since the introduction of Henry Ford's assembly line, the car
industry has been a symbol of alienation in work. The employers
claimed that the Taylorist methods of breaking jobs down into their
smallest elements, creating minimum skill repetitive work, was
necessary in order to control costs. Others argued that the control of
labour was a prime motivating force (Braverman 1974). Workers,
through their unions, attempted to push back the frontier of control.
In the car industry they did this by vigorously defending a large

number of differentiated job classifications and thus limiting management's ability to exercise arbitrary control, while retaining a semblance of self-respect and dignity in what would otherwise be a totally alienating situation.

It was back in 1937 when the UAW established bargaining rights with GM after a 44-day sit-down strike at the Flint Fisher Body plant (Fine 1969). It is significant, in the light of recent developments, that the UAW was able to resist GM's proposal to negotiate one plant at a time (Mann 1987: 47). Victor Reuther wrote: 'We understand that each individual Local was no match for the power of concentrated Capital. That was why we formed the UAW' (Mann 1987: 47). The national union acquired the right to approve local agreements in the 1942 GM–UAW national agreement (Katz 1985: 31–32). Substantial standardization in contract terms was maintained through the efforts of both the national union and GM corporate management.

Multiyear agreements were created in the 1948 negotiations, in which a formula governing future wage increases was agreed upon. One now familiar element of this formula was the annual improvement factor (AIF), an attempt to relate wage increases to technological progress by a linkage to estimated improvement in industry-wide productivity:[7] initially this was set at three cents per hour per year, approximately 2 per cent of an auto assembler's average wage. The other critical element was the Cost Of Living Allowance (COLA), established as an inflation linked cost of living protection, which was automatically added to basic pay at the rate of 1 per cent per hour for every 1.14 per cent rise in the Consumer Price Index (Katz 1985: 31–32).

Fortune Magazine dubbed the contract 'The treaty of Detroit', saying that 'GM may have paid a billion for peace (but) it got a bargain' (Mann 1987: 47). This 'treaty' lasted for almost thirty years, with the structure intact despite minor changes, in part because of its function in sustaining a relatively fixed relationship between wages and output, but also because it took wages out of competition amongst the 'big three'. This is not to say that there was an absence of industrial conflict. Periodic large-scale confrontations did occur, as in 1945 and 1970, but the terms of the challenge were essentially economic. The unions presented no challenge to management's basic right to manage but achieved, step by step, increases in pay, medical and dental benefits, supplemental unemployment benefit and pensions (Katz 1985: 20). At the same time the UAW restricted the worst excesses of machine paced production and protected the frontier of control, through their strict adherence to contractual language on such issues as job classifications and seniority provisions.

'The striking aspect of contract negotiation in the post war period,' comments Katz (1985: 30), 'is how strictly standardisation was imposed in work rules across the big three.' Plant agreements were essentially concerned with the interpretation and imple-mentation of national agreements, by specifying seniority ladders (e.g. job bidding and transfer rights), health and safety issues, plant specific job rules and production standards. Such plant agreements could diverge only slightly; the national union ensured parity by (i) establishing roving committees to check on equity across plants, and (ii) requiring national approval of individual wage rates on new jobs (Macdonald 1963). Locals were able to defend themselves in terms of work standards through binding arbitration on most local contract issues, but this was not the case for production standards, new job rates or health and safety rules. These are strikable issues at local level during the term of an agreement. The standardization of wages, terms and conditions across the corporation inhibited GM's ability to transfer production to areas with lower pay, or fewer restrictions on managerial control, such as the southern 'Sunbelt'.

Centralization of union control through the negotiation and administration of the national contract had the result of concen-trating union political power at the centre. Thus, as well as func-tioning to maintain the status quo, it facilitated the subsequent departure from it. From the time that the industry was organized it was characterized by 'adversarial' labour relations. This was a modus vivendi by which the UAW accepted the corporation's right to manage, and GM accepted that the union could negotiate on wages, terms and conditions. As Walter Reuther said: 'Gentleman, we understand that it is your pie, but our members are demanding a larger slice' (Mann 1987: 64). The relationship remained stable in the absence of significant competition and the oligopolistic pricing of the big three. A mutually acceptable system thus developed, and survived in large measure until 1975, because the economic environment did not challenge the status quo. Pay, it may be noted, was in no way linked to plant productivity or to employment levels, which experienced considerable fluctuations during the period.

However, beneath the surface the forces which were eventually to challenge this consensus were building up, as Fordism began to run out of steam in the face of market saturation and the initial challenge of overseas producers. By the late 1970s dramatic changes were afoot. In 1980 GM registered a loss of $763 million, its first since 1921 (Mann 1987: 38). Japanese manufacturers were estimated to be producing comparable cars at $1,500 to $2,000 less than their American counterparts (US Department of Labor 1987). Increased competition was also being applied through the growing number of 'transplants' which contributed to what has been termed the 'gathering glut'. The projection was that Japanese and Korean car makers would produce 1.6 million cars in North America by 1990 (*Wall Street Journal*, 4 February 1986: 1). The big three are also developing strategies of manufacture and assembly in low labour cost economies such as Mexico (*Auto Week*, 19 January 1987).

The US industry developed a variety of responses. In 1982, after Chrysler gained a concession package from its workforce, GM demanded a reopening of their contract in order to negotiate concessions. This was voted down at the UAW sub-council. GM subsequently announced the closure of four plants. Within months the UAW had agreed to contract reopening and GM presented an unprecedented $2.5 billion wage and benefits concession package. The AIF was eliminated, the COLA (cost of living allowance) deferred and the annual hours increased 4 per cent by the reduction of holiday entitlements. Nevertheless the UAW could, with some justification, claim that the basic package of rights (including comprehensive medical benefits) had been preserved, while contingent compensation was introduced by way of a profit sharing scheme and training funds.

The new phase, intensified since 1985, focuses on work rules changes at the plant rather than emphasizing economic concessions at the national level. These strategies revolve around the need to share in the Japanese success, and to deploy elements of their labour relations systems which were perceived to be at the root of their productivity. The 1980s have thus seen the introduction of a series of initiatives in GM which represent an alternative model of labour relations to that of the previous period. GM's commitment to the joint process is demonstrated in the appointment of Alfred S. Warren Jr, a prime mover in the JP and the first industrial relations head in GM's history to be promoted from outside their labour relations department. To get into top management, says one source close to GM, 'you now have to show that you can work co-operatively with the union' (US Department of Labor 1987).

It was of considerable significance that these initiatives involved the extensive dispersion of the JP across GM plants, but some plants, especially NUMMI, were standard bearers of the new system and of considerable symbolic importance. NUMMI was opened in 1984 as a joint GM–Toyota venture on the site of the GM assembly plant in Freemont, California which had closed two years previously. The closure resulted, it was said, from a combination of the world auto market situation, new consumer preferences and the effects of adversarial labour relations. During it's troubled twenty-year operation the plant had gone through four shutdowns. The UAW local was characterized as militant and the management authoritarian. When it closed there was a backlog of over 1,000 grievances, 50 disputed firings and absenteeism was running at 20 per cent. By 1987 NUMMI was producing 200,000 cars per year with 2,500 employees, as against 300,000 at its peak in 1978 with 6,500 employees. In two years under 20 grievances had been filed and overall attendance was at 98 per cent. Commentators have fallen over themselves in admiration for this venture, noting that it has been achieved with essentially the same workforce and technology as the previous inefficient and strife torn plant (US Department of Labor 1987 notes that with around 170 robots NUMMI has a lower level of automation than newer plants). An MIT study reported consistently high quality, rating 135–140 out of a possible score of 145. It also boasted productivity 50 per cent higher than other GM plants and nearly as high as the Toyota plant (*New York Times*, 4 December 1988).

The economic results are clear. The implications of the system are the focus of much dispute. Newsweek called NUMMI 'a model of industrial tranquillity', and the *Wall Street Journal* (27 March 1986) claimed it has 'managed to convert a crew of largely middle-aged, rabble rousing former GM workers into a crack force that is beating the bumpers off big three plants in efficiency and product quality'. The UAW Local view was expressed in their magazine *Solidarity*:

> To develop fully informed workers with a broad range of skills, the UAW agreed to just one job classification for all line workers and just three for trades. Critics say this historic reversal of protective job demarcation exposes NUMMI workers to the whims of management. But the UAW fought for the more than 100 job classifications in traditional auto plants precisely because workers had no control over job content on the shop floor. At NUMMI they do. If the lone job classification is a concession to Toyota, it is even more emphatically a

concession to the age old thirst of American workers for creativity, flexibility, and a degree of control.

(quoted in US Department of Labor 1987)

Parker and Slaughter's (1988) assessment is, however, more sceptical about the gains in worker control, pointing to tighter job specifications, monitoring of how the tasks are to be performed and no replacement for absentees. They argue that 'management by stress', differs from traditional Taylorism in that:

> Taylor believed that management's engineers and time study men could capture workers' knowledge of the production process all at once, after which workers would revert to being nothing but hired hands. Management by stress managers understand that workers continue to know more about the actual performance of their jobs than higher management does, and so make the process of appropriating that knowledge a never-ending one.
>
> (*New York Times*, 4 December 1988)

THE CASE STUDY

Fisher Guide Division GM (GMFG) Syracuse, New York is a dedicated components plant of the GM Motor Corporation, built in 1952 and employing 1,240 hourly and 230 staff personnel in 1989. The plant, once involved in metal stampings, is now dedicated to the injection molding of thermoplastics together with the associated trim, assembly, and paint lines. The major products are molded car trim components such as door panels, garnish moldings, exterior body panels, energy absorbing parts and fender panels. In 1988 the plant had sales of about $200 million, produced in 875,000 sq. ft. with 130 injection molding machines (700–3,300 ton capacity), 45 of which had robotic unloaders.

It is appropriate to trace the development of EI at GMFG in the words of the participants. They underline that the vocabulary of the 'joint process' was not new. It surfaced in 1973,

> when the union and the corporation sat down and negotiated another agreement. There was a real understanding that we needed each other – and no one side could go on into the future without the other. . . . They came up with what is the first language in the national agreement of what we now call

306

the JP. In 1973 it got its birth as a single memo in our national agreement . . . approximately 2 pages . . . that was entitled QWL, and established a national committee to look at it.

However, what transpired in 1973 needs to be understood in the context of the confrontation of 1970, when

we shut the Corporation down. In the previous years certain things backed both the union and management into a corner. On the Corporation side inflation was rampant. We had a COLA, which at that time, had a cap on it. The unions had already publicized that its demands were going to be quite extensive including a demand for a '30 and out' retirement package. The corporation was adamant on holding the line. The union had it's own turmoil that year [with the death of key leaders]. . . . After internal political struggle, Leonard Wood-cock ascended to the presidency. He had to be as tough as Reuther had been over the last thirty years. Everything fell into place for a confrontation. The circumstances and the players all meant that there had to be a strike. After that the corporation and the union understood that business had to be done a little different. Beginning in 1973 they sat down at the bargaining table and they began to talk about some of our goals and objectives not being quite so far apart as we had been led to believe. There began to be an understanding that organized labour needed GM just as much as, or more, than GM needed their employees. . . . It's not a giant step from there to realize that your employees have to be productive, have to turn a profit, have to come to work and have to do their work when they get here. All of these things are issues that most labour organizations had said [to management], it's your job, you confine your arguments and concerns to those particular areas, and what we will do is protect our people any way we can.

The accommodative stance portrayed here is not necessarily indicative of the absence of 'adversarial' industrial relations:

I would say that my job . . . was to come to work and do what I was told to do, as long as it fits into your job description, and no more. And if there was any deviation at all, then instead of refusing to do the job – the polite way to ask for your committeeman, and the supervisor would then be obligated to put in a call for your representative – and that's how we did business. The first thing you know when you come in is who your committeeman is – that's traditional – more important really than who your boss is, that could change at any time.

The supervision, however, had learned the rules of the game. 'Those guys are promoted on performance, and the best way to perform a lot of the time was to bang heads. Shoot one out of every ten to keep the other nine in line – and that's the way they did business.'

Although earlier moves prefigured the JP, the key developments came in the 1980s. Throughout the winter of 1985 the UAW residential centre at Black Lake, Michigan was host to an unprecedented series of week long meetings at which the president and full shop committee of each UAW local met with top management from each plant. This has to be seen in the context of the 1984 agreement, which contained a renewed commitment to QWL through the process of 'jointness'. Union members returning from Black Lake exhibited 'religious' fervour for the newfound JP:

> They came back with a mission. They were awakened or enlightened . . . they really got to know each other as people and really got to know that we both got a lot of common interest in the business.
>
> The first thing they did when they came back is they formed what is known as our plant joint local committee [JLC] . . . [with] the plant manager and his immediate staff, a couple of other selected people from his staff – and on the local union side we've got the shop chairman and his entire shop committee, along with the local union president and two members from his executive board. They are the decision making, policy making body for the joint activities in our plant. If you're going to do something jointly it goes before them and they have to bless it.

The JLC, which meets weekly, conforms with the national agreement and there was pressure on the plants from the regional level to conform. Simultaneously, the union hierarchy was meeting with plant management off-site, in unpaid weekend team building meetings.

> That body went through seven or eight Saturdays – just awareness sessions, just getting to know each other – of team building. We had 15–18 people in a room, and it's probably

something that you'd have to see, because when they first go in you've got management guys with ties sitting at one end, and you've got all the union guys sitting at the other – and if you call that joint, that's about as far from it as you can get, because the way that you're set up if you're traditional, the plant manager talks to the shop chairman, and that's it, everybody else shuts up. And when he (the chairman) nods his head and says yes, you nod your head – and that's how you work. But because we were going to become partners now, those fellas were taken through an extensive process just to get to know one another – to get to work together – it's what we now do with any teams which we put together.

TEAM S

During the 1984 negotiations the negotiating committee was informed that replacement molders were to be purchased and shown their proposed layout. On the return from Black Lake in January 1985, a joint UAW–GM letter was prepared and circulated to all employees. It began:

> Last week we were one of several plants that attended an informational conference at Black Lake Michigan to talk about 'quality of working life' [QWL]. We heard from Al Warren, GM vice president and Don Ephlin, UAW vice president. They each expressed their support for QWL and stated the time for decision is past – we have no choice, we must begin our QWL efforts or our plant, with all the people, will fall by the wayside. We then reviewed the 1984 memorandum of understanding in the national agreement, which is the basis for the QWL process throughout the corporation.[8]

Elsewhere the letter emphasized that 'we agreed that we do have many common goals . . . we need to get a great deal smarter at ways of working together . . . to attain our common goals.'

T-S, as an experimental area, employs approximately 75 people over 3 shifts, out of a total hourly population of about 1,240. It involves 24 advanced injection mold machines producing a selection of trim and garnish moldings for a variety of GM models. The layout is designed as an integrated work area conducive to teamworking. The structure of control in the area is flatter than elsewhere in the plant, having eliminated two management levels. Each shift has two team leaders, responsible to a superintendent who in turn reports directly to the plant manager. A committee member recounts:

> When they came back from Black Lake that letter was drafted and sent to the membership. This was the beginning. Something happened here in 1985 that really kicked us off. The corporation had authorised us to buy thirteen new 'state of the art' plastic injection molders. The people who went to Black Lake said wait a minute. This is a golden opportunity to put the joint process to the test. Lets see if we can't make the joint process work for us. The plant manager and the personnel director came to the local union – they came to our bargaining committee and told us: 'we've got this new equipment coming in, and we want to sit down and talk about it – what if we put them all together in one area and build a new plastic injection department in this plant. We'll talk about how we'll staff it and whether we could find some innovative ways to run it.' We agreed, understanding that at that time we were spending some time meeting at weekends – the shop committee and plant management – talking about just what our relationship ought to be.

The shop committee chair explained in a letter to the membership the rationale of involvement in T-S:

> The manager asked us . . . what we thought about locating all of these new molders in one area of the plant with the express purpose of then establishing a joint union–management committee charged with the responsibility of designing, from the ground up, a department more consistent with what we had earlier collectively said we would like our plant to be. Traditionally, a few salaried people would have laid out the plans . . . and then the rest of us . . . would have spent substantial amounts of our time and energies trying to 'improve' these plans. As far as I know, in our plant, this is the first time hourly people have been afforded this kind of an opportunity and I think this development potentially represents real progress. For the first time we, the hourly workers, have had the opportunity to have some real input into the solutions of potential problems and concerns before people were actually assigned to the area.

There were also meetings with engineering and plant management to hammer out technical issues:

> Out of these meetings on Saturdays grew an understanding that yes, there are some areas where there's always going to be an adversarial relationship, but maybe there are some areas where we can come to some understanding too. Out of that came T-S. We structured a whole new department. We invented a classification and a rate of pay and we structured the leadership in that department.

As the task force proceeded to plan the new area, it posted notices every two weeks to inform the membership of progress made. The task force developed both the structure of T-S and the strategies by which to sell it to the membership. When they asked for volunteers, they

> had an enormous number of applicants. Normally, for other classifications you'll find 20 to 30 applications. We had some 230 people apply. The vast majority were injection mold machine operators – it meant a raise of some 20 cents per hour, there was a monetary incentive. There was also something new about it. We really marketed the idea that it was going to be new – something different. The technology would be something you'd not seen before. Your participation would be at a level that you'd never had the opportunity to utilize before.

Persons selected for the T-S area were put through a four-week training session, the emphasis of which was on social/psychological aspects of teamworking, rather than on technical aspects of the new working systems. The plant QWL coordinator at the time explains how the philosophy of teamworking links with the training:

> T-S gives people the opportunity to think differently about themselves and to work and to grow to their potential. The first week of training deals with personal growth and self-image. The second develops team building, problem solving skills, and group dynamics. The third gives an overview of how the plant's departments function and where T-S employees fit in. The final week gives hands-on technical training for the area.

A key element in the T-S experiment is flexibility of the workforce. In order to execute short runs it is necessary to minimize tool changeover time. Traditionally special crews operating with rigid craft demarcations perform this work, and they might not be fully utilized all the time, or conversely might be occupied on a job when required to make a tool change for a new batch. A T-S superintendent explains how teamworking in this area changes all this:

> The machines themselves are laid out differently from the rest of the plant which allows for more efficient mold changes. In other sections . . . machines are separate systems. Here they are turned so they are parallel to each other with a track running down the centre for an automatic mold changer. In the rest of the plant molds have to be changed by hand using overhead bridge cranes. It's a difficult job that takes minimum two hours. Here they will be changed automatically in about ten minutes.

Early on a letter was put out by the action team addressed to the skilled trades. A vital paragraph identifies the change in philosophy:

> T-S has decided a total team concept must be maintained in this area. Skilled trades employees will receive not only necessary technological training, but the tradesman assigned to the area on a full-time basis will receive the complete group and personal development training that is being planned for all team members. It is important that everyone involved be given the information and background necessary to become the owners and managers of the area.[9]

A committee man elaborates on the changes which have occurred:

> Prior to T-S there was about seven classifications in the injection mold area: machine operator, tool-and-die setter, stockman, plastic mix controller, inspector, truck driver; all at very different rates of pay and all with very clearly drawn lines of job assignment which they would not go out of. And boy, if they went out of their area, we'd be down in a minute telling 'em 'you can't do that' – and filing appropriate grievances. We were very protective of our classification boundaries. In the T-S area there is one production grade classification, injection mold/technical setup [IMTS]. One classification does all the jobs.

Each day before the commencement of the shift the team meets with the leader of the previous shift. They discuss problems with the machines and allocate work roles amongst themselves. They also review production schedules, quality issues, training and scheduling of overtime. Decisions are subject to veto by the staff superintendent.

In practice most people want to stay with the same job, but jobs are now less individualized and broader in scope. The new technology gives the team the responsibility of controlling the various machine functions and monitoring all aspects of the operation.[10]

Job demarcation was always much more rigidly enforced in the craft areas, but the intention was that these divisions would cease in the T-S area.

> A tin smith is not gonna go out and do pipe fitters' work. Today it's not gonna happen except in this area. In this area we assigned two tradesmen, an electrician and a machine repairman. They cross lines of demarcation. The two skilled tradesmen handle 90 per cent of the trade related maintenance calls . . . and the IMTS assist them in that skilled work.

An interesting example of the breakdown of skilled demarcation involved repairs on the barrels employed to melt the plastic pellets before being fed into the mold machines. When the heater bands had to be repaired this traditionally involved a tin smith as well as the electrician, but:

> it doesn't make a whole load of sense. It doesn't take an expert tin smith to take them two screws out of that shroud and roll it back. So when we looked at that area we said that we're gonna let the electrician roll it back.

The T-S area was also established as a separate accounting base to track the efficiency of the new department and to make members aware of the performance and profitability of it on a regular basis.

Given that adversarial relations had characterized the plant for so long, it is pertinent to ask how a small group of local leaders could achieve a complete volte-face among the workforce. A committee-man recounts how the leadership approached the task:

> When you talk about change, it's slow. Just because Al and Dick told us that we were going to sit down and work with management now, well both sides took the, well show me. There was a lot of testing and close to the chest . . . it takes time. There were a lot of hustings and a lot of word of mouth from the committeemen. The T-S was really our first joint effort and the task force and plant leadership did a lot of marketing . . . in every way that we possibly could, to at least make our membership understand what we wanted to do.

Thus in the shop chair's letter to the workforce there is a clear message as to the imperative nature of the changes which were being proposed, but also suggestions that they were being presented with opportunities not to be rejected:

> Traditional rules and roles are significantly changing, and they are changing rapidly. It is important to me that you know that personally I am not totally comfortable with the fact of these changes. . . . But intellectually I know changes are necessary and they will occur whether I like it or not. . . . I believe the future of any auto plant, especially plants involved in our end of the business, will belong to those plant organizations . . . smart enough and daring enough to change and adapt to the challenges presented by the ever increasing competition both foreign and domestic. . . . The UAW leadership today wants and expects . . . me to spend the majority of time representing that other 90 per cent that come to work every day, do their jobs well, go home and are usually heard from by representatives serving in my capacity only on rare occasions.

The UAW shop committee was not confident that success would come easily. When there was a large response to the invitation for a position in T-S one committeeman recalls that: 'we were scared to death. Were we going in the right direction?' The novel ideas were not accepted without resistance from some quarters and indeed there remains scepticism, if not outright resistance in the plant. Reflecting on this, a committeeman explained the resistance as emanating from people who were taken on in the 1960s, 'the old guard' whose ideas are very difficult to change.

DISCUSSION

Contract compliance and flexibility

In principle the joint process and contractual issues are to be kept separate. Irving Bluestone, a former vice president of the UAW and a major proponent of EI programmes, wrote in 1980 that 'the provisions of the national agreement and of the local agreement . . . remain inviolable'; and further that 'the Local understands that normal collective bargaining continues' (Katz 1986). However, in the 1987 agreement, Attachment C specifically states that 'efforts of the local parties to improve operational effectiveness may require change or waiver of certain agreements or practices'. This appears to constitute authority to depart from negotiated agreements in the interests of the JP, thus blurring the boundaries between the two areas. This tendency is further developed in the plant's joint organizational development programme. A section of the programme is entitled, 'How do present national and local agreements apply and can we change them?'[11] and is followed by a series of nine sub-headings ranging from demarcation to discipline.

A committeeman comments on the problem in practice:

> Sometimes it's difficult to operate within the JP and not have an effect on some contractual issues. For instance, you couldn't use your JLC to negotiate your local agreement. Those activities should be, must be, kept separate. It's difficult to make a clear line though. Often when you talk about a project, it has ramifications for the national or local agreement.

Referring to the job of the shop committeeman of the past, a current member comments:

> if he was good at what he did, and most of our committeemen were – and are still – his job was to work under the guidelines of the local agreement that he was a part of negotiating, and to call management whenever they failed to dot an 'i' or cross a 't'. That's what they did – that's what his whole effort was based on. That's what his motivation was.

Such contract compliance has been important in the past as a protection from management arbitrariness. For example, by insisting on strict job demarcation and establishing 'ownership' rights to the job, management's ability to move people between jobs is restricted. Linked to this is the question of seniority. As much industrial employment is arduous, it has been important to the unions to ensure that there are specific jobs which are less physically demanding, to which members may progress by seniority as they get older and their stamina is reduced. In manufacturing plants this type of job will often exist in warehousing, but with the increasing emphasis on JIT these areas are often disappearing or being drastically reduced in size.

Seniority is a problem for management, not only because it limits their ability to select workers for particular jobs, but also because it undermines stability in the workplace. When, for example, people are laid off in one area of the plant, employees with seniority are removed to another area of work, where lower seniority workers are 'bumped' to lay-off, or more recently, to the jobs bank.[12] For T-S the seniority provisions of their agreement were set aside. The participants were selected, rather than being offered places according to seniority. Members of T-S cannot be 'bumped' out of the area regardless of their lack of seniority. This gives the company the dual advantage of choosing people deemed likely to thrive in the new environment plus the establishment of a stable workforce (save insofar as workers may wish to transfer).

Plastic panels for the exterior of some GM models are produced on a small 'paint line' in the plant composed of about twenty people. Under the joint process, the line in this area involves a variety of operations over and above the painting, including fitting fabric trim and inserting retainers and studs. Within this section 'tag relief' has been abolished and seniority provisions do not apply. The supervisor has authority to assign people to any job. With the emphasis of JIT on low stock levels this labour flexibility facilitates frequent changes of the product line.

The loss of 'tag relief' has important implications. It means continuously machine paced labour. The ability to maintain a semblance of control by varying the pace of work is lost in the relaxation of contract compliance. Under the old regime, the option of calling one's committeeman was available. This is less of an option today.

> In this plant, if you speed up a machine you have only one angry person (compared to the assembly line), so we've had an easier time resolving power speed-up issues. As a general practice we do not write up speed-up grievances . . . more and more in the last few years, production standards are set on the jobs. They run the job to the capability of the equipment – and it runs, and if there's a problem, we both (i.e. with management) look at it. Ninety per cent of the time there's not.

In 1984 there were still around 200 grievances being handled in the plant at any one time. By 1988 the number had fallen to around 25 to 30. This can be compared with the similar changes at NUMMI, cited above. The JP has brought changed attitudes to grievance handling. A committee member expresses the new union viewpoint: 'it's ridiculous to take some of these frivolous activities through grievance that we had in the past.' Similarly many issues which would have become a grievance in the past are now resolved at the shop floor level because supervision have accommodated to the new climate of industrial relations.

The joint memorandum of understanding on 'Goals and objectives of job security and operational effectiveness' in the 1987 agreement, part of JOBS program, 'lays the foundation for a new era of partnership between GM and the UAW' (Joint JOBS Document, 8 October 1987: 29). The essence of the JOBS Program is that it 'affords protection for eligible employees from virtually all permanent lay-offs except volume losses resulting from market conditions'; and gives the UAW a voice in 'outsourcing' decisions and the introduction of new technology, as a quid pro quo for union commitment to Attachment C. The programme is administered through a local JOBS committee composed of top plant management, the president of the local and the UAW Shop Committee.

The local committee's operations are monitored by a national JOBS committee of three people nominated by the UAW and three by GM. The local committee establishes a secured employment level (SEL) for both the 'skilled' and 'unskilled' workforce of each plant, equal to the number of employees with more than one year's service as of 26 October 1987, including any laid off after 14 September 1987. That level of employment is to be maintained during the term of the agreement, save for those reasons agreed, namely volume related, model change lay-offs or the sale of an operation. Essentially, jobs are protected insofar as the active workforce falls below the SEL due to improvements in technology or work methods.

Should the active workforce fall below the prescribed level, the employees effected retain full remuneration and employment rights. They may be assigned by the local committee to various training programmes or offered transfer to another GM plant. Additionally the local committee participates in discussions 'regarding sourcing decisions' and 'the introduction of new advanced technology'.[13] It also 'designs non traditional work assignments for employees in the Bank where practicable, both within and outside the bargaining unit' (GM–UAW 1987: 197, para. 10). Significantly, as a corollary of the SEL, it 'jointly develops and initiates proposals to improve operational effectiveness to secure existing jobs, and to attract customers and additional business, thus providing additional job opportunities' (GM–UAW 1987: 197, para. 13). Hence the language of Attachment C, that 'each committee will focus on cooperative efforts towards our common goal to improve effectiveness of operation and remove barriers to improvements, increase job opportunities and fully utilize the workforce'. It was thus mandated that an 'operational improvement plan' be produced within six months reviewing the plant's competitiveness and outlining plans 'indicating actions, and/or changes needed to improve quality and efficiency . . . of the existing workforce and attract new work' (GM–UAW 1987: 217).

Incorporation

Our data appears to confirm observations made by the Work In America Institute (1988) that 'these union leaders have crossed over from an arms length, non-participant reactive posture, with regard to management decisions, to a pro-active and involvement stance'. To what extent, then, will the union role become indistinguishable from management's, and what implications does this have for labour's vulnerability in the future?

There are two aspects of the question to be considered. First, to what extent is the trade union leadership being 'incorporated' into a 'unitarist' management frame of reference (Fox 1974) such that they will cease to be able to conceive of a unified resistance or to marshall effective collective action from the membership? Second, to what degree will the institutional structures which would allow resistance be eroded?

Insofar as each plant is developing its own particular accommodation with management, the potential for solidarity may be being undermined. There may be, as a consequence, no defences against whipsawing, which continues to be practiced by GM. Trade unionists referred to management's invitation to take on a product line provided that the terms of the working arrangements are satisfactory, and that unit costs can be kept below the level at which an alternative plant can produce.

Additionally, despite the statements that the processes of negotiating and the JP are to be kept separate, we find that the two are in practice enmeshed, both institutionally and substantively. The shop committee exists ostensibly to negotiate the local agreement, but it is this committee which, together with key management, constitutes the JLC, which initiated T-S and the other major innovations in the plant. The JLC meets monthly on a continuing basis. Since 1988 the shop chair also meets with the top management team at 7.30 a.m. each day. To further reinforce the institutional meshing of roles there are five training, joint organizational development (O/D) and quality people, recruited from among rank and file trade unionists, who are now full-time paid functionaries in those areas, reporting jointly to the shop chair and the relevant management executive.

One of these explained why committeemen would be spending time on the JP:

> because when I said we'd become partners in the business, we have, we're hooked up. There are staff people hooked up with a designated committee member, and their responsibilities are spelled out pretty definitively.

Furthermore, one UAW member is seconded half time to produce a twice weekly bulletin about developments in the joint process.

Are the statements made on the return from Black Lake mere rhetoric, then, or do they represent a meaningful adoption of a unitary frame of reference? It is instructive to note that whereas traditionally the grievance procedure was seen as central to trade union defences, this perception has been eclipsed. The perception is now one of problem solving. This is epitomized by the statement from one committeeman that 'if I knew how to go to management and get all my problems resolved, I wouldn't need a grievance policy'. He continues: 'we really don't need all the classifications that we had . . . we can be successful working together.'

Furthermore, 'integrating jobs in the plant,' as Katz and Sable (1985) note, 'allows workers to settle disputes informally. This makes it harder for unions to justify themselves as daily guarantors of worker's rights.' Reflecting on the setting aside of seniority in the T-S, a committeeman remarks

> it's one of those things that you make a decision, not as a union official any more; you make it as a union rep understanding the needs of the business . . . to make an analogy to the head doctor in an emergency ward – this is so important to the plant – this guy's bleeding to death, you gotta do something, whether it impacts upon a section of your agreement or not

As confirmed again by the Work In America Institute Report, each plant is encouraged to find its own particular mode of jointness. To the authors of that report, the 'crucial point' is that the 'value of local initiative and the ability to exercise choice have added to the increased trust and level of participation. Clearly participation has spiritual qualities which cannot be imposed or standardized' (Work in America Institute 1988: 1). The uniqueness of developments in different plants is not only a factor in whipsawing but in the acceptance of the JP. Whatever innovations develop, they will not have been imposed. The employees will all the more readily take 'ownership' of the new methods and structures, and the new areas of training. A committee-man remarked that before 1985 when management attempted to intro-duce predetermined innovations associated with QWL much resistance was generated. Now, however, 'we feel part of the process' (Work in America Institute 1988: 15).

Implications

It is arguable that the UAW stood to sink with GM had not changes been instituted in the traditional pattern of labour relations. The arms length adversarial relationship could not be maintained in the changed economic circumstances. As Hyman and Streek (1988: 5) have argued: 'paradoxically, an unfavourable economic environ-ment, by eroding traditional segmentation of production from industrial relations decisions, forces trade unions to address funda-mental issues of company strategy'. Management throughout the car industry decided that workforce flexibility on the shop floor was the key to increased productivity, quality and reliability. The con-tinuation of the traditional adversarial labour relations was clearly an option they ruled out. Two alternative models thus suggest themselves. One is the European (especially German) model of partial representative democracy, whereby elected worker repre-sentatives have a minority role in decision making bodies at the company level, and a somewhat stronger power of veto at the plant level over plant changes. In this model there is an acceptance of differences between the parties over both ends and means. Conflicts of interest, albeit within a participative structure, are a central premise. These conflicts of interest do not necessarily result in overt conflict. The system is characterized more by trade-off and com-promise, resulting both from the union's traditional means of exer-cising pressure on behalf of the membership, based in residual trade union solidarity, and its increased power derived from access to corporate information.

Given the pressures under which American unions are operating, together with their low level of public legitimacy, it is unlikely that this model would assume a central place on the union agenda in the foreseeable future. An alternative is the Japanese system of the unitary enterprise (Dore 1980). Here the company union rationale is premised on the mutually accepted goals of company profit and growth. The task for American management would be to move the UAW from an 'arms length' conflictual stance to a 'proactive' unitary involvement. Management has not relinquished the weapon of superior power epitomized by plant closures, nor arguably could it have done, given the state of the company in the early 1980s.[14] The clear emphasis now upon joint cooperation appears to represent the current stage of management's strategy of movement in this direction. GM, like other corporations remains subject to prevailing fashions, but it now appears to have a relatively coherent view of the nature of the labour relations to which it aspires.

A committeeman reflecting on the recent past put it this way:

> It seems to me that the corporation would catch wind of some quality programme somebody was selling . . . this was gonna be the answer. . . . Six months down the road it began to shatter – it couldn't be implemented, it wouldn't be implemented – there was no commitment to it. This happened three or four times.

More recently, however:

> The 1987 programme was negotiated as a concept. What we're attempting to do is make a cultural change within our organization.

The language of ownership is significant. As the case study shows, the relaxation of job control unionism has meant the breakdown of demarcation lines and seniority rules. The practical and immediate effects on the shop floor may in some cases be experienced as, in themselves, beneficial. Workers are, unsurprisingly, more satisfied in a job where they don't 'leave their heads at the gate'.

Some workers on the shop floor expressed satisfaction at having more control over their immediate work, and others at being consulted, after so many years of being treated as a 'pack animal'. In other cases flexibility has meant greater pressure. It has entailed working faster to cover for absenteeism and the peer pressure of teamworking. Some have lost their small degree of control to vary the pace of work, as a constant unremitting cycle of machine pacing has been instituted, while others experience the stress of lower levels of buffer stock under JIT systems (Klein 1989). For others the problem is the disappearance of the less strenuous jobs to which they could aspire by seniority. The question of whether, on balance, workers benefit in terms of intrinsic gains is not, however, our main concern here. It is rather with the implications of the new labour relations for the role of the union.

In the past the adversarial stance has ensured a distancing of the union's role from that of management. It could be argued that the unions have always had a role in the labour process insofar as they have limited and modified management control. However, this negative and defensive stance, important as it was, may also have kept unions from any positive involvement. Managements managed and unions grieved. The UAW wanted no hand in managing the corporation, but fought for an increased share of the economic rewards and the amelioration of the worst excesses of work degradation, speed-up and danger. Job security also became an issue, but involvement in the labour process was never systematically an issue.

What is to be witnessed now has the hallmarks of a dual process of incorporation. First, we see evidence, both at the national and plant level, of a unitarist stance. The union rationale becomes synonymous with that of the company (Fox 1974). The changing meaning of the grievance procedure has both practical and symbolic importance. It is no longer a means of defence, but is perceived instead as a problem solving mechanism. The second aspect, which moves the argument beyond the subjective arena, is the erosion of the separate and distinct institutional structure of the union. As demonstrated above, the key union personnel at the plant level are simultaneously representing the workforce in bargaining and in the JP. Given the institutional loss coupled with the pervasiveness of the unitary concept – the blurring of the division between management and union – will the union be able to marshall its defences in the future should the need arise? In an open letter two ex presidents and three ex vice presidents, recognizing that situations will arise in which the union needs to exercise countervailing power against the employer, still argued:

> In this uncertain period of challenge to our industries . . . of imports, slower sales growth, and curtailed capacity . . . these advances to protect the jobs of our members represent a major step forward on which to build even further protection in the future. Joint action does not mean an end to disputes, confrontation and conflict with management. Controversial issues will continue to exist and there will be situations when it will be necessary for workers to strike to obtain equity and economic justice. There is a host of issues in which labour and management 'have more in common than in conflict', as Walter put it in the years past, and in which, therefore, solving problems jointly is consonant with the union's goals.[15]

It is arguable that once the rationale of company success is accepted as the union's own, the logic of constant incremental improvement (kaizen) inevitably follows.[16] Competitive pressure is likely to increase rather than abate. In 1982 Roger Smith, chairman of GM, wrote that 'everyday we must decide whether to make a component ourselves or buy it in' (Wood 1988: 109), and before the contract negotiations of 1987 GM officials 'hinted that they could be forced to cut more than 50,000 jobs at components plants if those factories didn't boost efficiency' (*Business Week*, 27 March 1989).

There is nevertheless a small, though growing, resistance within the UAW to the 'administration'[17] mode of involvement with management, organized under the banner of the 'new directions' group. Proponents of the team concept at the GM assembly plant at Pontiac, Michigan suffered electoral defeat as delegates to the union's convention in June 1989. The proponents on the UAW executive who, intent on saving jobs by driving down costs, had fostered cooperation with management, the TC and flexible work rules, were overwhelmingly defeated by candidates lobbying against concessions and cooperation with the corporation (*Business Week*, 27 March 1989). Rank and file dissension organized under the banner of 'new directions' appears to be gaining ground, and may gain more leverage after the recent retirement of Donald E. Ephlin, UAW vice president for the GM department, who was a staunch supporter of the JP.

Cooperation from strength is to be distinguished from that stemming from weakness. The doubts of one rank and file unionist at the radiator plant are expressed this way:

> The concept of team from the union is that of the playground where one person brings the bat and ball. We can all play so long as we play to his rules. If we begin to win he then changes the rules. If we don't agree, he'll take his bat and ball away.

Strength can proceed from legal and constitutional guarantees such as in Sweden or Germany, or from organizational and institutional strength. Where the union's position is undermined by both the economic environment and the corporation's strategies such as whipsawing, the union decision leaders need to be particularly vigilant that the gains from the JP are not a trade-off on union strength. The danger, raised in the introduction to this chapter, is that initiatives such as the JP involve the erosion of individual protection and institutional strength, rather than a form of successful adaptation.

Acknowledgements

The interviews at the GM plant in New York were supplemented by observing and speaking with a variety of shop floor operators and skilled tradesmen on different shifts at the case study plant, by visits and discussions at two other auto-component manufacturers and by interviews with other UAW members across the US. This fieldwork was conducted by John Black who is deeply indebted to the UAW and to all the individuals who spoke so willingly with him and gave of their time so generously.

NOTES

1 UAW membership in 1986 was 83.3 per cent of what it was in 1978 (US Department of Labor 1987).

2 'Cell' manufacturing is to be distinguished from traditional plant layout in that machine tools, rather than being arranged with those of like function together, are arranged to facilitate the sequential movement of the product from machine to machine.

3 'Parallel structures' is a term employed to describe EI systems such as quality circles which leave undisturbed the traditional structure of the organization. See Rankin and Mansell (1986).

4 The UAW was successful in this endeavour. Up to the 1970s the UAW worker maintained wages 40 per cent above average industrial income, plus benefits.

5 Owen Bieber, the UAW president, has encouraged the process across the board. The particular 'push' at GM is through Donald F.Ephlin, vice president, and Al Warren, director UAW GM department.

6 Before the 1987 contract signing GM officials 'hinted that they could be forced to lose more than 50,000 jobs at components plants if those factories didn't boost efficiency' (*Business Week*, 27 March 1989: 110).

7 It has been calculated that the combined effect of the CPI and economy-wide production would have increased the $1.44 in 1948 to $11.11 in 1981. In fact it was $11.45, and total earnings included $8.20 in fringe benefits (Katz 1985: 20).

8 Joint Information Bulletin 1, produced by the joint organization development section in the plant. Copy in writer's possession.

9 Skilled Trades Information Bulletin 1, produced by the joint organization development section in the plant. Copy in writer's possession.

10 The duties of the IMTS, as listed in an information bulletin, cover: quality (start and stop production, inspect and guage parts, trim, assemble, pack and label, assist in colour changes); work with new technology (monitor machine functions, operate automatic mould changing system, change end of arm tooling); material handling (work with automatic guided vehicle system, handle containers, order crib supplies); and environment (house keeping, train new team members).

11 Joint UAW–GM O/D document entitled 'Team S', containing a mixture of letters and training material, produced for internal plant use.

12 'Bumping' is the process whereby employees of greater seniority having, for example, their own jobs displaced, take the jobs of persons of less seniority.

13 Dealt with respectively in Document 89 and the 'Statement on technological progress' of the 1987 GM–UAW *National Agreement.*

14 Plant closings have been and continue to be used. GM announced on 19 May 1989 that although 1988 saw record profits, plant closings were still possible.

15 Leonard Woodcock, Doug Fraser, Ken Bannon, Pat Greathouse and Irving Bluestone, 'An open response to Victor Reuther', February 1989: 6. This was an open letter framed as a response to Reuther's criticisms of the UAW policies on the JP.

16 The concept of kaizen became an important element in GM policies, and is central to 'Attachment C'. The jointly produced 'Summary of Attachment C plan' lists three major areas in the operational improvement plan – quality, price/cost, and customer satisfaction, and states that 'the philosophy is continuous improvement'. Copy in writer's possession.

17 This is the term employed to refer to that political group which is said to have occupied UAW top offices since Walter Reuther took office.

REFERENCES

Braverman, H. (1974) *Labor and Monopoly Capitalism,* New York: Monthly Review Press.

Brodie, D. (1985) *The American Labor Movement,* New York: Harper and Row.

Dore, R. (1980) *Japanese Factory–British Factory,* London: Allen & Unwin.

Fine, S. (1969) *Sit-Down: The GM Strike of 1936/7,* Ann Arbor: Michigan UP.

Fox, A. (1974) *Beyond Contract,* London: Faber & Faber.

GM–UAW *National Agreement,* 8 October 1987.

Hyman, R. and Streek, W. (eds) (1988) *New Technology and Industrial Relations,* Oxford: Blackwell.

Katz, H. C. (1985) *Shifting Gears: Changing Labor Relations in the US Automobile Industry,* Cambridge, Mass.: MIT Press.

—— (1986) 'Recent developments in US auto labour relations', in S. Tolliday and J. Zeitlin (eds) *The Auto Industry and Its Workers,* Cambridge: Polity Press.

Katz, H. C. and Sable, C. (1985) 'Industrial relations and industrial adjustment in the car industry', *Industrial Relations* 23, 3: 295–315.

Klein, J. A. (1989) 'The human costs of manufacturing reform', *Harvard Business Review* (March/April): 60–66.

Kochan, T. A., Katz, H. C. and McKersie, R. B. (1986) *The Transformation of American Industrial Relations,* New York: Basic Books.

Luria, D. (1986) 'New labour management models from Detroit?', *Harvard Business Review* (September): 22–33.

Macdonald, R. M. (1963) *Collective Bargaining in the Automobile Industry*, New Haven: Yale UP.

Mann, E. (1987) *Taking on General Motors*, Institute of Industrial Relations, UCLA.

Parker, M. and Slaughter, J. (1988) *Choosing Sides*, Detroit: Labor Notes.

Piore, M. and Sable, C. F. (1984) *The Second Industrial Divide*, New York: Basic Books.

Rankin, T. and Mansell, J. (1986) *National Productivity Review* (August).

US Department of Labor (1987) *Brief No. 10*, Bureau of Labor, Management Relations and Cooperative Programs, Washington.

Walton, R. E. (1985) 'From control to commitment in the workplace', *Harvard Business Review* (March): 77–82.

Wells, D. M. (1987) *Empty Promises: QWL Programs in the Labor Movement*, New York: Monthly Review Press.

Wood, S. (1988) 'Between Fordism and flexibility? The US car industry', in R. Hyman and W. Streek (eds) *New Technology and Industrial Relations*, Oxford: Blackwell.

Work In America Institute (1988) *Jointness in GM/UAW Relationships at Plant Level*, 15 December.

11

'JAPANESE' METHODS AND THE CHANGING POSITION OF DIRECT PRODUCTION WORKERS

Evidence from Brazil

John Humphrey

INTRODUCTION

It is increasingly evident that new methods of production organization, such as just-in-time, statistical process control (SPC) and total preventive maintenance, are capable of providing significant gains in the quality and productivity of manufacturing output. While these methods may not have originated in Japan, they have been developed furthest by Japanese companies, and the worldwide impulse towards their adoption is largely the result of Japanese manufacturing success.

It is clear that many firms are facing pressures to improve the performance and reliability of their products, increase the variability of products and respond more quickly to a wider range of customer orders. Such pressures affect companies using many different types of production process, from small batch production to continuous process (Bessant 1991: 24–33). It is also clear that many so-called Japanese practices can be applied widely in industry (albeit in different fashions) and transferred from country-to-country. Ideas such as quality at source and improved flows of materials are being applied in a wide range of industries and countries (see Humphrey (1993b) for a series of case studies from countries such as Brazil, Mexico, India and Zimbabwe).

A large part of the debate on the new methods of production organization has taken the form of a contrast between the production system characteristic of Western economies in the sixty or so years up to the 1980s and the systems found in Japan, parts of Italy and Germany and, to a lesser extent, Sweden. These new systems are sometimes differentiated or sometimes characterized as different embodiments of the same underlying principles –

flexibility, increased quality, product variability, etc. The contrast between the old and the new usually proceeds on the basis of a series of dichotomies. The old and the new are given different names: mass production/flexible specialization, Fordism/post-Fordism, machinofacture/systemofacture, or mass production/lean production (see Piore and Sabel 1984; Murray 1989; Hoffman and Kaplinsky 1988; Womack, Jones and Roos 1990). From here, a series of opposing attributes are specified. Schmitz, in a paper critical of the flexible specialization hypothesis, uses Murray's summing up of some of the differences between mass production and flexible specialization (1989: 11). These include:

Mass production	Flexible specialization
Large firms	Large and small firms
Specialized dedicated machinery	General purpose machinery
Hierarchical management	Flat hierarchy
High volume output	Large and small batch output, single units
Limited range of standardized products	Varied/customized products

These differences are also held to have a corollary in terms of labour use. Schmitz's summary refers to four aspects:

Mass production	Flexible specialization
Narrowly trained	Broadly trained
Conception and execution separated	Conception and execution integrated
Fragmented and routinized tasks	Multi-skilled and varied tasks
Narrow job classification	Broad job classification

On the basis of this kind of contrast, it is often argued that the success of new production systems depends upon raising the skills and understanding of workers and the creation of a more harmonious relation between capital and labour. Labour's active involvement with and consent to the new forms of work organization are an essential component for success. Labour becomes an asset – to be nurtured and valued as a key element of a company's competitive ability – rather than a cost which should be minimized.

In this paper, a discussion of changes taking place in Brazil will begin from two observations about the nature and impact of this process of industrial transformation. First, it is clear that there is a wide range of variation in the adoption of Japanese methods. Studies of British companies have shown a wide variation in the take-up of different Japanese methods. Statistical process control, for example, is much more widely introduced than just-in-time production or supply (Oliver 1990: 33). As important, once a term like just-in-time is broken down into constituent elements, then wide variations are also to be found.[1] Certain techniques are implemented much more than others. Oliver cites Voss and Robinson, who state:

> few companies are actually making a serious attempt to implement JIT. Where they are implementing JIT, many companies are implementing just a subset of JIT, and the data suggest that companies are focusing on the easy to implement techniques rather than those giving the greatest benefits.
>
> (Oliver 1990: 34)

To what extent, therefore, are Brazilian firms taking the 'easy' option? Will the legacy of authoritarianism, hire and fire policies, low skill and poor training rule out the use of new approaches to production management such as JIT and total quality control (TQC)? Will managements adopt only 'second-best' solutions which do not upgrade labour and do not rely on their involvement, or even fail to adopt JIT/TQC altogether?

Second, it has been argued that 'Japanese' methods intensify work and create a new form of subordination of labour to capital. It is argued that JIT/TQC, as practiced by Japanese firms in Japan and by Japanese transplants in other countries, particularly the United States, involves intensification of work, increased surveillance and control and the imposition of degraded employment contracts which allow compulsory overtime and use of temporary labour to ensure numerical flexibility (Delbridge, Turnbull and Wilkinson 1992; Berggren 1993). Attempts by firms to restrict union activities and workers' rights in the area of job control would indicate that JIT/TQC is based on giving management much greater power over productive activities. However, it also seems clear that workers often prefer to work under a 'Japanese' system rather than under standard Western work regimes. Which aspects of Japanese management will be more prevalent in Brazil – participation or control, coercion or consent, compliance or active involvement? Or will they both be evident at the same time?

This paper attempts to advance the debate on the impact of new forms of work organization on labour by discussing the changes taking place in Brazil. This offers the chance to study an economy undergoing rapid change as a result of trade liberalization, and, at the same time, examines the issues of institutional context and transferability in a society where pre-existing patterns of employment and labour relations were very different to those seen in advanced industrial economies. Fordism was very different in Brazil, compared to Europe (Silva 1991), so will a transformed or superseded Fordism be equally different? The next section of the paper considers how the 'Japanese' variant of new forms of work organization are meant to transform work, while the following ones consider the extent to which Japanese methods are being applied in Brazil, their impact on labour, and the implications of such methods for worker autonomy and participation.

LABOUR AND JAPANESE PRODUCTION MANAGEMENT

The challenge to established production systems has come above all from Japan, and it is worth considering some of the principles of Japanese production. There is no one standard Japanese approach to manufacturing. While Toyota is often taken as the exemplar of the 'Japanese model', its strategy is not adopted by even all of the leading firms in the motor industry (see Williams *et al.*, this volume, for different strategies in press shop production in two Japanese motor manufacturers). Indeed, it has been argued that Toyota is being forced to adjust its own strategy in the 1990s (Nomura 1993). It is important to realize that firms can only adopt the best practice they can attain in a given situation.[2]

In spite of this, there are some general principles which seem to guide manufacturing practice in those sectors of Japanese industry which produce large volumes of discrete products. Three, in particular, should be noted:

1 *A focus on the product.* Japanese firms tend to focus on the final product and meeting the demand of the client. As a result, great emphasis is placed on such indicators of performance as the time

taken to introduce new products and the time taken to respond to client orders. A product focus is designed to concentrate on the final outcome of the production process and is associated with greater integration of the various aspects of company activities – from design through production, to sales.

2 *Improve production flow.* The ideal factory is one where the product undergoes a continual process of transformation from the moment its component elements enter the plant until the point at which it is sent out to the customer. This idea is operationalized by such indicators as the distance and time materials take to pass through the factory and the proportion of time spent in the factory during which materials are actually worked upon.

3 *Trial and error.* Manufacturing practice should be defined by a process which accepts both continual improvement and the use of practical experimentation on the shop floor. If things work, they are incorporated; if not they are dropped or modified. The process of experimentation requires input from labour and a practical approach from managers.

These three notions have been presented in an abstract way because they are guiding principles. This means, first, that they do not define a single, best production strategy or method. Kanban cards, for example, are one way of operationalizing just-in-time but they are not necessarily the only way or the best way of putting just-in-time principles into operation (see Bessant 1991: 143, for discussion of the possible combinations of MRP and kanban). Second, these principles orient the search for improvement. Attention is focused on such indicators as lead time, setup time, lot size and stock reduction. These are usually operationalized at departmental level by means of physical indicators (Williams *et al.*, this volume), which are held to translate into overall company goals without each improvement having to be justified or costed. Where trade-offs exist, as in the case of machine utilization and cellular production, the emphasis on low stocks and fast throughput pushes strongly in the direction of cells. Where cells are inefficient, then their emphasis would be to work out how to overcome the inefficiencies rather than abandon cells. The problems which might arise from a blind adherence to certain basic techniques, such as stock reduction, may be held in check to some extent by the use of the trial and error approach. Management remains close to the process and can see quickly if it is going wrong.[3]

In more concrete terms, there are a number of methods which, when applied together, help to achieve the general aims of the Japanese system as outlined above. These are:

1 *The greater integration of different parts of the productive process.* One means of doing this is reducing stocks in general. Functional lay-outs are often abandoned. Within departments cellular production may be introduced with workers tending to more than one machine. Factories themselves may be divided up into 'mini-factories' specializing in particular product lines or in particular components or subassemblies. Within these mini-factories, workers may operate in cells or teams. These arrangements may require multitasking or flexible deployment of labour, as well as increased reliability of both quantity and quality of output.

2 *Control of quality by the operator.* If the aim of the Japanese system is to produce 'right first time', then the role of quality control as a check by an external agent, the inspector, after the work has been done has to be modified. Checks are still made, but increasing emphasis is put on the operator producing correctly first time and registering and responding to quality problems. This increased responsibility is reinforced by the use of cells, internal clients and reduced stocks. Poor quality is noticed much more quickly, is more easily attributable to a single person and is located by the production workers next working on the item rather than a quality control inspector.[4] The responsibility given to the worker can take many forms: visual inspection, 100 per cent testing by means of fixed gauges or measurement, as well as the possible use of statistical process control.

3 *Changing maintenance procedures.* In a low-stock system, organized along product lines, machine breakdown is much more disruptive than with functional layouts or buffer stocks. This increases pressure on maintenance, leading to two changes. First, specialized maintenance functions are decentralized and attached to particular production areas. Second, certain routine maintenance tasks may be transferred to the direct production workers. Once again, the idea is partly to free up maintenance worker time and partly to make the worker feel responsible for his/her machine. The worker may be expected to keep the machine (and the surrounding area) clean, lubricate parts and to draw the attention of maintenance workers to faults.

4 *Improvement groups.* The search for quality improvements, stock reductions and more rapid throughput of parts and products is never ending, and achieving smooth production requires attention to detail and continuous minor improvements. In many cases, these minor improvements can only be located by the direct production workers, as only they know the work they do in sufficient detail.

These new demands placed on labour are held to be associated with an increase in skill levels and a greater degree of cooperation and trust between management and labour. According to Kaplinsky:

> A highly skilled and, perhaps of even more significance, a multi-skilled labour force has become essential to compete in most global markets.
>
> (Kaplinksy 1988: 15)

> There are elements within the post-Fordist labour process which are inherently enhancing of the quality of work.
>
> (Kaplinksy 1990: 14)

Similarly, Hirst and Zeitlin refer to the fact that firms need 'to cooperate with their workforce', while they refer to Fordism in terms of 'hierarchical control of labour' (1989: 169, 171). The key words which occur repeatedly in the descriptions of the new system are, on the one hand, polyvalence (multiskilling or multitasking), work in groups and skill, and, on the other, involvement, trust, responsibility and commitment to the job. The latter can be extended to include participation and democracy as characteristics of the new managerial practice (Gitahy and Rabelo 1991: 3).

WILL 'JAPANESE' PRACTICES BE ADOPTED IN BRAZILIAN FACTORIES?

The introduction of Japanese methods appears to involve a major change in relations between capital and labour. Brazil would not seem, at first sight, to be fertile ground for this kind of change. Studies of capital–labour relations in the 1970s emphasized the high degree of management control over labour and the authoritarian attitudes displayed by management (Fleury 1982; Humphrey 1982). The failure of the first wave of Japanese experimentation, quality circles, in the early 1980s provided evidence of how difficult it might be to introduce innovations. Managements introduced certain aspects of quality circles, but without involving direct production workers to any great extent (Hirata 1983; Salerno 1985; Carvalho 1987: 202–203).

In an article written late in 1989, I argued that Brazilian firms would find it difficult to make the transition to 'Japanese management' – that they would prefer to adapt Japanese techniques to the patterns of skill, training and labour relations prevailing in the country. I used the term 'Taylorized just-in-time' to describe this phenomenon (Humphrey 1992: 251). This view is clearly wrong. Enormous changes have taken place, in no small way due to the opening up of the economy to external competition (or the threat of it), which began in 1990, and the promotion of quality and productivity by the Brazilian government. Brazilian industry has recently woken up to the issues of productivity and quality: a plethora of new acronyms fills the business pages of magazines and newspapers – JIT, TQC, TPM, ISO 9,000. Business, spurred on by the threat of international competition, is desperately seeking solutions which rapidly reduce the gap between Brazilian standards of price, quality and delivery and those prevailing in world markets.

There is now plenty of evidence to show that many leading firms are adopting some elements of Japanese practices. A study of seven leading firms in Rio Grande do Sul, in the South of Brazil, by Lima (1989) found firms using methods such as statistical process control, kanban, cellular production and mini-factories, and the results in terms of reductions in work in progress, lead time (taken to be either the time taken to produce an item, or the time between an order being received and the goods despatched), scrap and reworking appear to have been very significant (Lima 1989: 114–128). Further studies covering some of the same factories substantiate Lima's results (Ruas, Antunes and Roese 1992; Rodrigues and Antunes 1991).

The results of the IPEA survey of eighteen firms in 1991 (Fleury and Humphrey 1993) found an impressive catalogue of innovations inspired by Japanese management practices.[5] It documented the use of manufacturing cells, reorganization of layouts, the division of plants into 'mini-factories', the development of 'customer relations' between different sections of the factory, kanban, flexibility of labour and polyvalence. Even more important, it was clear that some managements had succeeded in introducing quality circles, multi-tasking, and operator responsibility for quality. Raising educational requirements and providing more extensive training were also part of the approach of companies reorganizing production around the principles of JIT and TQC. In some cases, such as Firm A and Firm C of the IPEA sample, the logic of cellular production was being pursued vigorously. Firms were seeking to create labour forces which were able to perform many different operations within cells (or in more than one cell), use measuring instruments and statistical process control, and perform routine maintenance functions. This meant raising educational requirements and investing heavily in training.

This experience suggests that an increasing number of firms in Brazil are willing to experiment with Japanese methods. However, evidence taken from the larger firms alone is misleading. Just as Voss and Robinson (see above, p. 329) found a tendency for firms in Britain to concentrate on the 'easy' applications of JIT, so there are clearly systematic differences between firms in Brazil. Suggestions schemes, periodic simple quality checks by workers and limited kanban schemes are much more widely diffused than SPC, total productive maintenance, cells and teamworking.

Ruas and Antunes distinguish between a systemic approach to JIT and a more limited partial focus, arguing that the systemic approach is adopted by firms who have an active market strategy and seek to gain competitive advantage through a combined process of technical, organizational and cultural change which affects the whole enterprise (1991: 3).[6] In contrast, firms which have a passive policy in relation to the market often adopt last-minute responses to crisis situations involving specific operational techniques such as group working, mini-factories or statistical process control, without a more global strategy. In this case, training is more limited, and the benefits offered to workers are more limited (1991: 3–4).

However, these differences are neither just the result of managerial choice or competence – between 'good' and 'bad' firms – nor merely the effect of viewing firms at different stages in the implementation of JIT/TQC. Ruas (1993) argues that clear differences between firms in different sectors arise from differences in management structures, ability to introduce new techniques and forms of competition prevailing in the sectors. It follows from this that the impacts of new practices on labour will also be differentiated. The IPEA study found considerable differences in approach between firms (Fleury and Humphrey 1993), and the work of Marx (1993) has highlighted the particular difficulties facing smaller firms when they seek to introduce methods such as JIT and TQC. The following factors would seem to restrict the depth and effectiveness of use of JIT and TQC:[7]

1 *Competition.* Markets not open to foreign competition (via exports or imports) will be under less pressure to develop sophisticated JIT/TQC systems.
2 *Competitiveness positioning.* Firms not aspiring to market leadership and taking a reactive stance will not develop comprehensive systems.
3 *Competitive patterns.* Firms in markets where competition is based on quality or delivery will tend to develop JIT and TQC further.
4 *Technical ability.* Firms which lack experience of management control systems and quality control find it difficult to develop JIT and TQC. They lack the management skills to develop indicators, establish goals and monitor progress. They may even lack the basic engineering capacity to bring processes under control and set about improving them.

These problems are deep rooted enough for differences in the adoption of JIT/TQC to persist for a long period. Focusing on the leading firms will provide a misleading impression of the overall pattern of use in Brazil.

THE IMPACT OF 'JAPANESE' METHODS ON DIRECT LABOUR

Does the adoption of Japanese methods lead to a change in employment conditions? The answer seems to be a definite 'yes' in the case of the firms which are developing systematic use of JIT and TQC. The areas of most marked change are training and education, stability of employment and the treatment of workers by lower level management.

The dynamics of education and training were seen clearly in the case of Firm A in the IPEA sample (see Acknowledgements, below), although it has only developed to a greater extent practices being adopted by other firms. Firm A had introduced a system of production cells, and it was aiming to have workers able to operate all the machines in one or more cells, and to be able to set up the machines, monitor quality and perform routine maintenance. It developed a new wage and occupational system to reflect this change. Production workers are now classified into six occupations, each defined according to a mixture of training on the job and formal training in the Company's training centre, and each requiring a minimal level of schooling. While the two days of training given to new recruits is largely motivational and introduces new workers to the concepts of quality control circles, kanban, total quality, etc., the content becomes increasingly technical. A worker needs twenty hours training with measuring equipment before passing to grade 2 (and at least six months experience on the job), while an operator/ setter on grade 4 would have to be able to prepare all the machines in the cell and be capable of carrying out routine maintenance on them. This involves courses in basic hydraulics and pneumatics (forty hours each), as well as extensive on-the-job training. Firm A has the ambitious aim of having all its workers on grade 6 by 1996. This means being able to set all the machines in a cell, carry out routine maintenance and use all of the measuring equipment and statistical methods needed for quality. Such a worker would have more than five years' experience and have accumulated 285 hours training. The level of pay for this grade is equivalent to that of an experienced toolmaker (for further discussion of education and training see Fleury and Humphrey 1993: 42–49).

The second major change concerns stability of employment. This could be seen as a consequence of increased operator responsibility and training. Turnover is disruptive because new workers have to be trained and the costs of inadequate training show up in poor quality and disruption to planned schedules. Any 'tightening' of the production system will raise the costs of inadequate performance. However, the major reason for stabilizing labour is to obtain the confidence and cooperation of the labour force. Stability of employment is both a major concern of Brazilian workers and a litmus test of management good faith, particularly so as the introduction of Japanese methods raises the fear of increased productivity and consequent job loss. Lima's study of firms in Rio Grande do Sul points to the centrality of this issue. In a number of cases, a commitment to stabilizing labour was a key element in the 'new era' of relations between company and workers (more often called 'collaborators' or 'functionaries'). This could mean an end to or reduction in seasonal fluctuations in employment and greater efforts to avoid dismissals (Lima 1989: 57–58, 90, 105). In the IPEA study, five firms out of 18 had turnover rates of less than 10 per cent per year in 1990–1991, and in contrast to past practices, firms were prepared to adopt measures such as stopping overtime, cutting the working week, bringing forward annual holidays, and giving workers leave (paid or unpaid) before resorting to dismissing labour. Firing workers became a last resort rather than an easy option.

This did not mean that firms offered guarantees of stability of employment. First, firms retained the right to dismiss workers who were uncooperative. In Firm V, 200 workers were dismissed when the programme was introduced as an initial measure to weed out potentially hostile workers (Lima 1989: 58). Similarly, Firm G's commitment to stabilize labour was suspended if the workers went on strike. Management acknowledged that they used strike periods both to dismiss activists and also to get rid of poorly performing workers. Second, five of the firms in the IPEA sample had made exceptional dismissals because of the severe recession in 1990–1991.

These large-scale dismissals indicated that labour's involvement with the new production practices was being obtained by means of an 'implicit bargain' of the type described by Coriat (1991: 22). There was a clear trade-off between involvement and stability of employment. The need for this in Brazil might not be apparent immediately. As Silva notes, even in one of the most unionized and organized of Brazilian plants – the Ford São Bernardo plant in the early 1980s – the introduction of employee involvement was facilitated by a lack of craft divisions, a positive attitude on the part of labour towards training and the long-established practice of shifting workers between jobs. It was much easier for Ford to introduce statistical process control, preventive maintenance and multitasking in Brazil than in Britain (Silva 1991: 345–346). However, managements in Brazil do need to motivate workers so that they follow procedures all the time and use their initiative when necessary. Managements can tell workers what to do and oblige them to do it by imposing strict supervision. It is much harder to persuade workers to want to do it even when the supervisor is absent. At the most basic level, firms may have to change the culture of labour relations. This may mean, for example, persuading workers that errors will not always be punished. As Posthuma argues strongly, the first obstacle to SPC can be workers' fear of registering a poor result (Posthuma 1991: 151). Beyond this, workers' involvement with new production methods may depend on a sense of having suggestions for improvement taken seriously, being given respect and having a sense that the firm cares. This is a big change from the pattern of labour relations prevailing in the 1970s. Small things such as improved leisure areas for coffee and the provision of cash dispensers in the workplace, as well as more obvious 'Japanese' innovations such as gymnastics and 'state of mind' panels can be a part of the process.[8]

The change is great enough for firms, in many cases, to declare a 'new beginning' and a 'new culture'. The 'implicit bargain' is part of this process. The bargain is implicit because it is not negotiated, and it constitutes a bargain because there is an exchange. In a number of the firms in the IPEA survey, failure to maintain employment led to a withdrawal of worker cooperation. Managers in some of the firms making dismissals reported a clear falling-off in worker commitment to the new systems. This was expressed by declines in the use of suggestion schemes, a falling-off of small group activities and falls in levels of quality. Similarly, in a detailed study of Firm V, Franzoi (1991) makes a direct link between mass redundancies in 1990 and widespread disillusion among the labour force with JIT. Following the dismissals, kaizen activities stopped completely (Franzoi 1991: 120).

The third aspect of change is the shift in patterns of supervision and labour–management relations. Part of this change has been mentioned above. Workers in Brazil have been devalued by their employers. Hire and fire policies, authoritarian management and the detailed division of labour were signs of this devaluation. The introduction of SPC, just-in-time, small group activities and suggestions schemes have put greater emphasis on the contribution that workers can make. In addition, there is evidence that firms introduced change with care. In the case of Firm S, for example, a new wage and occupational structure was introduced alongside a reorganization of production, but management made it clear that older workers would not be forced to shift to the new system if they did not wish to do so. In practice, the disadvantages of not moving to the new system persuaded most workers to accept it, but management caution was very clear (Roese 1992: 121). Similarly, Firm V wanted to substitute coffee breaks with informal stops, but refrained from doing this on the nightshift when workers voted against it (Rodrigues 1991). This cautious approach would have been unlikely in the 1970s.

In a number of firms in the IPEA sample, a major change in working and employment practices had taken place. Managements had sought to change the nature of work and the nature of employment relations. These are major changes. However, it is important to put them into perspective. Leite (1992) has recognized that there are signs of change, but she points to a number of issues as yet unresolved:

Are Brazilian industrialists really opting for systemic modern-ization based on job enrichment and more democratic labour relations? Up to what point will the position taken by the managements found in the studies by Gitahy and Rabelo and Fleury and Humphrey be extended to at least a significant part of Brazilian industry (if not the whole of it), or will it be restricted to a small number of technologically advanced firms? Is the current stage of research sufficient to allow us to talk of a new tendency among firms in relation to the manage-ment of labour? And, finally, if we assume that firms are in fact more inclined to adopt systemic modernization . . . it is neces-sary to ask to what extent these transformations are leading to more substantial changes in labour relations, particularly in terms of the adoption of a more democratic and participatory model of industrial relations.

(Leite 1992: 21)

Leite's questions cannot yet be answered. More research is required, particularly in-depth studies which examine the views of both labour and management. However, three points are clear:

1 There will be significant differences between firms and sectors in the adoption of JIT/TQC and its impact on labour. In less techno-logically advanced sectors and in smaller firms, the use of JIT/TQC will be less systemic and less likely to make demands on labour.
2 There are gains for labour in terms of stability of employment, training (and hence wages and promotion opportunities) and relations with supervisors.
3 Workers' enthusiasm for quality and productivity programmes is largely dependent on the benefits they expect to derive from them. It remains to be seen if management can deliver the promised benefits over a period of time.

A fourth point, concerning democracy, participation and the role of the union, requires more extensive discussion.

DEMOCRACY AND PARTICIPATION

If the factories implementing Japanese methods in Brazil are com-pared to those described by Fleury (1982) and Humphrey (1982), then the former are clearly less authoritarian and repressive. The reasons for this lie both in wider changes in society and internal factors. The growth of the labour movement and democratization have forced most firms, and certainly large firms, to treat labour better than in the 1970s. At the same time, Japanese methods appear to offer a new deal for labour, as indicated by the shift towards greater stability of employment. Will, therefore, the use of Japanese methods be associated with participation, and democracy, as has been suggested by Gitahy and Rabelo (1991: 3) among many others? The issue is a complex one, for while Japanese methods in the West have been linked to greater participation and involvement, some of the literature on Japan has stressed the oppression and control found in Japanese factories, and in particular, Toyota. Kaplinsky refers to the 'dark side' of the Japanese model (1991: 15–17).

On the basis of a study of the motor industry in the 1980s, Silva argues that the strengthening of the labour movement in Brazil has been the principle reason for improving conditions in the work-place. Citing a number of studies from the 1980s, she argues:

> In these studies workers appear to be efficient, to have improved their skills and abilities and to cooperate with management. It does not seem that this good will has made workers passive and more exploited than they were in the 1970s, for example. . . . This is mainly because Brazilian trade unions have become strong and workers have increased their power over matters relating to the workplace.
>
> (Silva 1991: 367)

However, the strengthening of trade union power, seen in the motor industry, has been restricted to a limited number of mainly larger firms located in the major industrial centres. The results of the IPEA survey suggest that even when the union is weak or has been marginalized by the management, improvements to employment and working conditions – increased stability of employment, better relations between workers and supervisors, and more training – are also in evidence.

On the whole, new production strategies have been introduced with little or no negotiation, and the unions have generally been hostile to such innovations, seeing them as a strategy to undermine union power. Negotiations between employers and unions on this issue have only taken place when resistance has forced manage-ment to bargain (Leite 1990). In most cases, managements have attempted both to convince workers that the changes will benefit them and to marginalize the union at the same time. Even when firms have successfully introduced new systems and have secured a degree of acceptance among workers, they continue to keep the union as far removed from the plant as possible and to neutralize activists within the plant (Roese 1992: 134–136).

In part, this is because managements fear the unions. Unions cannot be excluded completely from the scene. The Brazilian labour system still guarantees unions formal rights of representation and gives unions a role in collective bargaining. Managements associate union activity with militancy and opposition to change. Therefore, they try to pre-empt union demands by offering wages and conditions which are attractive to workers. In fact, one of the motivations for management adoption of quality circles, improvement groups, better and more open relations between management and labour ('open door' access to senior management, 'morning coffee with the boss', registers of workers' state of spirit, collective gymnastics, etc.) is precisely to catch worker discontent before the unions can mobilize around it.[9]

Does this mean, therefore, that the introduction of Japanese methods in Brazil is both anti-union and beneficial to labour? Will labour have any role to play in future? I have argued elsewhere (Humphrey, 1993a) that the relatively favourable conditions under which Japanese methods have been introduced in Brazil is the result of four factors: fear of the unions (rather than union power as such, as argued above), the need to implement changes predominantly in established plants, shortages of suitably educated labour, and the unsophisticated internal control mechanisms being used in Brazilian plants. These conditions may already be changing.

There are indications that managements in Brazil can develop the evaluation and control systems needed to increase pressure on workers. A clear example of this was seen in 1993 in a plant not included in the original IPEA survey. Significantly, this was located in a small town in the Interior of São Paulo where the union was weak. The firm had introduced annual assessments of performance based on three items: the training courses they had taken, the development of their operational skills and their attitude and behaviour (contributions to the suggestions scheme, effort, absenteeism, team spirit, etc.). A very good score meant promotion, but a poor score led to dismissal. At the same time, the firm was considering devolving responsibility to teams for accepting new team members and dismissing team members whose performance was not satisfactory. This was in a context where the team itself was set clear targets for quality and productivity, with sanctions being applied for failing to meet them.

The implications of this kind of arrangement are highlighted by Küsel (1990). In a Mexican auto plant, teams were made responsible for output and quality. If a team member was absent, the rest of the team had to compensate, working extra hours if necessary. As Küsel observes, this led quickly to repressive measures applied by team members to their own team:

> A [female] worker who was frequently absent had to wear a headband with the inscription 'Miss Absentee', and another had to clean up the whole working area after being absent on just one occasion.
>
> (Küsel 1990: 219)

Such punishments are more severe than managements themselves would exercise. Their severity arises from the fact that the burden of poor performance, absenteeism, etc., is placed directly on other workers. One would expect the same kind of practices to develop quickly in the Brazilian plant mentioned above.

Far from being democratic or participative, the development of group working under the constraints of both performance targets and the penalization of the group for the shortcomings of individual members places great pressure on workers. It is typical of Japanese management that total subordination to the aims of the company is demanded in exchange for stability of employment, training and promotion. In the case of Brazil, it is possible that once firms come to learn how to operate Japanese methods well, and once they develop better mechanisms of control, the balance between active consent and constrained compliance (or between commitment and control) will shift. The demands placed on workers will increase, and the level of conformance to company norms will be heightened. Brazilian workers might still prefer working in these conditions to those existing in the 1970s, just as workers in Japanese transplants in the USA seem, on the whole, to prefer the Japanese system to the traditional American way. However, the logic of JIT/TQC is to push these controls and the demands placed on workers as far as possible. In a just-in-time factory, as Berggren (1993) has noted, there is always a further demand for improvement. The demands only stop – or at least take on a new form – when resistance arises. As Nomura (1993) notes, even Toyota is being forced to attenuate the rigours of its system, and Robertson et al. (1992) describe how various aspects of the work regime at the CAMI plant in Ontario were modified in response to union pressure. In this type of situation, the need for a countervailing power and organization is more necessary than ever, and unions in Brazil will continue to have an important role in protecting workers from the worst excesses of management power.

Acknowledgements

This article is based on research carried out with the support of the Instituto de Pesquisas Econômicas Aplicadas (IPEA) in Brasília and the Overseas Development Administration of the United Kingdom Government. In the text, this research is referred to as the IPEA survey. The author acknowledges the support of the research team in Brazil, headed by Professor Afonso Fleury of the University of São Paulo.

NOTES

1 Just-in-time, which was defined abstractly above, could be implemented in a factory through techniques such as work in progress reduction, cells, setup time reduction, kanban, preventive maintenance and statistical process control. This list could be extended further.

2 On this issue of the transfer of 'best practice', see Tolliday's (1993) account of the failure of Ford in the United Kingdom in the pre-World War II period. The strategy which worked so well in the 1920s in the USA could not simply be transferred to a different product and labour market.

3 However, Nomura (1993) argues that a number of problems facing Toyota arise from pushing certain JIT principles to their limit.

4 It should be noted that while the focus in this paper is on direct production workers, all of the innovations described here will only work well if considerable attention is paid to such factors as design for manufacturability, simplification of layouts and increasing the reliability of production processes. The engineering investment needed for 'Japanese' methods is very great.

5 The 18 firms in the IPEA survey were designated by letters of the alphabet, and these designations have been retained in this chapter to facilitate cross-referencing. For a variety of reasons the letters used were A–H, J and P–X.

6 Such contrasts have been noted widely in the Third World. Kaplinsky (1993) has distinguished between the use of JIT as a technique and as a system, while Roldán (1993) has distinguished between 'high level', 'low level' and 'crisis' JIT in Argentina.

7 This presentation arises from discussions with Afonso Fleury, and draws on Fleury and Muscat (1992), as well as from Ruas (1993), although the author is solely responsible for its shortcomings.

8 A mundane example of this type of expression of commitment by management to labour was seen in Firm B in 1993. Prior to introducing cells and kanban in one part of the factory, management consciously decided to spend over 50,000 dollars upgrading the toilets. This was seen by management as an overt expression of concern with the quality of working life.

9 It is possible that a new climate is developing. Both the two main trade union confederations, CUT and Força Sindical, are adopting more pro-active policies on organizational change. Recession and an awareness of the need for industry to become internationally competitive have shifted attitudes. However, managements are likely to maintain a policy of not entering into agreements at plant level and excluding unions from day-to-day involvement in factory organization.

REFERENCES

Berggren, C. (1993) 'Lean production – the end of history?', in *Des Realités du Toyotisme*, Actes du Gerpisa, 6.

Bessant, J. (1991) *Managing Advanced Manufacturing Technology*, Manchester/Oxford: NCC/Blackwell.

Carvalho, R. (1987) *Tecnologia e Trabalho Industrial*, São Paulo: L & PM.

Coriat, B. (1991) 'Du Fordisme au post-Fordisme', in G.I.P. Mutations Industrielles, *Une décennie de modernisation. Quels modèles socio-productifs?*, Paris: CNRS.

Delbridge, R., Turnbull, P. and Wilkinson, B. (1992) 'Pushing back the frontiers: management control and work intensification under JIT/TQM factory regimes', *New Technology, Work and Employment* 7, 2: 97–106.

Fleury, A. (1982) 'Rotinização do trabalho: o caso das indústrias mecânicas', in A. C. C. Fleury and N. Vargas (eds) *Organização do Trabalho*, São Paulo: Atlas.

Fleury, A. and Humphrey, J. (1993). *Human Resources and the Diffusion and Adaptation of New Quality Methods in Brazilian Manufacturing*, Brighton: Institute of Development Studies, Research Report, 24.

Fleury, A. and Muscat, A. (1992) 'Sistemas de indicadores de qualidade e produtividade na indústria brasileira', São Paulo, University of São Paulo, Fundação Vanzolini, mimeo.

Franzoi, N. (1991) 'O Modelo Japonês e o conhecimento informal do trabalhador no chão-de-fábrica', unpublished MA dissertation, Post-graduate Programme in Administration, Federal University of Rio Grande do Sul.

Gitahy, L. and Rabelo F. (1991). 'Educação e desenvolvimento tecnológico: o caso da indústria de autopeças', DPCT/IG/UNICAMP, Textos para Discussão, 11.

Hirata, H. (1983) 'Receitas japonesas: realidade brasileira', *Novos Estudos Cebrap*, 2, 2: 61–65.

Hirst, P. and Zeitlin, J. (1989) 'Flexible specialisation and the competitive failure of UK manufacturing', *Political Quarterly* 60, 2: 164–178.

Hoffman, K. and Kaplinsky, R. (1988) *Driving Force*, Boulder, Col.: Westview.

Humphrey, J. (1982) *Capitalist Control and Workers Struggle in the Brazilian Auto Industry*, Princeton: Princeton UP.

—— (1992) 'L'Adaptation du "modèle japonais" au Brésil', in H. Hirata (ed.), *Autour du "modèle" japonais*, Paris: Harmattan.

—— (1993a). 'Japanese production management and labour relations in Brazil', *Journal of Development Studies*, 30, 1: 92–114.

—— (ed.) (1993b) 'Quality and productivity in industry: new strategies in developing countries', *IDS Bulletin* 24, 2.

Kaplinsky, R. (1988) 'Industrial restructuring in LDCs: the role of information technology', Paper presented to conference on Technology Policy in the Americas, Stanford, December.

—— (1990) 'Post-Fordist industrial restructuring: implications for an industrially advanced economy', Paper presented to conference on Canadian Political Economy in the Era of Free Trade, Carleton University.

—— (1991) 'The new flexibility: promoting social and economic efficiency', Paper presented to conference on The Efficient Society: Competition, Cooperation and Welfare, Budapest, September.

—— (1993) 'Implementing JIT in LDCs; from theory to practice', Paper presented to workshop on Intra-firm and Inter-firm Reorganization in Third World Manufacturing, Brighton, Institute of Development Studies, April.

Küsel, C. (1990). '"La calidad tiene prioridad número 1". Restructuración del proceso de trabajo e introducción de conceptos japoneses de organización en la industria automotriz mexicana', in J. Carrillo (ed.) *La Nueva Era de la Industria Automotriz en México*, Tijuana: El Colégio de la Frontera Norte.

Leite, M. (1990) 'A vivência operária da automação microeletrônica', unpublished Ph.D., University of São Paulo.

—— (1992) 'Modernização tecnológica e relaçes de trabalho no Brasil: notas para uma discussão', Paper presented to Seminar 'Work and Education', São Paulo, Fundação Carlos Chagas.

Lima, I. (1989) 'Análise das consequências da utilização das filosofias e técnicas japonesas de gestão da produção sobre o rendimento das empresas', unpublished MA dissertation, Federal University of Rio Grande do Sul.

Marx, R. (1993) 'Quality and productivity in small- and medium-sized firms in the Brazilian automotive industry', *IDS Bulletin* 24, 2: 65–71.

Murray, R. (1989) 'Fordism and post-Fordism', in S. Hall and M. Jacques (eds) *New Times: the Changing Face of Politics in the 1990s*, London: Lawrence & Wishart.

Nomura, M. (1993) 'Farewell to "Toyotaism"?', in *Des Realités du Toyotisme*, Actes du Gerpisa, 6.

Oliver, N. (1990) 'Human factors in the implementation of just-in-time production', *International Journal of Operations and Production Management* 10, 4: 32–40.

Piore, M. and Sabel, C. (1984). *The Second Industrial Divide*, New York: Basic Books.

Posthuma, A. (1991) 'Changing production practices and competitive strategies in the Brazilian auto-components industry', unpublished D.Phil., University of Sussex.

Robertson, D., Rinehart, J., Huxley, C. and the CAW Research Group on CAMI (1992) 'Team concept and kaizen: Japanese production management in a unionised Canadian auto plant', *Studies in Political Economy* 39: 77–107.

Rodrigues, M. B. (1991) 'Just-in-Time: Nova Forma de Organização do Trabalho', unpublished MA dissertation, Federal University of Rio Grande do Sul.

Rodrigues, M. B. and Antunes, J. A. (1991) 'Just-in-time: nova forma de organização do trabalho', Paper presented to XI Annual Meeting of Production Engineering, Rio de Janeiro, September.

Roese, M. (1992) 'Novas Formas de Organização da Produção e Relações de Trabalho na Indústria', unpublished MA dissertation, Federal University of Rio Grande do Sul.

Roldan, M. (1993). 'Industrial restructuring, deregulation and new JIT labour processes in Argentina: towards a gender-aware perspective?', *IDS Bulletin* 24, 2: 42–52.

Ruas, R. (1993) 'Notes on the implantation of quality and productivity programmes in sectors of Brazilian industry', *IDS Bulletin* 24, 2: 27–33.

Ruas, R. and Antunes, J. A. (1991) 'Mudança técnica e gestão de trabalho em indústrias tradicionais', Paper presented to 15th Annual Meeting of ANPOCS, Caxambú, October.

Ruas, R., Antunes, J. A. and Roese, M. (1992) 'Avancées et reculs du "modèle japonais" au Brésil: quelques études de cas', in H. Hirata (ed.) *Autour du "modèle" japonais*, Paris: Harmattan.

Salerno, M. S. (1985) 'Produção e participação: CCQ e kanban numa nova imigração Japanesa', in M. T. L. Fleury and R. M. Fischer (eds) *Processo e Relações de Trabalho no Brasil*, São Paulo: Atlas.

Schmitz, H. (1989). 'Flexible specialisation – a new paradigm of small-scale industrialisation?', Brighton: Institute of Development Studies, Discussion Paper 261.

Silva, E. (1991) *Refazendo a Fábrica Fordista*, São Paulo: Hucitec.

Tolliday, S. (1993) 'Transferring Fordism: the first phase of the diffussion and adaptation of Ford methods, 1911–1939', Paper presented to Gerpisa Meeting, 'Les Trajectoires des Firmes Automobiles', Paris, June.

Williams, K., Mitsui, I. and Haslam, C. (this volume) 'How far from Japan? A case study of management calculation and practice in car press shops'.

Womack, J., Jones, D. and Roos, D. (1990) *The Machine that Changed the World*, New York: Rawson Macmillan.

12

JAPANESE PRODUCTION TECHNIQUES IN BRAZILIAN AUTOMOBILE COMPONENTS FIRMS

A best practice model or basis for adaptation?

Anne Caroline Posthuma

INTRODUCTION

The subject of Japanese organizational practices has spawned great debate regarding their transferability to the West. One strand of the argument in this debate claims that Japanese methods have a universal applicability, whilst another strand has questioned the desirability or social acceptability of these new organizational techniques. This chapter, in contrast, is founded upon the perspective that certain features of the social organization of developing countries hinder the wholesale adoption of these techniques. In this chapter, I will draw on field research on the Brazilian auto-components industry to discuss the pattern and extent of the adoption of quality control (QC) programmes, quality control circles (QCCs) and just-in-time (JIT) among firms within this sector of the Brazilian economy. This will involve an analysis of the extent to which these new manufacturing practices are being adopted and the forms they take in this setting, the sorts of obstacles which hinder or discourage adoption, and the benefits and problems which result.

On the basis of this analysis, I will argue that the Japanese model, as interpreted in the Western industrialized countries, can be 'unpacked' and applied selectively by firms in developing economies. Furthermore, such innovations have been introduced in a manner which appears to improve the efficiency of existing production practices, in terms of both production and labour use, while avoiding significant changes in the existing mode of production and relations of production within the firm. In this respect, a key issue becomes how far the selective adoption of new practices represents a forging of adaptations tailored to local conditions, and whether

348

this may be seen as evidence of the emergence of specifically 'Brazilianized' adaptations.

Management consultants in the early 1980s voiced great optimism as to the transferability of Japanese manufacturing practices to enterprises outside the cultural milieu in which they emerged. Schonberger, one of the pioneers who brought an analysis and interpretation of Japanese methods to Western managers, was confident that Japanese practices were reducible to a few core management techniques which could be emulated:

> most management concepts and approaches are readily transportable, and the basic simplicity and logic of just-in-time and total quality control enhance their transportability from Japan to industry in America and the West generally.
>
> (Schonberger 1982: 3)

A related school of industry analysts refers to a superior 'best practice' model developed by the Japanese automotive industry and promotes its replication among Western firms. This model is shorthand for a collection of managerial, technological, organizational and institutional features associated with Japanese manufacturing. Such an approach, however, tends to overlook the historical and social factors which have shaped these practices as they have developed in Japan, and that this system only operates within a fraction of firms even in Japan. Adherents of this ahistorical view must recall that these practices themselves involved adaptations of techniques brought to Japan by American consultants in the 1950s. Even QC programmes and QCCs, often treated as quintessential Japanese inventions, were originally imported from the US (Cusumano 1985: 321; Fukuda 1988). If the Japanese imported, adapted and refined these QC techniques, there is no reason to expect that the pinnacle of manufacturing practice has been reached, nor can best practice models be treated as universal when they do not consider differing local political, economic and social conditions.

A more sceptical appraisal of universalistic notions of 'best practice' is reinforced by the findings of other analysts, who maintain that cultural specificity will block or severely limit the transferral of production methods (Fukuda 1988; Sethi *et al.* 1984). Such writers have emphasized their limited and selective spread in the advanced capitalist economies:

A survey of Japanese manufacturing subsidiaries operating in Europe, which was carried out in 1985 by Japan External Trade Organization, showed that few of the companies had tried to export Japanese management practices wholesale but had primarily chosen to adapt to local conditions.

(Fukuda 1988: 131)

Furthermore, Japanese multinational firms have had difficulty transferring their practices intact to subsidiaries not only in the West but in South-east Asia – a region with much greater historical and cultural affinity than Western countries:

Operating in an environment which is similar but not exactly the same as their own in the home country, few Japanese companies seem to have attempted to export wholesale Japanese-style management practices to Hong Kong. The majority have, in fact, chosen to adopt the local practices to a considerable degree.

(Fukuda 1988: 144)

Taking another approach to this issue, some authors leave aside the mechanisms of transfer and question the social acceptability of the Japanese model itself for the West (Dohse, *et al.* 1985; Sayer 1986).

In contrast to a number of other assessments . . . the Japanese system of industrial relations offers no counterweight to the power of management over individual workers and competition between them. . . . The Japanese organization of the labour process . . . is simply the practice of the organizational principles of Fordism under conditions in which management prerogatives are largely unlimited.

(Dohse *et al.* 1985: 140–141)

While considering that corporate unionism in Japan has allowed management to impose the mode of work organization which it desires, these authors argue that new organizational techniques will be more difficult to implant within most leading Western economies in light of the concessions won by organized workers.

IMPLICATIONS OF JAPANESE ORGANIZATIONAL PRACTICES FOR DEVELOPING COUNTRIES

More recently, a limited but distinctive body of work has emerged concerning the diffusion of these new organizational practices and their implications for production in developing countries. Hoffman (1989) argues that the fundamental features of organizational innovations and the resource constraints in finance and skill found in most developing countries provide an excellent match for upgrading Third World industrial practices and productivity. Among other outstanding features, organizational innovations are inexpensive to adopt (especially in relation to the costs of automation). Hoffman echoes the more universalistic emphasis of the management literature by arguing that these organizational techniques can be defined and easily transferred through books and management consultants:

> Four aspects of the new practices provide strong a priori grounds for our hypothesis concerning their applicability in developing countries. First, . . . most new practices are neither scale, product, sector nor function-specific. . . . Second, there is no mystery behind how these practices work. Indeed there are numerous 'how to' books that describe practically how firms should go about introducing the new practices. Moreover, most management consulting firms provide specific advice on the practices. In short, the new practices are codifiable and accessible.
>
> (Hoffman 1989: 87–88)

Such authors accept the 'best practice' vision unquestioningly as the model for developing country firms, despite the fact that it is based upon very different cost structures and a different labour force profile than those found in the Third World. Furthermore, as they approach organizational change as essentially a technical issue, they do not consider constraints to organizational change which arise on the shop floor, or are due to separate national systems of industrial relations, and fail to question whether management in developing countries will enthusiastically embrace these changes.

Despite their clear divergences, none of these schools of thought would deny that the adoption of new manufacturing practices has been slow; yet the various authors interpret this in different ways. The 'best practice' school is useful insofar as it provides a paradigm of manufacturing change and the interrelationships between different elements. Yet, when applied as a yardstick, it can merely judge success and failure, rather than offer tools to facilitate an improvement of manufacturing practices either in the industrialized or developing world. Alternatively, these difficulties encountered in the adoption of new techniques may be regarded as normal processes of socially mediated learning and adaptation to be expected in the learning process as firms adopt new techniques. Seen in this light, it is likely that different cultures and institutional structures will encourage continued adaptation and variations in approach. Although much can be gained from experiences in other countries, local adaptation is a necessary process: 'the diffusion process is limited by the degree of compatibility between the new methods of production and existing practices in the areas in which they are implanted' (Sayer 1986: 45).

Such techniques as zero defect and JIT were developed by Japanese firms in response to the conditions faced by their small island nation. Despite their emphasis on simplicity, these techniques were neither simple nor straightforward to develop, and took decades to refine. The high premium on scarce land and the fact that the majority of inputs required for automobile production had to be imported, meant that all resources, including land, had to be used to the utmost efficiency. In fact, the Japanese Ministry for International Trade and Industry defied strong recommendations to the contrary when it decided to sponsor national automobile production (Cusumano 1985). Frugality was valued uppermost in Japan under conditions of scarcity, in contrast to a country such as the US where all natural resources necessary for automobile production were present – steel, electricity, oil, plentiful land, a skilled labour force and a large, affluent consumer market. Moreover, due to the enterprise union system established among the 'core' labour force, Japanese management faced little resistance to the development and implantation of new techniques for the organization of labour.

Turning now to the setting for my own research, Brazil has the productive strength of an industrialized country, as the eighth largest economy in the world, yet contains the social and economic features of a developing country: enormous income disparity, high inflation and poor infrastructure outside of the few urban metropolises. Given this complex profile and the specific nature of industrial relations in Brazil, no single model of organizational change from the industrialized countries will entirely suit local conditions without adaptation.

This chapter draws upon field research conducted among twenty-one high exporting firms in the Brazilian auto-components sector, and examines QC programmes (involving both statistical process control and QCCs) and JIT to assess the diffusion and applicability of these Japanese practices in Brazil. I will discuss: (i) the extent to which these techniques are in use; (ii) the major obstacles in their transfer; and (iii) whether there are examples of 'Brazilianized' adaptations. Space constraints preclude discussion of other facets of the reorganization of production, such as cellular manufacturing, but quality programmes and JIT represent key features of Brazilian attempts to learn from Japan. In assessing the significance of these developments, I will discuss each of these areas of innovation in turn, and also seek to situate each of these Japanese management practices in the context of their development in Japan, to allow an appreciation of the significance of the findings collected in Brazil.

Contrary to both the authors which present a 'best practice' package of manufacturing techniques, and those who argue against the suitability of any elements of such a package, our research revealed a steady yet piecemeal adoption of QC techniques and JIT among Brazilian automobile components firms. Of particular importance is the fact that partial adoption yielded significant improvements in production performance and quality of output. Clear evidence was found that firms were unpacking certain features of the Japanese model and adapting them to suit existing production practices and social relations within the firm.

The first section of this chapter discusses the use which Brazilian firms make of statistical process control. I will argue that although there is evidence in some cases of great reluctance to change, the efforts of firms in developing countries to grapple with new techniques could prefigure yet another wave of adaptation of innovations to suit local socio-cultural, political and economic conditions. If this is the case, this also had interesting implications for industrial relations, the labour process and the competitive and investment strategies of developing country firms.

THE INTRODUCTION OF QUALITY CONTROL PROGRAMMES

As its name suggests, statistical process control (SPC) applies statistical methods to measure and monitor a product as it is being manufactured, to assure compliance with preset quality specifications. When the measurements used by each worker indicate that performance has drifted outside acceptable standards, the machine is adjusted and corrected before resuming its operation. This procedure is performed upon a determined number of parts, depending upon different features. These data are collected and an average is calculated by the machine operator, who records them on a chart posted at the workstation. When completed, the SPC charts are collected and sent to the QC department for analysis.

SPC is a widely used QC technique in the industrialized countries, and has proved highly effective as a technical tool for detecting quality problems as they arise in the course of production, rather than spotting them at the end of the production line. The initial one-off gains of SPC can be substantial, as experienced by one family owned firm in the research sample, which moved from a reject rate of 43 per cent before SPC, to 10 per cent in the first month of SPC, to 1.6 per cent after two years later. It is of particular interest that such dramatic improvements in product quality were achieved through the simple installation of SPC without any significant changes in the labour process itself. This is because SPC, as a diagnostic technique, provides immediate feedback on machinery performance and visible external product defects, yet the relative ease of its introduction and use contrasts with other preventative techniques which involve broader changes in the organization of production itself.

However, alongside tangible improvements in production and product quality as a result of introducing SPC, there was evidence that these work techniques could be altered in practice both by managers and workers, and that workers were suspicious of management's motives in implanting the new techniques because of the climate of mutual mistrust in existing labour–management relations.

SPC techniques were found to be in use in all Brazilian components firms visited. This finding alone is significant, since previous studies on the Brazilian automotive sector have not indicated such a high rate of utilization of this technique. Yet, merely measuring its quantitative use does not accurately assess the nature of QC practices among firms for two main reasons. First, all multinational automobile assemblers in Brazil have insisted that their component suppliers install SPC. Therefore, the widespread use of SPC among component producers is a reflection more of the QC policies of the assemblers than of the component producers. Second, measuring the scale of SPC use or of QC programmes fails to capture the qualitative features in their adoption. For example, the imposition of SPC use by the assemblers means that some components firms adopt it superficially as an end in itself. Finally, though the effectiveness of SPC as a technical device does bring swift visible results, any continued quality improvements continue to hinge upon how far these techniques are employed by the company and how far they are integrated with new forms of labour utilization, increased worker responsibility and training throughout the firm.

The automobile assemblers have played an important role in promoting quality practices among component suppliers in Brazil by offering introductory courses, monitoring SPC use and offering annual awards to outstanding suppliers. More than merely symbolic, these awards allow suppliers to deliver directly to the assembly line without inspection, and preferred suppliers are invited to participate in the design of new components, with exclusive sourcing rights for the first few years in production.

However, components producers shared the view that the auto assemblers were inconsistent and simplistic in their approach to defining responsibility for QC, and consequently sent mixed messages to their suppliers. First, suppliers complained that assemblers merely imposed SPC as an easy QC measure since a comprehensive programme of quality production would be difficult to decree among all parts producers. Second, QC programmes and standards imposed by assemblers varied widely – for example, while one required bureaucratically rigid documentation of QC techniques and results, another specified that one inspector be placed for every twenty machines on the production line. These differing requirements led many managers in components firms to the opinion that the automobile assemblers were satisfied with cosmetic rather than structural change to improve product quality. Finally, 'quality first' slogans which trickle down from company boardrooms were not necessarily embodied in criteria used by the assemblers' purchasing departments, which tended to be more interested in low price than top quality. The QC manager in one components firm summarized his dilemma in this way: 'Who am I to please – the purchasing or the QC department?'

One explanation for this inconsistent behaviour of automobile manufacturers toward component suppliers lies in the different structure of traditional assembler–supplier relationships in Japan and in the West. Typically, Japanese automobile producers and their components producers maintain a semi-permanent relationship through shared equity holdings, personnel exchanges and loans of operating capital and equipment. Mutual survival is critical since their fates are tied; consequently, assemblers and suppliers share ideas via a problem solving approach. In contrast, Western assemblers are accustomed to 'arm's length' relationships between several suppliers who must compete for sourcing contracts on the basis of price. Suppliers frequently decide to take a short-term loss to win a contract, hoping to recoup the loss over time. Consequently, it is not surprising that price concerns often outweigh quality factors.

Using SPC: cosmetic tinkering or tool for achieving structural quality improvements?

A divergence is notable among (QC) philosophies in the industrialized countries, generally split between quality practices which are corrective and those which are preventative – the former based upon inspecting quality, while the latter focuses upon producing quality. While both philosophies agree that a product must conform to design specifications, the short-run quality targets among Western firms presume an acceptable level of defects. In contrast, Japanese techniques are geared toward continuous quality improvement as an endless goal – by identifying and eliminating the root causes of poor quality, they seek to eliminate defects altogether. This divergence in philosophy marks a fundamental difference between the ways in which QC operates in the East and West.

In Brazil American and European companies dominate domestic motor vehicle production. Consequently, Brazilian component suppliers generally adopted the prevailing Western management culture, as well as attitudes toward QC. The Western QC style is geared principally toward inspecting quality rather than manufacturing quality. In this system, QC becomes a specialist function and the responsibility for quality performance becomes centralized in the hands of experts in the QC department, which may become top-heavy (Deming 1986: 134). For example, the QC department in the Brazilian subsidiary of an American axle producer had grown to 350 out of a total workforce of 2,200 employees (16 per cent), entrusted with monitoring activities in all departments. In another case, a leading family firm producing pistons reported levels of 12 per cent and 14 per cent respectively of QC staff involved in two different factories. The QC manager in this company described the quality policy, adopted in 1987, as following 'the old style of QC, with more policing control over the general as well as the specific' features of production.

In contrast, the Japanese logic of manufacturing quality catches defects at their source and eliminates them as they are produced. Hence, this approach requires the full participation and cooperation of production workers and reduces the need for a large, separate QC department. The research found a few cases where production workers were given a greater role in guaranteeing product quality. In particular, two firms had begun to install 'auto-control', which included passing greater responsibility to machinists for their work and providing the necessary testing equipment 'to deliver parts in good order and tested to the following sector'. These two cases, although incipient, demonstrate a commitment among some firms to deepen the process of quality improvement by involving workers rather than being satisfied with cosmetic changes.

Managers in some Brazilian firms also recognized that improved quality does not result solely from implanting new QC techniques, but is the fruit of increased control and responsibility by production workers over their individual operations. As one QC manager noted: 'SPC in itself doesn't resolve problems; rather, trained machine operators improve product quality and production.'

Such opinions suggest that increased use of QC techniques which require production workers to monitor product quality and machine performance will engender both a greater dependency of management upon workers to guarantee product quality and a greater value and respect for their labour force. Nevertheless, the treatment of shop floor workers in the majority of Brazilian firms interviewed showed that new production techniques did not improve work stability and conditions of work. This evidence suggests that there was a tension between established patterns of management–worker relations in Brazil and any strategy for exploiting the full potential of the new organizational techniques. The following section explores such tensions through an examination of some of the difficulties encountered in the introduction of SPC in the Brazilian components firms visited.

Obstacles encountered in the adoption of SPC in Brazil

Three major obstacles to the introduction of SPC were reported by the Brazilian components firms in the research sample: training and preparation of workers in the new techniques; fear or mistrust of workers toward management; and resistance to SPC use by managers themselves.

Training and preparation of workers

The principal difficulty encountered by all these firms was the high level of illiteracy among production workers. To measure a workpiece, calculate an average and record the results on a SPC chart requires abilities which are taken for granted in the industrialized countries, but which demand that basic mathematics and writing be taught by Brazilian firms prior to introducing the SPC course itself. Other authors concur that training is a fundamental problem in the transfer of new manufacturing techniques to developing countries (Ebrahimpour and Schonberger 1984: 429).

All firms in the research shouldered substantial training costs in the process of adopting SPC techniques. Most offered courses in both SPC and basic literacy simultaneously in order to meet the varied needs of workers. Nearly half the firms visited had contracted a management consultant to assist in the selection and implantation of new QC procedures. One local firm had prepared an initial course for two hours during one week, followed by an exam, ostensibly to test workers' comprehension of the material presented; yet the exam was actually designed to reveal their reading, writing and basic mathematics skills. The size of this firm meant most courses were held in-house and a refresher course in SPC techniques was offered regularly.

In another local firm producing axles, a forty-hour course was taught for two hours per day during a month. Upper level directors, managers and supervisors were trained first, and by the time of the interview, 80 per cent of production workers had been trained in SPC methods. Refresher courses were offered every six months for new employees or those wanting to revise their techniques. The course and the teaching style of the company were so well received that the machine operators themselves requested a special course in metrology (basic measuring and testing procedures).

Significantly, many companies not only adopted SPC, but adapted it to their own particular needs. As one manager reported:

It was difficult to introduce SPC as it was taught in courses such as Ford's, because they were developed for machining processes, and not for electric plastic injection moulding such as we have here in the factory. Therefore, we had to adapt the methods to suit our own particular product and production process.

Seven firms in the research sample (23 per cent) described how they had tailored their own courses and teaching materials to suit the company, its product and type of workers. Three had specially designed a booklet, with diagrams, exercises and even cartoons to clarify the new concepts and to practice numerical calculations.

While the development of in-house training materials and procedures is a sign of true local adaptation of a new technique, it may be equally true that local firms are diluting certain features of new QC techniques, making them more palatable to management, but at the risk of losing the full benefits of these new practices.[1] In either case, the effectiveness of local adaptation for management remains to be assessed, both in terms of the purposes to which these adapted techniques are put and in relation to the results obtained.

Workers' fear of management

Other problems arose during the implantation of SPC in Brazil in terms of the fear which workers expressed toward management and, consequently, their mistrust of any new production techniques introduced by management. In some cases, workers were suspicious or fearful that SPC techniques afforded the opportunity for management to survey even more closely the performance of each individual worker, and were concerned that they would be reprimanded or dismissed if management were not pleased with the results.

In one local firm, the initial SPC results appeared too good to be true, and indeed they were. As one manager summarized their situation:

> In the beginning, we had impeccable cards, because if workers encountered a poorly produced part, or a bad result, they wouldn't record it, but rather waited for a good result and then filled in the card. Therefore, we had to convince them that SPC wasn't introduced to monitor or punish them, but was a method to improve the production system.

In another case, an axle producer reported that occasionally a worker would recognize a problem and clearly understand its cause, but would avoid reporting such information on the SPC card, either out of fear that the supervisor would accuse him of negligence or from embarrassment about poor writing skills. These two brief examples emphasize that communication with workers is essential to successful implantation of quality programmes. However, these stories indicate that conditions specific to Brazilian industrial relations and economic development may pose road blocks to what have been described as 'readily transportable' techniques'.

Resistance by managers to SPC use

A final area of difficulty was encountered in resistance to QC practices by managers themselves. In our research workers were never cited as a source of resistance to the new SPC methods. In some cases, workers had requested more comprehensive and advanced courses from management. On the contrary, resistance was noted among some technicians and managers. This resistance was linked, in part, to the manner in which SPC and QC programmes were being introduced. When SPC was installed in isolated workstations, it implied few inherent changes in the production process. However, widening the scope of SPC into a comprehensive programme of quality improvement involved restructuring of traditional procedures and domains, which at times provoked resistance to its introduction among upper level staff who felt threatened by the new practices.

Technicians tended to focus upon the functional aspects of the procedures, such as the need to install an electrical system, improve the lighting system, or repair and reform machinery, but they did not perceive their normal duties to include the implantation of SPC. In these cases, the logic of SPC and QC needed to be introduced into the traditional range of technicians' activities, as well as new skills such as administration, cost accounting or shop floor reorganization, before engaging their efforts in introducing SPC to other areas in the firm.

Managers were cited, especially by technical staff, as the source of greatest resistance to changes in conventional manufacturing practices. If these changes in manufacturing practices were merely technical devices, as suggested by some authors, then there would be no reason for the resistance by management reported in the research. As one staff worker in a QC department observed, the installation of SPC differed according to the position held by an employee. Those with greater power in the firm tended to be suspicious of changes which could alter the existing order:

> One difficulty in the introduction of SPC is 'human nature'. It is difficult to accept change. Technicians, managers, chiefs, supervisors think 'he's introducing SPC because he isn't pleased with me and my work'.

In one extreme case, the QC manager himself was the major obstacle to advancing the SPC programme. Members of the QC department had attended various courses and had developed a comprehensive QC programme, including their own SPC and QC training manuals specifically designed for the firm. Yet this programme had been obstructed for five years by the QC manager. The small QC team quietly continued preparing the programme and training materials as they awaited a change; when this manager was replaced during a massive reorganization of the plant, the QC programme was ready for implementation. It was evident in this example that many years had been involved in preparing a comprehensive quality programme and the QC staff were quite sophisticated in their understanding of the concepts and procedures of QC.

Obtaining product quality without changing current practices

The experience of another firm demonstrated that high product quality can be obtained in unexpected ways. This family firm was renowned for its consistent product quality but had installed SPC in only 10 per cent of the factory. On the shop floor, there were few metal cutting or shaping operations and no automation. A highly fragmented division of labour reigned and most assembly tasks were conducted by female employees. To maintain exceptionally high quality standards, all raw materials and inputs were rigorously inspected, matched by 100 per cent final product inspection. Whereas such a procedure would be exorbitantly expensive for firms in the industrialized countries, this Brazilian company utilized low-wage labour not only for production but for cheap total inspection at the end of the line. In the opinion of the QC Manager:

> Product inspection is best done with the human eye; there isn't any machine yet which can detect superficial marks. This is an example of a competitive advantage which we have. If they could, producers in the industrialized countries would use human labour for inspection – but it is too expensive for them. . . . For now, cheap labour wins out and provides us with a clear advantage.

This manager acknowledged a limit to their strategy based upon low-cost labour, but was content to continue with this strategy while labour costs permitted. Already, the firm had obtained a rejection rate of between 0.2 and 0.3 per cent of total production at the end of the line. Using this combined approach, of conventional equipment and labour practices, matched with the limited introduction of new QC procedures and 100 per cent final inspection at the end of the line, this firm had obtained nearly total product quality. This example demonstrates that it is still possible to attain the objective of final product quality without implementing the structural changes in labour force use required by new QC techniques.

DO QUALITY CONTROL TECHNIQUES PROMISE TO UPGRADE THE LABOUR PROCESS?

As seen above, the success of any QC programme depends upon the attitude of managers toward the new techniques, and its outcome varies greatly according to the role workers play in its implementation. The need for training and in some cases for adaptation of SPC training materials in-house demonstrates the effort with which some firms implanted new quality procedures. It was noted in the research that workers enjoyed receiving training, and in some cases encouraged management or technical staff to provide additional courses. Meanwhile, management and occasionally technicians were found to be the greatest source of resistance to the introduction of these new techniques, clearly indicating that, more than mere technical procedures, they threaten to alter the existing relations within the firm.

The implantation of SPC among components firms relied to a large extent upon the willingness of firms to shoulder the costs of providing basic education in order to bring workers up to a level taken for granted in the industrialized countries. Many firms may be willing to absorb unanticipated costs in the short term, but will probably search for ways to reduce these costs in the medium to long term, and avoid instituting wider training programmes as normal procedure. Some of the companies interviewed had begun to require manual workers to demonstrate literacy in addition to machining skills. However, depending upon the type of quality philosophy in operation, firms may consider additional training unnecessary once workers are familiar with the fundamentals of SPC. Few firms availed themselves of the subsidies and benefits offered by the Brazilian government for training, since these benefits required the firm to reveal its accounts to the government, which few were willing to do. Hence, a tendency toward providing additional training for workers may be evident, but it can hardly be considered a harbinger of change toward a new attitude among firms where workers are valued, receive wider training opportunities and receive more stable employment in the firm.

Second, one might expect that firms would value and grant employment stability to workers in whom they have invested. However, certain features of the greater São Paulo manufacturing region where this research was conducted may offer wider flexibility to firms in their hiring and firing practices. The São Paulo region is an area of industrial concentration where hundreds of metalworking enterprises operate in close proximity. High labour turnover is the rule – around 40 per cent per annum overall and sometimes exceeding 30 per cent even for skilled workers (Humphrey 1989: 30).

Such conditions do little to foster a sense of loyalty to the firm. Companies can exploit these conditions, luring workers from neighbouring firms by offering marginally higher wages, rather than undertaking training themselves. It may be more reasonable to expect that they will continue this practice, perhaps more ruthlessly, in a new context where broader manual worker skill is at a greater premium. In some ways, therefore, the characteristics of the São Paulo industrial region may make it easier to perpetuate a high turnover, cheap labour production model.

Finally, eliminating the causes of poor quality at their source requires a level of worker participation which may be undesirable for a firm which treats labour as low-paid and disposable. Cosmetic QC techniques have been shown earlier to bring significant improvements in product quality, and they may be preferable to management, even though the full potential benefits of these methods would not be reaped in the long run, if the existing structure of authority survives untouched. Hybrids of imported techniques will most likely emerge in such a setting. A central question, regarding the transferability of the new production practices in Brazil, then becomes: to what extent will management find it can minimize structural change in the firm and reconcile the model of the multiskilled, high responsibility worker within the low-wage, high turnover environment in Brazilian industry, without sacrificing the productivity gains ascribed to the Japanese model?

The implantation of QCCs

Many schools of thought among management literature argue that QCCs increase worker involvement and participation in the firm and consequently improve their work satisfaction. Reflecting this view-point, an American subsidiary in the Brazilian components sector reported wide, 'well-motivated' participation from all parts of the factory, according to the QC manager, although pressure and prizes appeared to play an important role in stimulating participation. This manager emphasized that workers must feel gratified by their work and recognize that their ideas are valued. Therefore, management must be seen to respond quickly to suggestions, otherwise the interest in QCCs will wane. Consistent with job enrichment theories and industrial psychology (Fleury and Vargas 1987: 28–37), this manager avoided discussing any financial returns but insisted: 'QCCs are made for the development of workers, not for the results.'

In contrast, Hirata (1983) situates the emergence of QCCs in Japan within its historical context of political, economic and social crisis. Against this background it is notable that although the first QCCs appeared slowly in Brazil in the mid-1970s, their accelerated dissemination coincided both in Brazil and in France with the 1980–81 period of social and economic upheaval (Freyssenet 1985; Hirata 1985: 5). In addition to being a strategic response in order to increase productivity and to reduce costs under crisis, it has been suggested that Brazilian management was also interested in intro-ducing measures which would counterbalance the strengthened union and worker movement in the 1980s. The improvement of security and work conditions, however, received less attention (Salerno 1985: 41–42).

Despite the similar conditions under which they were intro-duced, the trade union response to the introduction of QCCs in Brazil diverged sharply from the experience in Japan. The weakness of the Japanese trade unions in the post-war period and the tacit acceptance of QCCs by the Japanese unions greatly facilitated their rapid diffusion. In contrast, QCCs met with resistance from the Brazilian industrial trade unions. For example, the Metalworkers Union of São Bernardo do Campo and Diadema took a strong position against QCCs, which had been introduced without consul-tation with the union. An edition of their newsletter was dedicated to a discussion of QCCs and their implications, drawing attention to management's intentions to establish new relations with workers outside of unions and proposed a boycott of the programme (Hirata 1983: 62).

By the mid-1980s, many firms indicated that QCCs had 'slowly died out' or were 'found to be unnecessary'. Aside from union resistance, one explanation for the low survival rate of QCCs in Brazil is that, to be effective, they must be inserted into a context where workers' contributions and discretion over production issues are considerably greater than that presently allowed by Brazilian management. It is worth noting that in most cases the failure of QCCs in this sector by the mid-1980s was followed by a new wave of QC initiatives by companies, raising the question whether QC programmes will constitute another short-lived management fashion, if they are not adopted in a structural manner which involves changes in labour use and management–labour relations.

Half of the firms in the research sample (six foreign subsidiaries and six Brazilian owned firms) indicated some programme of QCCs in use. Several large firms described particularly extensive QCC programmes. For example, one American subsidiary held an annual QCC convention in which reportedly 2,400 people from four separate plants had participated. The convention included sports and games between various factory teams, as well as an awards ceremony for outstanding QCC groups.

Two firms in the sample reported total participation by all workers in QCCs. In one of these firms, two types of groups had been established – homogeneous (workers from within the same sector) and heterogeneous (joining people across several departments) – with the intended purpose of facilitating the cross-fertilization of ideas. Meetings were held monthly, involving six to ten people, but no awards were given for successful suggestions or high performance, as this was seen to be contrary to the true philosophy of QCCs.

The only Japanese subsidiary in our sample had installed QCCs in 1975 and reported 60 per cent participation among machinists. Themes for discussion were defined in general terms such as work environment or economic performance and supervisors commonly attended the QCC meetings. The objective behind QCCs, according to the industrial manager, was to address the human problem that workers do not produce in the same manner or with consistent attention to detail every day. To avoid this unpredictability, workers were removed from their daily routine in order to think in larger terms about work and suggest ideas for improvement. This manager also indicated that the company enjoyed clear economic savings resulting from its effective QCC programme.

The production manager in another company echoed similar financial considerations behind their concern over 'human resources':

'conflicts must be avoided because tension between labour and management only results in damaging your production and product.' Seen in this light, QCCs can be employed by management as a mechanism to control volatile labour–management relations.

A German subsidiary had departed quite sharply from the normal rhetoric of QCC, and in this sense distorted it, by emphasising increased machine utilization. A reward system had been instituted which encouraged group effort, but also encouraged competition between workers:

> For example, we calculate that machinery should operate an average of 70 per cent of the time available. Therefore, using this measure, if the worker manages to increase the machine's operating time, then he receives a prize.

Rather than fostering the 'team spirit' so often expressed by supporters of QCCs, this reward system is divisive, encouraging individual effort for personal gain rather than for the work group or sector as a whole.

Upon closer scrutiny, half of the so-called QCCs among Brazilian owned firms were actually meetings of managerial and technical staff. In all these cases, the resolution of production problems was treated as a technical issue beyond the capability of production workers. One company maintained exceptionally high quality standards yet allowed little worker participation in QC procedures, by relying instead upon these technical staff 'circles'. The strategy employed by this firm demonstrated how management can appropriate the discretionary control involved in QC activities and continue using low-cost labour to obtain high product quality. The future life-span of such an approach may be limited, since machine operators do not become more involved or participate in assuring product quality more than in the previous regime. In the short term, however, management succeeded in retaining profitability and quality.

Despite the original enthusiasm with which management introduced QCCs, managers in several firms indicated that such arrangements had not delivered the anticipated results, arguing that Brazilian workers were not interested in resolving productivity problems but were only concerned with discussing soccer and parties. Several implications arise from this simple example. First of all, such a comment reveals the unrealistic expectation by management that workers will automatically provide insights which cut costs and increase productivity once QCC groups are established.

Second, management uniformly failed to recognize that while one could easily replicate a system whereby workers meet regularly to discuss production (and perhaps institute a reward system to encourage suggestions), the entire set of social relations which surround and support QCC activities in Japan, both inside and outside the workplace, was not transferred. For example, Brazilian workers may not be forthcoming with suggestions for greater efficiency in the production line, which commonly implies labour reduction, because they lack a secure employment system. On the one hand, the Japanese practice of life-time employment among large firms, pay increases and promotions related to seniority, plus a great emphasis on additional training opportunities, courses and travel, creates strong ties of dependency upon the place of employment (Hirata 1983: 64), though it should be emphasized that life-time employment is guaranteed only to full-time male employees of large firms – the large peripheral labour force, female workers in all firms, and the employees in small enterprises do not benefit from such a system (Freyssenet and Hirata 1985: 20). On the other hand, the lines between professional and personal life in Japan are blurred, whereas in Brazil the firm plays no role once the worker passes beyond the factory gates.[2]

Both Hirata (1983) and Salerno (1985) stress several problematic features of QCCs in Japan. First of all, they are not purely 'voluntary' as management argues; while not compulsory, participation in QCCs is considered as a factor in promotion. Second, despite the emphasis that QCCs help workers feel greater involvement and satisfaction in their work, QCCs do nothing to change the fundamental hierarchical relations within the firm. Nevertheless, despite the difficulties encountered in the implantation and sustained operation of QCCs and the control which is frequently exerted over workers in their use, the potential exists for the transformation of QCCs within a different context which could benefit workers and serve to advance their own interests in improving the workplace.

THE INTRODUCTION OF JUST-IN-TIME AMONG COMPONENTS FIRMS

Perhaps the aspect of Japanese production practices which has gained most attention and has stimulated greatest controversy is the JIT process of inventory reduction, and companies in the research sample demonstrated a high degree of selective adaptation of this feature of new organizational practice.

Conventional Western production practices use inventories in a 'just-in-case' approach, relying upon buffer stocks to safeguard the continuous flow of production. The Japanese, in contrast, have applied a JIT logic which reduces the build-up of stocks which hide organizational and technical defects throughout the production system, thereby exposing them for correction. Using the metaphor of a small boat in a rocky sea, the Japanese argue that only by lowering the water table can the rocks be exposed and removed. Nevertheless, it should be borne in mind that each Japanese assembler has its own JIT method, which has evolved depending upon differences in manufacturing processes, production design and component supplier relations, each finding an original solution which suits its needs (Shimokawa 1986: 238).

Fundamentally, JIT works at two levels: internal JIT, which focuses upon streamlining operations and eliminating work in progress within the factory, and external JIT, which includes both the receipt of inputs and the delivery of finished goods. Ideally, JIT production is arranged so that only one unit of work is in process at any point in time, by continually reducing inventories and batch sizes at all stages of production. Under this logic, production operates on a 'demand pull' basis, geared toward producing only what is needed. A principal tool employed in the process of slimming down to JIT has been the kanban system. 'Kanban' literally means 'card' and was originally based upon a system of cards which were used by production workers to signal to the previous machining stage when new parts were required for production. Instead of 'pushing' huge quantities of stocks down through production, Kanban works backwards by 'pulling' parts only as required through the production system. In practice, 'stockless production' is regarded as an ideal target, which is nearly impossible to achieve (and may be unsuitable for certain product lines). An important by-product of demand driven production is greater responsiveness to clients and changes in product design.

One major implication of successful JIT production is its challenge to conventional theories concerning scale economies, which are founded upon the use of ever larger batches and production runs in order to reduce unit costs. Another implication concerns production technology, as it requires that new machines be flexible to produce economically in smaller batches, encouraging a tendency toward (and the need for) automation. Despite its apparent simplicity, the JIT approach took nearly thirty years to develop and refine in the Japanese motor vehicle industry.

The obstacles facing JIT in Brazil

All components firms in the research sample were aware of or engaged in some form of preparation for JIT, and 50 per cent already had some degree of JIT in operation. In general subsidiaries had had to adopt such new organizational techniques on their own initiative, though one American subsidiary mentioned receiving help from its parent company. Yet all firms identified obstacles to the implantation of a replica of the Japanese JIT system in Brazil, and five areas of difficulty were mentioned most frequently. First, whereas the Japanese JIT logic posits that reduced inventories bring savings and higher quality products, most conditions in Brazil encourage firms to accumulate inventories for greater economy and security. Indeed, one manager challenged the received wisdom from Japan, arguing that high inventories also provided a form of flexibility. In a country where inflation reached nearly 1,600 per cent in 1989, initial inventories serve to protect the firm against unexpected price rises and act as a hedge against inflation. For example, prices of basic goods such as steel or rubber could jump between 50 and 200 per cent in one single price rise. If stocks run low, a serious risk exists that they cannot be replaced or can only be purchased at an exorbitant price.[3] Some firms in the sample reported up to ten-month inventories for certain items. In this context, initial inventories are not only a productive input, but also an investment, although this frequently led to speculation in raw materials, in addition to the more common financial practice of investing on the overnight market (a form of high interest, short-term investment which finances the Brazilian government's domestic deficit).

Second, the most frequently mentioned obstacle to the adoption of JIT concerned problems over the unreliability of upstream suppliers whose scheduled deliveries could be delayed because of difficulties caused by inflation and unreliable availability of raw materials. In addition to problems with the domestic economy and availability of goods, other cases were cited where deliveries from upstream suppliers were withheld to negotiate for a price increase or where firms simply halted production rather than produce at a loss. Similarly, a case study of the introduction of JIT into a small shoe producing firm in Venezuela reported that the company was confronted by a chronic shortage of raw materials, even those produced nationally (including leather). This report confirmed the conditions of uncertainty surrounding the delivery of inputs in developing countries, which encouraged firms to maintain large initial inventories (Cartaya and Medina, n.d.: 3).

Third, other difficulties were encountered in reducing inventories because it is often cheaper (and simpler for the purchasing department) to purchase materials in large quantities. Firms in our sample generally preferred to place several large orders for annual deliveries rather than numerous small orders. In Japan, even large orders are delivered by upstream suppliers in small, regular lots, but such purchase and delivery practices were not found to be operating in Brazil. Some small Brazilian firms reported receiving unfavourable treatment from raw materials suppliers who considered small orders too troublesome and costly. For example, a small components producer could not acquire any steel, and in desperation called on Ford – its major client – to intervene on its behalf. In the end, Ford solved the difficulty by increasing its own steel order to include that of the component supplier.

Fourth, the reduction of inventories is complicated by the import of inputs from overseas, for two primary reasons: imported goods are often ordered in large quantities and unexpected delays in deliveries from overseas could halt production. This issue is more acute in smaller and import dependent developing economies, with fewer natural resources than Brazil and a less developed manufacturing sector. Trade of goods between two developing countries often involves a greater margin of uncertainty regarding the precise timing of the order and receipt of goods. For example, one company which imported cork from Portugal ordered six-month quantities to compensate both for the cost of cargo and for delays in shipment by sea.

Finally, components firms complained that they were unable to plan their production and delivery schedules to suit fluctuations in the volume of orders from the assemblers. Although this would appear a strong argument in favour of the adoption of JIT to achieve a greater 'demand pull' system, a large proportion of firms cited unpredictable orders from the automobile producers as a constraining factor in any move to adopt JIT: 'For JIT to work, you must have a long-term perspective and the capacity to plan. In Brazil, nobody makes a fixed ordering programme.'

370

As an extreme example of a non-JIT approach, one large national family firm operates with high security stocks of finished goods as a deliberate feature of the firm's competitive strategy. This practice was justified principally for two reasons. First, they seek to retain high-scale economies. With no automation programme, they employ the traditional scale economies logic, using conventional equipment to produce in three-month batches. Second, as a quasi-monopoly and sole supplier for most automobile assemblers, this company holds over 80 per cent of market share in their product line. The burden of responsibility is substantial; consequently they believe the risk of change is great and resist altering current procedures: 'We can't let it happen even once that a client must stop the line because we were unable to fulfil an order or produced with poor quality.' Therefore they retain an average three month's inventory of finished goods for each client, although some plans to automate inventory control were discussed. Nevertheless, such strategies overlook the fact that conventional equipment can be very flexible when combined with organizational simplicity and that manufacturing efficiency is obtainable using a very simple technology base.

Other firms were slow in their implantation of JIT because they believed other techniques were precursors to JIT. The manager in one company was fully engaged in introducing QC techniques, yet had not begun to implement JIT techniques: 'For me, JIT comes after SPC and QCCs; it doesn't matter much now.' Yet this piecemeal approach overlooks the possibility that QC and JIT are mutually reinforcing principles within a much wider quality manufacturing programme.

Throughout the field research, the point was driven home repeatedly of the difficulties surrounding the adoption of a system which is founded upon predictability and stability by firms which operate within an external environment which provides little of these qualities. One manager expressed his view that low inventories were undesirable for most companies in Brazil: 'No one wants zero stocks. Everyone wants a little bit of security.' For Brazilian companies, this desire for security may be justified. JIT receipt of parts and primary materials is feasible within a stable external environment, but under economic and political uncertainty firms fend off chaos by erecting cushions of protection to assure that supplies will be at hand when necessary. A zero inventory policy under such conditions would court the risk of long down times, sporadic receipt of inputs and consequently unreliable deliveries to clients. Within this context, 'just-in-case' stocks of initial inventory do not necessarily mask poor internal quality, but act as a cushion against external crisis.

'Brazilianized' adaptations

Nevertheless, Brazilian auto-components firms have found ways to extract the benefits offered through JIT principles by adapting them to local conditions. Before discussing the adaptation of JIT in Brazil, it is useful to identify the three areas where buffer stocks accumulate: initial inventories received from the upstream suppliers or importers; intermediate inventories, work-in-progress within the enterprise; and inventories of finished goods, awaiting sale to national clients or export.

Inventories play different roles in the production process, depending upon where they occur, and it is important to understand the extent to which greater efficiency or benefits accrue even if the entire JIT 'package' is not adopted. As in the case of QC programmes, measuring the quantitative use of JIT or its success rate against a 'best practice' model diminishes our understanding of which factors may necessitate adaptation in a developing country environment or how new techniques may be successful in different contexts. Furthermore, when sights are set upon finding evidence of a best practice model, one risks overlooking the adaptive capability of firms to suit new techniques to conditions in their local environment. Indeed, some firms may be involved in implanting other QC programmes which delay the adoption of JIT practices, as noted earlier.

If the focus is turned, however, toward internal JIT and creating a more efficient, streamlined production system in-house, then reduction of intermediate inventories takes on central importance. The field research suggests that Brazilian components producers are channelling their principal innovative energies where they matter most – on the shop floor. Given unstable economic and market conditions, these firms can only safely initiate a process of organizational change – a very risky and delicate undertaking, especially if the company has no prior experience with this – within the protective buffers of initial and final inventories. In this way, a company may shield itself from external factors, and focus upon reducing work in progress, while proceeding cautiously with external JIT, but at a slower pace. Seen in this light, initial inventories are a necessary source of security to a firm undergoing change in an uncertain environment. Even the NUMMI joint venture between General Motors and Toyota in Fremont, California faced difficulties in reducing input inventories because of problems in coordinating deliveries of parts from the US Midwest and Japan, and focused first upon achieving smooth internal JIT, paired with controlled hourly feeding of materials. Similarly, Rocha (1989) describes how the firm most seriously engaged in organizational innovations in his sample of Brazilian automobile components producers, had modified JIT to include large inventories to make the implanted system less severe. In such cases, large initial inventories and productive efficiency are not mutually exclusive. Furthermore, these internal procedures will be facilitated further as more computerized purchasing, receiving and delivery techniques are adopted.

JIT delivery and exports

An important issue surrounding the transfer of the Japanese model to the Third World concerns whether developing country firms can continue to compete in international markets with the growing emphasis on JIT delivery. Speculation regarding a potential 'competitive advantage reversal' suggests that Third World firms will be unable to export just-in-time; consequently, customers in the industrialized countries will turn to components producers in their own backyard.

The extent to which JIT delivery is adopted by companies in the industrialized countries, however, will strongly determine whether large shipments of goods from Brazil will continue to be acceptable under new manufacturing practices. Shipments normally take one month to arrive at the factory of a client overseas, and government paperwork for exports can add several days to this delay. However, Brazilian components producers have developed flexible interim solutions to JIT exports. First, it should be borne in mind that not all components are equal. Of the thousands of parts which comprise the average automobile, certain components are more crucial and technologically sophisticated than others. The need for JIT deliveries of auto-components, therefore, will likely differentiate between different product types. For example, it is more important to receive pistons on time and with high quality than hubcaps. For this reason, three producers of more sophisticated products from our research sample – producers of pistons, piston rings and oil seals – are establishing production facilities in Europe and the United States.[4]

Second, successful JIT exports do not require that the shipments themselves depart from Brazil in regular and small batches. Many components firms in the research sample had developed a form of 'warehouse JIT'. Under this system, the Brazilian component producer sends large batches to a sales representative in Europe or the United States, who stores these goods in a warehouse and is responsible for delivering JIT as needed to different clients. This strategy for exporting JIT does not conflict with the objectives for in-house JIT, although it 'cheats' on the methods conventionally used to achieve a JIT delivery system. Lamming notes this method of short-cutting JIT delivery in the British automobile components industry, but warns against its consequences:

> This practice can degenerate into the pernicious custom of manufacturing in the same batches as before and then supplying JIT from finished goods stock. This corresponds to a transfer of inventory from the customer to the supplier – with no reduction in overall levels in the supply chain.
>
> (Lamming 1987)

The practice of 'warehouse JIT' cited above, as well as JIT delivery on the domestic market, permit companies to meet clients' demands for frequent delivery without necessarily acting as a stimulus to restructure internal production practices, reduce batch sizes or achieve streamlined work in progress. Since not all Brazilian exporters can establish production facilities overseas, warehouse JIT may prove a successful (although probably short-term) alternative for the delivery of technologically simpler and less critical components.

This discussion of JIT has shown how aspects of Japanese practices can be 'unpacked' and adapted to developing country conditions. For example, Brazilian components firms were found to be able to meet clients' demands for improved product quality or JIT delivery, while selectively introducing new organizational techniques and adapting them to specific needs. However, the long-term effectiveness of these adaptations relies largely upon whether they are applied cosmetically or provoke structural changes in production practices and labour–management relations.

CONCLUSIONS

Divergent views have clashed in the literature regarding the transferability of Japanese manufacturing practices to the West. Some authors question the suitability or social desirability of adopting the model outside of Japan, while the prevailing tone set by the management literature has been optimistic. More recent material which specifically addresses developing countries has echoed this positive perspective.

This chapter has addressed the introduction of QC programmes, QCCs and JIT in Brazilian automobile components firms. No firm in the research sample was found to have transferred any of these techniques as a whole. Instead, partial and selective local adaptation characterized the manner in which new organizational techniques were introduced. Even this limited introduction of new practices was found to have improved firm performance. However, the selective adaptation of new organizational techniques tended to deprive workers of some of their potential benefits, such as job security, multiskilling or a share in the financial returns enjoyed by the company as a result of the new practices.

Workers benefited from the introduction of new QC programmes to the extent that additional training and some short courses were offered by management. The material covered in these courses, however, was generally very basic. Nevertheless, practical experience in using techniques such as SPC could provide an advantage for workers seeking employment in another firm, as turn-over rates remain high in the metalworking sector in São Paulo. Firms which offered the most advanced courses to production workers had already established a tradition of offering additional training opportunities, and hence this could not be attributed to the adoption of Japanese techniques.

The introduction of QCCs was found to be a short-lived experiment in most Brazilian companies, largely because of the cosmetic manner in which they were implemented and the antagonistic nature of labour–management relations in Brazil. Participation in QCCs involved additional input and effort by workers, yet awards or benefits were generally received only by QCC teams whose suggestions were judged worthy of merit by management.

The introduction of JIT methods of inventory reduction may potentially bring indirect impacts upon workers. For example, through increased efficiency, reduced down time and improved utilization of existing resources, the use of JIT may result in a reduction in the total number of employees and an acceleration in the pace of work.

The lack of a clear position by the Brazilian metalworkers union regarding the introduction of most of these techniques, the conditions of their implantation or the negotiation of workers' associated rights and benefits, leaves a vacuum in which management can introduce and adapt them as required. Hence, adaptation of new techniques is neither a contested nor a consensual issue, but is left largely to the discretion, priorities and convenience of individual companies. As a result, labour was generally regarded by management as a technical problem, rather than as a participant in the modernization process – high turnover rates and limited training opportunities only reinforced this attitude. These circumstances highlight the need for dialogue among workers and with their union representatives to establish a clear position regarding the transfer and adaptation of new organizational techniques in Brazilian industry.

NOTES

1 Thus the establishment of worker centred responsibility was permitted in some cases only to the extent that it involved more worker effort in conducting SPC or other QC practices. Other activities such as tooling and machine setup were rarely passed on, and such additional tasks were not compensated financially.

2 In Japan, women are expected to take a greater share of domestic life to compensate for the man's dedication to the workplace. Women receive awards side by side with their husbands at annual ceremonies and are instructed to understand and forgive their husband's commitment to working late nights and on the weekend with activities related to the QCCs (Hirata 1983: 64).

3 Alternatively, it can be argued that inflation pushes up the cost of money and consequently makes inventories more expensive, meanwhile locking away productive capital. Material costs are a significant area for reduction since they can account for over 50 per cent of total unit costs (Lamming 1987). Hence, it must be borne in mind that conditions common to developing countries, such as inflation, shortages of essential inputs and general economic uncertainty produce complex and sometimes contradictory pressures which may have differing impacts on firms in different sectors, with different production processes and so on.

4 Nevertheless, the objectives behind the move overseas were different for each firm. For one company, the proximity to centres of leading-edge research and development and innovation in the automobile industry was crucial. For others, access to automated production equipment which is unobtainable in Brazil was a significant motive. Some companies emphasized that location was determined by the desire to have closer and more frequent contact with their major clients(s), whereas others stated that a low-wage production site within the industrialized country markets (such as the American South East, Ireland or Portugal) was a major consideration.

REFERENCES

Cartaya, V. and Medina, E. (n.d.) 'New organisational techniques: a case study from Venezuela', undated report from Brighton Polytechnic, mimeo.

Cusumano, M. (1985) *The Japanese Automobile Industry*, Massachusetts: Harvard University Press.

Deming, W. E. (1986) *Out of the Crisis*, Massachusetts Institute of Technology, Center for Advanced Engineering Study, Cambridge.

Dohse, K. *et al.* (1985) 'From "Fordism" to "Toyotism"? The social organisation of the labour process in the Japanese automobile industry', *Politics and Society* 14, 2: 115–146.

Ebrahimpour, M. and Schonberger, R. (1984) 'The Japanese just-in-time/total quality control production system: potential for developing countries', *International Journal of Production Research* 22, 3: 421–430.

Fleury, A. and Vargas, N. (1987) 'Aspectos conceituais', in A. Fleury and N. Vargas (eds) *Organização do Trabalho*, São Paulo: Editora Atlas.

Freyssenet, M. and Hirata, H. (1985) 'Mudanças tecnológicas e participação dos trabalhadores: os círculos de controle de qualidade no Japao', *Revista de Administração de Empresas* 25, 3 (July/September).

Fukuda, J. K. (1988) *Japanese-Style Management Transferred: The Experience of East Asia*, London: Routledge.

Hirata, H. (1983) 'Receitas japonesas, realidade brasileira', *Novos Estudos CEBRAP* 2, 2: 61–65 (July).

Hoffman, K. (1989) 'Technological advance and organizational innovation in the engineering industry', Industry and Energy Department Working Paper 4, The World Bank (March).

Humphrey, J. (1989) 'New forms of work organisation in industry: their implications for labour use and control in Brazil', Paper presented to conference on Pades tecnológicas e políticas de gestão, São Paulo, August 16–17.

Lamming, R. (1987) 'Towards best practice: a report on components supply in the UK automotive industry', Innovation Research Group, Brighton Business School, IRG Report No. 4, Autumn.

Rocha Lima, R. (1989) 'Difusão da automação e de novas formas de organização e gestão da produção no setor automobilístico', Masters thesis, Polytechnic School, University of São Paulo.

Salerno, M. S. (1985) 'Produção, trabalho e participação: CCQ e kanban numa nova imigração japonesa', Masters thesis, Production Engineering Department, Federal University of Rio de Janeiro.

Sayer, A. (1986) 'New developments in manufacturing: the JIT system', *Capital and Class* 30 (Winter) 43–72.

Schonberger, R. (1982) *Japanese Manufacturing Techniques: Nine Hidden Lessons in Simplicity*, New York: The Free Press.

Sethi, S. P. *et al.* (1984) *The False Promise of the Japanese Miracle: Illusions and Realities of the Japanese Management System*, London: Pitman Publishing Ltd.

Shimokawa, K. (1986) 'Product and labour strategies in Japan', in S. Tolliday and J. Zeitlin (eds) *The Automobile Industry and its Workers*, Oxford: Polity Press.

INDEX